A Companion to Lollardy

Brill's Companions to the Christian Tradition

A SERIES OF HANDBOOKS AND REFERENCE WORKS ON THE
INTELLECTUAL AND RELIGIOUS LIFE OF EUROPE, 500–1800

Edited by

Christopher M. Bellitto (*Kean University*)

VOLUME 67

The titles published in this series are listed at *brill.com/bcct*

A Companion to Lollardy

By

J. Patrick Hornbeck II

With

Mishtooni Bose
Fiona Somerset

BRILL

LEIDEN | BOSTON

Cover illustration: William Yeames (1835–1918), *The Dawn of the Reformation* 1867, oil on canvas, 1230 × 2000 mm, collection of The Suter Art Gallery Te Aratoi o Whakatu, Nelson, New Zealand: gifted by Mrs Amelia Suter in memory of her husband Bishop Andrew Burn Suter in 1895.

Library of Congress Cataloging-in-Publication Data

Names: Hornbeck, J. Patrick, 1982- author.
Title: A companion to Lollardy / by J. Patrick Hornbeck II, with Mishtooni Bose, Fiona Somerset.
Description: Boston : Brill, 2016. | Series: Brill's companions to the Christian tradition, ISSN 1871-6377 ; VOLUME 67 | Includes bibliographical references and index. | Description based on print version record and CIP data provided by publisher; resource not viewed.
Identifiers: LCCN 2015050995 (print) | LCCN 2015049645 (ebook) | ISBN 9789004309852 (E-book) | ISBN 9789004309791 (hardback : alk. paper)
Subjects: LCSH: Lollards.
Classification: LCC BX4901.3 (print) | LCC BX4901.3 .H67 2016 (ebook) | DDC 284/.3--dc23
LC record available at http://lccn.loc.gov/2015050995

Want or need Open Access? Brill Open offers you the choice to make your research freely accessible online in exchange for a publication charge. Review your various options on brill.com/brill-open.

Typeface for the Latin, Greek, and Cyrillic scripts: "Brill". See and download: brill.com/brill-typeface.

ISSN 1871-6377
ISBN 978-90-04-30979-1 (hardback)
ISBN 978-90-04-30985-2 (e-book)

Copyright 2016 by Koninklijke Brill NV, Leiden, The Netherlands.
Koninklijke Brill NV incorporates the imprints Brill, Brill Hes & De Graaf, Brill Nijhoff, Brill Rodopi and Hotei Publishing.
All rights reserved. No part of this publication may be reproduced, translated, stored in a retrieval system, or transmitted in any form or by any means, electronic, mechanical, photocopying, recording or otherwise, without prior written permission from the publisher.
Authorization to photocopy items for internal or personal use is granted by Koninklijke Brill NV provided that the appropriate fees are paid directly to The Copyright Clearance Center, 222 Rosewood Drive, Suite 910, Danvers, MA 01923, USA.
Fees are subject to change.

This book is printed on acid-free paper and produced in a sustainable manner.

Contents

Acknowledgements VII
List of Abbreviations IX

1 **Introduction: The Study of Lollardy** 1
    1.1   Developments in Lollard Studies 5
    1.2   Terminological Quandaries 15

2 **The People** 24
    2.1   John Wyclif 26
    2.2   "Fellows and Helpers" 35
    2.3   Lollard Knights 45
    2.4   Later Lollards 46
    2.5   Lollard Communities 51
    2.6   Conclusions 57

3 **Their Practices** 59
    3.1   Preaching and Teaching 61
    3.2   Lollard Spirituality 69

4 **Their Writings** 76
    Fiona Somerset
    4.1   Rapid, Large-Scale Production 79
        4.1.1 *The Floretum and Rosarium* 80
        4.1.2 *The Wycliffite Bible* 81
        4.1.3 *The Glossed Gospels* 81
        4.1.4 *The English Wycliffite Sermons* 82
        4.1.5 *Rolle's English Psalter, Revised Version (RV) 1, RV2, and RV3* 83
    4.2   Independent Projects 83
        4.2.1 *Spinoffs from Phase 1* 84
        4.2.2 *Works that Translate or Cite Wyclif* 87
        4.2.3 *Writings by Named Authors Associated with Wycliffism* 88
        4.2.4 *Anonymous Declarative or Confessional Writings* 89
        4.2.5 *Lollard Learning* 90
        4.2.6 *Writings in Verse* 94
        4.2.7 *Prose Dialogues* 96
        4.2.8 *Lollard Anthologies: Some Representative Lollard Manuscripts* 98

4.3 Recension and Diffusion 101
  4.3.1 *Individual Texts* 101
  4.3.2 *Compilation-Texts* 102
  4.3.3 *Manuscript Compilations* 102

5 Their Beliefs 105
 5.1 Salvation and Grace 111
 5.2 The Sacraments 117
  5.2.1 *Sacraments of Initiation: Baptism and Confirmation* 117
  5.2.2 *The Eucharist* 120
  5.2.3 *Penance* 125
  5.2.4 *Sacraments for States of Life: Marriage and Holy Orders* 126
  5.2.5 *Extreme Unction* 131
 5.3 The Church and Mainstream Religious Practice 132
  5.3.1 *Devotions and Other Religious Practices* 138
 5.4 Conclusions 141

6 Their Opponents 144
  Mishtooni Bose
 6.1 Chronology 146

7 Their Trials 159
 7.1 The Inquisitorial Process 161
 7.2 The Making of Records 167
 7.3 A Survey of the Extant Records 178
 7.4 Conclusions 186

8 Their Afterlife 188
 8.1 Lollards and Lollard Communities in the Sixteenth Century 189
 8.2 England and Bohemia 196
 8.3 Lollard Literature and the New Reforms 198
 8.4 Historiography and Lollardy 202

Conclusion 208
Bibliography 215
Index 242

Acknowledgements

It is impossible to produce a volume that seeks to summarize the state of a field of scholarly inquiry without incurring many debts to one's colleagues. I am especially grateful to two of them, Fiona Somerset and Mishtooni Bose, for each agreeing to contribute a chapter to the present volume. Specialists in the writings of those we have come to call lollards and in the opposition that John Wyclif and later lollards encountered from the representatives of the institutional church, these colleagues have penned chapters that far outshine anything that I could have written on these topics. Many other colleagues, including Andrew Cole, Jennifer Illig, Maureen Jurkowski, and Stephen E. Lahey, have helped to shape the structure and content of this book, though of course whatever errors may remain are my own responsibility.

To Julian Deahl and Christopher Bellitto, editors of Brill's Companions to the Christian Tradition series, I am thankful for the opportunity to contribute a volume on a medieval religious phenomenon that has captured my attention for more than a decade now. Lollardy has been for me an important context within which to pursue work on the Christian theological categories of heresy and dissent, as well as to see how those categories have been lived out concretely in the experience of actual women and men. While I imagine that this book will be my last major publication on lollards and lollardy, it would have been difficult for me to have chosen a field where scholars are more generous with their time and expertise, nor where colleagues work more collaboratively, rather than competitively, with one another. To those who have been my teachers and mentors in the study of lollardy—Mishtooni Bose, Anne Hudson, Stephen E. Lahey, Ian Christopher Levy, Fiona Somerset, Penn Szittya, and most recently Michael Van Dussen—I express my enduring gratitude. I am also thankful to the two anonymous readers for the press for their thoughtful, collegial, and challenging suggestions. Of course, any errors that remain are my own.

Fiona Somerset asks me to thank Mary Raschko, Anne Hudson, David Watt, and Fred Biggs for their assistance with her chapter, "Their Texts."

For me, this volume could not have come to fruition without support from my home academic institution. Fordham University provided a generous semester-long Faculty Fellowship to assist with the writing of the first draft. At various points, graduate students Amanda Alexander, John Garza, John Gleim, Lindsey Mercer, John David Penniman, and Zachary Smith all contributed to the tasks of tracking down references, helping to smooth the language of my arguments, and preparing the typescript for the press. The Brothers of the

Society of St. John the Evangelist—a monastic order so generous that I believe lollards would have spared it from their critiques—provided extraordinary hospitality as the final pages were being written.

Finally, my husband Patrick Bergquist has had to endure my talking about this book for far too long, and has not once been anything other than encouraging and patient, in equal measure. I am more grateful than I can ever tell for all his many gifts to me.

J. Patrick Hornbeck II
July 31, 2015
Feast of St. Ignatius of Loyola

List of Abbreviations

A&M	John Foxe, *The...Ecclesiasticall History Contaynyng the Actes and Monuments* (London, 1570) other editions of *Actes and Monuments* will be denoted by the year of publication
Arnold	Thomas Arnold, (ed.), *Select English Works of John Wycliffe*, 3 vols. (Oxford, 1869–71)
Books	Anne Hudson, *Lollards and Their Books* (London, 1985)
Companion	Ian Christopher Levy, (ed.), *A Companion to John Wyclif: Late Medieval Theologian* (Leiden, 2006)
Coventry	Shannon McSheffrey and Norman Tanner, (eds. and trans.), *Lollards of Coventry, 1486–1522* (Camden Fifth Series 23, 2003)
EETS	Early English Text Society
EWS	Anne Hudson and Pamela Gradon, (eds.), *English Wycliffite Sermons*, 5 vols. (Oxford, 1983–97)
FZ	W.W. Shirley, (ed.), *Fasciculi zizaniorum* (Rolls Series, 1858)
Influence	Fiona Somerset, Jill C. Havens, and Derrick Pitard, (eds.), *Lollards and Their Influence in Late Medieval England* (Woodbridge, 2003)
Kent	Norman Tanner, (ed.), *Kent Heresy Proceedings, 1511–12* (Kent Records 26, 1997)
Knighton	Henry Knighton, *Chronica de eventibus Angliae a tempore regis Edgari usque mortem regis Richardi Secundi*, ed. and trans. Geoffrey H. Martin (Oxford, 1995)
Lahey, *Wyclif*	Stephen E. Lahey, *John Wyclif* (Oxford, 2008)
Lechler	Gotthard Victor Lechler, *John Wycliffe and His English Precursors*, trans. P. Lorimer, rev. edn. (London, 1884)
Lollards and Reformers	Margaret Aston, *Lollards and Reformers: Images and Literacy in Late Medieval Religion* (London, 1984)
Lollardy and Gentry	Margaret Aston and Colin Richmond, (eds.), *Lollardy and the Gentry in the Later Middle Ages* (Sutton, 1997)
Matthew	F.D. Matthew, (ed.), *The English Works of Wyclif Hitherto Unprinted*, rev. edn. (EETS o.s. 74, 1902)
Netter, *Doctrinale*	Thomas Netter, *Doctrinale antiquitatum fidei catholicae ecclesiae*, ed. B. Blanciotti, 3 vols. (Venice, 1757–59)
Norwich	Norman P. Tanner, (ed.), *Heresy Trials in the Diocese of Norwich, 1428–1431* (London, 1977)

Ockham to Wyclif	Anne Hudson and Michael Wilks, (eds.), *From Ockham to Wyclif*, Studies in Church History Subsidia 5 (Oxford, 1987)
PR	Anne Hudson, *The Premature Reformation: Wycliffite Texts and Lollard History* (Oxford, 1988)
Selections	Anne Hudson, (ed.), *Selections from English Wycliffite Writings*, rev. edn. (Toronto, 1997)
Tanner, *Decrees*	Norman Tanner, (ed.), *Decrees of the Ecumenical Councils*, 2 vols. (Washington, 1990)
Text and Controversy	Helen Barr and Ann M. Hutchinson, (eds.), *Text and Controversy from Wyclif to Bale: Essays in Honour of Anne Hudson* (Turnhout, 2005)
Thomson, *Later Lollards*	J.A.F. Thomson, *The Later Lollards: 1414–1520* (Oxford, 1965)
Wilkins	David Wilkins, (ed.), *Concilia Magnae Brittaniae et Hiberniae*, 4 vols. (1737, repr. Brussels, 1964)
Wilks, *Wyclif*	Michael Wilks, *Wyclif: Political Ideas and Practice*, ed. Anne Hudson (Oxford, 2000)
Workman	H.B. Workman, *John Wyclif: A Study of the English Medieval Church*, 2 vols. (Oxford, 1926)
Wycliffite Controversies	Mishtooni Bose and J. Patrick Hornbeck II, (eds.), *Wycliffite Controversies* (Turnhout, 2012)
Wycliffite Spirituality	J. Patrick Hornbeck II, Stephen E. Lahey, and Fiona Somerset, (eds.) and trans., *Wycliffite Spirituality* (Mahwah, N.J., 2013)

CHAPTER 1

Introduction: The Study of Lollardy

It has been more than twenty-five years since the publication of Anne Hudson's magisterial work *The Premature Reformation* catapulted the study of lollardy into a central place in research on late medieval England.[1] Written by a literary historian exceptionally well-versed in the manuscript remains of the Oxford scholar John Wyclif, as well as in the writings of the women and men who came after him and in the records of their trials before ecclesiastical authorities, Hudson's book maintained that Lollardy (she wrote the word with a capital *L*, a choice whose consequences the present book will explore) was not a decisive forerunner of sixteenth-century evangelicalism, not the chief precursor of the Henrician Reformation that many of those who have pointed to its survival through long periods of persecution had envisioned. Nor was "Lollardy" a tired, dying force, having nothing at all to do with the religious changes of the sixteenth century. Instead, Hudson argued, it was a phenomenon worthy of attention in its own right and on its own terms: as a religious movement; as a textual culture; as a context for the writing of significant quantities of poetry, prose, and sermon literature; and as a force that unified and gave an identity to communities of dissenters scattered throughout England.

Much has changed in the study of lollardy since the appearance of *The Premature Reformation*, and while scholars have pointed out some gaps and inaccuracies in Hudson's accounts of Wyclif, Wycliffism, and lollardy (a triad of terms that this book will aslo interrogate), many of the trajectories of Hudson's work continue to set the agenda for researchers today. Her questions and categories have become entrenched in the study of late medieval English history, literature, and religion. Indeed, Fiona Somerset, a leader among the generation of scholars of lollardy that followed Hudson's, noted in 2003 that "within the last ten years or so in particular, Lollard studies have not only entered the mainstream, but come to occupy a central place."[2] In the year that Hudson's book appeared, forty-four books and articles on lollardy were published, and since then, there have been an average of more than thirty-one scholarly publications on lollardy each year, compared with an average of seven publications per year from 1900 to 1986.[3]

---

1 *PR*; for full details for this and other abbreviations, consult the Table of Abbreviations above.
2 Fiona Somerset, "Introduction," in *Influence*, 9–16, at 9.
3 The figures cited here are based on an analysis of the bibliography of secondary studies of lollardy and related topics published by the Lollard Society: "Bibliography of Secondary Sources," at http://lollardsociety.org/?page_id=10, accessed 5 July 2014.

In other quarters, however, there is skepticism about the significance of lollardy. Eamon Duffy, the Roman Catholic revisionist historian of the English reformations, aimed a direct critique at lollard studies when he wrote in the preface to the second edition of his now-classic study, *The Stripping of the Altars*, that "the impact of Lollardy on fifteenth- and early sixteenth-century religious awareness has been grossly exaggerated. The mainstream of fifteenth-century piety was indeed conventionally censorious of heresy, but not in my view greatly affected, much less shaped, by reaction to it."[4]

Stepping onto an often fiercely contested battlefield, the present book attempts to sum up, as best as is possible in the space of a few hundred pages, what we know about lollardy and what have been its fortunes in the hands of its twentieth- and twenty-first-century chroniclers. This book does not attempt to construct, nor to reinscribe, any particular meta-narrative about Wyclif or lollards. As a result, it reads in places less like a work of history than one of historiography. Nevertheless, in describing significant trends in the study of lollardy, it is also the goal of this volume to provide enough background information about the individuals, practices, texts, and beliefs that medieval and modern people have categorized as lollard to help introduce new readers to the field. If you have picked up this book with the expectation of putting it down secure in the knowledge of what lollardy was, and what role it played in English and Christian history, I am afraid that this volume will disappoint. If on the other hand you are willing to consider that the ways in which scholars and polemicists, literary critics and ecclesiastics have defined lollardy and evaluated its significance are interesting in and of themselves, then there may be something here to help deepen your understanding of the way in which lollardy has served as a window on religion, culture, and society in late medieval England.

I begin with a story that many readers will already know, indeed one that has circulated in various forms for nearly half a millennium. Having just foresworn master narratives, I nevertheless think it appropriate to start by conjuring up for our attention the tale that has traditionally been told about John Wyclif and those who have been called his "followers." What follows is cobbled together from medieval authors such as the influential Augustinian chronicler Henry Knighton, and evangelical propagandists such as John Foxe; this summary of the tales they told owes much to my colleagues Stephen E. Lahey and

---

4 Eamon Duffy, *The Stripping of the Altars: Traditional Religion in England, c. 1400–c. 1580*, 2nd ed. (New Haven, Conn., 2005), xxi. Among the most critical reactions to Duffy's work has been that of David Aers, "Altars of Power: Reflection on Eamon Duffy's *The Stripping of the Altars*," *Literature and History* 3rd ser. 3 (1994), 90–105.

INTRODUCTION

Fiona Somerset. As we move through the chapters of this book, we will see which elements of this account are true and which are false.

> Once upon a time, there lived a man named John Wyclif. Born in the 1320s or 1330s in Yorkshire, he entered the service of the church at what for us would have been a relatively early age. Bright and eager, he traveled to the south of England to pursue studies at the University of Oxford. He earned the respect of many of his colleagues there as one of the most skilled philosophers and theologians of his age, and key players at the royal court began to seek his counsel on political matters. After holding a series of lesser academic positions, in 1364 he was appointed master of Canterbury College, a community of monks and secular clergymen in Oxford recently founded by Simon Islip, the archbishop of Canterbury. When Islip died, his successor Simon Langham amended the college's statutes so that it would henceforth consist only of monks; he also deposed Wyclif from the mastership. Frustrated by this embarrassment, embittered by his inability to procure justice at the papal court, and angered further still when he was passed over for promotion to a bishopric, Wyclif began to formulate a series of progressively more controversial theological opinions.
>
> At first, Wyclif confined his pronouncements to the abstract language of academic theology, and likewise he kept discussion of them to the university where he lived and worked. Yet soon, they spilled out into the open. Wyclif and a group of scholars who gathered around him began to speak publicly, sometimes in English rather than Latin, about their views. In 1377, Pope Gregory XI sent a letter to the king of England in which he listed nineteen erroneous teachings of Wyclif's and ordered the king to suppress them. Wyclif, however, was protected by his patron John of Gaunt, the duke of Lancaster, who was effectively ruler of England early in the reign of his young nephew Richard II; initially, therefore, he was able to remain in Oxford. But when he publicly rejected the doctrine of transubstantiation—the official explanation of the miracle by which the consecrated bread and wine in the Mass were believed to turn into the body and blood of Christ—Wyclif took a step too far. He was offered the choice to remain in Oxford in silence or to leave the university forever. Opting for the latter path, he took up full-time the position of parish priest in Lutterworth, Leicestershire, where he had been serving in absentia since 1374. In Lutterworth, he continued to produce even more heterodox writings, right up until his death on New Year's Eve, 1384.

At some point, Wyclif and his followers acquired the name "Lollards", a word drawn from the New Testament parable of the wheat and the tares (*lolia*). They developed an extensive theological system, rejecting traditional understandings of the sacraments, denying the authority of the pope and his power of excommunication, criticizing the right of church institutions to own property and urging earthly lords to confiscate the church's goods, and denouncing such traditional practices as pilgrimage and the adoration of images of Jesus, Mary, and the saints. Either Wyclif alone, or Wyclif with some of his followers, translated the Bible into English, an act that made the gospel accessible to all, rather than merely the clerical elite. They produced dozens of commentaries, sermons, polemical texts, and devotional writings, the majority of them also in the vernacular tongue.

For all these deeds, Wyclif and his followers were persecuted, punished, and in many cases executed. A council of bishops and scholars met in London in 1382 to formally condemn Wyclif's opinions; he was posthumously pronounced a heretic at the general council of the western church that met in Constance in 1415. Trials of suspected Lollards began to take place around the time of Wyclif's death and continued through the early sixteenth century. Nevertheless, the number of people who subscribed to Wyclif's views only grew. Early on, Wyclif's followers received support from knights, perhaps even some nobles, at the royal court, who sheltered them and provided them with opportunities to preach. One Lollard knight, Sir John Oldcastle, went so far as to foment a rebellion against the crown. Later, when the failure of Oldcastle's short-lived revolt made gentry support for Lollardy more scarce, heresy was passed down from generation to generation in close-knit communities in (among other places) Norwich, Bristol, London, Coventry, and the Kentish Weald. In fact, heresy investigations early in the reign of Henry VIII uncovered moderately sized Lollard communities in many of the same places where they had first been detected a century earlier. Some of these later Lollards became early Protestants, helping to disseminate Lutheran texts, produce the first printed English Bibles, and spread evangelical teachings at the royal court. When Henry made the decision to break from the church of Rome, these Lollard-Protestants rejoiced that the vision that they had inherited from Wyclif and sustained through decades of persecution had finally come to pass.[5]

---

5 This account draws upon and significantly expands that of the introduction to *Wycliffite Spirituality*, 2–3.

This story relies upon a series of assumptions—conjectures, for instance, about Wyclif's psychological motivations, about the uniformity of lollard belief, about the origins of the Wycliffite translation of the Bible, about the survival of lollardy into the sixteenth century, and about its relationship with the reformation of King Henry. Each of these assumptions, especially the last, may reveal more about the religious and historical worldviews of the persons who made them than about the actual situation of late medieval England. The chapters that follow will hold up for closer examination the latent theological and historiographical claims implied in the traditional account of Wyclif and his followers. We will begin, in Chapter 2, with the individuals whose names are most closely linked with Wyclif and lollardy, before turning to consider lollard religious practices (Chapter 3), lollard writings (Chapter 4), and lollard beliefs (Chapter 5). The placement of practices before writings and beliefs may be surprising to some readers, but in keeping with the findings of the modern theological discipline known as practical theology, it reflects the fact that practices shape beliefs at least as often as beliefs shape practices. The remaining three chapters chronicle the institutional church's response to lollardy, as well as the fate of lollards, their texts, and their beliefs in the years leading up to the English Reformation. We will meet some academic and ecclesial opponents of lollardy (Chapter 6), consider when, how, and by whom lollards were tried in church courts (Chapter 7), and look at the afterlife of lollardy in a variety of contexts, English and continental (Chapter 8). A brief conclusion at the end of the book returns to the overarching historiographical questions of this introductory chapter.

1.1   Developments in Lollard Studies

In a very real sense, the study of lollardy can be traced back to the early 1380s, when chroniclers and other writers began to describe the existence of a sect of individuals who had gathered around Wyclif, appropriating his theological and philosophical positions as their own.[6] These authors were participating in a centuries-long tradition of polemical confrontation between self-consciously orthodox Christians and those whom they deemed religiously other. Since the second century, when the Greek word *hairesis* began to be used

---

6   I will be considering in some detail below the implications of calling lollards a sect; for the best treatment of this topic, see Margaret Aston, "Were the Lollards a Sect?" in *The Medieval Church: Universities, Heresy, and the Religious Life: Essays in Honour of Gordon Leff*, (eds.) Peter Biller and R.B. Dobson, Studies in Church History, Subsidia 11 (Oxford, 1999), 163–91.

by ecclesiastical writers to denote not simply an individual's morally neutral choice between competing schools of thought, but rather her or his fundamentally erroneous and evil choice to deviate from the true faith, Christianity had developed an extensive discourse about heresy.[7] Early writers such as Epiphanius of Salamis produced catalogues of the heresies that church leaders and fellow believers should avoid; the tradition was carried on in the year 429 by that most formidable of Christian scholars, Augustine of Hippo.[8] His *De haeresibus* (*On Heresies*) was in many ways a typical contribution to the emerging genre of heresiography, that is, writing about heresy. Just as church fathers like Augustine traced their beliefs through a succession of church leaders back to Jesus' apostles, they also traced the development of seemingly new heresies through a succession of their erroneous predecessors back to Simon Magus, the so-called "magician" of the Acts of the Apostles, whom they denounced as the first heretic.

The earliest medieval writers to mention Wyclif and his associates—canons regular such as Knighton, secular priests such as Adam Usk, and clerks who worked in the papal and royal chanceries—therefore perceived the rise to prominence of a heterodox Oxford scholar as yet another iteration of the perennial conflict between the faith of Christ and the snares of the devil. Many of these authors clothed "the Wycliffites" in the trappings of other known heresies, past as well as present. They assumed that Wyclif, like his reviled predecessors, must have sought to recruit a corps of followers, as well as that Wycliffites must possess a set of mutually agreed upon doctrines, must have developed covert structures of religious authority, must have held secret gatherings for prayer and reading, and must have conducted outreach to others with the intent of converting them to their heterodox beliefs. The result of such assumptions was often a portrait of Wycliffism sketched in far greater detail than the evidence available to medieval writers ought to have permitted; as a result, there often are substantial differences between what the authorities

---

7 On the origins of the Christian concept of heresy, see among others Alain Le Boulluec, *La notion d'hérésie dans la literature grecque*, 2 vols. (Paris, 1985); Rebecca Lyman, "A Topography of Heresy: Mapping the Rhetorical Creation of Arianism," in *Arianism after Arius: Essays on the Development of the Fourth-Century Trinitarian Conflicts*, (eds.) M.R. Barnes and D.H. Williams (Edinburgh, 1993), 45–62; and Lyman, "Heresiology: The Invention of 'Heresy' and 'Schism'," in *The Cambridge History of Christianity, Volume 2: Constantine to c. 600*, (eds.) Augustine Casiday and Frederick W. Norris (Cambridge, 2007), 296–313.

8 See *The Panarion of Epiphanius of Salamis*, trans. Frank Williams, 2 vols. (Leiden, 1987–94); Augustine, *Heresies*, in *Arianism and Other Heresies*, (ed.) John E. Rotelle, trans. Roland J. Teske (Hyde Park, N.Y., 1995).

of their day expected of Wycliffites and what Wycliffites may actually have believed, done, and preached.

For convenience, it is possible to speak of three broad phases in the history of writings about Wycliffism or, as it quickly came to be called, lollardy. The heresiographical work of late medieval chroniclers and scribes represents the first of these phases. With the religious, social, and cultural changes introduced in the wake of Henry VIII's reformation, the study of lollardy entered a second, confessional phase. Here, writers on both the "Catholic" and "Protestant" sides of the reformation divide employed lollardy as an example in their attempts to prove that their particular church was the true successor of the church founded by Christ.[9] For evangelical writers such as John Foxe, the church historian, propagandist, and author of the *Actes and Monuments* (known in its abridged version to generations of Protestant worshippers as Foxe's *Book of Martyrs*), lollardy represented the survival of the gospel amidst the corruption of the medieval institutional church:

> For to say the truth, if tymes had bene well searched, or if they which wrote histories had without partiallitie gone vpright betwen God, and Baal, halting on neither side, it might well haue bene found the most part of all this Catholicke corruption intruded into the Church...al these (I say) to be new nothings lately coyned in the minte of Rome, without any stampe of antiquitie, as by readyng of this present history shall sufficiently, I trust, appeare. Which history therfore I haue here taken in hand, that as other storywriters heretofore haue employed their trauaile to magnifie the Church of Rome: so in this history might appeare to all Christen readers the Image of both Churches, aswell of the one, as of the other: especially of the poore oppressed and persecuted Church of Christ. Which persecuted Church though it hath bene of long season trodden vnder foote by enemies, neglected in the world, nor regarded in histories, &

---

9 To use the terms "Catholic" and "Protestant" with regard to early sixteenth century religion is to risk anachronism, as the word "Protestant" was not used in its modern sense until, at the very earliest, the reign of King Edward VI (1547–1553). The word "Catholic" was likewise contested: as Diarmaid MacCulloch has written about the sixteenth century, "in fact there were very many different Reformations, nearly all of which would have said that they were simply aimed at recreating authentic Catholic Christianity" (*Reformation: Europe's House Divided* [London, 2003], xix). Following MacCulloch, in this book I will be using the term "evangelical" to describe the movement of late medieval and early modern religious reform that produced today's Protestant churches.

almost scarce visible or knowne to worldly eyes, yet hath it bene the true Church onely of God.[10]

Seeking to demonstrate the continuity between his own Church of England and the primitive church of Jesus' apostles and their immediate successors, Foxe portrayed Wyclif and lollards as members of the "secret multitude of true professors" who had descended from the apostles, preserving authentic Christian doctrine and practice in the face of opposition from increasingly venal prelates and their enforcers.[11] As we will see, Foxe's interest in lollardy had more to do with its place in his theologically inflected narrative of the progress of the gospel and less to do with actual lollards' intellectual and theological positions, which he sometimes whitewashed in order to remove whatever did not cohere with his depiction of Wyclif and his associates as forerunners of sixteenth-century evangelicalism.[12]

Of course, not everyone who lived during the tumultuous years of the English reformations saw things Foxe's way. Catholic polemicists condemned latter-day reformers for associating themselves with Wyclif, whose teachings had been anathematized at the Council of Constance. Thomas More, for instance, alleged that the sixteenth-century biblical translator and evangelical preacher William Tyndale was a disciple of "Wyclyffe, the fyrst founder here of that abominable heresye, that blasphemeth the blessed sacrament."[13] Anti-Lutheran writings of the sixteenth century employed the same tropes that had been used against Wycliffites, as well as against earlier heretics, and many criticized Luther for the kind of embitterment against the church that they also believed had characterized Wyclif.[14]

---

10   *A&M*, 2–3. For further discussion of the portrayal of lollards by Foxe, see Chapter 8 below, and on early modern church history more generally, see Joseph H. Preston, "English Ecclesiastical Historians and the Problem of Bias, 1559–1742," *Journal of the History of Ideas* 32 (1971), 203–20.

11   *A&M*, 945.

12   On this point, see J.A.F. Thomson, "John Foxe and Some Sources for Lollard History: Notes for a Critical Reappraisal," in *Studies in Church History* 2, (ed.) G.J. Cuming (London, 1965), 251–57; see also additional discussion in Chapter 7 below.

13   Thomas More, *The Confutation of Tyndale's Answer*, in *The Complete Works of St Thomas More*, (eds.) Louis A. Schuster, Richard C. Marius, et al., vol. 8 (New Haven, Conn., 1973), part ii, 587; see also Polydore Vergil, *Anglica historia*, 2 vols. (Ghent, 1556–58), II, i, 1016–17, quoted in James Crompton, "John Wyclif: A Study in Mythology," *Transactions of the Leicestershire Archaeological and Historical Society* 42 (1966–67), 6–34, at 9.

14   See "A Most Stupid Scoundrel: Some Early English Responses to Luther," in John Edwards and Edward Wesley, (eds.), *Literatures of Luther* (Eugene, Ore., 2014), 1–25.

It would not be difficult to recall other instances where early modern writers presented lollards in the light most conducive to their theological agendas. Indeed, to borrow a metaphor from the reformation historian Peter Marshall, it is not unfair to remark that in early modern hands lollardy was often little more than an "ideological football," a name with which to conjure visions of either the persecution of the gospel or the spread of heresy in the years leading up to the break between England and Rome.[15] Many subsequent historians, especially prior to the mid-twentieth century, likewise allowed their own religious convictions to color their views of Wyclif and his associates. Wyclif's early biographers, including Thomas James, who served as the first librarian of Thomas Bodley's library in Oxford, pronounced Wyclif "an absolute Protestant" before his time.[16] By the mid-nineteenth century, especially in Anglican circles, "Wyclif had been well launched as a hero."[17] His growing prominence coincided with the publication of a series of texts related to the movement he was thought to have led. The five hundredth anniversary of Wyclif's death was marked by the foundation of a Wyclif Society dedicated to printing his whole corpus of Latin works, and editions of bishops' registers and inquisitorial court books containing the records of medieval heresy trials appeared in increasing numbers from the early twentieth century onward.

It has only been in the last fifty years or so that scholars have, in the main, moved beyond confessional approaches to the study of lollardy. This is not to say, however, that such scholarship is no longer being produced.[18] Most contemporary work on lollardy instead reflects what I will be calling the mindset of the historical professional. I deliberately choose this phrase as an alternative to the more popular designation "post-confessional." As Marshall has eloquently pointed out in a recent essay, the emergence of postmodern perspectives on western historical writing and its debts to the epistemological norms of the academy renders it impossible for any historian to write from a standpoint of total objectivity.[19] While contemporary historians may consciously forswear the theological master-narratives of writers like Knighton, Foxe, and More, their identities as Roman Catholics, Marxists, Anglicans, atheists, women, men,

---

15   For a detailed account of the confessional agendae of scholars of Wyclif and lollardy in the late nineteenth and early twentieth centuries, see Peter Marshall, "Lollards and Protestants Revisited," in *Wycliffite Controversies*, 295–318, at 315.
16   Quoted in Crompton, "John Wyclif," 14.
17   Crompton, "John Wyclif," 16.
18   See, for instance, John Stacey, "John Wyclif as Theologian," *Expository Times* 101 (1990), 134–41.
19   Peter Marshall, "(Re)defining the English Reformation," *Journal of British Studies* 48 (2009), 564–86.

British, American (or, most likely, more than one of these) cannot help but continue to influence the ways in which they think and write.[20] What most distinguishes professional from confessional scholarship is that in the former, the temptation to produce a totalizing, value-laden account of lollardy and its significance is set aside in favor of more circumscribed intellectual goals. As a result, one of the most salient characteristics of this newest phase in the study of lollardy is that its practitioners tend to be interested in lollardy not primarily on account of its relationship, real or imagined, to the events of the English reformations. Rather, most of the time, they are interested in lollardy for its own sake. To borrow the words of one scholar who has been vocal in his opposition to writings on lollardy that overemphasize its relationship to later reformations, even critical or skeptical accounts of lollardy have begun to take it as their goal "to appreciate what lollardy was and what it meant to its adherents and its opponents."[21] It will not be surprising that, as a result, most contemporary writers on lollardy are specialists primarily in the literature, history, and theology of the middle ages rather than those of the Reformation or the early modern period.

The boundaries between the three phases of scholarship I have delineated are not, however, nearly as distinct as this account might suggest: heresiography was produced well into the nineteenth century, and some confessional historians and theologians continue to write today. Nevertheless, it has been through the work of two Oxford scholars, Margaret Aston and Anne Hudson, that professional scholarship on lollardy has flowered. Aston, an ecclesiastical historian trained under K.B. McFarlane, wrote her doctoral thesis on the career of Thomas Arundel, the archbishop of Canterbury dubbed by one lollard writer "þe grettist enmy þat Crist haþ in Ynglond."[22] She published widely on the dissemination of lollard ideas in the fourteenth, fifteenth, and sixteenth centuries; on the careers of individual lollards; and on the survival of Wyclif's memory

---

20   See also Marshall's observations on the religious backgrounds of professional Reformation scholars who have contested the role of lollardy in the English reformations: "Lollards and Protestants Revisited," 314–15. There is not space here to address the important, and complex, debates among historians about subjectivity, the so-called linguistic turn, and the historian's social and academic roles. For one recent account of the state of the historical profession in relation to these and cognate topics, see Gabrielle M. Spiegel, "The Task of the Historian," *American Historical Review* 114 (2009), 1–15.
21   Richard Rex, *The Lollards* (Basingstoke, 2002), 149.
22   *Tractatus de oblacione iugis sacrificii*, in Anne Hudson, (ed.), *The Works of a Lollard Preacher* (EETS o.s. 317, 2001), line 405.

INTRODUCTION   11

into the reformation period.²³ Her book on opposition to religious images in the middle ages, *England's Iconoclasts, Volume 1*, remains a standard reference work.²⁴ Hudson, on the other hand, has brought to the study of lollardy the tools of textual criticism and analysis. From her early work on medieval English chronicles, she has established, through a series of groundbreaking essays, articles, and critical editions, a place as unquestionably the preeminent living scholar of Wycliffite texts. Her monograph *The Premature Reformation*, with which I introduced this chapter, both summarized the findings of her work on lollard writings and provided a point of entry to the study of lollardy for scholars working in a range of cognate fields. More recently, she has published a collection of essays on the survival and transmission of Wyclif's Latin writings and has produced an edition and investigation of the Wycliffite Glossed Gospels.²⁵

If Aston, Hudson, and their contemporaries constituted the first generation of historical-professional students of lollardy, then it may be fair to say that the majority of currently active scholars in the field comprise a second generation. Like all children, they have both learned from and yet in some ways rejected the ideas of their scholarly parents. In the main, second-generation lollard scholars work in departments of English language and literature. A substantial majority of them are female. Many are professionally interested in lollard texts and history at the same time as they investigate the works of other, better-known writers like Geoffrey Chaucer, John Gower, and William Langland. For them, lollardy is part of the broader literary and intellectual history of fourteenth- and fifteenth-century England. There are a number of prominent exceptions to this profile, as we will see in later chapters: some of the best work on the identification and trial of heresy suspects has been done by more conventional ecclesiastical and religious historians, while at the same time a small but prolific cadre of theologians has begun to investigate anew the theological and philosophical content of Wyclif's writings.²⁶

---

23   Many of Aston's classic essays have appeared in two collections of her writings: *Lollards and Reformers*; and *Faith and Fire: Popular and Unpopular Religion, 1350–1600* (London, 1993).
24   Margaret Aston, *England's Iconoclasts: Volume 1: Laws against Images* (Oxford, 1998).
25   Hudson's publications are too numerous to list here, but the most significant are PR; the collections of her essays *Books* and *Studies in the Transmission of Wyclif's Writings* (Aldershot, 2008); and her editions EWS; *Selections*; *The Works of a Lollard Preacher*; and *Two Wycliffite Texts* (EETS o.s. 301, 1993). Most recent is *Doctors in English: A Study of the Wycliffite Gospel Commentaries* (Liverpool, 2015). Fiona Somerset discusses these and other lollard writings at length in Chapter 4 below.
26   Among historians, I am thinking especially of Jeremy Catto, whose work on the history of the University of Oxford has provided a valuable context for Wyclif's and Wycliffite

Like the blurry lines between major phases in the historiography of lollardy, first-generation and second-generation lollard scholars are not as rigidly separable as the distinction might suggest. Broadly speaking, there are at least five characteristics that typically differentiate recent contributions to the study of lollardy from their predecessors. First, whereas earlier scholars were often ready to accept medieval chroniclers' and polemicists' characterizations of lollardy as a primarily negative tradition, one interested more in the rejection of institutional religion than in the building up of alternative forms of Christianity, recent work has explored the positive spiritual and theological ideals of lollard writers; emphasized the continuities, rather than the discontinuities, between lollards and mainstream Christians; amd sought to explain lollardy's appeal at a time when it had the potential to lead to a death sentence. Somerset has led the way in this regard, producing a book on lollard spirituality and contributing to a collection of translations of lollard spiritual writings into modern English.[27] Second, while much scholarship on lollardy remains unabashedly interdisciplinary, a number of specifically disciplinary voices have begun to assert themselves, arguing that historical, literary, or theological methods can reveal details about lollards and lollardy that interdisciplinary approaches might overlook. This trend has been especially visible in the use among scholars of English literature of formalism, a type of literary analysis that takes as its starting point the relationship of a particular text to the genres of texts being produced during the same time period.[28] Next, just as in the study of the English reformations broad generalizations about the impact of reform have given way to local and microhistorical studies, so also has much recent work on lollardy focused on prosopography (the study of individual persons), on the social relationships

---

theology, and of Ian Forrest, whose monograph *The Detection of Heresy in Late Medieval England* (Oxford, 2005) is invaluable for studies of its topic. Among theologians, the many publications by Stephen E. Lahey and Ian Christopher Levy cited in this volume are evidence of their great productivity in retrieving Wyclif as a late medieval scholastic theologian.

27 Fiona Somerset, *Feeling Like Saints: Lollard Writings after Wyclif* (Ithaca, N.Y., 2014). See also Jennifer Illig, "Through a Lens of Likeness: Reading *English Wycliffite Sermons* in Light of Contemporary Sermon Texts" (Ph.D. diss., Fordham University, 2014), and *Wycliffite Spirituality*.

28 See for instance, Ian Forrest, "Lollardy and Late Medieval History," and Shannon Gayk, "Lollard Writings, Literary Criticism, and the Meaningfulness of Form," both in *Wycliffite Controversies*, 121–34 and 135–52. On formalism, see also Bruce Holsinger, "Lollard Ekphrasis: Situated Aesthetics and Literary History," *Journal of Medieval and Early Modern Studies* 35 (2005), 67–90.

and interconnections within particular lollard communities, and on the local economic activity of those identified as or suspected of being lollards.[29]

Fourth, scholars of lollardy have taken more seriously the impact on late medieval England of a range of religious phenomena that were occurring contemporaneously on the European continent.[30] Kathryn Kerby-Fulton's 2006 monograph *Books under Suspicion*, for instance, argues that the study of lollardy can ill afford to ignore the traditions of apocalyptic and visionary writing, such as those associated with Joachim of Fiore and the Spiritual Franciscans, that remained influential in fourteenth- and fifteenth-century England.[31] Other scholars have called for greater attention to the relationship between lollardy in England and the Hussite movement in Bohemia, suggesting that ideas flowed both ways across the English Channel, rather than unidirectionally from Oxford to Prague.[32] Still others have recommended that lollard scholars question more assertively other long-held assumptions about insularity, such as that only the Middle English, rather than also the Anglo-Norman, vernacular is implicated in the phenomenon of lollardy; or that there were few heretics in England prior to the time of Wyclif.[33]

Finally, specialists in other European dissenting movements, such as the so-called "Cathars" of southern France and Italy, have suggested both that medieval churchmen employed against lollards a series of tools that had already been forged in campaigns against continental heretics, and that the study of lollardy could benefit from some of the methods developed in the study of

---

29 Among the most recent work that falls into this category, see Maureen Jurkowski, "Lollardy and Social Status in East Anglia," *Speculum* 82 (2007), 120–52; and Robert Lutton, *Lollardy and Orthodox Religion in Pre-reformation England: Reconstructing Piety* (London, 2006).

30 See especially John van Engen, "A World Astir: Europe and Religion in the Early Fifteenth Century," in *Europe After Wyclif*, (eds.) J. Patrick Hornbeck II and Michael Van Dussen (New York, forthcoming 2016).

31 Kathryn Kerby-Fulton, *Books under Suspicion: Censorship and Tolerance of Revelatory Writing in Late Medieval England* (South Bend, Ind., 2006). See also, more recently, John H. Arnold, "The Materiality of Unbelief in Late Medieval England," in *The Unorthodox Imagination in Late Medieval Britain*, (ed.) Sophie Page (Manchester, 2010), 65–95.

32 See, for instance, Michael Van Dussen, "Conveying Heresy: 'A Certayne Student' and the Lollard-Hussite Fellowship," *Viator* 38 (2007), 217–34, and Van Dussen, *From England to Bohemia: Heresy and Communication in the Later Middle Ages* (Cambridge, 2012).

33 On lollardy and Anglo-Norman literature, see Nicholas Watson, "Lollardy: The Anglo-Norman Heresy?" in *Language and Culture in Medieval Britain*, (eds.) Jocelyn Wogan-Browne et al. (York, 2009), 334–46. For the most recent investigation into pre-Wycliffite heresy, which focuses on the University of Oxford, see Andrew E. Larsen, *The School of Heretics: Academic Condemnation at the University of Oxford, 1277–1409* (Leiden, 2011).

these groups.³⁴ Among the methodological moves these historians have recommended is to apply to the study of late medieval heresy the insights of twentieth and twenty-first-century critical theory, most commonly the ideas about power, punishment, and confession articulated by Michel Foucault. Scholars of Catharism such as John H. Arnold, James Given, and Mark Gregory Pegg have deployed Foucault's analysis of the power differentials operative in the coercive environment of a heresy trial in order to argue for the instability not only of individual trial records but even of the very concept of a discrete heresy or heretical movement.³⁵ We will see later in this book that some scholars of lollardy have evinced a similar kind of skepticism in their reading of documents prepared by the opponents of putative heretics: R.N. Swanson, for instance, has used the theoretical framework of James C. Scott's writings on resistance movements to characterize lollard practices as a form of "hidden transcript" performed by those too disempowered to resist the medieval ecclesiastical system directly.³⁶

In these and other ways, the study of lollardy today is qualitatively different from the pioneering work of Hudson and Aston. Yet despite these and other methodological developments, many of the questions asked by first-generation lollard scholars remain very much alive. What did it mean in the Middle Ages, and what does it mean now, to call someone a lollard, or a Wycliffite? What theological ideas that lollards believed in set them apart from mainstream Christianity? How did lollard groups disseminate their ideas and recruit new members? What sorts of religious practices did they engage in? And perhaps the most perennial question of all: did late medieval lollardy survive in any meaningful sense into the sixteenth century, and if it did, did lollardy exert any discernible influence on the shape of King Henry's reformation?

---

34   For an excellent representative of these trends, see John Arnold, "Lollard Trials and Inquisitorial Discourse," in *Fourteenth Century England II*, (ed.) Christopher Given-Wilson (Woodbridge, 2002).

35   See, for instance, John H. Arnold, *Inquisition and Power: Catharism and the Confessing Subject in Medieval Languedoc* (Philadelphia, 2001); Arnold, "Inquisition, Texts, and Discourse," in *Texts and the Repression of Medieval Heresy*, (eds.) Caterina Bruschi and Peter Biller (Woodbridge, 2003), 63–80; James B. Given, *Inquisition and Medieval Society: Power, Discipline and Resistance in Languedoc* (Ithaca, N.Y., 2001); and Mark Gregory Pegg, *The Corruption of Angels: The Great Inquisition of 1245–1246* (Princeton, N.J., 2001); Pegg, *A Most Holy War: The Albigensian Crusade and the Battle for Christendom* (New York, 2008). Claire Taylor, in *Heresy, Crusade, and Inquisition in Medieval Quercy* (York, 2011), uses local evidence to refute some of the stronger forms of this argument.

36   R.N. Swanson, "'Lollardy', 'Orthodoxy', and 'Resistance' in Pre-reformation England," *Theological Journal* (Tartu, Estonia) 64:1 (2003), 12–26.

1.2 Terminological Quandaries

Before answering any of these questions, however, it is necessary first to interrogate more closely some of the terms that we have already been using. What, after all, is a "lollard"? Is a "lollard" the same thing as a "Wycliffite"? Must a person, or a text, possess a particular set of attributes to be judged a "lollard"? Are there characteristics that, if a person possessed them, would put that person beyond suspicion of lollardy altogether?

These and similar questions have fueled some of the longest standing debates among scholars of English religion in the later Middle Ages. Even the etymology of the term *lollard* remains disputed, with some arguing that it came into use in England after having been applied to the beguines and beghards, communities of semi-lay, semi-religious men and women in France and the Low Countries; others suggesting that it was originally a pun on the Latin word *lolium*, referring to the tares in the New Testament parable of the wheat and the tares; and yet others tracing it back to a Middle Dutch word that originally referred to mumbling.[37] The timing of its first use in England has also been a matter of some uncertainty: was "lollard" coined specifically in response to the controversies that surrounded John Wyclif and his early academic followers, or was it a term of abuse already in circulation?[38] Finally, is it helpful—or even meaningful—to distinguish between lollards, Lollards, and Wycliffites?

The assumption that Wyclif's views and those of later dissenters formed a coherent theological program—an assumption that as we have seen underpinned the religiously confessional polemics of both the evangelical Foxe and the traditionalist More—remained influential through the late nineteenth and early twentieth centuries. At that point, a majority of scholars began to distinguish, more or less sharply, between Wyclif and those who came after him. The German historian Gotthard Lechler, for instance, described an "inner circle" of Wyclif's closest followers and an "outer circle" of those who may have been

---

37 For the biblical parable, see Matt. 13:24–30. Widely divergent accounts of the application of the term to late medieval English heretics can be found in Andrew Cole, "William Langland and the Invention of Lollardy," in *Influence*, 37–58, and Cole, *Literature and Heresy in the Age of Chaucer* (Cambridge, 2008); Wendy Scase, *'Piers Plowman' and the New Anti-clericalism* (Cambridge, 1989), 150–51; and Michael Wilks, "Wyclif and the Great Persecution," in *Wyclif*, 179–203, among many studies.

38 For some answers to these questions, see Cole, *Literature and Heresy*; Wendy Scase, "'Heu! quanta desolatio Angliae praestatur': A Wycliffite Libel and the Naming of Heretics, Oxford 1382," in *Influence*, 19–36, and the earlier works cited there; and John Scattergood, "The Date of Sir John Clanvowe's *The Two Ways* and the 'Reinvention' of Lollardy," *Medium Aevum* 79 (2010), 116–20.

inspired by his reforming ideas but nevertheless did not endorse all of them.[39] The distinction became more pronounced in the next few decades of work on the subject: Ezra Kempton Maxfield, writing in 1924, was following the terminological fashion of his day when he suggested that not all "Wyclifian" ideas were carried over into the theologies of "later Lollardry."[40] Nevertheless, the suggestion that medieval heretics be separated into theologically aware, Latinate "Wycliffites" and somewhat less sophisticated, vernacular "Lollards" was never unanimously embraced.

In the opening pages of her magisterial work *The Premature Reformation*, Hudson opined that the distinction between "the academic disciples of Wyclif" and "the later, provincial Lollard[s]" is ultimately untenable.[41] Indeed, she soon argued elsewhere, Wyclif's own contemporaries saw the two words as roughly equivalent.[42] Throughout her many publications, Hudson has treated the terms *Lollard* and *Wycliffite* as interchangeable.[43] Many of her contemporaries and students have followed the same practice, and in the late 1980s, 1990s, and early 2000s it was familiar to discover in the first footnote of a scholarly book or article the statement that the two terms would be used interchangeably.[44] Nevertheless, a number of voices have been raised to challenge this consensus. Richard G. Davies, in a well-received 1990 address to the Royal Historical Society, distinguished between the academic enterprise conceived by Wyclif and the reformist views and activities of the local communities of religious dissenters that continued to dot the English landscape through the early sixteenth century. As Davies memorably put it, "If Wyclifitism [*sic*] was what you knew, Lollardy was whom you knew."[45] The Oxford historian Jeremy Catto has argued that the category of lollardy is "effectively meaningless," because most of the people who have been described as lollards would not have acknowledged the label as naming more than a single, often secondary, facet of their

---

39   Lechler, 439.
40   Ezra Kempton Maxfield, "Chaucer and Religious Reform," *PMLA* 39 (1924), 64–74 at 67, 68.
41   *PR*, 2.
42   Anne Hudson, "*Laicus Litteratus*: The Paradox of Lollardy," in *Heresy and Literacy, 1000–1530*, (eds.) Peter Biller and Anne Hudson (Cambridge, 1994), 222–36.
43   This remains Hudson's position in a recent scholarly article, "Five Problems in Wycliffite Texts and a Suggestion," *Medium Aevum* 80 (2011), 301–24; see especially n. 7.
44   In the interest of full disclosure, it is worth admitting that many of my first publications on lollardy employed this convention: see for instance "*Lollard* Sermons? Soteriology and Late Medieval Dissent," *Notes and Queries* 53 (Mar. 2006), 26–30.
45   Richard Davies, "Lollardy and Locality," *Transactions of the Royal Historical Society*, 6th ser. 1 (1991), 191–212.

identity.[46] Putting the case against the equivalence of lollardy and Wycliffism perhaps most forcefully of all, Andrew Cole argued in a 2008 study that in late medieval England, lollardy denoted not merely and not always adherence to a particular set of theological views, but rather the rhetorical and social status of an outcast. For Cole, "[t]he term 'lollard' is a curse word generated by persons who, in the first instance, are intent on marshaling the greatest resources of secular and ecclesiastical institutions against individuals at Oxford and elsewhere. It is also bandied about by those who are sympathetic to such an approach."[47] Analyzing the works of a range of authors to show that the category "lollardy" testifies to the existence of a complex politics of religious and ecclesiastical identity in late medieval England, Cole's book drew a firm distinction between the blurry semiotics of lollardy and the specific intellectual and religious claims of Wycliffism.

Is it possible to move beyond this impasse? It is helpful to point out that each of the terminological practices I have been describing has its advantages. For Hudson, on the one hand, treating lollardy and Wycliffism synonymously freed her to present more straightforwardly the results of her meticulous work among the archives of lollard texts and trial records. Her practice also reflects the usage of some medieval writers, such as the Carmelite prior provincial and anti-Wycliffite polemicist Thomas Netter, who often spoke of lollards and Wycliffites in the same breath.[48] For Cole, on the other hand, drawing a sharp distinction between Wycliffism and lollardy allows him to underscore the extent to which the category of lollardy possessed a wider and more complicated valence in late medieval society than did the category of Wycliffism.[49]

Without wishing to imply that mine is the only viable approach, in this book I will be writing primarily about lollards and only rarely about Wycliffites. This is because, following a number of recent specialists in this area, I take "Wycliffism" to be a term both of heresiography and intellectual history: it is

---

46 Jeremy Catto, "Fellows and Helpers: The Religious Identity of the Followers of Wyclif," in *The Medieval Church: Universities, Heresy, and the Religious Life: Essays in Honour of Gordon Leff*, (eds.) Peter Biller and R.B. Dobson, Studies in Church History, Subsidia 11 (Oxford, 1999), 141–62; likewise, see Catto, "Religious Change under Henry V," in *Henry V: The Practice of Kingship*, (ed.) G.L. Harriss (Oxford, 1985), 97–115, at 113.

47 Cole, *Literature and Heresy*, 72.

48 Wyclif's opponents are treated at length by Mishtooni Bose in Chapter 6 below; for Netter, see especially Kevin Alban, *The Teaching and Impact of the Doctrinale of Thomas Netter of Walden (c. 1374–1430)* (Turnhout, 2010), as well as the collection of essays, *Thomas Netter of Walden: Carmelite, Diplomat and Theologian (c.1372-1430)*, (eds.) Johan Bergstrøm-Allen and Richard Copsey (Faversham, Eng., 2009).

49 Cole, *Literature and Heresy*, 72–74.

the word that the supporters of institutionally sanctioned orthodoxy used to denote the "school" of individuals who followed Wyclif into his heterodox beliefs, and it is likewise a word that modern scholars can usefully continue to use to refer to people and texts that reflect the influence of Wyclif and his ideas. The number of such people and texts is not as great as one might imagine, however: once the assumption that every religious dissenter in late medieval England must have some connection to Wyclif and his associates is set aside, it is not always easy to demonstrate a relationship, direct or indirect, between Wyclif's ideas and any particular individual or text. "Lollardy," on the other hand, is a more capacious word: it is a subjective term, a term of abuse used both by dissenters against their clerical antagonists and by clerics against dissenters, whether Wycliffite or otherwise.[50] Therefore, the while the vast majority of Wyclif's controversial works, and those promoted by him, were treated as (and here are called) lollard, not every text or individual that was reviled as lollard is demonstrably Wycliffite.

I must hasten to add that in this book, as in many recent studies, the word "lollard" does not function like an on/off switch. Hudson, Jill C. Havens, and others have written of a "grey area" between the totalizing orthodoxy demanded (at least in theory) by the institutional church, and the position of utter heterodoxy imputed by some medieval ecclesiastics to Wyclif and his followers.[51] On the view of these scholars, there is something of a continuum or sliding scale between heresy and orthodoxy, a spectrum on which it is possible to situate particular individuals and texts. However, as I have argued elsewhere, despite its many merits, even this model runs the risk of oversimplification.[52] A person might be theologically orthodox yet have become suspect of lollardy on account of her associations with prominent lollards, or her unusual religious practices; likewise, another person might hold a position of church leadership and conduct himself unimpeachably as a leading member of his community, yet privately hold heterodox views. Borrowing from the philosophical work of Ludwig Wittgenstein the notion of "membership gradience," that is, the idea

[50] For help in clarifying my thinking on the subjective nature of "lollardy," I am hugely indebted to Mishtooni Bose and am grateful to her for sharing with me a prepublication draft of her essay "The Trouble with Lollardy." There are some instructive parallels with the term "Gnosticism," as presently employed in a qualified manner by historians of early Christianity: see, for instance, Karen L. King, *What is Gnosticism?* (Cambridge, Mass., 2005).

[51] Jill C. Havens, "Shading the Grey Area: Determining Heresy in Middle English Texts," in *Text and Controversy*, 337–52.

[52] This is the thesis of the first chapter of my book *What is a Lollard? Dissent and Belief in Late Medieval England* (Oxford, 2010).

that within a group, some individuals may fall closer to or further away from those who best exemplify the group as a whole, I have suggested that the study of lollardy runs the risk of anachronism when too strict a distinction between lollards and non-lollards is employed, or when lollardy is thought to have a single, fixed meaning.[53] Therefore, my decision in this book to write the word "lollard" without the traditional capital L (except where the word is capitalized by those I am quoting) is an attempt to avoid implicitly attributing too much coherence—intellectual, theological, political, or otherwise—to the religious phenomena I will be discussing.

After all these preliminaries, then, we can say that this book is about lollards, about a not particularly well-defined set of individuals whose beliefs, actions, and social affiliations caused them to be thought of as suspect by the religious authorities of late medieval England. Some of the individuals I will be discussing have names that are known to us; others, like the writers of the majority of extant lollard texts, do not. Some of them professed beliefs quite similar to those that landed Wyclif in trouble; others, like the fifteenth-century mystic Margery Kempe, who in her autobiographical *Book* recalls at least half a dozen accusations of lollardy made against her, described their faith in terms that would likely have satisfied even the strictest inquisitor.[54] Some were bound together as members of local or regional communities of reformers who recognized one another as fellow dissenters from the ecclesiastical *status quo*; others appear together in this volume only on account of the shared experience of persecution that binds them across expanses of time and distance.

Yet the meaning of "lollard" and "Wycliffite" is not the only terminological issue that scholars have had to confront. Lollards have often been described as members of a heretical sect that was founded in an academic environment and gradually emerged as a popular heresy: these terms, too, deserve unpacking.

What does and what does not constitute heresy is not as simple a question as it may seem. Consider, for instance, that in the wake of the 1431 council of Basel-Ferrara-Florence, it was not orthodox for a western Christian to believe

---

53 A more detailed discussion of Wittgenstein's philosophy and its relevance to the classification of heretics in late medieval England is in *What is a Lollard?* 10–18. For insight into the significance of "membership gradience," I remain indebted to Daniel Boyarin's study *Border Lines: The Partition of Judaeo-Christianity* (Philadelphia, 2004).

54 On Kempe's relationship to lollardy, see Cole, *Literature and Heresy*, Chapter 7, and Ruth Shklar, "Cobham's Daughter: *The Book of Margery Kempe* and the Power of Heterodox Thinking," *Modern Language Quarterly* 56 (1995), 277–304. The authorship of Kempe's *Book* is too complex a question to entertain here.

that non-Christians living after the time of Christ could be saved.[55] The Second Vatican Council of the 1960s, however, affirmed the possibility of salvation for all human beings, including those non-Christians who died unaware that they would be saved through the death and resurrection of Christ.[56] Did the latter decree render heretical the more than twenty generations of putatively orthodox Roman Catholics who lived and died between the two councils?

It is helpful here to distinguish between *heresy* and *heterodoxy*. In the Middle Ages, as in contemporary Roman Catholic canon law, heresy does not simply entail belief in one or more erroneous theological propositions about truths of the faith. Rather, heresy has traditionally been defined as the impertinent refusal of a person to recant such an erroneous belief when confronted by an authoritative teacher. Hence, the thirteenth-century bishop of Lincoln, Robert Grosseteste, wrote that heresy is "an opinion chosen by human perception contrary to Holy Scripture, publicly avowed and obstinately defended."[57] In this sense, as A.S. McGrade has put it, heresy in the Middle Ages was "thought of as willful disruption of a saving awareness of God previously shared with others. It involved choice *for oneself*...but the choice was *self-deceptive*, a personally motivated choice that was not only uncommon but misdirected."[58] Heresy, therefore, was (and still is) a highly personal offense, which in a technical sense can only be committed by living people and only with regard to errors judged to be serious; in contrast, the broader category of heterodoxy includes all theological claims at variance with authoritative teaching.

Thus, heterodoxy is the opposite of orthodoxy, whereas heresy is the opposite of submission.[59] It may be possible, given the right kinds of historical

55 The council took this position in its decree on union with the Greek churches: for the text, see Tanner, *Decrees*, 1:478. For discussion of this question throughout the history of Christianity, see the first part of Jacques Dupuis, *Toward a Christian Theology of Religious Pluralism* (Maryknoll, N.Y., 1999).

56 This is the theological force of the final sentences of paragraph 4 of the council's decree *Nostra aetate*; see Tanner, *Decrees*, 2:971.

57 Malcolm Lambert, *Medieval Heresy: Popular Movements from the Gregorian Reform to the Reformation*, 2nd ed. (Oxford, 1992), 5. For contemporary Catholic canon law, see Canon Law Society of America, *Code of Canon Law, Latin-English Edition, New English Translation* (Washington, 1999), can. 751.

58 A.S. McGrade, "The Medieval Idea of Heresy: What are We to Make of It?" in *The Medieval Church: Universities, Heresy, and the Religious Life: Essays in Honour of Gordon Leff*, (eds.) Peter Biller and R.B. Dobson, Studies in Church History, Subsidia 11 (Oxford, 1999), 135, original emphasis. See also M.-D. Chenu, "Orthodoxie et hérésie: le point de vue du théologien," in *Hérésies et sociétés dans l'Europe pré-industrielle* (Paris, 1968), 9–17.

59 This is a shorthand statement of the view of R.N. Swanson, "Literacy, Heresy, History, and Orthodoxy: Perspectives and Permutations for the Later Middle Ages," in *Heresy and Literacy, 1000–1530*, (eds.) Peter Biller and Anne Hudson (Cambridge, 1994), 279–93.

evidence, to determine if the content of a written document or a person's beliefs was heterodox within the context in which the document was written or the person lived. It is likewise possible to determine if those views or that document would be heterodox according to the teachings of a particular theological system today. On the other hand, it is *not* always easy to determine if a person committed the crime of heresy, especially if no trace remains of that person's appearance before an ecclesiastical tribunal or an authoritative figure or figures.[60]

Finally, it is worth pointing out that notwithstanding the formal, legal definition of heresy that I have been rehearsing and that will guide my use of the term throughout this book, accusations of heresy were bandied about quite loosely by almost all parties to the controversies surrounding Wycliffism and lollardy. Lollard writers inveighed against the "heresies" of monks and friars; defenders of institutional orthodoxy likewise denounced the "heresies" of Wyclif and those they took to be his followers.[61] Like "lollard," "heresy" is a slippery fish of a term. Used too liberally or anachronistically, it risks perpetuating a facile bifurcation of the world between the righteous defenders of orthodoxy and the misguided, prideful, and even diabolical heretics.

The terminological situation does not become much clearer when we consider the implications of the word "sect," another perennial descriptor for lollards and their associates. In an influential essay published in 1999, Aston applied to the study of lollardy the traditional sociological distinction between a church (an organized, often hierarchical religious organization, weaving other social structures into its own way of being) and a sect (a looser religious community, often organized specifically for the purpose of protest against a dominant church).[62] She concluded that in these terms, lollardy was neither a church nor a sect; nevertheless, in recounting the long history of the application of the word *sect* to lollards, she struggled to create an alternative terminology: "what else can we call Wyclif's Lollard followers?"[63]

As Aston pointed out, polemicists and propagandists had been calling lollardy a sect long before nineteenth-century sociologists of religion developed their categories. Even Wyclif himself, in writing a defense of his theology of the

---

60　This position stands in contrast to that of Ian Levy, "Were the Lollards Heretics?" an unpublished paper delivered at the 2004 International Medieval Congress in Leeds, U.K. I am grateful to Professor Levy for sharing a copy of his paper with me.

61　This phenomenon is explored in greater detail in Chapters 4 and 6 below.

62　For the classic formulation of this distinction, see Ernst Troeltsch, "Stoic-Christian Natural Law and Modern Secular Natural Law," in *Religion in History*, trans. James Luther Adams and Walter F. Bense (Minneapolis, 1991), 321–42 at 324–26.

63　Aston, "Were the Lollards a Sect?" 191.

eucharist in 1381, referred to his associates with the Latin phrase *secta nostra*, and lollard writers regularly called the religious and monastic orders sects.[64] Yet the medieval notion of a sect is not that of modern sociology, and the anachronistic application of the church-sect typology to the study of lollardy has often resulted in an overemphasis on the coherence of lollard theology and social structures, in overexaggerated claims about the extent to which lollards developed a formal program for evangelizing their contemporaries, and in false assumptions about the political and cultural significance of lollardy.[65]

The pairs of binary terms that I have been describing all purport to distinguish lollards from Wycliffites, the heretical from the orthodox, and the lollard sect from the institutional church. It should be clear from the preceding discussion, however, that none of these binaries can do justice to the complex cultural and religious situation of late medieval England. The same observation holds true of one last pair of terms, *academic heresy* and *popular heresy*. In the historiography of medieval Christianity, especially in the mid-twentieth century, scholars have often attempted to distinguish heterodox views that had their origins in academic and ecclesiastical settings from heretical movements that flowered among supposedly illiterate, theologically uneducated laypeople.[66] Given this framework, and likewise given the long-standard distinction between academic Wycliffites and rustic lollards, lollardy has sometimes been held up as a rare example of an academic heresy that became a popular one. On this account, although Wyclif and his early associates were all clerics and Oxford scholars, they decided to preach and write in English as a way of spreading the gospel as widely as possible, including by translating the Bible into the vernacular tongue. Often implicated in claims of this sort is the assumption that lollardy is "Wycliffe's teachings reduced from scholastic to popular terminology."[67] While this point is not without some merit—Wyclif's associates certainly did, on a number of documented occasions, leave the university and preach in the

---

64   John Wyclif, "*De eucharistia confessio*," in *FZ*, 125.

65   Such assumptions can be found, for instance, in H.L. Cannon's article "The Poor Priests: A Study in the Rise of English Lollardry," *Annual Report of the American Historical Association for the Year 1899*, 2 vols. (Washington, D.C., 1900), 1:451–82.

66   For examples of this distinction, see Gordon Leff, *Heresy in the Later Middle Ages: The Relation of Heterodoxy to Dissent, c. 1250–c. 1450*, 2 vols. (Manchester, 1967); Lambert, *Medieval Heresy*; and *Heresies of the High Middle Ages*, (eds.) and trans. Walter L. Wakefield and Austin Evans (New York, 1991). A helpful critique of this binary is Herbert Grundmann, "Hérésies savantes et heresies populaires au moyen age," in *Hérésies et sociétés dans l'Europe pré-industrielle, 11e–18e siècles*, (ed.) J. Le Goff (Paris, 1968), esp. 212–13.

67   A.G. Dickens, "Heresy and the Origins of English Protestantism," repr. in *Reformation Studies* (London, 1982), 363–82.

vernacular, and some English texts are rough translations of the master's Latin—we will see that the dissemination of Wyclif's views did not involve only their simplification for lay audiences.[68] Scholars such as the literary critic Nicholas Watson have actively challenged the view that lollard writings in English are merely distilled versions of more sophisticated, Latin originals. Much to the contrary, Watson has argued, lollard writers' use of the English language opened up for them the possibility of making new theological claims, indeed opened up the possibility of an entire "vernacular theology" better suited to English than to Latin.[69]

These terminological remarks have all sought to problematize at least some elements of the traditional account of Wyclif and lollardy. That story, as I recounted it at the beginning of this chapter, involves the foundational assumptions that Wyclif and lollards constituted at least a coherent, if not in fact an organized, movement of dissent against the medieval church; that rebellious, iconoclastic, anti-institutional lollards are easily distinguished from pious, devout non-lollards; and that Wyclif's ideas, whether in their original form or else in some simplified version, furnished the intellectual energy for lollardy from the late fourteenth century through the time of the early English reformations. In the chapters that follow, I hope to demonstrate just how seductive, and how fallacious, these assumptions are.

---

68 See, for instance, A.K. McHardy, "The Dissemination of Wyclif's Ideas," in *Ockham to Wyclif*, 361–68.

69 See especially "Censorship and Cultural Change in Late-Medieval England: Vernacular Theology, The Oxford Translation Debate, and Arundel's Constitutions of 1409," *Speculum* 70 (1995), 822–64; and "Visions of Inclusion: Universal Salvation and Vernacular Theology in Pre-reformation England," *Journal of Medieval and Early Modern Studies* 27 (1997), 145–87. For one important critique of Watson's notion of vernacular theology, see Alastair Minnis, "Making Bodies: Confection and Conception in Walter Brut's 'Vernacular Theology,'" in *The Medieval Translator: The Theory and Practice of Translation in the Middle Ages*, (eds.) Rosalynn Voaden, René Tixier, et al. (Turnhout, 2003), 1–16.

CHAPTER 2

The People

Traditionally, the story of lollardy has begun with John Wyclif, a Yorkshire-born, Oxford-educated philosopher and theologian whose academic speculations allegedly gave rise to widespread heresy, sedition, and revolt. For centuries, Wyclif has occupied a unique place in the historiography of English Protestantism. Lionized by evangelical bibliophile John Bale as the "morning star" (*stella matutina*) of the Reformation, Wyclif's name became synonymous with a characteristically English kind of religious reform: committed to the use of the vernacular language, suspicious of foreign involvement in national affairs, and opposed to any hint of superstition.[1] In the eyes of Bale and his colleagues, Wyclif was one of the "secret multitude of true professors" who facilitated the hidden, underground survival of the gospel in the face of popish ignorance, tyranny, and heresy.[2] Over the centuries, Wyclif's purported involvement in the first complete translation of the Bible into English has earned him and the movement he was believed to have founded particular praise. "None has done more to attach Englishmen to the cause and issue of the Reformation than the belief that they are indebted to it for the open Bible. Nothing has worked more powerfully to divorce their hearts from the mediaeval type of discipline and authority than the fact that the first translators of the English Bible achieved their task under the censure of authority."[3]

For others, of course, Wyclif has represented something far more sinister. Beginning with his condemnation by the monastic chronicler Thomas Walsingham as a "diabolical instrument, enemy of the Church, confusion of the common people, idol of heretics, mirror of hypocrites, instigator of schism, sower of hatred, [and] inventor of falsehood," his medieval opponents reviled

---

[1] John Bale, *Illustrium maioris Britanniae scriptorum…summarium* ([Wesel], 1548), fol. 154v, quoted in Margaret Aston, "John Wycliffe's Reformation Reputation," *Past and Present* 30 (Apr., 1965), 23–51, at 25; see also Aston, "Wyclif and the Vernacular," in *Ockham to Wyclif*, 281–330. On distinctively English religion more broadly, see Patrick Collinson, "A Chosen People? The English Church and the Reformation," *History Today* 36 (March 1986), 14–20.

[2] *A&M*, 945.

[3] Anonymous (Arthur Ogle), "Dr. Gasquet and the Old English Bible," *Church Quarterly Review* 51 (1901), 138–46, at 139; for similar sentiments, see J. Radford Thomson, *The Life and Work of John Wyclif* (London, n.d.). Even in the immediate aftermath of Wyclif's death, some lollards labelled him a saint: see Christina von Nolcken, "Another Kind of Saint: A Lollard Perception of John Wyclif," in *Ockham to Wyclif*, 429–43.

Wyclif as the most recent in a long line of heretics whose appearances have marked the assaults of Antichrist upon the church.[4] Their attacks were often personal as well as intellectual: some critics ascribed his descent into heresy to the anger that accompanied his failure to obtain the bishopric that he supposedly desired, while others charged him with hypocrisy because he criticized clergymen who held more than one benefice yet held multiple livings himself.

What we know of the historical John Wyclif, however, does not quite measure up to either of these competing mythologies. In the last three decades, a number of scholars have set out to produce new biographies of the man who provided the early intellectual impetus for lollardy, and as we will see in this chapter, their portraits of Wyclif are in some ways clearer, yet in other ways more tentative, than those of the past.[5] They depict a man deeply indebted to conventionally medieval ways of thinking about philosophical and theological questions, as well as a man who, for all the polemic that he directed against the institutional church, seems not to have played an active role in organizing a movement of popular protest. At the same time, scholarly investigations into the lives and careers of Wyclif's earliest followers have turned up new information about the men who learned from him and took his ideas into the English countryside; they have emerged as far more autonomous, intellectually as well as socially, than previously thought.[6] Finally, much new work has been done on the communities of dissenters that these men may (or may not) have inspired. We have learned more about their social and economic standing, about their relationships with those of their neighbors who did not adopt heterodox theological positions, and about the connections that they made with one another. This chapter, then, serves as an introduction to the people of lollardy, those whose names we know and those we do not.

---

4 Thomas Walsingham, *The St. Albans Chronicle: The Chronica Maiora of Thomas Walsingham*, 2 vols., (eds.) John Taylor, Wendy R. Childs, and Leslie Watkiss (Oxford, 2003–11), 1:736: "organum diabolicum, hostis ecclesie, confusio uulgi, hereticorum ydolum, ypocritarum speculum, scismatis incentor, odii seminator, mendacii fabricator."

5 The most recent attempts at comprehensive treatments of Wyclif's life and thought are Anthony Kenny, *Wyclif* (Oxford, 1985); Gillian R. Evans, *John Wyclif: Myth and Reality* (Downer's Grove, Ill., 2006); Andrew E. Larsen, "John Wyclif, c. 1331–1384," in *Companion*, 1–65; and Lahey, *Wyclif*. For the historiography and indeed mythology that have grown up around Wyclif, see J. Crompton, "John Wyclif: A Study in Mythology," *Transactions of the Leicestershire Archaeological and Historical Society* 42 (1966–67), 6–34.

6 The use here and throughout this chapter of the gender-exclusive term "men" is intentional: as we will see, few if any women can be counted among the most active participants in the history of lollardy. For further discussion of lollardy and gender, see below, 54–56.

2.1   John Wyclif

First, let me share some important facts. The date and place of Wyclif's birth remain unknown; many scholars point to the Yorkshire village of Wycliff-on-Tees as the most likely location, and to 1328 as the most likely year. His parents, lesser nobles, were married in 1319, and thus it is probable that Wyclif, a younger son, followed other younger sons of the gentry into an ecclesiastical career. He likely came to Oxford in the 1340s and received his bachelor's degree in arts in 1356, the same year that he first appears in the records as a fellow of Merton College. Five years earlier, in 1351, he had been ordained sub-deacon, deacon, and finally priest, in Yorkshire. He became the third master of Balliol College sometime between 1356 and 1360, then spent a short period in pastoral work in the diocese of York before returning to Oxford in 1363. From there, his academic and political prominence grew considerably. Wyclif earned his bachelor's degree in theology in 1369 and received his doctorate in 1372, no fewer than twenty and perhaps as many as twenty-five years after first arriving at the university.[7] In the meantime, in 1365 the archbishop of Canterbury, Simon Islip, had appointed him warden of Oxford's newest foundation, Canterbury College, a position from which he was removed the following year by a new archbishop, John Langham.[8]

The most recent assessments of Wyclif's career all agree that the primary context within which he lived, and from which he acquired his strongest sense of personal identity, was that of the late medieval university system in general and the University of Oxford in particular. As Ian Christopher Levy has put it, "As a medieval theologian, John Wyclif was by definition a *magister sacrae paginae*, a licensed biblical expert uniquely qualified to interpret the most authoritative text in Christendom. If the Bible was the foundation of orthodoxy, then the theologian was charged with discerning and defending the faith of the Church."[9] Before turning to Wyclif's writings and ideas, then, it will be essential to understand more clearly the academic world he inhabited.

---

7 Medieval academic degrees typically required many more years of study than their modern counterparts. For discussion of the medieval academic system, see Evans, *John Wyclif*, 18–89, and the references cited there.

8 These facts, along with others cited in the following few paragraphs, are drawn from the overview of Wyclif's early life in Lahey, *Wyclif*, 3–7, and from Andrew Larsen's biographical essay, "John Wyclif," 1–65.

9 Ian Christopher Levy, "A Contextualized Wyclif—*Magister Sacrae Paginae*," in *Wycliffite Controversies*, 33–57. On the ways in which Wyclif created greater scholarly interest in the Bible, see William J. Courtenay, "The Bible in the Fourteenth Century: Some Observations," *Church History* 54 (1985), 176–87.

Gillian Evans' 2006 biography of Wyclif and Stephen E. Lahey's 2010 introduction to his philosophical and theological ideas both strongly emphasize his formation in the conventions of the medieval university.[10] In brief, the University of Oxford that Wyclif knew was patterned after the preeminent academic institution of its day, the University of Paris. As at Paris, the university was divided into the "higher disciplines" of theology, medicine, and law, subjects that could be approached only after a student had first mastered the "lower" arts disciplines, the *trivium* (grammar, rhetoric, and logic) and the *quadrivium* (mathematics, geometry, music, and astronomy). Evans has traced Wyclif's progress through the medieval curriculum, noting the privileges and responsibilities that accrued to him at each of its stages. As a candidate for the degree of Master of Arts, for instance, Wyclif would have lectured to younger students on subjects including grammar and logic; would have set questions for public disputations; and would have participated in the governance of the university. Once he began his studies in theology, he would have started with the great systematic textbook of his age, the *Sentences* of Peter Lombard, and finally moved on to what for him and his colleagues was the ultimate source of truth, the Bible. Eventually, he prepared a commentary (the technical term is *postilla*) on the whole Bible.[11] The portrait of Wyclif that emerges from Evans' biography is not that of the evangelical hero of later Protestant mythology but rather that of a diligent, hard-working scholar who was thoroughly steeped in contemporary academic debates and, perhaps as a consequence, was often confused by the rough-and-tumble nature of life outside the university's walls. "The real Wyclif was an able academic, not untypical of his times in the subjects which interested him and the lines he took in his teaching and writing."[12]

Evans has pointed to the year 1374, after Wyclif had earned the degree of Doctor of Theology and when he undertook a diplomatic mission to Bruges on behalf of King Edward III, as a turning point. Upon returning from Bruges, where he had deployed his emerging theories about the relationship between church and crown in defense of the king's resistance to paying papal taxes, Wyclif may have believed himself due a promotion. He did not get it; both the episcopal see of Worcester and a prebend in Lincoln diocese went to others.[13]

---

10 See n. 5 above. In this vein, see also Levy's "A Contextualized Wyclif" and his recent book *Holy Scripture and the Quest for Authority at the End of the Middle Ages* (Notre Dame, Ind., 2012).

11 Beryl Smalley, "John Wyclif's *Postilla super totam bibliam*," *Bodleian Library Record* 4 (1953), 185–205.

12 Evans, *John Wyclif*, 255–56.

13 M.E.H. Lloyd, "John Wyclif and the Prebend of Lincoln," *English Historical Review* 61 (1946), 388–94. That Wyclif held a series of ecclesiastical benefices, sometimes simultaneously,

While several of his opponents later attributed his slide into heresy to his failure to have obtained a bishopric, for her part, Evans has hypothesized that Wyclif "woke up at this point, if he had not done so before, to the corruptness of the world and the way big organizations work."[14] Whether for this or another reason, Wyclif's writings after 1372 grew more polemical.[15]

Public, extramural controversies about Wyclif's theology began in the middle of the 1370s, when he began to publish his Oxford lectures on divine and civil dominion. The concept of dominion was to figure prominently in his thought; for Wyclif and his contemporaries, it referred to the claim by one person to be able to wield temporal or spiritual power over another. These ideas of Wyclif's, which may have reached the papal court at Rome through the politicking of an English Benedictine, Adam Easton, were likely responsible for his earliest public censure.[16] In February 1377, he was summoned to appear before the convocation of the ecclesiastical province of Canterbury, but a timely intervention by his protector, John of Gaunt, Duke of Lancaster, spared him a full public interrogation. Later that year, in May, Pope Gregory XI sent five bulls to England, in which he ordered the archbishop of Canterbury and the bishop of London to conduct a secret investigation into Wyclif's teachings, required them to imprison Wyclif while they were doing so, and commanded the chancellor of Oxford to hand Wyclif over to church authorities. The university demurred, noting that it did not lie in its power to imprison "a man of the King of England"; it did, however, delegate to its masters of theology the task of assessing the theological claims attributed to Wyclif and ruling on their orthodoxy.[17] Wyclif was released following a brief incarceration in one of Oxford's halls and continued his academic work.

---

was in many ways typical for the age. Nonetheless, his non-residence in several of the livings to which he was appointed, and his apparent failure to provide a vicar for at least one of them, has prompted charges of hypocrisy. See J.H. Dahmus, "Wyclyf was a Negligent Pluralist," *Speculum* 28 (1953), 378–81, and more recently Nicholas Orme, "John Wycliffe and the Prebend of Aust," *Journal of Ecclesiastical History* 61 (2010), 144–52.

14   Evans, *John Wyclif*, 146.
15   There is not space here to review the contested chronology of Wyclif's many writings; for detailed discussion, see Lahey, *Wyclif*, 7–21, and many of the papers in Anne Hudson, *Studies in the Transmission of Wyclif's Writings* (Aldershot, 2008), especially item IV, "Cross-referencing in Wyclif's Latin Works."
16   Easton, later created a cardinal, published a formal refutation of Wyclif's views on dominium in his *Defensorium ecclesiasticae potestatis*, presented to Pope Gregory IX in 1378. See W.A. Pantin, "The *Defensorium* of Adam Easton," *English Historical Review* 51 (1936), 675–80.
17   Quoted in Evans, *John Wyclif*, 174.

By all accounts, the straw that finally broke the camel's back and led to Wyclif's departure from Oxford had little to do with the questions about dominion that had first attracted the hostile attention of authorities. Evans has argued that after the events of 1377, "[h]e had of course reached a stage of 'demonization', where almost any opinion he put forward was likely to be challenged as dangerous merely because he said it."[18] This may be true, but for his part, Wyclif could not have chosen for the site of his next confrontation with the institutional church a theologically more sensitive topic than the sacrament of the eucharist. The central ritual of late medieval Christianity, the eucharist had provided fertile ground for theological controversy in the centuries leading up to Wyclif's day. Detailed discussion of this point will have to wait until Chapter 5, but suffice it to say that not a few scholars with reputations better burnished than Wyclif's had found eucharistic questions politically as well as theologically complicated.[19]

In 1379, Wyclif began to lecture on the eucharist in the Oxford schools. What precisely he said to his audiences there is not clear. The orthodoxy of his statements, however, was ambiguous enough for Oxford's chancellor William Barton, long an opponent of Wyclif's, to convoke a committee of twelve doctors of theology, four secular priests and eight members of the monastic and fraternal orders, to investigate Wyclif's ideas. Their verdict, rendered in a decree read publicly in the schools in May 1381, was that Wyclif had crossed the line in his teaching on the sacrament. The committee specifically censured two of Wyclif's statements as erroneous: that "in the sacrament of the altar the substance of the material bread and wine, which was previously there before the consecration, truly remains after the consecration" and that "in this venerable sacrament the body and blood of Christ are not [present] essentially or substantially, nor even corporeally, but figuratively or as in a trope…because Christ is not present here in his own corporeal person."[20]

Wyclif appealed the committee's decision not to his colleagues, as would have been usual, but instead to King Richard II. John of Gaunt, now the young king's protector after the death of his grandfather Edward III, had previously

---

18 Evans, *John Wyclif*, 185.
19 On the complex history of eucharistic theology prior to the Fourth Lateran Council, see Gary Macy, *The Theologies of the Eucharist in the Early Scholastic Period: A Study of the Salvific Function of the Sacrament according to the Theologians* (Oxford, 1984).
20 *FZ*, 110, quoting the committee's presentation of Wyclif's propositions: "in sacramento altaris substantiam panis materialis et vini, quae prius fuerunt ante consecrationem, post consecrationem realiter remanere"; "in illo venerabili sacramento non esse corpus Christi et sanguinem, essentialiter nec substantialiter, nec etiam corporaliter, sed figurative seu tropice; sic quod Christus non sit ibi veraciter in sua propria persona corporali."

been able to save Wyclif from a public interrogation, but this time he chose not to intervene. One version of the story has Gaunt making a nighttime visit to Oxford to meet with the embattled theologian, telling Wyclif that nothing short of retracting the condemned theses and remaining silent on the eucharist for the foreseeable future could save his career, and possibly his life.[21] Whether or not Gaunt paid such a call on Wyclif, the writing was on the wall. Academic year 1380–1381 was Wyclif's last in Oxford, and the summer of 1381 saw him return to the parish of Lutterworth, in the county of Leicestershire, where since 1374 he had been rector. Not a few commentators have observed that Wyclif's long absence from his parish had made him into precisely the sort of absentee pluralist that he condemned in his written works; this was, nevertheless, the normal arrangement for secular clergymen who lived and taught in the university towns, who would not have been able to support their academic careers without income from their parishes.[22]

Wyclif's Lutterworth years were marked by, on the one hand, extraordinary scholarly productivity, and, on the other, growing resentment and vitriol toward anyone who upheld the theological positions he associated with friars, monks, and other elements within the church that he saw as corrupt. The extent to which Wyclif was able to keep in contact with colleagues from his Oxford years remains unclear, and he almost certainly did not supervise, as a day-to-day occupation, either the translation of the Bible or the activities of the preachers who had begun to spread some of his ideas in parts of the English countryside. Wyclif suffered at least two strokes in Lutterworth; the last one, on 28 December 1384, marked the beginning of his final illness, and he died three days later, on 31 December.

Many of his early biographers portrayed Wyclif as a man of action as well as of ideas; they depicted him laying the foundations for a network of "poor preachers" commissioned to disseminate his ideas throughout the countryside.[23] As we have been observing, however, more recent writers have emphasized that

---

21 For references to Wyclif's relationship with John of Gaunt, see Joseph H. Dahmus, *The Prosecution of John Wyclyf* (New Haven, 1952), 14, 21, 60–61, 156–57.

22 K.B. McFarlane, *John Wyclif and the Beginnings of English Nonconformity* (London, 1952), 15.

23 On Wyclif's "poor preachers," see H.L. Cannon, "The Poor Priests: A Study in the Rise of English Lollardry," in *Annual Report of the American Historical Association for the Year 1899*, 2 vols. (Washington, 1900), 1:451–82. Already by 1949, cracks in the traditional story were beginning to show: James Crompton, "Lollard Doctrine, With Special Reference to the Controversy over Image-Worship and Pilgrimages" (B.Litt. thesis, University of Oxford, 1950), 226. More broadly, see also Geoffrey Martin, "Wyclif, Lollards, and Historians, 1384–1984," in *Influence*, 237–50.

Wyclif's primary identity was that of a scholar, albeit one whose work positioned him at the intersection of contentious political, philosophical, and theological issues. Current scholarship has also sought to temper the oversimplified, often extreme accounts of Wyclif's philosophical and theological positions that have frequently been put forward since the revival of scholarly interest in Wyclif in the late nineteenth century. New studies have also sought to curb the historiographical effects of what Ian Christopher Levy has called the process of "Netterization," referring to the penchant of many scholars, following in the footsteps of Wyclif's great Carmelite opponent Thomas Netter, to "read everything Wyclif says as tending toward some heretical end."[24] It would be foolhardy to attempt, in the space available here, even a cursory summary of Wyclif's thought, but I hope that in touching briefly on a few of the broad principles that undergirded his treatment of particular topics, it may be possible for us to trace the development of scholarly attitudes toward Wyclif as well as the intellectual contributions he himself made.[25] We will return to Wyclif's views on specific theological issues, such as salvation, the eucharist, and the papacy, in Chapter 5.

First, commentators have traditionally given pride of place among Wyclif's principles to his realist epistemology or, in other terms, his belief that all things that exist derive their being from "universals" which, in turn, ultimately have their origin in the mind of God. In writing on the question of universals, Wyclif was taking sides in the perennial debate in Western philosophy between those who believe the nature of a thing, that is to say, what makes that thing the kind of thing that it is, exists independently of its instantiation in a particular being, and those who, to the contrary, believe that our categories are simply helpful tools that we use to relate to the complexities of the world. As J.A. Robson put it in a 1961 study that sought to systematize Wyclif's philosophical views, "Wyclif's metaphysics start from the cardinal assumption that everything possesses intelligible being eternally known to God by ideal exemplars; from which he deduced that all actual things have also an ideal being that knows neither past nor future, but only a 'present' and unchanging essence."[26]

Why have Wyclif's views on universals been the subject of so much attention over the past six centuries? For scholars like Robson, Wyclif's metaphysics are interesting not simply in and of themselves; they are also significant because they laid the groundwork for many of Wyclif's more controversial

---

24 Levy, "A Contextualized Wyclif," 55.
25 The most recent survey of Wyclif's thought is Lahey, *Wyclif*; other book-length analyses of his philosophy and theology include J.A. Robson, *Wyclif and the Oxford Schools* (Cambridge, 1961); Kenny, *Wyclif*; and the essays collected in *Companion*.
26 Robson, *Wyclif*, 163; on what follows, see Lahey, Wyclif, 93–101.

theological claims. With regard to the eucharist, for example, a series of commentators starting in the late nineteenth century have argued that Wyclif's ideas about universals led him to deny the possibility that any substance can be annihilated, even by God. This conviction, in turn, provided the intellectual basis for his opposition to the doctrine of transubstantiation.[27] Since Wyclif believed that transubstantiation must necessarily involve the annihilation of the substances of the bread and wine present on the altar, it would also involve the annihilation of the universals that gave rise to those substances. And since, according to Wyclif, particular universals themselves derive their being from higher-order universals, and ultimately from ideas in the mind of God, to annihilate one substance would entail the annihilation of all substances. Scholars have likewise linked Wyclif's views on universals to his ideas about predestination, scripture, and the governance of the church and civil society.[28]

Yet careful attention to Wyclif's writings, others have more recently argued, reveals that for him, universals did not possess the significance that has been attributed to them in much of the scholarly literature. Even though more could be said about this debate, Stephen E. Lahey has argued that perhaps too much has *already* been said:

> Many of Wyclif's metaphysical works have been in modern editions for almost a century. But the philosophy of some of his predecessors…only began to be widely understood in the latter half of the twentieth century. Without a secure grasp of their ontological programs, Wyclif's positions could not hope for a fair hearing, and the result has been an undue attention to the question of universals, to the exclusion of his wider program of a metaphysics of being.[29]

On Lahey's account, Wyclif's philosophical writings contain a softer form of realism than scholars have commonly believed—a form of realism that

---

27 Among others, John Thomas McNeill, "Some Emphases in Wyclif's Teaching," *Journal of Religion* 7 (1927), 447–66; Workman; and S.H. Thompson, "The Philosophical Basis of Wyclif's Theology," *Journal of Religion* 11 (1931), 86–116.

28 See, for instance, John Stacey, *John Wyclif and Reform* (London, 1964), 99–100; Beryl Smalley, "The Bible and Eternity: John Wyclif's Dilemma," *Journal of the Warburg and Courtauld Institutes* 27 (1964), 73–89, repr. in Smalley, (ed.), *Studies in Medieval Thought and Learning from Abelard to Wyclif* (London,1981), 399–415. Revisionist views include Anthony Kenny, "Realism and Determinism in the Early Wyclif," in *Ockham to Wyclif*, 165–78.

29 Lahey, *Wyclif*, 100. On this point, see also Ian Christopher Levy, "John Wyclif and Augustinian Realism," *Augustiniana* 48 (1998), 87–106.

specifically rejects the more extreme stances of Wyclif's contemporaries like the Merton College thinker Walter Burley and instead takes as its starting point Wyclif's doctrine of *ens in communi* (being in common). "The reason we are able to abstract being from our thinking of any given thing, Wyclif explains, is that there is an ontological connection between any true thought and Truth as such."[30] All things that exist participate in the same ultimate source of being, namely, God, and God uses God's divine ideas both to create and to know the universe. Divine ideas correlate with universals, of which Wyclif distinguished three kinds: universals by causation (in the sense that universals are the proximate causes of the things they instantiate), universals by commonality (in the sense that a universal is shared by many particulars), and universals by signification (in the sense that a single thing may be represented in many ways, as in the case of a person whose portrait is painted by multiple artists).[31] An individual thing that exists, such as my friend's dog Russell, can be explained in terms of multiple kinds of universals: his formal cause, for instance, is the universal "dog," in which all dogs in the world participate in common.

Lahey's focus on Wyclif's notion of being in common has allowed him to place Wyclif's ideas about universals within the broader context of his metaphysics, a strategy that Lahey has also used to explore another of Wyclif's influential (and infamous) themes, that of sovereignty, lordship, or, in Latin, *dominium*.[32] As with his realism, earlier research linked Wyclif's views on *dominium* with his most controversial theological positions. For instance, in the 1960s the British historian Gordon Leff argued that because Wyclif believed that only those in a state of grace can properly exercise *dominium*, his theological system as a whole was "an unceasing attack on the life and claims of the contemporary church."[33] According to Leff, not only did Wyclif's allegedly strict doctrine of predestination make it impossible to determine who was and was not capable of rightly exercising ecclesiastical authority, but Wyclif was also effectively a Donatist with regard to the administration of the sacraments, holding that only ministers free from sin can validly baptize, consecrate the eucharist, or grant absolution.[34]

---

30 Lahey, *Wyclif*, 84.

31 Lahey, *Wyclif*, 94–95.

32 In addition to Chapter 7 of Lahey, *Wyclif*, for a detailed analysis of the historiography of Wyclif's views on *dominium*, see Lahey, *Philosophy and Politics in the Thought of John Wyclif* (Cambridge, 2003), Chapter 1.

33 Gordon Leff, *Heresy in the Later Middle Ages: The Relation of Heterodoxy to Dissent, c. 1250–c. 1450*, 2 vols. (Manchester, 1967), 2:527. For similar, if earlier critiques, see Lowrie Daly, S.J., *The Political Theory of John Wyclif* (Chicago, 1962).

34 E.g., Leff, *Heresy*, 2:515–27. The charge of Donatism has been effectively refuted by, among others, Anne Hudson, "The Mouse in the Pyx: Popular Heresy and the Eucharist," *Trivium*

In a series of writings published since 2003, Lahey has again led the way in articulating a new interpretation of Wyclif's views on *dominium*. He has contextualized Wyclif's theories by tracing their background in the writings of Augustine, Giles of Rome, the Spiritual Franciscans, Marsilius of Padua, and Richard FitzRalph, concluding that Wyclif's writings on *dominium* "contain the essence of his theological vision, uniting his metaphysics to his sociopolitical and ecclesiological thought."[35] Wyclif was distinctive among medieval theologians in closely tying his realism, which required him to posit that any instance of earthly *dominium* is an instantiation of God's divine *dominium* over creation, to specific claims about the church and civil society. On Lahey's account, Wyclif admits that civil *dominium* and, in particular, the ownership of private property are inadequate analogues to God's divine *dominium*. Civil *dominium* is in fact only a necessary evil, created as a result of the Fall, which deprived human beings of the natural *dominium* of Eden, where love reigned and private property was unnecessary and unknown.[36] Because civil *dominium* "is a phenomenon that arises from original sin and is not likely to result in justice in itself," Wyclif argues that the church should not entangle itself with the ownership of property; any goods that it acquires should immediately be given to the poor. Likewise, Wyclif's most controversial political claims also follow as necessary consequences of his views on the evils of civil *dominium*: lords should see themselves not as owners but as stewards of property on behalf of God; hereditary monarchies should be abolished; and civil lords should intervene to divest the church of its wealth.[37]

As I have been showing, Wyclif's metaphysical realism and political-ecclesiological claims about *dominium* have provided the context for recent re-evaluations of his thought. A third theme in Wyclif's writings, the relationship between visible signs and invisible theological realities, has been the site of greater continuity in scholarly assessments. Starting with his late nineteenth and early twentieth century biographers, such as Gotthard Lechler and H.B. Workman, Wyclif's theology has been thought to posit a sharp dichotomy between observable, often tangible phenomena, such as the sacraments and pronouncements of the church, and the unseen grace

---

26 (1991), 40–53; and Ian Christopher Levy, "Was John Wyclif's Theology of the Eucharist Donatistic?" *Scottish Journal of Theology* 53 (2000), 137–53.

35   Lahey, *Wyclif*, 200; more extensively, see Lahey, *Philosophy and Politics*.

36   Lahey, *Wyclif*, 210–12; on Wyclif's views on Eden, see Alastair Minnis, "Wyclif's Eden: Sex, Death, and Dominion," in *Wycliffite Controversies*, 59–78.

37   Lahey, *Wyclif*, 213–21; quote at 213.

that God communicates.[38] Standing in this tradition, Leff declared that Wyclif had chosen "to discount the visible church in the name of the invisible church," a decision that for Leff resulted in a range of ambiguities and inconsistencies in Wyclif's writings.[39]

While the three topics we have been exploring—realism, *dominium*, and the relationship between the visible and the invisible in theology and the church—hardly do justice to the full range of Wyclif's thought, they do illustrate the complex ways in which the Oxford master brought together philosophical, theological, and political ideas. They also highlight the changing fortunes of Wyclif's views in the hands of successive generations of his critics, who have over time come to appreciate Wyclif less as an idiosyncratic, radical thinker and more as a relatively conventional philosopher and theologian deeply embedded in the scholarly arguments of his own day.

2.2 "Fellows and Helpers"

If Wyclif was, above all else, a late medieval academic, then it is not surprising that many of the individuals whose names are prominent in the early history of lollardy were also scholars of the University of Oxford.[40] In recent years, the

---

38 Consider, for instance, Lechler's emphasis on Wyclif's definition of the church as "the whole number of the elect," rather than "the visible Catholic church." Lechler, 315. See, likewise, Workman's discussion of the relationship between Wyclif's ecclesiology and soteriology: Workman, 2:7–16.

39 Leff, *Heresy*, 2:519. For instance, Leff pointed to the ways in which Wyclif distinguished between God's invisible decree that a person is no longer a member of the true church on the one hand, and a visible decree of excommunication by the pope on the other. *De officio regis*, 147; *Dialogus sive speculum ecclesie militantis*, 34; for discussion, see J. Patrick Hornbeck II, *What Is a Lollard? Dissent and Belief in Late Medieval England* (Oxford, 2010), 150–54. Likewise, Wyclif compared God's communication of grace to a person whom God wished to make a priest on the one hand, and the visible rite of ordination on the other. For Wyclif, the church is a minister or steward of God's grace and God's decisions, not a body capable of making autonomous theological determinations on its own authority.

40 This section takes its subtitle from Jeremy Catto's influential essay "Fellows and Helpers: The Religious Identity of the Followers of Wyclif," in *The Medieval Church*, (eds.) Peter Biller and R.B. Dobson, Studies in Church History, Subsidia 11 (Oxford, 1999), 141–61. In two magisterial articles, Catto has traced in detail the role that Wyclif and his associates played in fourteenth- and fifteenth-century theology and academic life: "Wyclif and Wycliffism at Oxford, 1356–1430" and "Theology after Wycliffism," both in *The History of the University of Oxford*, Volume 2: Late Medieval Oxford, (eds.) J.I. Catto and Ralph Evans (Oxford, 1992), 175–261 and 263–80.

emergence of new evidence has allowed historians to delve more deeply into their individual biographies, rather than treating them, as medieval chroniclers like Knighton and Reformation propagandists like Foxe did, as mere mouthpieces for Wyclif's ideas.

Four Oxford scholars were especially visible as Wyclif's ideas gave impetus to a nascent movement of church reform. Nicholas Hereford, who was possibly born in the city after which he was named, was approximately ten years behind Wyclif in his academic career. A fellow of The Queen's College by 1369, he earned his doctorate in theology in 1382; earlier that year, while still a bachelor of theology, Hereford preached two sermons against friars, monks, and canons. One of them, on Ascension Day, he delivered in English and addressed to the townspeople as well as the scholars of Oxford.[41] Even more radical than his choice of language was his call in this sermon for the laity to work toward the disendowment of the religious orders. Archbishop William Courtenay suspended Hereford, a secular priest, from his duties, and ordered him, along with Philip Repingdon and John Aston (about whom more shortly), to appear before the council of church leaders that was soon to consider Wyclif's controversial opinions at the house of the London Dominicans, the "Blackfriars." There, Hereford and Repingdon refused to recant their views in a way that satisfied the archbishop, and when they failed to appear at a later hearing, both were excommunicated.[42] Alone of Wyclif's early followers, Hereford somehow made his way to Rome and argued his case before Pope Urban VI and his cardinals. They were, to say the least, not a sympathetic audience, and they imprisoned Hereford for life. He escaped in 1385, returned to England, and was recaptured in January 1387. But somehow he was free again by August, when the bishop of Worcester issued a decree that proscribed Hereford from preaching in his diocese.[43] It was during this time, as well as during his earlier years of residence in Oxford, that Hereford likely contributed to the ongoing Wycliffite project of translating the Bible into English. A note in one manuscript (not echoed in others) famously alleges that "Nicholay de herford" was the translator of the Old Testament from Genesis through Baruch 3:20, though this may

---

41   Printed in Simon Forde, "Nicholas Hereford's Ascension Day Sermon, 1382," *Mediaeval Studies* 51 (1989), 205–41. On Hereford, see also Forde, "Hereford, Nicholas," in *Oxford Dictionary of National Biography* (Oxford, 2008) [http://www.oxforddnb.com/view/article/20092, accessed 21 August 2011].
42   *FZ*, 318–26; Wilkins, 3:165–68; Knighton, 277–81.
43   Wilkins, 3:202–3; Forde, "Hereford, Nicholas."

be an exaggeration.[44] Despite his lollard activities, Hereford reconciled himself with the institutional church at some point before 1391, when he was taken into the king's protection as a reward for preaching against Wyclif's ideas and followers. According to a letter preserved in a contemporary bishop's register and later printed by John Foxe, Hereford was reproached later in the 1390s by one of his former co-religionists, who called him "maister of the Nicholitanes" and upbraided him for having "left or forsaken the infallible knowledge of the holy Scripture."[45] He held a series of ecclesiastical positions, including those of chancellor of St. Paul's Cathedral in London and of the diocese of Hereford, before resigning them all and entering a Carthusian monastery.

Like Hereford, Philip Repingdon eventually made his peace with the church after a period of heterodox evangelizing. Also like Hereford, Repingdon had earned his doctorate in theology in 1382, preached Wyclif's ideas inside and outside Oxford, and was summoned to and excommunicated by the Blackfriars Council later that year. Unlike Hereford, however, Repingdon was an Augustinian canon, and he had arrived at Oxford with political support in the form of the longstanding patronage his abbey received from the noble house of Lancaster.[46] It may have been at the urging of his friends in ecclesiastical and civil office that Repingdon chose not to prolong his confrontation with the institutional church. He recanted his heresies late in 1382 and returned to what seems to have been an ordinary life of university teaching and study in Oxford. Ten years later he began his ascent up the ecclesiastical hierarchy, becoming abbot of his abbey in Leicester, chancellor of Oxford University, chaplain and confessor to King Henry IV, and ultimately bishop of Lincoln. If he was now playing a prominent role in the church, he was no strident opponent of heresy; his former colleagues, nonetheless, saw him as a turncoat.[47] As several scholars have noted, Repingdon's episcopacy saw him undertake reforms in the diocese of Lincoln that would have delighted Wyclif, including the prosecution of clerical absenteeism.[48]

---

44   Oxford, Bodleian Library MS Douce 369.1. I am grateful for this detail to the anonymous reader for the press.

45   *A&M*, 598. "Nicholaitanes" is likely a reference to Revelation 2:6. I am grateful to Asher Harris for this reference.

46   Simon Forde, "Repyndon, Philip," in *Oxford Dictionary of National Biography* (Oxford, 2008) [http://www.oxforddnb.com/view/article/23385, accessed 21 August 2011].

47   Forde, "Repyndon, Philip."

48   See, for instance, M. Archer, "Philip Repingdon, Bishop of Lincoln, and His Cathedral Chapter," *University of Birmingham Historical Journal* 4 (1954), 81–97; Simon Forde, "Theological Sources Cited by Two Canons of Repton: Philip Repyngdon and John Eyton," in *Ockham to Wyclif*, 419–28.

He maintained social links with the so-called "Lollard knights," whom we will soon meet, and temporized when ordered by the Council of Constance to unearth and burn Wyclif's body. Among the many pieces of evidence for the persistence of his reforming convictions, perhaps the most striking is Repingdon's will, which asked for little in the way of pomp and directed that his goods be given away, in their entirety, to the poor.[49]

About the career of a third Oxford follower of Wyclif's, John Aston, we know comparatively little. He did not have time to complete his doctorate before being summoned before and censured at the Blackfriars Council, but he was reputed as a great disseminator of Wyclif's ideas. In May 1382, the same month that Hereford and Repingdon delivered their notorious sermons in Oxford, Aston preached in Odiham, a small town outside the university in Hampshire. At the council, Aston, unlike Hereford and Repingdon, refused to put his beliefs in writing and declined to speak in Latin.[50] Although he was expelled from the university, he shortly thereafter recanted his support of Wyclif's ideas. But within eighteen months he had returned to preaching and teaching controversial ideas in locations as distant as Bristol, London, and Gloucester. In a royal decree of 1388, his name was mentioned, alongside those of Wyclif, Hereford, and John Purvey, as an author whose works were to be sought out and burned.[51] The date of his death is unknown, but as we shall shortly see, in 1407 his colleague William Thorpe claimed that Aston had maintained his dissenting views "right perfectly unto his life's end"; in contrast, he disparagingly observed that Repingdon had been "riȝtwise...and prudent" only early in his career.[52]

As the monastic chronicler Knighton numbered the leaders of lollardy, fourth among them, after Wyclif, Hereford, and Aston, was John Purvey.[53] (Ever concerned for the reputation of his abbey, where Repingdon was a canon and later abbot, Knighton remained cautiously silent about the future

---

49 Margaret Aston, "'Caim's Castles': Poverty, Politics, and Disendowment," in *Church, Politics, and Patronage in the Fifteenth Century*, (ed.) B. Dobson (New York, 1984), 45–81, repr. in Aston, *Faith and Fire*, 95–132.

50 Maureen Jurkowski, "Aston, John," in *Oxford Dictionary of National Biography* (Oxford, 2008), from which this paragraph is drawn [http://www.oxforddnb.com/view/article/824, accessed 21 August 2011]

51 Wilkins, 3:204.

52 A.B. Emden, *A Biographical Register of the University of Oxford to AD 1500*, 3 vols. (Oxford, 1957–59), 1:67, quoted in Jurkowski, "Aston, John"; *The Testimony of William Thorpe*, in Anne Hudson, (ed.), *Two Wycliffite Texts* (EETS o.s. 301, 1993) lines 572–75.

53 Knighton, 290–93. For a biographical survey, see Anne Hudson, "Purvey, John," in *Oxford Dictionary of National Biography* (Oxford, 2008) [http://www.oxforddnb.com/view/article/22908, accessed 21 August 2011].

bishop of Lincoln's involvement in heresy.)[54] Purvey, originally of Lincoln diocese, was ordained a priest in the late 1370s, but his academic and ecclesiastical background remains for the most part enigmatic. Some have suggested that he belonged to a second generation of academic lollards, rather than to the circle of scholars who immediately surrounded Wyclif in Oxford.[55] It is clear that by 1387, the authorities had become aware of Purvey's involvement in heterodox preaching, since in that year and the following year, bishops directed their clergy to stop Purvey from preaching and to confiscate his heretical books. His name does not appear in the records again until 1401, when he was interrogated by Archbishop Thomas Arundel of Canterbury and abjured his heresies at Paul's Cross in London; the topics on which he admitted himself to be in error included the eucharist, the power of priests to absolve penitents of their sins, clerical celibacy, and the priesthood of all believers.[56] His conversion to orthodoxy may have won him a benefice as rector of West Hythe in Kent, though not the admiration of his former fellows: the lollard preacher Thorpe denounced Purvey as someone who no longer "holdiþ feiþfull wiþ þe lore þat he taught and wroot biforehonde" and instead "schewiþ now himsilf to be neiþir hoot ne coold."[57] Anne Hudson has speculated that the proximity of Purvey's new living to Arundel's residence at Saltwood Castle may have allowed the archbishop to keep an eye on him.[58] Perhaps such supervision proved too much, for Purvey had left his position by the autumn of 1403 and was involved in Sir John Oldcastle's rebellion in 1414. Captured soon thereafter, he died in Newgate prison.[59] Successive generations of historians exaggerated the significance of Purvey's involvement in lollardy, not least because Netter, in his great anti-Wycliffite work the *Doctrinale*, described Purvey as *glossator Wicleffi* ("commentator on Wyclif") and *librarius lollardorum* ("librarian of the

---

54 James Crompton, "Leicestershire Lollards," *Transactions of the Leicestershire Archaeological and Historical Society* 44 (1968–69), 11–44, at 15.

55 Anne Hudson, "John Purvey: A Reconsideration of the Evidence for His Life and Writings," *Viator* 12 (1981), 355–80, repr. in *Books*, 85–110.

56 The heresies abjured by Purvey, as well as a list of eleven errors attributed to Purvey by the Carmelite friar Richard Lavynham, appear in FZ, 383–407; see also Hudson, "Purvey, John."

57 *The Testimony of William Thorpe*, in Hudson, (ed.), *Two Wycliffite Texts*, 40; see also Hudson, "Purvey, John."

58 Hudson, "John Purvey," 358.

59 For additional details on Purvey's life, his involvement in the Oldcastle revolt, and his books, see Maureen Jurkowski, "New Light on John Purvey," *English Historical Review* 110 (1995), 1180–90.

lollards").[60] On the basis of epithets like these, eighteenth-century scholars attributed to Purvey first the authorship of the General Prologue to the Wycliffite Bible and then parts of the translation itself; however, no extant work can with certainty be said to come from Purvey's own pen.[61]

Hereford, Repingdon, and Aston, like Wyclif, were all fellows or students of Oxford colleges. It must be remembered that in the middle ages, such foundations were more fluid in their structure and membership than they are today. Especially in the late fourteenth century, Wycliffite sympathizers were able to leverage the privileges attached to their college affiliations in order to further their theological goals. Individual colleges may have played specific roles: in a fascinating essay, Jeremy Catto has proposed that groups of lollards at the different Oxford colleges invested themselves differently in the work of church reform. Those at The Queen's College, for instance, may have been more interested in providing resources for the vernacular translation of the Bible and other religious texts than in developing heterodox doctrinal claims; those at Merton College, on the other hand, seem to have been more radical and outspoken in their views.[62] The research of Maureen Jurkowski and Alison McHardy confirms this characterization of Merton lollards: fellows of the college may have disseminated ideas while undertaking visits to college lands outside Oxford, and the authorities of Merton and other colleges may knowingly have appointed lollards to ecclesiastical benefices in their gift.[63]

Beyond the formal structures of Oxford colleges, other well-educated men played significant roles in the dissemination of Wyclif's views and the emergence of lollardy as a phenomenon widespread enough to attract repression. There is not space here to describe all of them, but several deserve special mention. First, William Thorpe was a Yorkshire preacher who, unusually for an English heresy suspect, produced a written account of his examination before Archbishop Arundel.[64] Important details about Thorpe's background remain

60 For the latter of these epithets, see Netter, *Doctrinale*, 3: col. 732. Hudson has argued that the "tantalizingly vague" title "librarius lollardorum" has given rise to the greatest number of misconceptions about Purvey: "John Purvey," 365.

61 Hudson, "Purvey, John." On writings ascribed to Purvey, see the discussion and citations in Mary Dove, *The First English Bible* (Cambridge, 2007), 76–79.

62 Jeremy Catto, "Fellows and Helpers," 153–54.

63 Maureen Jurkowski, "Heresy and Factionalism at Merton College in the Early Fifteenth Century," *Journal of Ecclesiastical History* 48 (1997), 658–81; A.K. McHardy, "The Dissemination of Wyclif's Ideas," in *Ockham to Wyclif*, 361–68.

64 On the rhetorical strategies of Thorpe's text, see Chapter 7, 167–171, below; Elizabeth Schirmer, "William Thorpe's Narrative Theology," *Studies in the Age of Chaucer* 31 (2009), 267–99; Fiona Somerset, "Vernacular Argumentation in the Testimony of William

vague, and his text is not necessarily a reliable source. Thorpe reported that he had traveled to Oxford prior to Wyclif's expulsion in 1381 and there learned his theological opinions from the master and his associates. That he soon thereafter became an energetic preacher of lollard ideas is clear from the charges of heresy that the bishop of London laid to his account at some point between 1382 and 1386; his responses to the accusations survive, but no document concerning the outcome of the trial is extant.[65] It may be that Thorpe was the man of the same name who was appointed, by Arundel no less, to a vicarage in north Yorkshire in 1395, though the relationship between the heresy suspect and the man who held this benefice has not been firmly established.[66] It is certain, however, that in June 1407, Arundel summoned Thorpe to Westminster after he had preached against the adoration of images, pilgrimage, and tithing at St. Chad's church in Shrewsbury.[67] As to the content and outcome of Thorpe's examination before Arundel, we have only his own record.[68] The three topics mentioned in Arundel's summons also appear in Thorpe's text, and the text includes passages in which Thorpe praises Wyclif and reports on the activities of fellow lollards, several of whom had returned to orthodoxy. *The Testimony of William Thorpe* ends with its subject being returned to Arundel's prison without a verdict having been rendered against him; as to what became of the historical Thorpe, we can only surmise. On the basis of a possible scribal error in the text that purports to be Thorpe's will, Richard Rex has proposed that Thorpe died in captivity, while Hudson has suggested that he may have made his way to Bohemia, where there are some traces of his influence in extant manuscripts.[69]

Thorpe," *Mediaeval Studies* 58 (1996), 207–41; and Anne Hudson, "William Thorpe and the Question of Authority," in *Christian Authority: Essays in Honour of Henry Chadwick*, (ed.) G.R. Evans (Oxford, 1988), 127–37.

65   Anne Hudson, "Thorpe, William," in *Oxford Dictionary of National Biography* (Oxford, 2008) [http://www.oxforddnb.com/view/article/27387, accessed 15 January 2012]; John Fines, "William Thorpe: An Early Lollard," *History Today* 18 (1968), 495–503, dates Thorpe's trial in London to 1397.

66   Hudson, "Thorpe, William."

67   Maureen Jurkowski, "The Arrest of William Thorpe and the Anti-Lollard Statute of 1406," *Historical Research* 75 (2002), 273–95.

68   Hudson, "Thorpe, William."

69   Richard Rex, "Thorpe's Testament: A Conjectural Emendation," *Medium Aevum* 75 (2005), 109–13; Hudson, (ed.), *Two Wycliffite Texts*, liii. See also Jamie K. Taylor, *Fictions of Evidence: Witnessing, Literature, and Community in the Late Middle Ages* (Columbus, Ohio, 2013), 153, 184.

The other early lollard who penned an account of his examination was the priest Richard Wyche, who wrote a letter to an unknown sympathizer sometime after his trial before Bishop Walter Skirlawe of Durham.[70] It is likely that Wyche was educated at Oxford, but few claims about his background can be made with certainty. His trial ended with Wyche being sentenced to prison, but he was later released; at some point he began to correspond with and send books to the Czech reformer Jan Hus.[71] He also seems to have been affiliated with Oldcastle: although he avoided being directly implicated in the rebellion of 1414, he was questioned in its wake about Oldcastle's finances. Wyche was committed to the Fleet prison in 1419, was released from prison in 1420, and by 1423 had been appointed to the first of a series of church positions. Two decades later, in 1440, he was found guilty of heresy, degraded from the clerical state, and burned.[72] According to the extant London city chronicles, the place of his execution attracted a number of his sympathizers, some of who allegedly attempted to preserve his ashes as relics. Scholars have regularly noted the discrepancy between these practices and supposedly longstanding lollard opposition to the veneration of relics; recently, the revisionist historian Richard Rex has proposed that in the absence of firm evidence that Wyche's condemnation was on account of genuine heretical beliefs, the crowd's behavior connoted "not endorsement of heresy, but fellow feeling for an innocent man wrongfully convicted.... [T]hose who venerated Richard Wyche were not Lollards but Catholics."[73]

Just as Wyche was involved in the dissemination of Wyclif's ideas to Hus and his Czech co-religionists, so also was another, slightly later Oxford scholar,

---

[70] Printed in F.D. Matthew, "The Trial of Richard Wyche," *English Historical Review* 5 (1890), 530–44.

[71] John A.F. Thomson, "Wyche, Richard," in *Oxford Dictionary of National Biography* (Oxford, 2008) [http://www.oxforddnb.com/view/article/50263, accessed 21 August 2011].

[72] Thomson, "Wyche, Richard"; Anne Hudson, "Which Wyche? The Framing of the Lollard Heretic and/or Saint," in *Texts and the Repression of Medieval Heresy*, (eds.) Caterina Bruschi and Peter Biller (Woodbridge, 2002), 221–37, at 224–25.

[73] Richard Rex, "'Which is Wyche?' Lollardy and Sanctity in Lancastrian London," in *Martyrs and Martyrdom in England, c. 1400–1700*, (eds.) Thomas Freedman and Thomas Maye (Woodbridge, 2007), 88–106. H.A. Kelly has agreed that Wyche's trial was procedurally flawed: it "was uncanonical in many ways, and probably would not have passed muster if his entirely legitimate appeal to the pope had not been brushed away." See H.A. Kelly, "Inquisition, Public Fame, and Confession: General Rules and English Practice," in *The Culture of Inquisition in England, 1215–1515*, (eds.) Mary C. Flannery and Katie L. Walter (Woodbridge, 2013), 8–29. For further discussion of Thorpe and Wyche, see Chapter 7 below, 167–171, and Taylor, *Fictions of Evidence*, 170.

Peter Payne. Payne arrived in Oxford approximately two decades after Wyclif had departed, during the period of increased institutional and political concern about heresy that led to the passage of the statute *Contre les lollardes*.[74] Given Wyclif's books by an Oxford contemporary, Peter Partridge, Payne became "the most outspoken Wycliffite in Oxford," as Czech scholar František Šmahel has dubbed him.[75] Among his dissenting acts was a feat of genius: whether by political persuasion or by stealing the university seal's outright, Payne was able to arrange for the seal to be attached to a document that described Wyclif as a wise, honest man of good repute.[76] The letter was published in Prague in 1409, and it is possible that Payne also helped to convey letters from Wyche and Oldcastle to Bohemia.[77] After a brief academic career, which saw him become principal of an Oxford hall of residence but later brought before a committee investigating Wycliffite influence on the university, Payne left England in 1413; eventually he arrived in Bohemia, where he contributed to the development of Hussite theology. We will explore the relationships between English and Hussite dissenters in Chapter 8.

Finally, it remains to mention briefly two rather shadowy figures who came to the attention of church authorities soon after Wyclif rose to notoriety. The activities of one of them, William Swinderby, were first mentioned in the register of John Buckingham, bishop of Lincoln, in 1382.[78] Swinderby may have been a priest; he certainly was a popular preacher who may have had some backing from the Augustinians of Leicester Abbey, where at the time Repingdon was a canon.[79] When he began to publicly preach ideas that sounded reminiscent of Wyclif's, he was apprehended first in Lincoln diocese and then, after he had been released on a pledge not to preach without a license, in Hereford diocese. Summoned to trial before Bishop John Trefnant of Hereford in 1391, Swinderby sent his inquisitors two lengthy written defenses of his theological positions. He ultimately evaded capture by the bishop's officials, and his final appearance in the records is dated 1392. Despite the similarities between his

---

74 On the name of the statute, as distinct from the writ *De heretic comburendo* that sent convicted heretics to the stake, see Forrest, 66.
75 F. Šmahel, "Payne, Peter," in *Oxford Dictionary of National Biography* (Oxford, 2004) [http://www.oxforddnb.com/view/article/21650, accessed 21 August 2011]; for additional background, see A.B. Emden, *An Oxford Hall in Medieval Times: Being the Early History of St Edmund Hall*, rev. ed. (Oxford, 1968), 133–37.
76 Wilkins, 3:302. On this episode, see further Emden, *An Oxford Hall*, 138–42.
77 Šmahel, "Payne, Peter."
78 Crompton, "Leicestershire Lollards," 21–23.
79 Anne Hudson, "Swinderby, William," in *Oxford Dictionary of National Biography* (Oxford, 2004) [http://www.oxforddnb.com/view/article/38041, accessed 21 August 2011].

views and Wyclif's on topics such as the eucharist, tithing, and church endowments, it remains unclear how Swinderby came to hold these and other positions; likewise, the sources of his considerable theological and biblical learning are unknown.[80]

Tried before Trefnant in the same year as Swinderby was a second man whose history has proven difficult to trace. Walter Brut, possibly a Welsh associate of Swinderby's, identified himself as a "literate layman" (*laicus litteratus*) and defended, in writing, a series of theological propositions that were similar to those that Swinderby had been accused of teaching.[81] Whether Brut was indeed a layman, where he learned to write, and where he acquired his theological training all remain open questions, but it is clear that Brut was treated quite seriously by his interrogators, who produced no fewer than four written refutations of his ideas. Alastair Minnis has argued that Brut must be regarded "as one of the most radical thinkers among the early Lollards, who added much to the doctrine he acquired from his associate William Swinderby."[82] A series of recent studies has focused in particular on Brut's views on the ordination and priestly powers of women. Although the topic occupies only a few pages of the records of the proceedings against him, it features prominently in his inquisitors' responses. Brut proposed, for instance, that since a woman, Mary, made the body of Christ in her womb, so also can women confect the body of Christ in the sacrament.[83] He also argued that if women are able to baptize and baptism is the most necessary of all the sacraments, then there is no reason why women should not be able to administer a less necessary sacrament, the eucharist.[84] Minnis has argued that for Brut, these arguments were largely hypothetical, designed primarily to ridicule the official theology of ordination against which he was protesting; his opponents, however, dedicated many pages to refuting them. "Perhaps Trefnant's team pushed certain crucial principles of Brut's Lollard theology to extremes of which the Welshman himself was innocent, thereby coming up with propositions which might have

---

80   Ian Forrest, "William Swinderby and the Wycliffite Attitude to Excommunication," *Journal of Ecclesiastical History* 60 (2009), 246–69, at 247.

81   Anne Hudson, "*Laicus Litteratus*: The Paradox of Lollardy," in *Heresy and Literacy, 1000–1530*, (eds.) Peter Biller and Anne Hudson (Cambridge, 1994), 222–36.

82   Alastair Minnis, "Making Bodies: Confection and Conception in Walter Brut's 'Vernacular Theology,'" in *The Medieval Translator: The Theory and Practice of Translation in the Middle Ages*, (eds.) Rosalynn Voaden, René Tixier, et al. (Turnhout, 2003), 1–16, at 10.

83   Minnis, "Making Bodies," 6.

84   Hereford reg. Trefnant, 364.

surprised the figure who had occasioned them."[85] Below, we will be returning to the treatment of gender in scholarship on lollardy.

2.3 Lollard Knights

The men whose biographies we have been reviewing—Wyclif himself; his initial associates Hereford, Repingdon, Aston, and Purvey; later Oxford Wycliffites such as Thorpe, Wyche, and Payne; and sympathizers like Swinderby and Brut—all came from the clergy or the commons, the first and third estates of medieval society. A few members of the second estate, the nobility, were also associated by their contemporaries with Wyclif and lollardy. Chief among them was John of Gaunt, Wyclif's patron and protector who served as *de facto* ruler of England during the old age of King Edward III and the minority of his grandson, King Richard II. As we have already seen, Gaunt early on shielded Wyclif from being interrogated or arrested by church authorities and later may have urged him to withdraw from Oxford rather in the face of fierce opposition to his views on the eucharist.[86]

In addition to Gaunt, a number of knights at the court of Richard II came under suspicion of favoring or patronizing lollards and lollard ideas.[87] Chroniclers Knighton and Walsingham listed between them a sizeable group of men who, they believed, had in one way or another sought to advance the cause of heresy. Walsingham named Sir Richard Stury, Sir Lewis Clifford, Sir Thomas Latimer, and Sir John Montaigu as the authors of the Twelve Conclusions, a lollard manifesto supposedly published during the parliament of 1395.[88] Knighton denounced Stury, Clifford, Latimer, and three other knights

---

85 Alastair Minnis, "'Respondet Walterus Bryth...': Walter Brut in Debate on Women Priests," in *Text and Controversy*, 229–49, at 248–49.

86 On the relationship between Gaunt and the English bishops, see McFarlane, *John Wycliffe*, 102.

87 For a summary of recent scholarship on the lollard knights, see Charles Kightly, "Lollard knights (act.c.1380–c.1414)," in *Oxford Dictionary of National Biography* (Oxford, 2008) [http://www.oxforddnb.com/view/article/50540, accessed 7 August 2011]; this paragraph is indebted to Kightly's survey, as well as to his doctoral dissertation, "The Early Lollards: A Survey of Popular Lollard Activity in England, 1382–1428" (Ph.D. diss., University of York, 1975).

88 Kightly, "Lollard knights"; Walsingham, *St. Albans Chronicle*, 1:818–22. For more on the *Twelve Conclusions*, see 89 below.

for protecting lollard preachers.[89] It is certain that many of the knights singled out in this way were associated with one another socially: their names regularly appear together in legal documents such as wills, and five of them served in the chamber of King Richard II. Whether they also all subscribed to heterodox religious views has been a disputed question: a 1913–14 biography of the knights by W.T. Waugh sought to position them as victims of malicious gossip, whereas in his classic work *Lancastrian Kings and Lollard Knights*, published in 1972, K.B. McFarlane argued that the knights had used their positions at court to advance lollard ideas.[90] For McFarlane, their success in doing so may be attributed to the fact that lollard views "found more than an echo in many hearts, even those of some of the higher clergy."[91] Literary scholars have paid particular attention to one of the knights, Sir John Clanvowe, who unusually for a man of his rank wrote a treatise on Christian morality, using the Ten Commandments, a favorite lollard text, to organize the bulk of his exposition.[92] Whatever their sympathies for lollard ideas, however, the knights' involvement seems to have waned as the persecution of heresy intensified.

2.4 Later Lollards

The activities of Wyclif's academic followers, a few itinerant preachers, and the lollard knights represent one side of the story of early lollardy. For them, Wyclif's death did not constitute an immediate crisis. He had already been gone from Oxford for three years, during which time his sympathizers continued to occupy positions of academic prominence, and the public preaching of lollard ideas and the production of lollard texts had increased. Even after the master had breathed his last, writers inspired by his ideas were likely already at

---

89 Knighton, 292–97; on the knights' protection of heresy suspects, see also Peter McNiven, *Heresy and Politics in the Reign of Henry IV* (Woodbridge, 1987), 55–56.

90 Kightly, "Lollard knights." Some decades ago, Mairi Anne Cullen developed this point further in a neglected Oxford M.Litt. thesis, "The Lollards of Northamptonshire, 1382–1414" (1989), esp. 38–95.

91 W.T. Waugh, "The Lollard Knights," *Scottish Historical Review* 11 (1913–14), 55–92; K.B. McFarlane, *Lancastrian Kings and Lollard Knights* (Oxford, 1972), 224.

92 The treatise has been edited and printed by V.J. Scattergood, "*The Two Ways*—An Unpublished Religious Treatise by Sir John Clanvowe," *English Philological Studies* 10 (1967), 33–56. K.B. McFarlane has noted, however, that the text does not treat such controversial issues as confession, pilgrimages, the saints, or the priesthood; thus, in Clanvowe's treatise, "The only trace of lollardy is in the silences": *Lancastrian Kings*, 205. On the treatment of the ten commandments in *The Two Ways*, see Chapter 3 below.

work on the vernacular translation of the Bible, an interlinear commentary on the gospels, and an extensive cycle of sermons.

Nevertheless, the signs of coming repression were beginning to gather on the horizon, and the actions of churchmen and civil political leaders constitute another side of our story. In 1381, groups of farmers and artisans had marched on London from the surrounding counties of Kent and Essex, demanding relief from the poll tax and improvement in the working conditions set forth in the 1351 Statute of Labourers.[93] One of the rebel leaders, the priest John Ball, had preached ideas reminiscent of Wyclif's, and even though Wyclif and his Oxford contemporaries denounced the revolt, irreparable political damage had been done. The following year, Archbishop Courtenay assembled at the London house of the Dominicans the council whose decrees condemned as heretical or erroneous twenty-four propositions that were clearly, although not explicitly, associated with Wyclif. An earthquake shook London during the council, a sign of divine displeasure that each side interpreted to its own advantage. For the churchmen, it was a symbol of God's wrath at Wyclif's and his followers' heresies, whereas for Wyclif, it was an endorsement of the need for reformation in the church.[94]

The years after Wyclif's death saw a gradual constriction of the boundaries of orthodoxy. His followers began to be referred to with a new, derogatory epithet—"lollards"—which as we learned in the previous chapter was a term of abuse that predated the controversies involving Wyclif, both in England and on the continent.[95] Bishops and archbishops began to conduct formal investigations into the beliefs and activities of suspected heretics. In 1389, for instance, Courtenay undertook a visitation of the whole of the ecclesiastical province of Canterbury and discovered at least one cohort of lollards residing in Leicestershire, not far from Wyclif's former parish at Lutterworth.[96] It was during this period that several of the more colorful characters we have met, such

---

[93] This event is traditionally known as the Peasants' Revolt, but more recent scholarship has emphasized that its leaders and many of its participants were of higher socioeconomic status. The most recent treatment of the relationship between lollardy and the revolt is Steven Justice, *Writing and Rebellion: England in 1381* (Berkeley, 1994), especially Chapter 2; see also Margaret Aston, "Corpus Christi and Corpus Regni: Heresy and the Peasants' Revolt," *Past and Present* 143 (1993), 3–47.

[94] For an important revisionist interpretation of the proceedings of the Blackfriars Council, see Andrew Cole, *Literature and Heresy in the Age of Chaucer* (Cambridge, 2008), Chapter 1.

[95] The origin of the English term *lollard* remains, as we saw in Chapter 1, a site of some contestation: see 15–19 above.

[96] Joseph Dahmus, (ed.), *The Metropolitan Visitations of William Courtenay, Archbishop of Canterbury, 1381–1396* (Urbana, Ill., 1950), 48–50, 164–67, 170–72.

as William Swinderby and Walter Brut, came to the attention of church officials, and likewise during this period that lollard supporters may have posted the Twelve Conclusions on the doors of Westminster Hall. But there was not yet a coherent strategy on the church's part for responding to the perceived threat of heresy.

The ongoing political turmoil that led to the accession of King Henry IV in 1401 prevented a full-fledged campaign against lollardy from taking shape. But with a new king came a new archbishop of Canterbury—or, rather, a restored archbishop, since Thomas Arundel had briefly held the office under Richard II. Arundel's opposition to heresy was as much a political as a theological matter. Paul Strohm has forcefully argued that the new Lancastrian dynasty found in lollardy a convenient and easy enemy, an opportunity to rally loyal, God-fearing subjects around a common cause.[97] In 1401, Parliament moved to enact the statute *Contre les lollardes*, which established the death penalty for heresy and in that regard brought England into line with other major European kingdoms. That same year, but before the statute's formal approval, the priest William Sawtre, who had previously been tried for heresy in Norwich diocese, was sent to the stake in London by a special royal writ of execution.[98]

As the campaign against lollardy intensified, Arundel presented to the convocation of Canterbury province a set of laws, or constitutions, that limited unlicensed and unorthodox religious practices.[99] Translations of the Bible or of any portion of the biblical text now required episcopal approval; wandering preachers now needed to obtain licenses from local clergy; and the colleges of Oxford and Cambridge were to be subjected to monthly investigations into the theological opinions of their masters and students. In an influential 1995 article, the literary historian Nicholas Watson pointed to Arundel's constitutions as an important moment in the history of censorship; he emphasized their chilling effect on the production of orthodox as well as lollard religious literature, writing that in their wake, "it is fair to say that original theological writing

---

[97] Paul Strohm, *England's Empty Throne: Usurpation and the Language of Legitimation, 1399–1422* (New Haven, 1998); likewise Strohm, "The Trouble with Richard: The Reburial of Richard II and Lancastrian Symbolic Strategy," *Speculum* 71 (1996), 87–111. On the broader relationship between secular and ecclesiastical politics in this period, see also Margaret Aston, "Lollardy and Sedition," *Past and Present* 17 (1960), 1–44, repr. in *Lollards and Reformers*, 1–47, and McNiven, *Heresy and Politics*.

[98] A.K. McHardy, "*De heretico comburendo*, 1401," in *Lollardy and Gentry*, 112–26; McNiven, *Heresy and Politics*. For Sawtre's earlier trial, see John Ridgard, "From the Rising of 1381 in Suffolk to the Lollards," in *Religious Dissent in East Anglia*, (ed.) David Chadd (Norwich, 1996), 9–28.

[99] Wilkins, 3:314–19.

in English was, for a century, almost extinct."[100] Whether as a direct result of the constitutions or an indirect consequence of the attitude toward heresy they represented, few new lollard texts were composed after the first decade of the fifteenth century, and the copying of existing works also seems to have slowed dramatically.[101]

As official mechanisms for the repression of lollardy continued to take shape, so also did the persecution of individuals connected with heresy. Sawtre's hastily organized execution in 1401 was followed by that of John Badby, in 1410, who became the first officially to die under the terms of the new statute.[102] Building on the precedent set by Archbishop Courtenay, bishops began to search their dioceses for hidden heretics, though it was not until later that they began to put on trial large groups of putative lollards.

At this point, it is fair to say that lollardy was perceived primarily as a religious problem—perhaps even a religious problem that, given Wyclif's views on the disendowment of the church, might be able to be exploited by the Lancastrian state. As we have seen, in the reign of Richard II there were a number of "lollard knights" at court, and a few of them maintained their positions into the reign of Henry IV. Henry's son, the future King Henry V, counted among his close friends another courtier with heterodox religious views: Sir John Oldcastle, a minor knight and successful soldier who had married into a prominent Kentish family, the Cobhams. It was Oldcastle's actions that most associated lollardy with political as well as religious dissent. When the knight was accused of heresy during the Canterbury convocation of March 1413, Henry sought to convince his friend to submit to orthodoxy, to no avail: Oldcastle fled to his own lands and only at the king's command consented to appear for his trial. He was found guilty of the crime of heretical depravity, and when Henry asked the court to allow his friend time to reconsider, Oldcastle escaped from

---

100   Nicholas Watson, "Censorship and Cultural Change in Late-Medieval England: Vernacular Theology, The Oxford Translation Debate, and Arundel's Constitutions of 1409," *Speculum* 70 (1995), 822–64, at 835; important responses to Watson are Fiona Somerset, "Professionalizing Translation at the Turn of the Fifteenth Century: Ullerston's *Determinacio*, Arundel's *Constitutiones*," in *The Vulgar Tongue: Medieval and Postmedieval Vernacularity*, (eds.) Fiona Somerset and Nicholas Watson (University Park, Penn., 2003), 145–57; and Michael G. Sargent, "Censorship or Cultural Change? Reformation and Renaissance in the Spirituality of Late Medieval England," in *After Arundel: Religious Writing in Fifteenth-Century England*, (eds.) Vincent Gillespie and Kantik Ghosh (Turnhout, 2011), 55–72. See also Ian Forrest, "English Provincial Constitutions and Inquisition into Lollardy," in *The Culture of Inquisition in England, 1215–1515*, (eds.) Mary C. Flannery and Katie L. Walter (Woodbridge, 2013), 45–59.
101   See *PR*, Chapter 9.
102   For details, see McNiven, *Heresy and Politics*.

the Tower of London and plotted to overthrow the king. Unfortunately for Oldcastle, his conspiracy was discovered, and his ragtag army was overthrown in early January 1414. It was not until almost four years later that royal troops captured Oldcastle, who was condemned to death by hanging as well as burning.[103]

While some Oxford-educated lollards continued to preach and teach privately, Oldcastle's rebellion and execution marked the beginning of a new phase in the history of lollardy, where lollard ideas were firmly associated in the minds of England's leading men with rebellion and treason. A 1414 parliamentary statute declared heresy an offense against common law as well as canon law, and many of Oldcastle's followers went to their deaths or made public recantations.[104] Another, far less successful, attempt to revive lollard political ideas was made about fifteen years after Oldcastle's rebellion, when a bailiff by the name of William Perkins, operating under the pseudonym Jack Sharp, sought to enact the program of ecclesiastical reform that earlier lollards had proposed to Parliament. Riots broke out in London, Abingdon, and Salisbury, and were severely repressed. Perkins himself was captured and beheaded as a traitor, although, significantly, not burned as a heretic.[105]

After Perkins' rebellion, few events of national significance punctuate the remainder of the history of lollardy. As we will see in Chapter 7, a number of bishops conducted large-scale campaigns against heresy beginning in the late 1420s, and collectively, they put on trial several hundred heresy defendants from that time through the early sixteenth century. We will also see that the years in which bishops were most active in their investigations into lollardy often coincided either with periods when heresy was figuring prominently in the discourses of the broader European church or with periods when the English monarchy was most interested in self-definition and self-promotion. Finally, in Chapter 8, we will take up the complicated history of the interrelationships between lollardy and the English reformations, and consider the ways in which ideas about lollardy shaped the English government's early

---

103   The earliest modern biography of Oldcastle is W.T. Waugh, "Sir John Oldcastle," *English Historical Review* 20 (1905), 434–56, 637–58; more recently, see J.A.F. Thomson, "Oldcastle, John," in *Oxford Dictionary of National Biography* (Oxford, 2008) [http://www.oxforddnb.com/view/article/20674, accessed 21 August 2011].

104   J.A.F. Thomson, *The Later Lollards: 1414–1520* (Oxford, 1965), 5–19; see also Eleanor J.B. Reid, "Lollards at Colchester in 1414," *English Historical Review* 20 (1914), 101–4.

105   John A.F. Thomson, "Perkins, William," in *Oxford Dictionary of National Biography* (Oxford, 2008) [http://www.oxforddnb.com/view/article/25210, accessed 21 August 2011].

responses to Luther and his contemporaries, as well as shaped the stories that later English reformers told about themselves.

2.5 Lollard Communities

For much of its history, however, the word "lollard" did not primarily conjure up the image of an Oxford scholar or a courtier with a penchant for dissenting religious beliefs and activities. With a few exceptions, the history of later lollardy is one of dispersed lay groups rather than prominent individuals. As we have already seen, many of Wyclif's early academic colleagues had either returned to orthodoxy or fled the country by the first decade of the fifteenth century, and with the enactment of Archbishop Arundel's constitutions, lollards found Oxford to be an increasingly inhospitable venue for preaching and writing. The scattering of individuals and ideas that followed meant that only a few names of leading lollards from this period have come down to us. Some do appear in the fifteenth- and sixteenth-century records, such as William White, a priest whose itinerant preaching made converts in both Canterbury and Norwich dioceses, and John Stilman, who early in the sixteenth century visited the homes of a number of lollards in Winchester diocese.[106] But these and a few other instances aside, the majority of the extant records for later lollardy emphasize the networks that like-minded individuals formed with one another.

What to call these groups of individuals remains a matter of some dispute. In recent scholarship the word most commonly used has been *communities*, but the term is difficult to define for any period. When the community in question is a group of individuals who may have been brought together on account of shared heterodox beliefs that could, if detected, have landed them in court or worse, definitions are harder still to formulate.[107] Medieval chroniclers and inquisitors used the word *conventiculum* ("conventicle," literally meaning "little gathering") to denote groupings of heresy suspects, and lollards sometimes referred to themselves as a "sect."[108] Many modern scholars who have chosen

---

106 For White, see *FZ*, 417–32; for discussion of Stilman's activities, see J. Patrick Hornbeck II, "*Wycklyffes Wycket* and Eucharistic Theology: Cases from Sixteenth-Century Winchester," in *Wycliffite Controversies*, 279–94.
107 As Christine Carpenter and others have noted, the word "community" has frequently been over-employed in the study of premodern societies. See Carpenter, "Gentry and Community in Medieval England," *Journal of British Studies* 33 (1994), 340–80.
108 See Patrick Collinson, "The English Conventicle," in W.J. Sheils and Diana Wood, (eds.), *Voluntary Religion*, Studies in Church History 23 (Oxford, 1986), 223–59.

not to speak of lollard communities or sects have frequently described lollard "clusters" or "networks" instead, pointing to patterns of familial, social, trade, and intellectual relationships that formed webs that connected people to each other.[109] Whatever terms are used—and in this book I will cautiously use the shorthand label "community" to refer to groups whose members recognized one another as fellow-travelers who differed from traditional religious beliefs and practices—lollards seem to have interacted most often in small meetings, often for the purpose of reading aloud from vernacular translations of the scriptures or devotional texts. Meetings may have been more or less frequent, and the size of a particular group may have expanded or contracted to reflect the induction of new members, the arrival of trusted visitors from other regions of the country, or the departure of members who no longer wished to participate in potentially dangerous activities.

To the extent that lollards formed communities, they seem to have been textual communities, in the sense that the theorist Brian Stock has given that phrase.[110] The opportunity to participate in the reading and exposition of texts—the biblical text especially, but also other spiritual and devotional writings—commonly provided the impetus for lollards to gather together. As Stock has explained, a member of a group did not personally need to possess the capacity to read and write, since all members took part in an orally mediated encounter with the text. What was essential was at least one "individual who, having mastered [the text], then utilized it for reforming a group's thought or action."[111] R.N. Swanson has observed that some leading lollards, such as William White, were texts unto themselves, possessing an "incarnate textuality" that they communicated to others through their preaching, reading, and leadership activities.[112]

In Chapter 7, we will examine in more detail the ways in which the interwoven webs of relationships that comprised lollard communities were partially brought to light in the course of anti-heresy investigations. Here, it will have to suffice to mention some of the locations where such communities were uncovered in the fifteenth and early sixteenth centuries; they may of course

---

109   See, for instance, Jurkowski, "Lollard Networks"; Davies, "Lollardy and Locality"; and McSheffrey, "Heresy, Orthodoxy," 76–77.
110   See, for instance, Brian Stock, *The Implications of Literacy* (Princeton, N.J., 1987); Stock, *Listening for the Text: On the Uses of the Past* (Philadelphia, 1997).
111   Stock, *Implications of Literacy*, 90.
112   R.N. Swanson, "Literacy, Heresy, History and Orthodoxy: Perspectives and Permutations for the Late Middle Ages," in *Heresy and Literacy*, 279–93, at 286.

have flourished elsewhere, undetected.[113] Several towns and cities witnessed extensive or repeated investigations concerning heresy: these locales included Leicester, Amersham, Coventry, Norwich, and especially London.[114] Heresy appeared to be strong in a number of regions outside cities and towns as well: the Weald of Kent, a wooded area between the North and South Downs, saw prosecutions as early as the 1410s and as late as the 1510s. In Lincoln diocese, heresy was found in Philip Repingdon's visitation of 1413, in isolated cases through the middle of the fifteenth century, in a major investigation undertaken by John Chedworth in the 1460s, and in another major inquisition under John Longland in the 1520s. East Anglia saw a substantial number of heresy trials in the late 1420s and early 1430s, as well as in the early sixteenth century; these cases appear to have emerged primarily from villages in rural Norfolk. The Gloucester Vale produced not a few heresy suspects, and the nearby Forest of Dean was reputed to be a hiding place from the authorities.[115] Some regions, especially outlying areas such as Cornwall, Devon, Wales, and the northern counties of England, remained largely untouched by heresy trials during the same period; in Scotland, there was only one major heresy prosecution, that of the so-called "Lollards of Kyle," in 1494, although there were some scattered cases early in the fifteenth century.[116]

Where lollard communities can be found, by no means were they always comprised of the same kinds of people, nor did their members always relate in the same way to one another and to their orthodox contemporaries. In contrast to earlier scholarship that focused primarily on lollard beliefs and the manner of their investigation and repression and that assumed that lollardy after the Oldcastle revolt was a lower-class movement, a few recent studies have concentrated on the social and economic status of lollards, their families,

---

113 An excellent overview and analysis of later lollardy is Shannon McSheffrey, "Heresy, Orthodoxy, and English Vernacular Religion 1480–1525," *Past and Present* 186.1 (2005), 47–80.

114 Traditionally, this list would also have included the city of Bristol: see, e.g., Thomson, *Later Lollards*, Chapter 2. However, Clive Burgess has argued that Bristol was "nothing much more than a hotbed of cold feet": "A Hotbed of Heresy? Fifteenth Century Bristol and Lollard Reconsidered," in *Authority and Subversion*, (ed.) Linda Clark (Woodbridge, 2003), 43–62.

115 On Gloucester and its environs, see now Ben Lowe, *Commonwealth and the English Reformation: Protestantism and the Politics of Religious Change in the Gloucester Vale* (Farnham, 2010).

116 T.M.A. McNab, "The Beginnings of Lollardy in Scotland," *Records of the Scottish Church History Society* 11 (1953), 254–60; W. Stanford Reid, "The Lollards in Pre-reformation Scotland," *Church History* 11 (1942), 269–83.

and those who opposed them.[117] Shannon McSheffrey has suggested that church authorities were more sympathetic to the possession and reading of vernacular books when they were owned by individuals of high status.[118] Likewise, in Norwich, where Bishop William Alnwick put on trial more than eighty defendants in the late 1420s and early 1430s, Maureen Jurkowski has found that "[n]ot only were the Lollards prominent figures in their local communities, but in one Norfolk village (Earsham, in the Waverney Valley) they actually formed the elite and were so in control of the manor court as to constitute a ruling faction."[119] Jurkowski has traced these elite lollards back to the arrival in Norfolk of lollard sympathizers who were displaced as a result of Oldcastle's abortive revolt.[120] Socially prominent members of other communities were also sympathetic to lollardy: studies by Richard G. Davies, Robert Lutton, and Andrew Brown have demonstrated that prominent lollards were also sometimes prominent members of their local communities, men and women (usually men) who contributed financially and in other ways to the common good.[121] Likewise, two of the heresy suspects tried in Coventry and Lichfield diocese in 1511 were the widows of former mayors of Coventry.[122] While more research concerning the social and economic standing of lollards remains to be done, it now appears reasonable to set aside earlier assumptions that lollardy appealed primarily to the poor. Lollards came from nearly all ranks of medieval society, and as the habits of independent thinking that lollardy cultivated may have been especially attractive to the upwardly mobile.[123]

For many lollards, community began at home: family members taught one another their beliefs, and new members joined the community through marriage. A number of the extant sets of trial records portray wives being tried alongside their husbands, children alongside their parents, and domestic

---

117   For the earlier historiography, see Maureen Jurkowski, "Lollardy and Social Status in East Anglia," *Speculum* 82 (2007), 120–52, at 120.
118   McSheffrey, "Heresy, Orthodoxy," 68–70.
119   Maureen Jurkowski, "Lollardy and Social Status in East Anglia," *Speculum* 82 (2007), 120–52, at 121.
120   Jurkowski, "Lollardy and Social Status," 131.
121   Davies, "Lollardy and Locality," esp. 203–06; Lutton, *Lollardy and Orthodox Religion* Brown, *Popular Piety*.
122   *Coventry*, 27. Other examples of this phenomenon can be multiplied; for instance see Maureen Jurkowski, "Lollardy in Oxfordshire and Northamptonshire: The Two Thomas Compworths," in *Influence*, 73–95.
123   Jurkowski, "Lollardy and Social Status," 152.

servants alongside their masters.[124] Nevertheless, the attitudes that lollards possessed about family and social relationships remain contested among scholars. Lollard views on women, in particular, have provided much fodder for debates in the past few decades. In the 1970s, several scholars believed that lollardy, like other medieval religious movements such as those of the beguines and so-called Cathars, offered to women the opportunity to engage in forms of religious practice and religious leadership that would otherwise have been denied them. On the basis of the records of several heresy trials, a few scholars even went so far as to propose that lollards were willing to ordain women as priests.[125] These last arguments coincided with battles over women's ordination in The Episcopal Church in the United States of America and the Church of England and, ultimately, seem to have been overstated. More recent research has revealed that many supposed references to women's ordination were explicitly or implicitly hypothetical in nature, and no conclusive evidence has yet been offered that a lollard community ever ordained a woman.[126] (As we will see in Chapter 5, the attitudes of many lollards toward the sacrament of orders may explain why there is little evidence that they ever ordained men, either.) Earlier assessments of lollard views on gender have also been called into question: in 1995, the historian Shannon McSheffrey published a book-length study in which she contended that far from experiencing a greater degree of religious freedom within lollard communities, women lollards encountered many of the same limitations that they would have experienced in orthodox religious contexts.[127] Her findings have not been universally accepted, but they serve as an important counterweight to the conclusions of

---

124 See, for instance, the cases of Robert and Katherine Hachet of Coventry, Laurence and Elisabeth Swaffer of Mattingley, and Hawisia and Thomas Mone of Loddon. Agnes Grebill of Tenterden was tried in 1511 alongside her husband and two sons, and ultimately burned. Thomas Mone's servant John Burell had also appeared in court. *Coventry*, 232, 237–38; Winchester reg. Fox, fols. 74v-75v; *Norwich*, 138–44, 175–81; *Kent*, 16–32; *Norwich*, 72–78.

125 Margaret Aston, "Lollard Women Priests?" *Journal of Ecclesiastical History* 31 (1980), 441–62, repr. in *Lollards and Reformers*, 49–70; Claire Cross, "'Great Reasoners in Scripture': The Activities of Women Lollards 1380–1530," in *Medieval Women*, (ed.) Derek Baker, Studies in Church History, Subsidia 1 (Oxford,1978), 359–80.

126 Alastair Minnis, "Making Bodies: Confection and Conception in Walter Brut's 'Vernacular Theology,'" in *The Medieval Translator: The Theory and Practice of Translation in the Middle Ages*, (eds.) Rosalynn Voaden, René Tixier, et al. (Turnhout, 2003), 1–16, and Minnis, "'Respondet Walterus Bryth.'"

127 Shannon McSheffrey, *Gender and Heresy: Women and Men in Lollard Communities 1420–1530* (Philadelphia, 1995).

her predecessors.[128] For McSheffrey, lollardy, like medieval Christianity more broadly, was governed by the interests of men; a few women, such as widows of high social status, might have been allowed to exercise leadership within their communities, but they were exceptions rather than the rule.[129]

Outside the home, lollards also socialized and came to know one another through many of the same social structures that connected other medieval men and women. In some cases, ties of godparenthood, a relatively little studied feature of medieval religious life, bound lollard groups together.[130] In others, lollards interacted with each other and disseminated their views through networks of commerce and trade. Evidence from a few trial records suggests that when some lollards traveled for commercial purposes, they made connections with fellow dissenters in other towns. There may have been signs, coded language, or social networks that helped lollards to identify like-minded people in other locations; without them, it is unlikely that individuals like Joan Wasshingburn *alias* Warde, who was tried in Coventry and Lichfield diocese in 1512, would have been able to arrange to stay with fellow-believers in towns as widely dispersed as Northampton, London, and Maidstone.[131] It may also have been the case that certain trades counted larger numbers of lollards than others; in particular, some mid-twentieth-century historians pointed to the cloth trade as something of a hotbed for dissenting ideas.[132] Both the mobility enjoyed by traveling merchants and the ample opportunities for conversation

---

128 Fiona Somerset, in *"Eciam Mulier*: Women in Lollardy and the Problem of Sources," in *Voices in Dialogue: Reading Women in the Middle Ages*, (eds.) Linda Olsen and Kathryn Kerby-Fulton (Notre Dame, Ind., 2005), 245–60, questions whether McSheffrey's reliance on trial records perhaps led her to reinscribe the biases of inquisitors (p. 247). Likewise, Kathryn Kerby-Fulton has urged that Aston's and Cross's vision "of women active as oral biblical instructors in the home" not be discarded completely. See Kerby-Fulton, "*Eciam Lollardi*: Some Further Thoughts on Fiona Somerset's '*Eciam Mulier*: Women in Lollardy and the Problem of Sources,'" in *Voices in Dialogue: Reading Women in the Middle Ages*, (eds.) Linda Olsen and Kathryn Kerby-Fulton (Notre Dame, Ind., 2005), 261–68.

129 More recently, see David Lavinsky, "'Knowynge Cristes speche': Gender and Interpretive Authority in the Wycliffite Sermon Cycle," *Journal of Medieval Religious Cultures* 38 (2012), 60–83, for discussion of the earlier historiography and of the attitudes to gender to be found in several classic lollard texts.

130 Robert Lutton, "Godparenthood, Kinship, and Piety in Tenterden, England, 1449–1537," in *Love, Marriage, and Family Ties in the Middle Ages*, (eds.) I. Davis, M. Muller, and S. Rees Jones (Turnhout, 2003), 217–34.

131 *Coventry*, 239.

132 John F. Davis, "Lollard Survival and the Textile Industry in the Southeast of England," in *Studies in Church History* 3, (ed.) G.J. Cuming (Oxford, 1966), 191–201; Davis, *Heresy and Reformation in the South-East of England, 1520–1559* (London, 1983), 2.

provided by work at the mill and the loom may explain the correlation between the cloth trade and heresy, but it is important to avoid the *post hoc ergo propter hoc* fallacy that there is something innate about any particular kind of work that predisposes a person to hold and disseminate heterodox views.[133]

Finally, even as lollards formed communities that participated collectively in the reading of texts, the discussion of ideas, and perhaps the concealment of itinerant preachers, they also continued to take part in many of the civil and religious practices of mainstream medieval religion. As we will see in the next chapter, the majority of lollards likely continued to attend church services; some even served in positions of lay leadership in their parishes. As Robert Lutton has shown so effectively in his study of testamentary piety in the heresy-prone Kentish village of Tenterden, some lollards made gifts and left bequests to the church, participating in the material dimensions of medieval Christianity in ways that made them indistinguishable from their orthodox contemporaries.[134] The portraits of lollards and lollard communities that continue to emerge from studies like Lutton's highlight the similarities, rather than the differences, between lollardy and mainstream religion.

2.6   Conclusions

The women and men who were—or who, had they been detected, might have been—called lollards in late medieval England fit no single pattern. They included Oxford scholars such as John Wyclif and his early associates, knights and courtiers such as Sir John Clanvowe, and also relatively ordinary artisans whose only encounters with the theological debates of the schools came through listening to texts being read by the better educated members of their communities. Lollard ideas were present at both the upper and lower extremes of the social and economic spectrum, as well as in a number of disparate regions of England.

The sheer variety of individuals who were accused of lollardy may seem to provide further support for the arguments against the coherence of lollardy as an historical category, much less an actual social movement, that we encountered in Chapter 1. William Thorpe, John Oldcastle, and the Norwich suspect Margery Baxter, whom we will meet later, operated in vastly different social contexts and might have found little in common with one another if their

---

133   I owe this point to Ian Forrest.
134   Robert Lutton, *Lollardy and Orthodox Religion in Pre-reformation England: Reconstructing Piety* (London, 2006).

paths had ever crossed. Nonetheless, whether their assessment was valid or not, medieval churchmen saw these and other lollards as heirs of the same tradition of heresy, sedition, and protest, and they proceeded against them in roughly similar terms. In future chapters, we will investigate the texts that lollards and their sympathizers wrote, the beliefs they articulated and were accused of holding, and the opposition they experienced from the institutional church. All of these factors will help to further nuance our assessment of the capacious category of lollardy. First, though, we need to explore in greater detail how lollards practiced their adopted form of Christianity.

CHAPTER 3

Their Practices

What lollards believed—or at least what others have *thought* they believed—has been the focus of most polemical and scholarly work on Wyclif and lollardy. Since it was their erroneous beliefs that earned them censure as heretics, and since the writings in which they expressed their beliefs, and those in which their opponents condemned those same ideas, constitute the primary archive for the study of lollardy, scholarly accounts have frequently taken lollard texts and lollard beliefs as a starting point.[1] As a consequence, the biographies of most known lollards have received less attention than the theological propositions that such women and men defended or abjured, with the inevitable result being that in some accounts, many individual lollards seem reducible to their ideas—indeed primarily, if not exclusively, reducible to those of their ideas that were, or would have been, judged heterodox.[2] And if scholars have not always fully pursued the matter of who lollards were, the question of how lollards lived out their beliefs has been explored more infrequently still.

This chapter seeks in part to serve as a corrective to writings about lollardy that privilege the intellectual over the personal and social. It rests on assumption drawn from the sub-discipline of Christian theological study known as practical theology, namely, that for most people, most of the time, religious practice exists prior to religious belief and prior to the inscription of beliefs and ethical guidelines in sacred and religious texts.[3] Practical theology originated

---

[1] To take just three examples, more than half of each of the extant modern studies dedicated to Wyclif is concerned with his thought; the longest single section of Anne Hudson's magisterial study *Premature Reformation* (PR) is entitled "Lollard Ideology" and consists of three chapter-length parts that together run to more than 150 pages; and all but one of the contributions to a collection of essays marking Wyclif's sexcentenary focus on what can broadly be called theological and intellectual history. See Lechler; Workman; Anthony Kenny, *Wyclif* (Oxford, 1985); Gillian R. Evans, *John Wyclif: Myth and Reality* (Downer's Grove, Ill., 2006); and Lahey, *Wyclif*, among many others. PR, Chapters 6–8. Anthony Kenny, (ed.), *Wyclif in his Times* (Oxford, 1986). In contrast, the 1990s and the early twenty first century have witnessed the publication of a number of prosopographical and practice-based studies, many of which are cited below.

[2] On the "intellectualist bias" in the study of medieval heresy more generally, see many of the writings of Mark Gregory Pegg, including most recently "Albigenses in the Antipodes: An Australian and the Cathars," *Journal of Religious History* 35 (2011): 577–600, esp. 585, 596.

[3] For overviews of the field, see Richard Osmer, *Practical Theology: An Introduction* (Grand Rapids, Mich., 2008), and the essays collected in Bonnie J. Miller-McLemore, (ed.), *The Wiley-Blackwell Companion to Practical Theology* (Oxford, 2012).

in the late eighteenth century in Protestant seminaries and universities in continental Europe, and the discipline has experienced substantial development in the late twentieth and twenty-first centuries in both Roman Catholic and Protestant contexts. It is now a mainstay of academic theological scholarship in and beyond the English-speaking world, serving a range of religious communities and encompassing a diverse set of scholarly methodologies.

The key insights of practical theology—that practices shape beliefs at least as often as beliefs shape practices, and that practices and beliefs are connected with each other in a mutually interdependent way—undermine the intellectual approach to the study of medieval heresy that I have described above. They invite scholars of lollardy to form at least as deep an understanding of how lollards practiced Christianity as of what specific doctrines they accepted or rejected. (I will momentarily address the difficult question of how it is possible to determine how lollards practiced Christianity.) As we will see in this chapter, there is much evidence to suggest that lollards came to their beliefs through practices, both the ordinary practices of what has been called traditional religion and the clandestine practices condemned by the institutional church that flourished within lollard communities. For instance, we will discover that some individuals began to think more critically about the teachings of the institutional church after reading books, participating in private readings from English translations of the scriptures and polemical texts, or listening to sermons. It is not at all clear that these individuals held the heterodox beliefs they were later accused of holding *prior* to taking part in these practices; rather, the practices shaped their beliefs, and the support that they received from others created conditions where they could hold such beliefs despite the potential costs. Were they not participating in such practices, it is difficult to believe that many of those who were identified and punished as lollards would have acted and believed as they did.

Practical theologians emphasize that, important though it is to challenge the age-old assumption that theological beliefs always create religious practices, we must be equally wary of claiming with a similar level of certainty that religious practices always create theological beliefs. Instead, practical theologians explain, practices and beliefs are like chickens and eggs: it is not always possible to determine which came first, and they cannot exist without each other. For that reason, in this volume, this chapter and the two that follow seek to present a fairly integrated portrait of lollard practices, texts, and beliefs. The present chapter, on practices, appears prior to the other two, on texts and beliefs, as a riposte to intellectualist accounts of lollardy and as a word of encouragement for us to begin the study of lollardy as close as possible to the flesh-and-blood lives of the people we study.

There is, of course, a substantial difficulty with this approach: by their nature, religious practices leave fewer traces in the historical record than do heterodox texts, the individuals identified as owners and readers of them, and the beliefs those owners and readers may have held. Whereas texts can be confiscated; beliefs can be formulated as theological propositions, written down, and condemned; and persons can be arrested, tried, and burned, practices enter documentary history only insofar as those who engaged in them recorded what they did, or those who observed them wrote down what they saw. In either case, of course, it is impossible to avoid persistent and often unanswerable questions about the relationship between a practice as it actually took place and the description of that practice in written accounts.[4]

Unfortunately for our purposes, neither lollards nor their opponents left behind much evidence concerning lollard religious practice. As we will see in this chapter, we do know that many groups of lollards gathered together in one another's homes, at least sometimes for the purpose of reading aloud and discussing vernacular scriptural, devotional, and polemical tracts, both orthodox and heterodox in content. A small number of texts provide fleeting glimpses into what may have been lollard liturgical celebrations, though what we can learn of these events is usually limited to the perspective of those who judged them to be illicit and erroneous. Finally, and perhaps most importantly, we can identify some of the ideals that lollards had for their own spiritual and devotional lives. Through the careful reading of their texts, separate from what their antagonists said about them, it is possible to discern the outlines of a practical spirituality centered on the proper reading of the Bible, on the observance of God's commandments (especially the ten commandments of the Hebrew Bible), on the cultivation of proper kinds of affect, on the imitation of Christ, and on work for social change.

3.1   Preaching and Teaching

The first modern historians of lollardy, like medieval chroniclers before them, considered preaching and teaching to have been its most characteristic practices. H.L. Cannon, for instance, writing in 1900, took it as incontrovertible that Wyclif had sent groups of preachers around the English countryside: "That Wiclif's Poor Priests were designed to give the people not merely sermons in English, as the friars had done, but were intended to present to the people the

---

4   For useful theoretical perspectives on the relationship between practice and discourse, see Michel de Certeau, *The Practice of Everyday Life* (repr. Berkeley, 2011).

gospel itself as clearly as possible, and hence in English, as the other preachers had not done, goes almost without argument."[5] For these writers, lollardy was an organized movement, directed if not by Wyclif himself—as Cannon had it—then at least by a core group of individuals who had studied with Wyclif in Oxford. In the mid- to late twentieth century, a much looser picture began to emerge of the organizational structures of the lollard "movement," as it was usually still termed, but preaching and teaching remained the practices most commonly associated with Wyclif and his followers. A.K. McHardy argued in 1987 that Wyclif did not need to establish his own cadre of preachers, because instead he was already at "the centre of a ready-made network, that of ecclesiastical patronage." McHardy identified a number of Oxford scholars who were associated with Wyclif at the university, were subsequently presented to ecclesiastical livings in the gift of their Oxford foundations, and were then accused of preaching or facilitating the preaching of heterodox ideas in their parishes.[6] A decade later, Maureen Jurkowski showed that several fellows of Merton College who were affiliated with Wyclif undertook journeys to college lands, mostly in the north of England, and may have preached Wycliffite ideas to congregations there.[7] For both of these scholars, existing academic and ecclesiastical channels permitted early lollards to disseminate their ideas, and the existence of such arrangements made it unnecessary for scholars to hypothesize the existence of an independent, centrally organized body of lollard missionaries.

That Wyclif's "poor priests" have been shown to be largely mythological has not lessened the role that scholars have assigned to preaching in the practice of lollardy. Examples of itinerant preachers abound for nearly all periods of lollard history, beginning with the journeys of Merton fellows and the activities of other roving evangelists, such as William Swinderby, in the late fourteenth century. In 1428, the priest William White, on trial for heresy in Norwich, was accused of having preached in the Kentish villages of Gillingham and Tenterden, "and many others in the diocese of Canterbury," before he arrived in East Anglia

---

5   H.L. Cannon, "The Poor Priests: A Study in the Rise of English Lollardry," in *Annual Report of the American Historical Association for the Year 1899*, 2 vols. (Washington, 1900), 1:451–82, at 458. Cannon was heavily indebted to medieval chroniclers and other early anti-lollard sources: for one account strikingly similar to his, see Walsingham, *Historia anglicana*, (eds.) Matthew Parker and Henry Thomas Riley, 2 vols. (London, 1863–64), 1:324–26. The writings of many of Cannon's contemporaries contain similar views of Wyclif's "poor priests"; see, for instance, G.M. Trevelyan, *England in the Age of Wycliffe*, 4th edn. (London, 1909), 339.

6   A.K. McHardy, "The Dissemination of Wyclif's Ideas," in *Ockham to Wyclif*, 361–68, quote at 362.

7   Maureen Jurkowski, "Heresy and Factionalism at Merton College in the Early Fifteenth Century," *Journal of Ecclesiastical History* 48 (1997), 658–81.

and converted to his views many of those who, beginning that same year, were summoned before William Alnwick, the bishop of Norwich.[8] At some point in Canterbury, White had been tried and had abjured his heretical opinions before Archbishop Henry Chichele, and thus, he was promptly burned in Norwich as a relapsed "heretic and lollard."[9] Another example of a peripatetic lollard evangelist was John Stilman, who figured prominently in the trials of seven men and women brought before Bishop Richard Fox of Winchester in 1512.[10] Stilman had earlier abjured heterodox opinions before Bishop Edmund Audley of Salisbury, in 1508, and was later apprehended again, in 1518, by the officers of Bishop Richard Fitzjames of London, at whose command he was imprisoned in the Lollards' Tower and eventually burned as a relapsed heretic.[11]

Not all lollard communities benefited from exposure to itinerant preachers such as these, however. For many individuals, conversations with like-minded neighbors constituted their only means of practicing an alternative form of Christianity, and for them, "preaching" was not necessarily a formal activity.[12] Early on, authorities suspected lollards of meeting together in secret conventicles for the purpose of discussing heterodox ideas and reading, or hearing readings from, forbidden books. Indeed, the preface to the 1401 parliamentary statute that authorized the death penalty for obdurate and relapsed heretics charged that lollards "make conventicles and confederations, hold and conduct schools, compose and write books, wickedly instruct and teach and exhort the populace to sedition or insurrection, to the extent that they can, and create great dissentions among the people."[13] That "conventicles" and "schools" featured so prominently in this list was no coincidence: authorities believed that groups of lollards were doing what they thought heretics had done for centuries before them, that is, meeting together secretly and spreading erroneous and seditious opinions. Later evangelical propagandists, for their part, believed that the existence of such groups served an entirely opposite purpose: to

---

8   *FZ*, 418: "et aliis quampluribus infra diocesim Cantuariensem."
9   *FZ*, 432: "haereticum et Lollardum."
10 For discussion of these trials, see below, 185–86.
11 J.A.F. Thomson, *The Later Lollards: 1414–1520* (Oxford, 1965), 88–89; *A&M*, 979–80. For Stilman's activities in Winchester diocese, see the records printed in *Wycliffite Spirituality*, 341–66, and analysis in J. Patrick Hornbeck II, "*Wycklyffes Wycket* and Eucharistic Heresy: Two Series of Cases from Sixteenth-Century Winchester," in *Wycliffite Controversies*, 279–94.
12 Simon Forde, "Lay Preaching and the Lollards of Norwich Diocese, 1428–1431," *Leeds Studies in English* 29 (1998), 109–26.
13 *A&M*, 700: "Conuenticulas & confederationes faciunt, scholas tenent & exercent, libros conficiunt atque scribunt, populum nequiter instruunt & informant, & ad seditionem seu insurrectionem excitant, quantum possunt, & magnas dissentiones in populo faciunt."

provide places of refuge where the true gospel of Christ could survive underground, in order that it might emerge again at the appointed time, during the early stages of the Reformation.[14]

While medieval church authorities and early-modern evangelicals both interpreted the existence of lollard conventicles according to their own lights, evidence from the records of heresy trials confirms that such small, easily concealed, usually domestic meetings comprised for most lollards a primary space for their religious practice. Records of such "scoles of heresie" appear as early as 1382, when they were first described by Henry Knighton, and continue through the early Reformation.[15] In some cases, a "meeting" comprised only a single married couple and their carefully chosen intimates, as in the case of the Norwich defendant Margery Baxter, who allegedly asked her neighbor, Joan Clifland, to join her "secretly in her bedroom at night, where she might hear her husband read to her from the law of Christ, which was written in a book that her said husband was accustomed to reading to Margery at night."[16] In other cases, groups were larger, and some lollards traveled long distances to be present in one another's homes. The Kentish villages of Benenden, Boxley, and Maidstone are as many as nineteen miles apart, but as the register of Archbishop of Canterbury William Warham notes, lollards from all three villages met in December 1510 at Edward Walker's home in Maidstone, where

> the wife of the same Walker commyned [conversed], herd, assentid and affirmed without contradiccion ayenst the blessed sacrament of the aulter.... And as they were so commynyng...the wif of yat said Walker said, "Sires, it is not good that ye talke moche here of this maters for the jaylors will take hede of you yf ye come huder. And also beware for som folks will comyn hider anon [soon]." And thereupon forthwith came yn the jaylors wif and they cessed of their communicacion.[17]

Accounts of similar meetings can be found in the majority of surviving court records, though (as we will see in greater detail in Chapter 7) these records vary widely in terms of the details they preserve about the size of a group, the names of those present, and the topics discussed.

In the records, two practices stand out as the most common agenda items for lollard meetings: the reading aloud of vernacular biblical and spiritual texts and

---

14   See for instance *A&M*, 699, 759, 946, among many others.
15   The phrase is from *Norwich*, 28.
16   *Norwich*, 47–48; translation in *Wycliffite Spirituality*, 333.
17   *Kent*, 55.

the discussion of theological ideas. With regard to reading, there is substantial evidence that lollards read not only heterodox literature, such as tracts arguing in favor of unorthodox positions on the eucharist, other sacraments, and the papacy, but also texts that originated in the milieu of mainstream religion, above all the Bible. Rita Copeland has noted that a number of heresy defendants owned vernacular primers, that is, the lay-oriented Books of Hours that figured prominently in the traditional piety of the later Middle Ages.[18] She has observed that while the records do not reveal which parts of the primer lollards may have read aloud, "[h]owever these primers were used in Lollard circles, the ecclesiastical authorities viewed them with suspicion, and indeed English primers disappear after the middle of the fifteenth century, because ownership of them was linked with heresy."[19] Yet primers were not the only orthodox books named in heresy trials; so also were books of scripture, whose unauthorized translation was forbidden under the terms of Archbishop Arundel's constitutions of 1409. We have already seen the charge against Margery Baxter, that her husband "read to her from the law of Christ," and in Bishop Fox's trials in early sixteenth century Winchester diocese, defendants admitted to having read from "the books of the New Testament translated into English," "an English book of Luke and John translated out of Latin into English," and other "English books prohibited by the church."[20]

Precisely how a lollard gathering was conducted remains an open question, indeed a question unlikely ever to be resolved in the absence of new evidence. Lollards may have prayed together, may have offered one another support in the midst of persecution, and may have traded gossip and information about recent events in the parish, diocese, and town or village community. Copeland has argued that one of the distinctive features of many lollard conventicles was the way in which they permitted open-ended discussion of theological and religious matters. Unlike memorizing and reading texts, which were common medieval educational practices, discussion was "pedagogically unorthodox," and in Copeland's view, inquisitors saw even informal discussions among lollards as "as the first step towards planting theologically unorthodox ideas" in the heads of the unsuspecting.[21] However, beyond naming conventicles as sites for reading and conversation, most trial records show little interest in the

---

18   On primers, see Duffy, *Stripping of the Altars*, and *Marking the Hours: English People and Their Prayers, 1240–1570* (New Haven, Conn., 2011).
19   Rita Copeland, *Pedagogy, Intellectuals, and Dissent in the Later Middle Ages* (Cambridge, 2001), 16.
20   *Wycliffite Spirituality*, 355–66.
21   Copeland, *Pedagogy*, 11.

mechanics of the meetings of such groups, focusing instead on the specific beliefs that lollards were charged with holding and sharing with one another.

In contrast to the meetings I have been describing, it seems unlikely that lollard practices regularly included rituals designed either to replicate or to mock the sacraments of the official church. Scholars have traditionally identified a few exceptions to this claim, among them most famously the record of the 1389 trial of William Ramsbury, who was brought before the bishop of Salisbury on a range of purported heresies having to do with the priesthood, the eucharist, the adoration of images, and sexual licentiousness. At his trial, Ramsbury confessed to having been ordained by a certain Thomas Fishbourn, about whom no other records survive. Ramsbury was also accused of having performed an unauthorized version of the Mass "in diverse places" in the diocese. The ritual described in the record of Ramsbury's trial resembled in many ways the conventional Sarum Rite liturgy widely used in medieval England, but with a few adjustments: he either omitted several prayers (the *Adiutorium*, the *Agnus Dei*, and the *Gloria*) altogether, or moved them to unusual places in the ritual; he did not speak the words of consecration, though he elevated the host; and he omitted the words of blessing over bread at the end of Mass, although bread was still distributed to the congregation. Commenting on Ramsbury's trial, Anne Hudson observed in 1972 that while some of the changes in Ramsbury's liturgy may have been inspired by Wycliffite theology, his ritual was not unequivocally heterodox. "The use of the established liturgy, albeit abbreviated, for this mass goes some way to explain how Lollards could often survive a long time unsuspected by their orthodox fellows."[22]

Responding to Hudson's essay nearly forty years later, the historian Richard Rex offered an alternative assessment of Ramsbury's case, claiming that he was not so much a lollard priest as a confidence artist. As evidence that Ramsbury was not in fact indebted to lollard ideas, Rex has pointed to the incongruities between Ramsbury's version of the liturgy and the articles about the eucharist that he abjured at his trial: "Why should a Lollard, who believed that only those of his sect had a true understanding of the words of consecration, omit those words while including in his liturgy the elevation, a gesture which summed up the rival theology of the eucharist which as a Lollard he would have to condemn as idolatry?"[23] Rex has proposed instead that Ramsbury was simply

---

[22] Anne Hudson, "A Lollard Mass," *Journal of Theological Studies* n.s. 23 (1972), 407–19, repr. in *Books*, 111–23, at 118. See also Andrew Brown, *Popular Piety in Late Medieval England: The Diocese of Salisbury, 1250–1550* (Oxford, 1995), 210–11.

[23] Richard Rex, "Not a Lollard Mass After All," *Journal of Theological Studies* n.s. 62 (2011), 207–17, at 211.

interested in convincing others that he was a priest in order to earn a living by celebrating masses for the souls of the dead. Since all the portions of the liturgy that Ramsbury omitted were those said privately by the priest, while all the portions he retained were those said publicly in the sight and hearing of the congregation, Rex has argued that Ramsbury's revised liturgy simply provided him with an expedient way of saying as many "masses" as possible in the shortest length of time. For Rex, then, Ramsbury was never a lollard. Instead he "was a rogue and a rascal. When caught he admitted everything. His judges, cynically or from conviction (for there was a moral panic over the spread of Lollard ideas), chose to see him as more than a mere rogue, and tarred him with the brush of heresy."[24]

So, which was it: was Ramsbury a lollard priest, or simply a clever fraud? In the absence of further evidence it is impossible to say for sure, but it is certainly worth concluding that Ramsbury's case may not present the kind of unambiguous evidence for distinctive lollard liturgical practice that has traditionally been claimed. It may prove to be more important that whether or not they also had their own distinctive liturgies, some, if not in fact many, lollards also continued to participate in at least some of the ritual practices of the institutional church. Whether out of fear of being detected as heretics, out of curiosity about what the local priest was saying, or without any ulterior motives, many lollards continued to attend mass and to take part in the other sacraments and rituals of medieval Christian life. Some found subtle ways of distancing themselves from the ways in which mainstream liturgies reflected official theological positions: thus some heresy defendants admitted to not raising their eyes at the elevation, or said that they looked up to heaven rather than gazing on the consecrated host.[25] Finally, still others took more defiant stances, for instance remaining at home instead of going to church, avoiding the mandatory annual confession to a priest, or (in the most extreme cases) desecrating the consecrated host.[26]

---

24 Rex, "Not a Lollard Mass," 214–15. Rex's discussion of the veneration of Richard Wyche by citizens of London proceeds along similar lines to his discussion of Ramsbury's liturgy. See Rex, "'Which is Wyche?' Lollardy and Sanctity in Lancastrian London," in *Martyrs and Martyrdom in England, c. 1400–1700*, (eds.) Thomas Freedman and Thomas Maye (Woodbridge, 2007), 88–106.

25 PR, 149–50. For examples of these phenomena, see among others *Coventry*, 69; Netter, *Doctrinale*, 2:341.

26 Hudson discusses a range of such cases in PR, 150–52. In addition to the examples she cites there, see the cases of Robert Winter, Winchester reg. Fox 3: fol. 76v, and William Moress, Rochester reg. Fisher, fol. 57r.

In the absence of formal liturgical rituals, it would seem that the practice of lollard forms of Christianity revolved around the kinds of teaching and preaching I have been describing. That the majority of the evidence describes practices of reading and conversation among individuals who already acknowledged one another as members of a distinctive underground religious group, though, does not mean that lollards did not at times preach publicly. References to a number of public sermons and pronouncements by prominent lollards, especially those directly connected with Wyclif, appear in medieval chronicles and the records of heresy trials. These include the controversial vernacular Ascension Day sermon preached by Wyclif's early collaborator Nicholas Hereford in Oxford in 1382; the sermon that William Taylor preached at Paul's Cross in London on 21 November 1406; and at least one sermon preached by William Thorpe in Shrewsbury at around the same time.[27] Other public preachers included William Swinderby, several of the Merton fellows described by McHardy and Jurkowski, and the anonymous but well-educated preacher of the "Egerton sermon" edited by Anne Hudson.[28] All these public sermons date from the first three decades of the Wycliffite controversies, however, and as persecution intensified, the preaching and teaching of lollard ideas became a more private, domestic matter. When John Stilman taught the Winchester heresy defendants Thomas Wattes and Laurence Swaffer in 1513, for instance, he visited each of their homes and read aloud "various English books prohibited by the church."[29]

Practices like public preaching, private teaching, and informal discussion among members of lollard communities helps us see how, as Copeland has argued, lollardy was simultaneously theologically and pedagogically unorthodox. Not only did lollards articulate positions about the sacraments, the ecclesiastical hierarchy, and other religious and theological topics that were at variance with those of the institutional church, but lollardy was "also radical, or indeed heterodox, in its educational ideologies. The constitution of a discourse about pedagogy from antiquity onwards represents a kind of institutional orthodoxy that is distinct from theological rules."[30] For Copeland, then, lollards were interested in the development of alternative modes of teaching

---

27 Further details about these sermons can be found in Simon Forde, "Nicholas Hereford's Ascension Day Sermon, 1382," *Mediaeval Studies* 51 (1989), 205–41; and Anne Hudson, (ed.), *Two Wycliffite Texts* (EETS o.s. 301, 1993).

28 No text or *reportatio* of Swinderby's sermons survives, but see Hereford reg. Trefnant, 237–51, for Swinderby's account of some of his teachings. See also nn. 6–7 above, and Anne Hudson, (ed.), *The Works of a Lollard Preacher* (EETS o.s. 317, 2001).

29 *Wycliffite Controversies*, 362.

30 Copeland, *Pedagogy*, 6.

and learning, combining for instance "the recent theological respect for the literal sense of Scripture with the ancient pedagogical utility of literal explanation." Lollards therefore presented "'literal' expositions of Scripture to lay audiences whose own literacy may have been at an elementary level. In other words, they converted a theological preference for the 'plain sense' of Scripture to the pedagogical purpose of introducing the biblical text to vernacular audiences."[31] In the kinds of pedagogies they chose to develop, lollards demonstrated a preference for modes of instruction that, in some respects, resemble the "modern radical pedagogies" of scholars like Paolo Freire.[32] Projects like the *Glossed Gospels*, about which we will say more in the next chapter, constituted the heart of these pedagogies, and indeed, the layout of the surviving manuscripts of these gospel commentaries suggests that they may have been intended for use in the kind of group instruction described in some records of heresy suspects' trials.[33] Likewise, new research on the *English Wycliffite Sermons* has uncovered evidence, such as tables of lections prefixed to some manuscripts of the sermon-cycle, that these sermon texts were at least sometimes intended for liturgical use.[34]

3.2   Lollard Spirituality

If readings from and discussions of the scriptures and other vernacular religious texts were at the heart of lollards' spiritual practice, then what did lollards learn from engaging in such activities? As we have been observing throughout this chapter, lollardy has traditionally been described in both intellectual and negative terms: following in the footsteps of lollards' medieval opponents, scholars have perceived lollardy, at least in its early stages, to have been a form of academic theological dissent. Thus, as we have seen, a majority of studies have focused on the ways in which lollards rejected orthodox theological claims. Yet at least two limitations of this approach, one historical and one methodological, have become apparent over time. First, it is unclear what attraction a

---

31   Rita Copeland, "Lollard Instruction," in Miri Rubin, (ed.), *Medieval Christianity in Practice* (Princeton, N.J., 2009), 27–32, at 30.
32   Copeland, *Pedagogy*, 22.
33   Anne Hudson, (ed.), *Doctors in English: A Study of the Wycliffite Gospel Commentaries* (Liverpool, 2015).
34   We await the publication of Jennifer Illig's research on the *English Wycliffite Sermons*, which includes a survey of the manuscripts that present the sermons in the order of the liturgical year. See Illig, "Through a Lens of Likeness: Reading English Wycliffite Sermons in Light of Contemporary Sermon Texts" (Ph.D. diss., Fordham University, 2014).

religious movement that was overwhelmingly negative in its ideology—that is, one that consisted largely of the denial and rejection of traditional beliefs and practices rather than in the affirmation of constructive alternatives—would have had for the individuals who risked their lives and livelihoods to disseminate and preserve lollard ideas. Though few heresy suspects in late medieval England were ultimately executed for their beliefs, the stake cast its shadow not only across every heresy defendant but also across those engaged in the activities of reading, copying, and distributing lollard literature. It stands to reason that those who took their lives and reputations in their hands by partaking in such practices must have had positive reasons to risk suffering and death, and the attracts of lollard spirituality may explain much of the appeal that lollardy had to its practitioners. Second, as Somerset has repeatedly observed, the reason most accounts of lollard theology and spirituality focus on lollard denials, rather than lollard affirmations, is that scholars have usually relied on the "extrinsic" accounts of lollardy produced by its opponents, rather than on the "intrinsic" evidence for lollard belief available in the more than 250 extant manuscripts with lollard affiliations. "It is as if we were to begin our research on Franciscans by reading antifraternal writings or base our study of Christianity on what Muslims affected by the Crusades have to say about Christians."[35] Somerset's most recent study, *Feeling Like Saints*, aims to trace the shape of a coherent lollard "pastoral program" by observing what actions, feelings, and imaginings lollard writers intended to prompt in their readers.

Following Somerset's lead, recent work on lollardy has attempted to reconstruct the positive spiritual ideals that lollards embraced as their own, although more research in this area is needed. One finding to have already emerged is that the differences in spiritual and devotional practice between lollardy and mainstream Christianity are not nearly as wide as previously imagined.[36] As we will see in greater detail in the next chapter, lollards employed a range of traditional literary forms, writing commentaries on prayers such as the Pater Noster and Ave Maria; composing guidelines for how clerics, lords, and commoners should live; and even producing a formula for making one's confession. These similarities notwithstanding, however, lollard devotional writings also possess distinctive emphases that mark them out as texts written by lollards or by others affiliated with lollardy. With her two collaborators on a recent set of

---

35 Somerset, *Feeling Like Saints*, 3; see also Somerset, "Wycliffite Spirituality," in *Text and Controversy*, 375–86; and *Wycliffite Spirituality*, 7–52.
36 The same is true about the content of sermon literature: see Illig, "Through a Lens of Likeness."

translations of lollard writings, Somerset has identified eight sets of ideas and methods that, together, characterize lollard spirituality.[37]

First, lollard spiritual writings often refer to "God's law" and "Christ's law." With these phrases, lollard texts seem to point not only generally to the wide range of commandments contained in the Bible but, in particular, to the ten commandments of the books of Exodus and Deuteronomy. A range of lollard writings, even those which ostensibly cover other topics, are structured around the ten commandments, and expositions of the commandments often occupy unusually prominent positions: "it is common, rather than as a sign of especially bad planning, for this section to bulge out of proportion and distort the shape of the work as a whole."[38] Many lollard writers take the commandments to include within their terms all possible sins, as well as all possible virtues, and in many cases, they present breaking a single commandment as tantamount to breaking them all. Lollard authors are distinctive in relying on the commandments as an orienting principle, rather than, as was conventional, structuring their writings around the seven deadly sins and the seven virtues.

Second, lollards emphasized continuous prayer as a means of turning oneself toward God and keeping the commandments, since they believed that when people pray, they are better able to withstand the temptations of the devil and to serve as an example to other Christians. The text *On Holy Prayers* observes that "in the gospel of St. Luke, Christ says that it is necessary to pray at all times, and St. Paul commands Christian men to pray without ceasing and without delay."[39] In one lollard commentary on the Ave Maria, those who pray this prayer are said to find in it encouragement to live a life of "meekness, chastity, charity, modesty, and seriousness," rather than "evil speech, especially of lechery…evil conduct and sin, debauchery, and discourtesy."[40]

Third, not unlike the spiritual writings of other medieval groups who were perceived to inhabit the margins of orthodoxy, lollard spiritual writings encourage their readers to imitate Christ.[41] A number of lollard writers specifically

---

37   The following paragraphs paraphrase the long account of these ideas and methods available in *Wycliffite Spirituality*, 7–52.
38   *Wycliffite Spirituality*, 9.
39   "De Precationibus Sacris," in Arnold, 3:219; translation in *Wycliffite Spirituality*, 182–90.
40   "The Ave Maria," in Matthew, 204.
41   The classic case, of course, is Thomas à Kempis' *The Imitation of Christ*, of which the most recent edition is trans. E.M. Blaiklock (London, 2009). À Kempis was affiliated with the Brothers and Sisters of the Common Life, also known as the *Devotio moderna* or Modern-Day Devout: on this group, see John van Engen, *Sisters and Brothers of the Common Life: The Devotio Moderna and the World of the Later Middle Ages* (Philadelphia, 2008). For Wyclif's views on the imitation of Christ, see David Aers, "John Wyclif's Understanding of

looked to Christ as a model for perseverance in the face of persecution. One text, the "Dialogue between a Wise Man and a Fool," famously applies the abusive epithet "loller" to Christ himself:

> As for where they call men lollers for speaking God's word, I read of two kinds of lollers in the law of grace. Some loll toward God, and some toward the fiend. I intend to talk about both of these kinds. The most blessed loller that ever was or shall be was our Lord Jesus Christ, who lolled for our sins on the cross. Wearing his livery and belonging to his retinue were Peter and Andrew and others as well. These were blessed lollers, lolling on the right hand of Jesus with the repentant thief, trusting in God's mercy, to whom our Lord promised the bliss of paradise on the same day. But, good friends, what was the reason why Christ and his followers were lolled in this way? Certainly, because of their faithful speaking out against the sins of the people. And especially because they spoke against the covetousness and sins of untrue bishops and of the false, feigned religious.[42]

The message to this writer's contemporaries was clear: the best way to follow Christ is to imitate him, and likewise to imitate his first disciples, in crying out against corruption and patiently suffering persecution at the hands of sinful men. Likewise, a range of lollard texts describe the ways in which Antichrist continually mounts assaults on Christ's church; they depict persecution as an opportunity to join oneself to Christ and the saints.

Next, lollard spirituality looks beyond the self to the community and, in doing so, calls upon the church to practice the works of mercy and justice that God has commanded. Many lollard writers stress the responsibility of each member of a community to speak out against social and communal injustices, even when to do so is to invite opposition and persecution. It may have been that early, academic lollard writers borrowed from Wyclif the idea, derived from his realist metaphysics, that a sin against any one person is a sin against the whole of humanity and, by extension, the whole of creation.[43] Certainly, a number of lollard writers articulated theories of social consent to sin whereby

---

Christian Discipleship," in *Faith, Ethics, and Church: Writing in England, 1360–1409* (Woodbridge, 2000), 119–48.

42   "Dialogue between a Wise Man and a Fool" [Cambridge Tract XII], in Mary Dove, (ed.), *The Earliest Advocates of the English Bible: The Texts of the Medieval Debate* (Exeter, 2010), 131; translation in *Wycliffite Spirituality*, 247–63.

43   On Wyclif's realism, see above, 31–33.

failure to point out an injustice is a sin in itself.[44] Fifth, spiritual writings by lollards display interest in the dichotomy between those who will and those who will not be saved. Even though most lollards did not believe in predestination, at least not as later reformers understood the term, lollard texts do frequently distinguish between true and false clerics, between the few who are chosen and the many who are called, and between the members of their group and the broader population who call themselves Christian.[45] The *Lanterne of Liȝt*, for instance, is structured around a series of distinctions between the mystical "churches" of God and the devil; its author dedicates more than two thirds of his text to a detailed analysis of the ways in which church officials, ministers, and laypeople behave in God's and the devil's churches, respectively.

Lollards' interest in the distinction between the saved and the damned did not stop them from articulating hopes for social reform, the sixth characteristic of lollard spirituality identified by Somerset and others. For most lollards, "social reform" meant returning to the earliest (and therefore best) days of Christian history; in this regard, lollards joined many other medieval reformers in advocating a return to the example of the apostolic church, from which they believed the contemporary church had gradually fallen away.[46] Lollards looked favorably upon what they took to be the practices of the early church, when there were neither friars nor monks, when priests and bishops were content to be servants rather than worldly lords, and when the sacramental rituals instituted by Jesus had not yet been defiled by the speculations of scholastic theologians.

A seventh characteristic of lollard spirituality concerns its abiding interest in biblical exegesis. In the next chapter, we will explore the proposal made by several modern scholars that lollards developed and employed a "sect vocabulary," a set of terms and ways of using them that identified lollards to one another.[47]

---

44   See Fiona Somerset, "Before and After Wyclif: Consent to Another's Sin in Medieval Europe," in J. Patrick Hornbeck II and Michael Van Dussen, (eds.), *Europe After Wyclif* (New York, forthcoming 2016).

45   For further discussion of lollard ideas about salvation and predestination, see 111–117 below.

46   On this point, see the still classic study of Scott H. Hendrix, "In Quest of the *Vera Ecclesia*: The Crises of Late Medieval Ecclesiology," *Viator* 8 (1977): 347–69.

47   See Anne Hudson, "A Lollard Sect Vocabulary?" in M. Benskin and M.L. Samuels, (eds.), *So Meny People, Longages, and Tonges: Philological Essays in Scots and Mediaeval English Presented to Angus McIntosh* (Edinburgh, 1981), 15–30, repr. in *Books*, 164–80; Matti Peikola, *Congregation of the Elect: Patterns of Self-Fashioning in English Lollard Writings* (Turku, Finland, 2000); and Jill C. Havens, "Shading the Grey Area: Determining Heresy in Middle English Texts," in *Text and Controversy*, 337–52.

If there were such a vocabulary, then the pair of Middle English terms *groundid* and *ungroundid* would have to count among its most frequently used components. For lollards, a belief, practice, or text was "grounded" if it could trace its arguments back to scripture, which Wyclif had exalted as identical with Christ: "I have often said that the entire Holy Scripture is the one word of God, and that every one of its parts should be condensed into the totality of that Word in whom the blessed in heaven see the multitude of truths spoken by God."[48] Since lollards were so keenly interested in the biblical legitimacy of theological claims, many of their writings focus on the exposition of scripture, ranging from simple translation and exposition to interpolation and commentary.

Finally, lollards' interests in the keeping of God's law, in social reform, and in biblical exegesis are all relevant to a final characteristic of lollard spirituality. Many of the surviving records of the trials of heresy suspects, about which we will learn more in Chapter 7, suggest that lollards were strongly committed to what modern Christians might call the dignity of the human person and the cultivation of spiritual simplicity. Several heresy defendants admitted to encouraging their neighbors and acquaintances to focus not so much on the externalities of Christian observance as on Christ's command to love one's neighbors. For instance, Margery Jopson, on trial in Winchester diocese in 1512, rebuked a gentlewoman who came to her house and refused to accept a drink of water before she had made an offering to the Rood in the local church: "Why will you drink so sparingly? Why should you offer your money to the Rood? Give to a poor body, for priests have enough money!"[49] Like other suspects from the fifteenth and early sixteenth centuries, Jopson drew an explicit comparison between the wooden body of Christ on the crucifix and the fleshly bodies of one's neighbors, privileging the living bodies over the inanimate one. In doing so, she gave voice to a broader concern of lollard theology, namely, a concern that idolatry will inevitably arise from overvaluing specific religious practices and thereby not attending to the image of God that exists in all human persons, especially the materially poor.

By way of concluding this survey of lollard spirituality, it is worth recalling that, of necessity, the glimpses we have of the ways in which lollards thought about and lived out their faith are momentary at best. Until recently, the nature of the evidence that scholars have relied upon has not permitted us to observe more than a few isolated moments in the life and religious practice of an individual or community. As a result of the recent growth of interest in the content

---

48   John Wyclif, *On the Truth of Holy Scripture*, trans. Ian Christopher Levy (Kalamazoo, Mich., 2001), 264.

49   Winchester reg. Fox 3: fol. 72r, translated in *Wycliffite Spirituality*, 351.

of lollards' own spiritual writings, however, exciting new evidence for the ways in which lollards believed, lived, and prayed will surely continue to be found. We may learn more about how groups gathered to read (or be read to) from the vernacular Bible and other English religious texts, how preachers delivered their occasional public sermons, and how lollards put into practice their disdain for unnecessary ceremonies and observances. More importantly, we may learn more about the spiritual ideals that undergirded all such practices, as well as about the practices that gave rise to the spiritual ideals. First, though, in the next two chapters we must turn to more traditional ways of studying lollards: through literary analysis of their writings (Chapter 4) and theological analysis of their beliefs (Chapter 5).

CHAPTER 4

Their Writings

Fiona Somerset

This chapter will survey the many texts written, translated, or interpolated by lollard writers, nearly all of them anonymous. It makes no pretense to originality, but relies heavily on the work of others as well as my own previous work.[1] In the light of significant advances in our understanding of the social networks and locales in which religious books were produced and circulated in medieval England, it attempts to describe not just texts themselves, but the life histories of the kinds of books in which they appear.

In the forms in which they now remain to us, most lollard texts are as uninformative about their original date and circumstances of production as they are about their authorship.[2] Some are only extant in much later copies. Their study has been complicated by difficulties of identification and definition. What counts as a lollard text? Scholars have sought to isolate doctrinal claims, polemical points, vocabulary, or stylistic characteristics that are distinctively lollard. On the other hand, they have also sought to identify characteristics that rule out the possibility of lollard influence. These tasks are made more difficult by three tendencies in lollard textuality strongly prevalent in their

---

1 In addition to studies cited in this chapter, I draw upon Ernest W. Talbert and S. Harrison Thomson, "Wyclyf and His Followers," in *A Manual of the Writings in Middle English 1050–1500*, vol. 2, (ed.) J. Burke Severs (Hamden, CT, 1970), 354–80, as updated by Anne Hudson, "Contributions to a History of Wycliffite Writings" and "Additions and Modifications to a Bibliography of English Wycliffite Writings" in *Books*, 1–12 and 249–52. This overview gives a fuller account of Latin writings and of verse than was possible in my "Wycliffite Prose" in *Middle English Prose: A Critical Guide to Major Authors and Genres*, (ed.) A.S.G. Edwards (Woodbridge, 2004), 195–214, itself an update of an eponymous article by Anne Hudson in *A Companion to Middle English Prose*, (ed.) A.S.G. Edwards (New Brunswick: Rutgers University Press, 1984), 249–70. Funded by the Social Sciences and Humanities Research Council of Canada, and with David Watt, Mary Raschko, and others credited in the document, I have compiled an open access online resource to accompany this chapter, in which a list of the extant manuscripts of every item discussed may be found: http://digitalcommons.uconn.edu/eng_suppub/3/. This resource will be regularly updated: corrections and additions are requested.

2 In contrast with an earlier phase of scholarship when many writings in English were confidently attributed to John Wyclif or to John Purvey on the basis of similarity of dialect or expression, most now agree that the only solid reason for authorial attribution is identification of the author in the work itself. However, most writings are anonymous.

books, and indeed to a greater or lesser degree in every manuscript book written out laboriously by hand. These are tendencies toward repeated revision in successive copies; toward the more or less thorough interpolation and adaptation of existing writings; and toward the miscellaneous gathering within one book's covers of widely varying materials.

Far from helping us pick out which texts are lollard, these habits of manuscript book production often blur the line between lollard writings and the religious mainstream. A seemingly distinctive word or phrase present in one extant copy of a text might be removed in other copies. Interpolation or adaptation of a mainstream text may produce an ideological position that seems incoherent or at the very least inconsistent. What looks to us like a text with very obviously objectionable content may nonetheless appear without alteration in a manuscript owned by a religious house and otherwise consisting of prayers and devotional writings that seem entirely ordinary. These phenomena suggest that medieval readers were often as uncertain as we are about the boundaries between lollard and mainstream writings—though the readers who *were* sharply aware of them, and meticulous in their revisions and adaptations, can be very helpful to us in deciding where to draw them. Moreover, many medieval readers did not much care about these boundaries, and some at least saw little risk in incorporating materials of unknown provenance within their compilations. Ownership of books containing English writings or reports of clandestine group reading may sometimes (especially among lower-status laity) have been the grounds for an investigation for heresy. Far more rarely, the content of a specific English book may have been investigated under trial.[3] But more often lollard writing seems to have flown under the radar.

This complexity and even confusion need not invite despair, even for those new to this field of study. Rather, it should impel us to move as quickly as we can beyond introductory, thematic anthologies of shorter texts and excerpts—valuable as these are as a starting point—toward the study of the books from which these writings come.[4] This chapter shows the way: the survey provided here places the texts it examines within a roughly chronological account of three overlapping phases in the production and reception of lollard writings

---

3 See Chapter 7 of this volume.
4 Still widely used are the anthologies by Arnold and Matthew. Their ascriptions of works to Wyclif are now rejected, but their principle of selection was not unsound: they gathered polemical and pastoral materials found together in a small group of manuscripts then sought other items like them. More recent anthologies with better quality texts and more commentary include Hudson, (ed.), *Selections*; Helen Barr, (ed.), *The Piers Plowman Tradition* (London, 1993); Mary Dove, (ed.), *The Earliest Advocates of the English Bible: The Texts of the Medieval Debate* (Exeter, UK, 2011); *Wycliffite Spirituality*.

and the books in which they appear.[5] First, we examine an early phase of rapid, large-scale collaborative production that produced five massive works designed variously to promote more comprehensive learning and teaching among newly broadened audiences. Especially early on, these works typically appear in large, single-purpose volumes that often show signs of standardized format or even mass production. Second, we survey a concurrent but longer-lived phase in which individual and often idiosyncratic labors produced texts extant in one or a few copies. Some of these are spinoff projects from the large-scale collaborative projects of Phase 1, while others are imitations or translations of Wyclif's writings. They typically appear as the single work in a volume, or within an anthology where all or most items are clearly closely associated with lollard concerns. Third, we trace the reception or recension of material from Phase 1 and Phase 2 and their characteristic idioms in a variety of contexts where they are diffused among mainstream writings, influencing them and being influenced in turn. The distinguishing feature of Phase 3 is the diffusion of its texts within more miscellaneous books, and frequently these are books whose concerns overlap extensively with the mainstream. A fourth phase, the reception and even printing of lollard writings in the sixteenth and seventeenth centuries, is covered in Chapter 8 of this volume.

More should be said about the means by which this survey identifies texts as lollard. On the whole it follows the general consensus in the field. Occasionally, though not without fair warning, it expands the canon to embrace what others have considered dubious or unlikely cases. The basis for identification in these cases is the intrinsic characteristics of the writings themselves, and most especially what they draw from Wyclif's works, rather than external criteria such as later protestant expectations or even tenets of belief sought by bishops at contemporary heresy trials.[6] However, readers whose set of criteria is different, or whose investigations center around a particular point of doctrine or claim or practice, will find this introductory survey equally valuable as a roadmap for their investigations of the corpus. All will find ample confirmation of a point first made by Christina von Nolcken as the modern rediscovery of a fuller range

---

5 In addition to critical editions and studies of materials in Phase 1 and 2 cited below, Anne Hudson has recently drawn important general conclusions about Phase 1 book production: see "Five Problems in Wycliffite Texts and a Suggestion," *Medium Ævum* 80.2 (2011): 301–24. I have focused mainly on Phase 2 and on Phase 3, whose books have often been studied from the point of view of mainstream religion rather than lollardy: see for example Vincent Gillespie, "Vernacular Books of Religion," in Jeremy Griffiths and Derek Pearsall, (eds.), *Book Production and Publishing in Britain 1375–1475* (Cambridge, 1989), 317–44.

6 On the identification of lollard writings, and suggested terminology for describing them, see my *Feeling Like Saints: Lollard Writings After Wyclif* (Ithaca, N.Y., 2014), esp. 1–22.

of lollard writings was just beginning.[7] When we attend to the full range of lollard writings, rather than only a thin slice of them, we find not the narrow stridency and lack of imagination that Duffy has attributed to them, but wide variation in genre, purpose, audience, style, and tone.[8]

4.1 Rapid, Large-Scale Production

In Wyclif's final years in Oxford, and in their wake, collaboration amongst teams of scholars who in the early phase at least had access to well-stocked libraries produced five massive works, each now extant in a number of versions and recensions.[9] Two, the *Wycliffite Bible* and *English Wycliffite Sermons*, have been in print since the nineteenth century and have recently been extensively studied.[10] The other three are less well known, largely because they have so far seen print only in part. One, the interpolated commentaries on Rolle's *English Psalter*, has just been published in a critical edition of its two principal complete versions, while the remaining two, the *Glossed Gospels* and the Latin encyclopedia the *Floretum* and its redaction the *Rosarium*, are large reference works with complex textual traditions that may never be printed in full.[11]

---

7   Christina von Nolcken, "An Unremarked Group of Wycliffite Sermons in Latin," *Modern Philology* 83 (1986): 233–49. This modern rediscovery was led by Anne Hudson and Margaret Aston, and has continued in the work of many of their students.

8   Eamon Duffy, "Preface to the Second Edition" in *The Stripping of the Altars: Traditional Religion in England, c. 1400–1580* (New Haven, 2005), xiii–xxxvii, and see further Somerset, *Feeling Like Saints*.

9   Anne Hudson makes the case that these five works are especially significant for understanding large-scale production in the early lollard movement: see "Five Texts."

10 On the *Wycliffite Bible* see Mary Dove, *The First English Bible: The Text and Context of the Wycliffite Versions* (Cambridge, 2007). There is no modern critical edition of the entire work; instead we rely on J. Forshall and F. Madden, (eds.) *The Holy Bible…[made] by John Wycliffe and his Followers,* 4 vols. (Oxford, 1850), and on newer editions of individual manuscripts by Conrad Lindberg. For the *English Wycliffite Sermons*, see EWS.

11 For the interpolated psalter commentaries see Anne Hudson, (ed.), *Two Revisions of Rolle's English Psalter Commentary and the Related Canticles*, 3 vols., EETS o.s. 340, 341, and 343 (2012–14). On the *Glossed Gospels* see Henry Hargreaves, "Popularising Biblical Scholarship: The Role of the Wycliffite Glossed Gospels," in The Bible and Medieval Culture, (eds.) W. Lourdaux and D. Verhelst (Leuven, 1979), 171–89 and *PR*, 248–58. On the *Rosarium* and *Floretum* see Anne Hudson, "A Lollard Compilation and the Dissemination of Wycliffite Thought," *Journal of Theological Studies* n.s. 23 (1972): 65–81 (repr. in *Books*, 13–29); and "A Lollard Compilation in England and Bohemia," *Journal of Theological Studies* n.s. 25 (1974): 129–40 (repr. in *Books*, 30–42). See also Christina von Nolcken, "Notes

In working to reconstruct where these five large-scale works were compiled and copied, Hudson has drawn out the broad similarities between these projects.[12] She points, for example, to their biblical focus; links with Wycliffism; close reliance on but also augmentation and correction of sources; complex revision history involving addition and reorganization as well as redaction; and reliance on trained scholarship, collaboration, and access to an extensive library. Especially given the movement's beginnings there, Oxford is the most likely location where these labours and resources might have been gathered. Equally, the waning or withdrawal of certain forms of support in Oxford may help explain how and why the scope and focus of lollard book production shifted, as well as its location. With this in mind, in what follows I survey these five works in what may be their chronological order of inception, beginning with those most closely dependent in their early stages on extensive library resources and close collaboration.

4.1.1 *The Floretum and Rosarium*

Drawing its alphabetical organization by keyword from its principal source, the early fourteenth century *Manipulus Florum*, the *Floretum* is a sort of encyclopedia of doctrinal, ecclesiological, and other religious topics, each accompanied by extensive quotations or citations of biblical passages, canon law, and patristic and more recent authors (Wyclif is heavily quoted). There are four English manuscripts extant, and eight Bohemian ones.[13] Its later redaction the *Rosarium* is more tightly organized: its entries typically proceed by distinguishing a term's use "in bono" (often a figurative or earlier, broader sense) from "in malo" (often in more recent innovations), and it cuts or shortens many of the *Floretum*'s more expansive quotations while adding still more. Sixteen English copies are extant, and eleven Bohemian ones. Eight more manuscripts (five Bohemian, three English) reveal more revisions and adaptations, one of them a translation of the *Rosarium* into Middle English.[14] The compilation of the *Floretum*, no less the *Rosarium*, must have relied upon coordinated research

---

on Lollard Citation of John Wyclif's Writings," *Journal of Theological Studies* n.s. 39.2 (October, 1998): 411–37.

12 Hudson, "Five Texts."
13 On the manuscripts see Hudson, "A Lollard Compilation" and "Lollard Compilation in England and Bohemia."
14 On the Middle English *Rosarium* see Christina von Nolcken, (ed.), *The Middle English Translation of the "Rosarium theologie": A Selection* (Heidelberg, 1979).

efforts and access to a very substantial library.[15] The collaborators' efforts were rewarded, for it was much consulted by later writers and compilers.

4.1.2 *The Wycliffite Bible*

The efforts of a team of translators working between the 1370s and 1390s produced a translation of the full Vulgate bible, together with prologues to individual books by Jerome and from other sources, and two original prologues.[16] These original prologues to Prophets and to the bible as a whole are found in a limited range of manuscripts, and comment (perhaps at some remove) on the process of establishing and translating the text. Extant copies reveal at least two stages of revision known as the Earlier and Later versions, and perhaps further intermediary stages in between. Despite efforts to restrict the proliferation of biblical translations produced "recently since the time of the said John Wyclif" in Archbishop Thomas Arundel's provincial *Constitutions* of 1407/1409, this bible was seemingly late medieval England's most popular book, with over 250 full or partial copies extant as well as any number of extracts and quotations copied into other manuscripts.[17] However, it is difficult to be certain whether the translators envisaged only the production of expensive, bulky copies of the whole text, as is sometimes assumed, or whether they hoped for the broader range of uses that did develop.[18] It is also hard to be sure whether and to what extent this biblical translation's uses and users are lollard, for many extant copies were owned by readers with no known connections with lollardy. While ownership or quotation of the *Wycliffite Bible* is insufficient to prove any further affiliation with lollardy, however, there is no question that many of this bible's early uses, its manuscript glosses, and its prologues, are inflected by lollard concerns.

4.1.3 *The Glossed Gospels*

The simple title of these related works conceals complex textual reworkings. Extant are shorter and longer versions of glosses compiled verse by verse on

---

15 Hudson, "Five Texts."
16 On the dating and process of composition see Dove, *First English Bible*, 79–82; for an edition of the prologues see Dove, (ed.), *Earliest Advocates*, 3–85, 86–88. For a different view see H. Ansgar Kelly, *The Middle English Bible: A Reassessment* (University of Pennsylvania Press, forthcoming). I thank Kelly for discussing his research with me and allowing me to read some of it in draft.
17 The *Constitutions* are printed in Wilkins, 3:314–19. For this phrase, a translation of "jam noviter tempore dicti Johannis Wycliff" from article 7, see 3:317.
18 For an index of manuscripts briefly describing the contents of all known copies, see Dove, *First English Bible*, 281–306.

the gospel of Matthew (two complete copies of short version survive, two of an intermediate version, and one of a yet longer version), Mark (one copy of a short version), Luke (two copies of a short version and one of a much longer version) and John (two copies of a short version). One further manuscript, in York, compiles only the sections from all four gospels used as Sunday lections, but adds even more commentary, and indexes at the end seventeen topical excurses embedded amidst the commentary. The topical discussions are not unique to York: some also appear within the serial treatment of gospel verses in the other manuscripts, where yet more excurses may be found.[19] For all but the longest commentary on Matthew, the *Catena Aurea* is the source.[20] Yet in many places it seems the compilers have returned to the original passages and augmented the quotations. Like the *Floretum* and *Rosarium*, the *Glossed Gospels* were much used by subsequent writers, as were their prologues.[21]

4.1.4 The English Wycliffite Sermons

These 294 model sermons cover all preaching needs across the liturgical year of the Sarum use (the version of the liturgy used in southern England until the sixteenth century). The five sets provide 54 sermons on the Sunday gospels; 31 sermons on the gospel readings assigned for feast days for types of saints such as apostles, evangelists, or martyrs; 37 sermons on the gospels for feast days for specific saints; 120 sermons on the gospels for ordinary weekdays; and 55 sermons on the Sunday epistle readings. (Liturgical scholars would term these sets respectively the Dominical gospels, Common of Saints, Proper of Saints, Ferial gospels, and Dominical epistles.) The sermons follow the "ancient" rather than "modern" sermon style, providing a detailed exposition of the liturgical reading that while it may digress, returns to explaining the same biblical passage rather than pursuing the "modern" method of linking biblical and other quotations in pursuit of a theme.[22] Many draw on Wyclif's own sermons on the same topics.[23] Their composition seems to have involved collaborative division of labor, between for example exegesis and commentary of various kinds, and not all sermons are finished to the same extent. The Sunday gospel and epistle sermons are most fully developed; some of the sermons for

---

19 For details see Hargreaves, "Popularising Biblical Scholarship," 185–88. For more on the *Glossed Gospel* versions and their sources see Hudson, *Premature Reformation*, 249–54.

20 On the sources of the longest Matthew commentary, see Hargreaves, "Popularising Biblical Scholarship," 182.

21 The prologues are edited in Dove, *Earliest Advocates*, 172–86, who gives details of their later use in *Wycliffite Bible* and *Oon of Foure* manuscripts, lx-lxvi.

22 For more on the liturgical occasions and expository modes of medieval English sermons, see H. Leith Spencer, *English Preaching in the Late Middle Ages* (Oxford, 1993).

23 On the relationship with Wyclif's sermons see the notes on each sermon in vol. 5 of *EWS*.

individual saints, and some of the Ferial gospel sermons, are brief or even perfunctory.[24] The polemical tracts *Of Mynystris* and *Vae Octuplex* frequently travel with the sermons in manuscripts, and may from the beginning have been intended as companion pieces. More than any other work in Phase 1, the early manuscripts of this sermon cycle provide evidence of standardized production and oversight, of a kind that suggests the authors aimed to provide comprehensive sets of sermons in a standard format.[25] However, their sermons were repurposed in a variety of ways in the fifteenth century.

4.1.5 Rolle's English Psalter, Revised Version (RV) 1, RV2, and RV3

These lollard revisions are derived from Rolle's translation and commentary upon the Psalter, which they variously interpolate, paraphrase, or depart from entirely.[26] They augment as well Rolle's commentary on seven canticles, adding commentary on five more canticles. Each of the three versions, RV1, RV2, and RV3, is successively revised from the previous ones rather than by returning to Rolle's text. The manuscripts of RV1 and RV2 exhibit ongoing revision over time; RV2's revisions mostly tone down the content of RV1. The unevenness of revision in each version and manuscript copy suggests a collaborative enterprise involving stints of work as well as division of tasks: one person might render Rolle's commentary while another adds further comment, for example, but each might hand his task on to another as the work proceeds. RV3 is extant in only two copies, each in its manuscript setting copied as a continuation of RV1, and covers only Psalms 84:6–118:1: this version, as yet unprinted, diverges from Rolle and RV1 to expatiate at length.[27]

4.2 Independent Projects

As well as the large-scale collaborations of early lollardy, we find in the corpus a good scattering of more independent projects probably pursued by individuals working alone, and typically extant in a handful of copies at most—sometimes only one. Many are scholarly enough that their author must have had access to

---

24 On the production of the sermons see *EWS*, 1:189–202.

25 Anne Hudson, "Middle English," in *Editing Medieval Texts: English, French, and Latin Written in England; Papers Given at the Twelfth Annual Conference on Editorial Problems, University of Toronto*, (ed.) A.G. Rigg (Toronto, 1977), 34–57.

26 The following simplified overview of their variance is derived from Anne Hudson, "Introduction," in *Two Revisions*, 1:xxi–xxx, cx–cxxxvi.

27 A modernisation of RV3's commentary on Psalm 86 appears in *Wycliffite Spirituality*, 229–41.

a good library at some stage. Some derive from the large-scale collaborative projects of Phase 1, while others imitate, heavily cite, or translate Wyclif's writings. Their production was probably more geographically scattered, in locations where their authors could find time for writing and the resources for book production through local patronage networks: some present themselves as written in prison, others as the products of itinerant pastoral ministry.[28] In contrast with the diffusion of Phase 3, where some of these texts reappear, books containing Phase 2 texts are are more unified in purpose: sometimes their only or principal content is the text in question, while sometimes they present a coherent anthology where most items display lollard concerns.

4.2.1 Spinoffs from Phase 1

Some spinoff projects from the five large-scale works just described may be readers' responses; others may be independent efforts by the participants. The line between coordinated effort in Phase 1 and independent development in Phase 2 may indeed be difficult to draw neatly: the Middle English translation of the *Rosarium*, the liturgical adapatation of the *Glossed Gospels* now in a York manuscript, and the third revision of Rolle's *English Psalter*, RV3, might more appropriately be discussed in this section, for example.

Yet clearly there are uses of the *Rosarium* that are far more independent of the work itself. Single entries, or multiple selected entries, are extracted and modified into freestanding works in some manuscripts.[29] The *Unremarked Sermons* draw on both the *Floretum* and *Rosarium*, while the *Lollard Sermons* draw extensively on the *Rosarium*, sometimes using multiple entries to complete a single sermon.[30] There may be any number of other cases where consultation of the *Rosarium* or *Floretum* may underlie a work's citation of Wyclif or of other authors popular with lollard writers.[31]

---

28   On local patronage networks see Maureen Jurkowski, "Lollard Networks," in *Wycliffite Controversies*, 261–78. See also Robert Lutton, "Geographies and Materialities of Piety: Reconciling Competing Narratives of Religious Change in Pre-Reformation and Reformation England," in *Pieties in Transition: Religious Practices and Experiences, c.1400–1640*, (eds.) Robert Lutton and Elisabeth Salter (Aldershot, 2007), 11–39. Texts written in prison include the *Opus Arduum* (see pp. 90–91) and *Letter of Richard Wyche* (see pp. 88–89) texts concerned with pastoral ministry include the *Letter of Richard Wyche* and *Omnis Plantacio* (see p. 92).

29   For examples see Christina von Nolcken, "Some Alphabetical Compendia and How Preachers Used Them in Fourteenth-Century England," *Viator* 12 (1981): 271–88, 276.

30   Von Nolcken, "Alphabetical Compendia," 276–77. On both these collections of sermons, see below, pp. 90–92.

31   For some possible cases see von Nolcken, "Notes on Lollard Citation."

As for the *Wycliffite Bible*, Cardinal Gasquet's 1890s contention that this translation of the full bible into English is not Wycliffite has recently been renewed.[32] Indeed, the collaborative effort involved is likely to have got under way before Wycliffism was hereticated and to have included persons with a range of views, just as may have been the case for the *Floretum* as well. But rather than imposing a separation that may belong more to our own purposes than those of the bible's readers, it would seem more useful to describe and appreciate the full range of the translation's uses. The extant copies reflect the wide range of ways that people wanted to make use of translated scriptures in medieval England, and found the resources to do so. There are five complete copies of the Earlier Version, fifteen of the Later Version; surviving extant parts of larger wholes would add five more Earlier Version copies, and twelve more of the Later Version.[33] Large, illuminated volumes of this kind would be owned by kings and nobles, and we know the owners of some of them.[34] These massive books were not necessarily what everyone could afford or even what they wanted: many copies instead present a small selection of biblical books, in a format and size far more easily carried and passed from hand to hand and read aloud.[35] The most popular (or at any rate most frequently preserved) selections were the most commonly read biblical materials, heavily used in the liturgy. Thus the Psalms appear in 48 manuscripts, some part of the New Testament in 176 (of which 109 contain no selections from the Old Testament).[36] Many books containing parts of the *Wycliffite Bible* also contain parabiblia and glosses and summaries or loose translations of other parts of the bible. Excerpts from this biblical version are not typically quoted within polemical works, whose authors typically produce their own purpose-built translations on the fly. But they are used, for example, in the *Glossed Gospels*, in a cluster of Books of Hours in Middle English, in a concordance to the bible extant in a single copy, in manuscripts of the gospel harmony *Oon of Foure*, and in the very long summary of the bible found uniquely in Oxford, Trinity College MS 93.[37]

---

32   Kelly, *Middle English Bible*.
33   Dove, *First English Bible*, 17–18.
34   Dove, *First English Bible*, 44.
35   For some examples see Kathleen E. Kennedy, *The Courtly and Commercial Art of the Wycliffite Bible* (Turnhout, 2014), 35–51.
36   Dove *First English Bible*, 18.
37   See K.E. Kennedy, "Reintroducing the English Books of Hours, or 'English Primers,'" *Speculum* 89 (2014): 693–723; S.M. Kuhn, "The Preface to a Fifteenth-Century Concordance," *Speculum* 43 (1968): 258–73; Mary Raschko, "Oon of Foure: Harmonizing Wycliffite and Pseudo-Bonaventuran Approaches to the Life of Christ," in *The Pseudo-Bonaventuran Lives of Christ: Exploring the Middle English Tradition*, (eds.) Ian Johnson and Allan F. Westphall (Turnhout: Brepols, 2013), 341–73; "A Middle English Summary of the Bible: An Edition of

The *Glossed Gospels*, too, were variously redacted and excerpted, and perhaps used in lay biblical reading as well.[38] Quotations from them appear in the margins of two Wycliffite Bible manuscripts, alongside the gospels they annotate; they are quoted as "þe glos" in the polemical *Of Mynistris* that often travelled with the *English Wycliffite Sermons* ; and Cambridge University Library MSS Ff.6.31 and Ii.6.55 include extracts from them.[39] The *Pore Caitif* draws on them extensively; and so may the *Lollard Sermons* (though there may be some intermediary source).[40]

Despite efforts to standardize the content and layout of early copies, it is evident that the *English Wycliffite Sermons* quickly spread to audiences that found their outspoken content objectionable. Yet they did not all object to the same things: Oxford, Bodleian Library MS Don. C.13 omits all criticism of friars but retains some discussions of the sacraments, for example, while Bodley 95 retains criticism of the friars but eliminates the sacraments.[41] Among later adaptations of the cycle into other works, Sidney Sussex 74 incorporates nearly the whole Sunday gospel set into sermons on the Sunday epistles that also provide a comprehensive program of pastoral instruction, while the miscellaneous sermon compilation in London, British Library MS Royal 18 B xxiii includes a limited selection, but becomes increasingly nervous about their content as it goes.[42]

The revisions of Rolle's English Psalter are especially fluid. In addition to composite copies of the revised versions of Rolle's English Psalter that combine parts of different revisions or even Rolle's original version, there are ten more manuscripts that contain all or part of the lollard-interpolated canticles,

---

Trinity College (Oxon) MS 93," (ed.) Robert Reilly (Ph.D. diss., University of Washington, 1966), and Somerset, *Feeling Like Saints*, Chap. 5, 166–202.

38   Henry Hargreaves, "The Wycliffite *Glossed Gospels* as Source: Further Evidence," *Traditio* 48 (1993): 247–51. For the suggestion that a heresy suspect with highly unusual views on prayer may be drawing on commentary on Matthew 6 popularized by the *Glossed Gospels* or another vernacular commentary, see Somerset, *Feeling Like Saints*, 130–33.

39   Henry Hargreaves, "Popularising Biblical Scholarship." See also entries for these manuscripts in Margaret Connolly, *The Index of Middle English Prose, Handlist XIX: Manuscripts in the University Library, Cambridge (Dd-Oo)* (Cambridge, 2009).

40   Hargreaves, "Wycliffite *Glossed Gospels*," Sr. M. Theresa Brady, "Lollard Sources of the Pore Caitif." *Traditio* 44 (1988): 389–418.

41   For these modifications, and descriptions of each manuscript containing a significant portion of the sermon cycle, see Hudson, *English Wycliffite Sermons*, 1:51–123. See also Anne Hudson, "The Expurgation of a Lollard Sermon Cycle," *Journal of Theological Studies* n.s. 22 (1971): 435–42 (repr. in Hudson, *Lollards and their Books*, 201–15).

42   See Helen L. Spencer, "The Fortunes of a Lollard Sermon Cycle in the Later Fifteenth Century," *Mediaeval Studies* 48 (1986): 352–96.

and five more than contain only the revised prologue: clearly these items in particular were of broad interest.

4.2.2   Works that Translate or Cite Wyclif

Many translations and citations of Wyclif appear in the *English Wycliffite Sermons* and *Floretum* and *Rosarium*, and achieved broad currency through the dissemination of those works. But there are more. Another widely disseminated work is the Ten Commandments (or decalogue) commentary commonly referred to as the "Standard Orthodox Commentary," which draws extensively on a decalogue commentary by Wyclif incorporated within his Sermons, volume 1.[43] There are twenty other known copies of this version, with some variation and adaptation visible among them; what is more, these twenty copies lie at the center of a much larger cluster of related decalogue commentaries that adapt this version's prologue in varying directions and are incorporated in a wide range of contexts. Clearly, more about Wyclif's reflections on the decalogue than his most sharply polemical conclusions was of interest to his pastoral-minded followers.

Works of more limited circulation that adapted Wyclif's writings for new audiences include the *Dialogue between Reson and Gabbyng* and *Five Questions on Love*. Each incorporates new content into a free but substantially faithful rendition of one of Wyclif's works. *Reson and Gabbyng* follows Wyclif's *Dialogus* fairly closely across the course of its first twelve chapters, while the *Five Questions* translates Wyclif's letter *De Amore*.[44] Similarly, the *Tractatus de regibus* in Douce 273 relies extensively on Wyclif's *De officio regis*.[45]

---

43   This commentary, also known as the 'standard version,' is printed as Appendix I in W. Nelson Francis, (ed.), *The Book of Vices and Virtues*, EETS, o.s. 217 (London, 1942), 316–33. Wyclif's commentary begins at *Sermones*, (ed.) Johannes Loserth, 4 vols.,Wyclif Society (London, 1887–90), 1:89/22–24, then occupies part of this sermon and the nine that follow. For this discovery, and a thorough study of this commentary and its related versions, see Judith Jefferson, (ed.), "An Edition of the Ten Commandments Commentary in BL Harley 2398, and the Related Version in Trinity College Dublin 245, York Minster XVI.L.12 and Harvard English 738 Together with Discussion of Related Commentaries," 2 vols. (Ph.D. diss., University of Bristol, 1995); on the relationship to Wyclif, see 1: cxli.

44   The notes to *Reson and Gabbyng* in Fiona Somerset, (ed.), *Four Wycliffite Dialogues*, detail its relationship with Wyclif's *Dialogus*; on the *Five Questions* and *De Amore* see Fiona Somerset, "Wycliffite Spirituality," in *Text and Controversy from Wyclif to Bale: Essays in Honour of Anne Hudson*, (eds.) Helen Barr and Ann M. Hutchison (Turnhout, 2005), 375–86.

45   J.P. Genet, (ed.), *Four English Political Tracts of the Later Middle Ages* Camden Society, fourth series, vol. 18. (London: Royal Historical Society, 1977), 1–21.

4.2.3 *Writings by Named Authors Associated with Wycliffism*

Two such writings are sermons from specific occasions: Nicholas Hereford's Ascension Day (15 May 1382) sermon on the disendowment of the clergy, given in Oxford but preserved only in a hostile *reportatio* or set of detailed notes in Latin in a single manuscript; and William Taylor's 21 November 1406 sermon calling for the reform of the church given at St Paul's Cross in London, preserved in one English and one Latin copy.[46] Judging from Richard Maidstone's two Latin responses to John Ashwardby's public preaching at St Mary's Church in Oxford at some point in the early 1380s, Ashwardby too seems to have been preoccupied by ecclesiastical reform: his special focus seems to have been the problems caused by religious mendicancy, but Ashwardby's sermons themselves do not survive.[47]

Four authored works present themselves as the product of heresy trials. Walter Brut's lengthy Latin defense of his views, as well as the preacher William Swinderby's shorter English defenses and appeals, are preserved in the record of their trials in the register of bishop Trefnant.[48] The *Testimony of William Thorpe* is one of the clearest and most comprehensive expositions of lollard belief, purportedly as affirmed by Thorpe under examination by Archbishop Thomas Arundel and two of his clerks in 1407 (although the account is clearly somewhat fictionalized).[49] Its extant medieval copies include one Middle English manuscript and two Latin copies preserved in Bohemian manuscripts, each within larger compilations of Wycliffite and Hussite texts. Preserved only in a Latin copy of what seems to have been a Middle English original in the same Bohemian manuscript as Taylor's sermon is the *Letter of Richard Wyche*. Like Thorpe's *Testimony* (which may have imitated it), the letter presents a

---

46   For Taylor's sermon see Anne Hudson, (ed.), *Two Wycliffite Texts: The Sermon of William Taylor 1406, The Testimony of William Thorpe 1407* EETS, o.s. 301 (Oxford, 1993), 3–23; see also "William Taylor's 1406 Sermon: A Postscript," *Medium Aevum* 64:1 (1995): 100–06. For Hereford's sermon see Simon Forde, "Nicholas Hereford's Ascension Day Sermon, 1382" *Mediaeval Studies* 51 (1989): 205–41.

47   For Maidstone's responses see Chapter 6 in this volume, pp. 148, 154.

48   *Registrum Johannis Trefnant Episcopi Herefordensis*, (ed.) W.W. Capes, Canterbury and York Society 20 (1916). On problems with this edition see Anne Hudson, "The Problems of Scribes: The Trial Records of William Swinderby and Walter Brut." *Nottingham Mediaeval Studies* 49 (2005): 80–104. For more on Walter Brut see Maureen Jurkowski, "Who Was Walter Brut?" *English Historical Review* 127 (2012): 285–302. On the intellectual influences behind Brut's defense see Ruth Nisse, "Prophetic Nations," *New Medieval Literatures* 4 (2001): 95–115.

49   For more on Thorpe's text, see Chapter 7 in this volume, 167–69.

narrative, first-person account of Wyche's examinations for heresy; one that in this case also reveals to his followers his failings and physical weakness.[50]

John Clanvowe's devotional treatise *The Two Ways* is less argumentative than these works, unsurprisingly given its different genre. But like Thorpe's *Testimony* and Wyche's *Letter*, its aims include religious instruction and exhortation toward an alternative mode of living in the world, on the narrow way of extraordinary effort toward virtue rather than the broad way followed by most ordinary men.[51]

4.2.4 *Anonymous Declarative or Confessional Writings*

There are other declarative or confessional texts whose authors we do not know, but whose textual anonymity must have been a transparent fiction for some readers, at least, at the time when they were writing. Most claim to voice the views of a group, "we pore men" or "trewe Christen men." The *Apology for Lollard Doctrines* is unusual in making its assertions in the first person, while in the *Thirty-Seven Conclusions* the claims themselves take center stage: "this sentence is preuid;" "this sentence is open."

The *Twelve Conclusions* is more a manifesto than a full exposition of belief, as befits its celebrated status as a bill nailed to the doors of Westminster Hall and of St Paul's Cathedral. It is extant in both English and Latin, but only within hostile responses.[52] Its language is academic in tone, but brisk in exposition: each conclusion is shortly stated, elaborated, proved, and provided with corollaries. Similar in its mode of argumentation are the *Thirty-Seven Conclusions*, extant in a brief Latin version in a single copy and in a longer elaboration in English with added corollaries.[53] Steeped in canon law, this work was plainly

---

50   See F.D. Matthew, (ed.), "The Trial of Richard Wyche," *English Historical Review* 5 (1890): 530–44, and the translation with commentary in Christopher G. Bradley, (ed. and trans.), "The Letter of Richard Wyche: An Interrogation Narrative," *PMLA* 127 (2012): 626–42. See also Anne Hudson, "Which Wyche? The Framing of the Lollard Heretic and/or Saint." In *Texts and the Repression of Medieval Heresy*, (eds.) Caterina Bruschi and Peter Biller (Woodbridge, 2002), 221–37.

51   See John Clanvowe, *The Two Ways*, in *The Works of John Clanvowe*, (ed.) V.J. Scattergood (Cambridge, 1967), 57–80. A modernization appears in *Wycliffite Spirituality*, 164–82. One full copy is extant, and a fragment of another, both in devotional compilations.

52   "The Twelve Conclusions" in *Selections*, 24–29. See Chapter 6 in this volume for responses within the *Fasciculi Zizianorum* and Roger Dymmok's *Liber contra duodecim errores et hereses lollardorum*.

53   For the Latin version see H.F.B. Compston, (ed.), "The Thirty-Seven Conclusions of the Lollards," *English Historical Review* 26 (1911): 738–49. For the English, see [*The Thirty-Seven Conclusions*] *Remonstrance against Romish Corruptions in the Church*, (ed.) J. Forshall

intended for an educated audience, but seemingly a wider audience than that of the schools. The *Apology for Lollard Doctrines*, extant only in TCD 245, is likewise a litigious, contentious text focused on ecclesiastical controversy.[54] Yet it disapproves of canon law, despite its familiarity with it, and cites original sources rather than the familiar citations from Gratian's *Decretum* from which they are typically quoted.

Two further works in this genre focus on rebuttal rather than on self-generated assertions. The *Sixteen Points* distinguishes the positions that it says bishops impute to "men whiche þei clepen [they call] lollardis" from what true Christian men should meekly and thoughtfully answer, denying each point in turn on the grounds that it mixes truth with falsehood, but granting some parts of it in a carefully qualified sense. It is extant in a single copy in Trinity College Cambridge B.14.50. The *Twenty-Five Articles* derives its longer list of imputed lollard beliefs from a source something like the list provided in Henry Knighton's *Chronicle*: the full text is extant only in Douce 273, but two articles are also excerpted in Trinity College Dublin 245.[55] While the authors profess their willingness to be corrected, their replies are anything but conciliatory. While they refine many points put to them, and deny some, their main effort is dedicated toward elaborating their positions on ecclesiastical reform.

4.2.5 Lollard Learning

A surprising number of other lollard writings beyond the five works of Phase 1 are lengthy, learned, and rely upon (or attempt to foster) learning in their readers. Prominent in accounts of learned lollard writing, but little read by scholars, are the Latin prose works the *Opus Arduum* and a sermon collection we will title the *Unremarked Sermons*.[56] The *Opus Arduum* is a lengthy commentary on Revelations, broad in its range of citations, that purports to explain the literal sense of the serially quoted passages interspersed within it. However, the author's expansive understanding of the literal sense allows the biblical text to pertain directly to concerns of the present day, occasioning sprawling

---

(London, 1851). Extant are two fifteenth-century manuscripts, a sixteenth century copy, and a modernized transcription.

54 J.H. Todd, (ed.), *Apology for Lollard Doctrines* Camden Society (London, 1842).

55 On Knighton's *Chronicle* see Chapter 1. For the *Twenty-Five Articles* see Arnold, 454–96.

56 For a very thorough account of the *Opus Arduum* and its manuscripts (on which this draws) see "A Neglected Wycliffite Text," *Journal of Ecclesiastical History* 29 (1978): 257–79 (repr. in Hudson, *Lollards and their Books*, 43–65). On the *Unremarked Sermons* see Christina von Nolcken, "Unremarked Group."

and digressive polemical commentary.[57] The work is extant in thirteen copies made in Bohemia, none in England. The author does not identify himself, but provides much circumstantial detail, claiming he has been imprisoned for his views at the time of writing and dating his text to 1389. The *Unremarked Sermons* are more homogeneous in their content: each provides line by line exegesis and moral interpretation in the "ancient" sermon style followed by a more "modern" exposition of a topic divided into two or three parts and explained though other prooftexts. They comprise 42 sermons on the Sunday gospels and for other occasions in the liturgical year between Advent and Trinity, then thirteen sermons for saints' feasts from Andrew to John the Baptist: what remains may be only part of a larger collection.[58]

The vernacular *Lollard Sermons* have received more notice, partly in the form of dispute over their lollard affiliations.[59] Certainly the sermons are not polemical, but their references to the persecution of true Christian men, and emphasis upon spiritual rather than customary observance, as well as their citation of favorite lollard authorities (Grosseteste, Augustine, pseudo-Chrysostom, and indeed the lollard *Rosarium*) are suggestive. Many cross-references between the sermons provide evidence that they are part of a coherent set that may have been larger, and may have been completed in stages. Like the *English Wycliffite Sermons* they are clearly model sermons, rather than sermon scripts, in that in some places they give directions to a potential preacher. Sixteen of them treat gospel lections, most for Sundays, for two important sequences in the liturgical calendar: Advent to the feast of Circumcision on 1 January, and Lent together with the three Sundays before it. The seventeenth sermon is a funeral sermon, the *Sermon of Dead Men*. They are filled with engaging similitudes, and some passages in high style are heavily alliterative.[60] Of the three

---

57 For this extended understanding of the literal sense in later medieval exegesis, see Christopher Ocker, *Biblical Poetics before Humanism and Reformation* (Cambridge, 2002).

58 One manuscript contains all the sermons as its sole contents, another ends incomplete after the first thirty-six; the other four contain selections and combine them variously with the *Rosarium* and two of the lollards' principal sources, Peraldus's *Summa de Vitiis* and pseudo-Chrysostom's *Opus Imperfectum*. See Christina Von Nolcken, "Unremarked Group"; see also Siegfried Wenzel, *Latin Sermon Collections from Later Medieval England* (Cambridge, 2005), 91–94 and 528–33.

59 For an edition see Gloria Cigman, (ed.), *Lollard Sermons* EETS o.s. 294 (Oxford, 1989). For the dispute, see e.g. J. Patrick Hornbeck II, "Lollard Sermons? Soteriology and Late Medieval Dissent," *Notes and Queries* 53.1 (Mar. 2006): 26–30.

60 On the formal qualities of the *Lollard Sermons* and other lollard writings see Shannon Gayk, "Lollard Writings, Literary Criticism, and the Meaningfulness of Form," in *Wycliffite Controversies*, 135–52.

manuscripts, one contains the sermons alone (yet it is incomplete), and the other two combine the sermons (in one case only the *Sermon of Dead Men*) with the *Pore Caitif.*

Two lengthy vernacular anonymous works bristling with learned citations refer to current events that probably place them between 1407 and 1414: these are *Omnis Plantacio* (c.1407–1413) and the *Tractatus de oblacione iugis sacrificii* (c.1413-?1414).[61] The second claims authorship of the first. *Omnis Plantacio* is a very long sermon providing an extensive exposition of arguments against ecclesiastical endowments; the shorter, related tract printed as "The Clergy May Not Own Property" is most probably an earlier work, likely by the same author, from which the longer sermon derives. All extant medieval copies of each work (three of the sermon, one of the tract) are the sole contents of small, easily portable books.[62] The sermon addresses its audience in closing, proposing to leave a written copy with them for further discussion and asking that any arguments opposed to his own should be passed on to him.[63] This audience must have been remarkably attentive, however, all the more so if the same readers also encountered the *Tractatus de oblacione*. The *Tractatus* is lollardy's most extended treatment of arguments for proper belief about the eucharist, replete with authoritative citations and and closely conversant with the idioms and topics of current academic argumentation.[64]

The *Lollard Chronicle of the Papacy* relies on a rather different base of authoritative knowledge than other works listed here. It facilitates argumentation and religious instruction about ecclesiastical history rather than theology, providing a highly selective account of the wrongdoings of past popes and the good deeds of secular rulers. The two extant copies are each separate revisions of a prior source. The much longer version is of special interest: it is derived largely from Ranulph Higden's *Polychronicon* and chronicles emperors and kings and major events as well as popes, including many references to England.[65]

---

61 For a thorough account of the dating, manuscripts, and versions, see Anne Hudson, (ed.), *The Works of a Lollard Preacher* EETS o.s. 317 (Oxford, 2001). Derivative later printed works are discussed in Chapter 8 of this volume.

62 Hudson, *Works*, xvii–xxvii; there is also a sixteenth century transcription.

63 For the passage see Hudson, *Works,* 138/2938–139/2962. This passage has been much discussed: see also *PR*, 184–85; Rita Copeland, *Pedagogy, Intellectuals, and Dissent in the Later Middle Ages: Lollardy and Ideas of Learning* (Cambridge, 2001), 127–29.

64 On academic learning in the *Tractatus* see Kantik Ghosh, "Wycliffite 'Affiliations': Some Intellectual-Historical Perspectives," in *Wycliffite Controversies*, 13–32.

65 Dan Embree, (ed.), *The Chronicles of Rome: The Chronicle of Popes and Emperors and The Lollard Chronicle* (Woodbridge, 1999), see especially 15–26 on the two extant versions of *The Lollard Chronicle*.

The *Tretise of Miraclis Pleyinge* has been rather more controversial. Lawrence Clopper is certainly correct that the staging of biblical plays is not the work's only or main concern.[66] Yet while lollard writers oppose dramatic representations elsewhere only rarely, the work's mode of biblical exposition is characteristically lollard.[67] The single copy is in London, British Library MS Additional 24202, whose other contents are multiply affiliated with lollardy but similarly quirky (nowhere else does a lollard manuscript contain a work opposed to dice playing, for example).[68] The work's two parts may be successive recensions by two authors: the first is argumentative, asserting that no man should use in play the miracles and works that Christ did in earnest for our salvation and refuting opposing arguments, while the second offers religious instruction and advice in something like the manner of a religious manual, surveying examples of false and true play found in the bible and suggesting in conclusion that David's dancing before the ark in 2 Samuel 6 provides an exemplar of true play for contemporary Christians.

Religious manuals combining guidance on life in the world with biblical exegesis and basic pastoral instruction proliferated in the fifteenth century: John Clanvowe's *The Two Ways* is by no means the only lollard work in this genre, nor the *Tretise of Miraclis Pleyinge* the only tract inflected by it. The *Lanterne of Liȝt* is also a pastoral manual of sorts, but one whose identification as lollard has never caused any difficulty.[69] Its exposition of pastoral basics is folded within or interpolated by polemical exegesis throughout; and it was the center of the 1415 heresy trial of the London skinner John Claydon.[70] Thirteen chapters explain what antichrist is, distinguish the everyday "material church" in which good and bad are mixed from the true church of God and the devil's church, and give guidance on distinguishing the two. There are two extant manuscripts, one now incomplete, in which it is the sole item.

That the *Book to a Mother* too is a religious manual is not in doubt.[71] However, its relationship to lollardy has been. Ostensibly written by a son for his mother, it advises against taking vows and joining a religious order, showing lay readers how they may instead live a virtuous life in the world. On the basis of its dating

---

66 Lawrence Clopper, "Is the *Tretise of Miraclis Pleyinge* a Lollard Tract against Devotional Drama?" *Viator* 34 (2003): 229–71.
67 Ruth Nisse, "Reversing Discipline: The *Tretise of Miraclis Pleyinge*, Lollard Exegesis, and the Failure of Representation," *Yearbook of Langland Studies* 11 (1997): 163–94; Somerset, *Feeling Like Saints*, 147–50.
68 For a similar assessment see Hudson, *Books*, 186 n. 1.
69 *The Lanterne of Liȝt*, (ed.) L.M. Swinburn EETS o.s. 151 (London, 1917).
70 See *PR*, 211–14, and Chapter 5 in this volume, p. 116.
71 *Book to a Mother*, (ed.) A.J. McCarthy (Salzburg, 1981).

to the 1370s in its edition, the *Book to a Mother* has been presented as the limit case for "reformist" orthodoxy that demonstrates how far a work can share lollard concerns without itself being lollard.[72] However, the evidence for an early date is poor. The work shows Wyclif's influence, incorporates or is the source of another short lollard work, and presents arguments on organized religion and the sacraments that are characteristically lollard.[73] In its earliest extant copy, now incomplete, the work was copied alone in a hand-size volume for personal reading and circulation. Three further copies, among them the only one that is now complete, appear within larger collections of religious writings of interest to mainstream readers as well as lollards.[74]

4.2.6 *Writings in Verse*

Writings in verse that express characteristic lollard concerns are far less common than writings in prose. Yet most have been printed over and over since the early modern period, and are better known than most of the prose corpus. Typically, those that have received repeated attention have done so owing to their long-term association with a major literary author. Not only the *Plowman's Tale*, but *Jack Upland* in the *Upland Series*, were printed among Chaucer's collected works, in 1542 and 1602 respectively, as part of efforts to demonstrate Chaucer's protestant leanings.[75] *Piers the Plowman's Creed* and *Mum and the Sothsegger*, for their part, have each at one time or another been ascribed to the author of *Piers Plowman*.[76]

The *Plowman's Tale* is not extant in any medieval manuscript. The language and content of the bulk of the text, a verse dialogue between a griffin and a pelican, suggest that it is probably medieval; the opening frame, in which the

---

72 See e.g. Nicole Rice, *Lay Piety and Religious Discipline in Middle English Literature* (Cambridge, 2008), 106–11.

73 On the dating and contents see Somerset, *Feeling Like Saints*, 239–72.

74 On the manuscripts see Elisabeth Dutton, "Textual Disunities and Ambiguities of Mise-en-Page in the Manuscripts Containing *Book to a Mother*," *Journal of the Early Book Society* 6 (2003): 140–59.

75 On the *Upland Series* and *Plowman's Tale* see the Introduction provided for each work in James M. Dean. (ed.), *Six Ecclesiastical Satires*, TEAMS Middle English Texts (Kalamazoo, MI, 1991), available in the Robbins Digital Library, http://d.lib.rochester.edu/teams/publication/dean-six-ecclesiastical-satires

76 On *Piers the Plowman's Creed* see Dean, (ed.), *Six Ecclesiastical Satires*; on *Mum and the Sothsegger* see James M. Dean, (ed.), *Richard the Redeles and Mum and the Sothsegger*, TEAMS Middle English Texts (Kalamazoo, MI, 2000), available in the Robbins Digital Library, http://d.lib.rochester.edu/teams/publication/dean-richard-the-redeless-and-mum-and-the-sothsegger. See also Barr, (ed.), *Piers Plowman Tradition*.

Canterbury Tales Host asks the Plowman for a tale, was probably added later. Like lollard dialogues in prose (see below) the debate is decidedly one-sided: the Griffin speaks for the Pope, but has little defense to offer against the Pelican's complaints about ecclesiastical corruption and calls for reform. Instead he threatens the Pelican with burning, drawing, and quartering, then flies away. After a brief exchange with the Plowman observer in which he expresses his readiness for martyrdom, the Pelican finds that the Griffin has returned with many allies—but the Pelican returns with the Phoenix, who destroys them all.

The *Upland Series* consists of *Jack Upland*, sixty-five questions about fraternal abuses posed from the perspective of a naive rural observer in alliterative prose; *Friar Daw's Reply*, replies to the *Jack Upland* questions in alliterative verse; and *Upland's Rejoinder*, further ripostes against some of Friar Daw's replies, again in verse. There are two copies of the English version of *Jack Upland*, as well as several early and later printed copies and a Latin version embedded within a refutation by Wyclif's opponent William Woodford.[77] The single manuscript of *Friar Daw's Reply*, a university notebook in which these poems are the first item, had *Upland's Rejoinder* written into its margins before the volume was bound.

Piers the Plowman's Crede, like the *Upland Series*, is chiefly concerned with the abuses of the friars, yet plainly attuned to broader lollard concerns: indeed, the poem names Walter Brut (see above) as someone pursued by the friars as a heretic for speaking the truth (657–61).[78] The author is heavily indebted to the lengthy allegorical alliterative poem *Piers Plowman*, yet his own effort adopts its dialogical structure without its dream vision frame or its characteristic indirection. The Plowman who finally teaches the poor narrator his Creed is unequivocally a speaker of truth, in stark contrast with the friars from all four orders that the narrator had previously interviewed without success, receiving only their criticism of one another and appeals for funds for his pains.

Mum and the Sothsegger likewise draws heavily on *Piers Plowman*, and similarly involves an extended narratorial quest in pursuit of a speaker of truth—in this case through a range of secular as well as clerical occupations that ought to contribute their expertise to the common good by speaking truth, but fail to do so. At length the narrator falls asleep, and finds a garden whose keeper has

---

77 For full details and a redating of the text see Fiona Somerset, *Clerical Discourse and Lay Audience in Late Medieval England* (Cambridge: Cambridge University Press, 1998), 135–78, 216–20. See also Chapter 6 in this volume, 144–48. On Woodford see Chapter 6 below.

78 The poem is extant in two sixteenth century paper manuscripts and a fragment of a fifteenth-century copy.

much to tell him about horticulture, and especially about his bees (as is often the case, the beehive is a political allegory). Even though the poem is incomplete at beginning and end in its single extant manuscript, it seems clear that it more fully embraces *Piers Plowman*'s use of personification, riddling, and questionable or inconclusive assertion in order to engage readers in evaluating its less unambiguous truth claims.

Shorter lyrics and Latin satirical poetry are more difficult to classify firmly as lollard in their sympathies when they may instead simply share in a broader antifraternalism or give voice to academic debates and rivalries. Still, the "Layman's Complaint" and "Friar's Answer" (on facing pages in their single copy) and "Of Thes Frer Mynours," (extant in a single copy) are worth attention for their use of a questioning lay voice, and in the case of the first pair of poems, of unequal dialogue, as in each of the longer poems just discussed.[79] "Of Thes Frer Mynours" shares its "O and I" refrains with a number of Middle English and Latin satirical poems produced in imitation or response to one another in late fourteenth century Oxford.[80] These poems are similarly difficult to classify, especially since some of them are highly allusive. But "Heu quanta desolacio" is certainly Wycliffite and produced directly in the wake of the Blackfriars Council that condemned Wyclif and some of his academic followers in 1382, and other poems may be products of this controversy as well.[81]

4.2.7   *Prose Dialogues*

In contrast with the frequently printed and anthologized dialogic poems, lollard prose dialogues have received very little attention until recently. Even though the *Dialogue between Jon and Richard*, the *Dialogue between a Friar and a Secular*, and the *Dialogue between Reson and Gabbyng* appear in three of the lollard manuscripts most heavily used by nineteenth-century editors, they were all overlooked by Arnold and Matthew and other early anthologists.

79 For these poems see James M. Dean, (ed.) *Medieval English Political Writings*, TEAMS Middle English Texts (Kalamazoo, MI: Medieval Institute Publications, 1996), available in the Robbins Digital Library, http://d.lib.rochester.edu/teams/publication/dean-medieval-english-political-writings.

80 See A.G. Rigg, "Two Latin Poems against the Friars," *Mediaeval Studies* 30 (1968): 106–18; Penn R. Szittya, "'Sedens super flumina': A Fourteenth-Century Poem against the Friars," *Mediaeval Studies* 41 (1979): 30–43.

81 Wendy Scase explains the literary context for "Heu quanta desolacio," suggesting that "Sedens super flumina" and "Vox in Rama" may be motivated by the same sequence of events, in "'Heu! quanta desolatio Angliae praestantur': A Wycliffite Libel and the Naming of Heretics, Oxford 1382," in *Influence*, 19–36. See also A.G. Rigg, *Anglo-Latin Literature* (Cambridge, 1992), 269–76.

So, despite its facing-page modernization and commentary in the seventeenth century by William Crashawe, who presented it to James I, was the *Dialogue between a Clerk and a Knight*. These four have now been published as *Four Wycliffite Dialogues*.[82] Other dialogues with lollard affiliations include the *Dialogue between A Wise Man and a Fool*, the *Lucidarie*, and the *Life of Soul*.

The *Four Wycliffite Dialogues* present a range of dialogue types drawing on different traditions, from the literary products of quarrels between religious orders (*Jon and Richard*), to the written record of a staged oral disputation (*Friar and Secular*), to often topical arguments over papal authority produced by publicists across Europe (*Clerk and Knight*). *Reson and Gabbyng*, as already mentioned, is an abbreviated adaptation of Wyclif's *Dialogus*. Each presents an unbalanced debate where one side's arguments are obviously better and much lengthier than the other's. Two of them, *Reson and Gabbyng* and *Jon and Richard*, have a number of common traits that suggest the close association if not identity of their authors; several of these common traits are also found in *Book to a Mother*.

The remaining three dialogues *Wise Man and Fool*, *Lucidarie*, and *Life of Soul*, on the other hand, are all master-student dialogues providing moral and other instruction in something like the manner of a religious manual. *Wise Man and Fool* features the most resistant pupil, who brief as his objections are, manages to make a telling defense of the enjoyment of daily pleasures hallowed by tradition and criticized by few (beer, wrestling, storytelling) before his sudden conversion to acknowledging Christ and living by his law. The single copy appears in Cambridge University Library MS Ii.6.26.[83] The shorter of two extant copies of the *Lucidarie* follows in the same manuscript. A partial translation of Honorius Augustodunensis's *Elucidarium*, in its fuller form the *Lucidarie* covers Book I and the opening of Book II and adds twelve new questions and answers inflected with lollard concerns: the shorter copy is similar except that it is now missing several pages, some of which may have been cut out deliberately.[84] The *Life of Soul*'s three copies, in contrast, are each a different version of the text, one between two friends in Christ (a common lollard locution), one between a brother and sister who appear to be in religious life, and one between a father and son. The first, in Bodleian Library MS Laud Misc. 210, is most obviously lollard in its concerns: five shorter questions and answers

---

82   Somerset (ed.), *Four Wycliffite Dialogues*.
83   For an edition see Dove, *Earliest Advocates*, 130–42.
84   See Anna Lewis, "Rethinking the Lollardy of the *Lucidarie*: The Middle English Version of the Elucidarium and Religious Thought in Late Medieval England," *Florilegium* 27 (2010): 209–36.

lead to a lengthy exposition, punctuated by instruction in pastoral basics, of the question of what food and drink nourish the life of soul.[85]

4.2.8   Lollard Anthologies: Some Representative Lollard Manuscripts

Not every manuscript that contains a miscellaneous collection of texts will reward investigation for its unity of purpose.[86] Indeed, sometimes what lies between two covers is not a single book at all, but rather two or more booklets bound together, perhaps many years after their separate production and circulation, and for arbitrary rather than thematic reasons.[87] Still, it is worth investigating the contents of manuscripts as a whole, for they often reveal relationships and influences that we might not have noticed. We should attend, furthermore, to their life histories across time, even if we can know them only partially: in what stages they were compiled and modified, who owned and circulated them, and what book collectors and libraries allowed them to survive to the present. Among the manuscripts already mentioned, Douce 274 and 273 are a case in point: they are two parts of the same book, unbound into separate volumes at some unknown later date.[88] A third portion of the same book came to light in the 1980s: the manuscript that is now Oxford, Bodleian Library MS Eng. th. e.181 contains lollard commentaries on the Pater Noster, Ave Maria, and Creed that are elsewhere interpolated into the mainstream *Lay Folks' Catechism*; a freestanding redaction of the *Lay Folks' Catechism*; and a form of confession. Douce 274 was made by extracting two contentious texts on priests and friars that stood before the form of confession, carrying the end of the *Lay Folks' Catechism* with them; Douce 273 then follows and completes the book.

---

85   For discussion and a modernisation of the Laud version, see Paul F. Schaffner, (ed.) and trans., *Life of Soul*, in *Cultures of Piety: Medieval English Devotional Literature in Translation*, (eds.) Anne Clark Bartlett and Thomas Howard Bestul (Ithaca, N.Y., 1999), 118–40. For Schaffner's Middle English edition see the *Corpus of Middle English Prose and Verse*: see http://quod.lib.umich.edu/cgi/t/text/text-idx?c=cme;idno=lifesoul

86   For similar cautions see Derek Pearsall, "The Whole Book: Late Medieval English Manuscript Miscellanies and their Modern Interpreters," in *Imagining the Book*, (eds.) Stephen Kelly and John J. Thompson (Turnhout, 2005), 17–29; Ralph Hanna, "Miscellaneity and Vernacularity: Conditions of Literary Production in Late Medieval England," in *The Whole Book: Cultural Perspectives on the Medieval Miscellany*, (eds.) Stephen G. Nicholas and Siegfried Wenzel (Philadelphia, 1996), 37–51.

87   Ralph Hanna, "Booklets in Manuscripts: Further Considerations," rev. and repr. in *Pursuing History: Middle English Manuscripts and their Texts* (Stanford, 1996), 21–34.

88   For details see Ralph Hanna, *Index of Middle English Prose Handlist XII: Smaller Bodleian Collections* (Cambridge, 1997), 12–14, and Anne Hudson, "The Lay Folk's Catechism: A Postscript," *Viator* 18 (1988): 307–09.

The consistent production values, sumptuous decoration, and high quality parchment of this volume suggest that it was carefully planned and executed for a reader with considerable resources. Without learning its life history we would lose the opportunity to consider the contents of the book as a whole.

A small sampling of the manuscripts that a reader new to lollard books may want to consider might include Cambridge, Trinity College MS B.14.50, Cambridge University Library MSS Ii.6.26, and Cambridge University Library MS Nn.4.12. Each merits attention for how it brings seemingly disparate parts together, and together they augment our understanding of lollard book production.[89]

Cambridge, Trinity College MS B.14.50 consists of two independent booklets bound together, yet seemingly by someone who appreciated their similarity of content and purpose: together they probably belonged to a university-trained cleric charged with preaching responsibilities.[90] Booklet I seems to be notes compiled to aid in writing sermons: following two sets of English notes and Latin quotations pertinent for writing sermons on the Sunday gospels (fols. 1–7v) and on saints' days (fols. 8–13v), it contains a compilation of brief notes and attributed quotations in prose and verse, most Latin but some English, with a general focus on pastoral reform: one is a quotation from Wyclif. Booklet II begins with four vernacular lollard tracts: *First seiþ Bois*, a defense of biblical translation derived from a longer treatise by Richard Ullerston; the *Sixteen Points*; a treatise on images, and the *Dialogue between Jon and Richard*. A short Latin text on the eucharist attributed to Wyclif follows, and then a series of position statements against clerical possessions, begging by friars, etc., derived from the *Rosarium* but altered so that they refer explicitly to friars. Among them is interspersed a copy of pseudo-Hildegard's *Insurgent gentes*, interpolated throughout and with an added conclusion. The combination of pastoral and polemical concerns visible here in each booklet and in the manuscript as a whole, and the compilation and adaptation of previous texts alongside the composition of new ones, are both very much typical of Phase 2 lollard book production.

Cambridge University Library MS Ii.6.26 is a well-known lollard compilation: this sparsely decorated small book copied clearly but unfussily on poor quality parchment is typical of lollard book production for lay audiences.[91]

---

[89] For more examples see Anne Hudson, "Lollard Book Production," in *Book Production*, (eds.) Griffiths and Pearsall, 125–42.

[90] For a full description see Somerset, *Four Wycliffite Dialogues*, xvii–xxiii.

[91] See Dove, *Earliest Advocates*, for description of the manuscript and more details on other copies of the texts (xxxiv–xlix) and an edition of the twelve tracts on translation (89–142).

Twelve texts that advocate for biblical translation or lay biblical reading are followed by an incomplete copy of the Middle English translation of Honorius Augustodunensis's *Elucidarium*, the *Lucidarie* (see above). Some of the twelve texts on translation are derived from prior sources, lollard or otherwise: the eleventh reworks the second prologue to Robert of Gretham's c.1250 *Miroir*, the tenth repurposes the bulk of the epilogue to the *Glossed Gospel* on Matthew, the seventh adapts a lollard Pater Noster commentary (unless the commentary was adapting this text). The twelfth text, the *Dialogue between a Wise Man and a Fool*, provides a generic link to the *Lucidarie* that follows; the whole manuscript is copied in the same hand, but the size of the script increases markedly at the start of the *Lucidarie*.[92]

Cambridge University Library MS Nn.4.12 might not at first seem to merit attention as a designedly lollard book, for none of its contents are overtly polemical. Yet each of them is strongly associated with lollard texts elsewhere, and interpolated or reworked in ways that reflect lollard concerns: the versions found in this volume appear exclusively, or nearly so, with other lollard writings.[93] The volume begins with a shorter version of the decalogue commentary whose many versions were mentioned among works that translate or heavily cite Wyclif; it then incorporates more pastoral instruction by including the first two parts of *Pride, Wrath, and Envy*, presenting the sins, commandments, and gifts of the Holy Spirit interleaved with polemical digressions.[94] Next it includes lollard commentaries on the Pater Noster, Ave Maria, and Crede; the *Visitation of the Sick* version E; *The Seven Works of Mercy*, found elsewhere within the second chapter of *Book to a Mother* and in manuscripts with other lollard contents; catechetical lists that include the "six manners of consent" (the topic of a verse frequently quoted by Wyclif and in lollard writings); and finally an unpublished text commenting on the "Wordes of Poule" on tribulation.[95] Only

---

92 On the shift in layout see Lewis, "Lollardy of the *Lucidarie*," 222–23.

93 See Connolly, *Manuscripts in the University Library, Cambridge*, 348–51; and a correction in Margaret Connolly, "Preaching by Numbers: The 'Seven Gifts of the Holy Ghost' in Late Middle English Sermons and Works of Religious Instruction," in *Preaching the Word in Manuscript and Print in Late Medieval England: Essays in Honour of Susan Powell*, (eds.) Martha W. Driver and Veronica O'Mara (Turnhout, 2013), 83–100.

94 On this decalogue commentary see Jefferson, "An Edition," clxxxi–xlxxxiv; Somerset, *Feeling Like Saints*, 68–73. On *Pride, Wrath, and Envy* see the forthcoming edition by Arthur Russell and Richard Newhauser.

95 The prayer commentaries are printed by Arnold, 98–110, 111–13, 114–16. On *Visitation E* see Amy Appleford, *Learning to Die in London* (Philadelphia, 2015), 18–54. On the *Seven Works of Mercy* see Fiona Somerset, "Textual Transmission, Variance, and Religious Identity," in *Religious Controversy in Europe, 1378–1536: Textual Transmission and Networks of*

Visitation E and the "Wordes of Poule" appear elsewhere in contexts with no apparent lollard affiliation. Yet clearly in the versions found here they are closely compatible with typical lollard preoccupations—indeed *Visitation* E is excerpted in the longest lollard decalogue, as well as appearing in other manuscripts containing lollard writings.[96]

4.3 Recension and Diffusion

Of necessity this discussion of complex variation will be representative rather than comprehensive: an attempt to describe every extant manuscript with any lollard affiliation would fill volumes. We might characterize complex variation as centered around three centripetal poles: individual texts, compilation-texts, and manuscript compilations.

4.3.1 *Individual Texts*

The ways in which individual texts morph provide us with insight into textual creativity, as well as tolerance and intolerance of differing ideas. Tracing interpolations or alterations within an individual text is a straightforward if bulky exercise, but the texts themselves are not always easy to find. Alteration of their opening or closing words may make it difficult to find them in a manuscript catalogue that records incipits and explicits; they may be embedded within longer texts; and thus even their form and genre may shift. A relatively straightforward example of a variable text is the *Schort Reule of Lif*: as Mary Raschko has demonstrated, some of its seven copies are thoughtfully altered to fit their surroundings, as when an apocalyptic conclusion is added for a manuscript preoccupied throughout its length with the end of time, while others demonstrate a certain obliviousness, as when more contentiously worded version is copied into a trilingual manuscript of prayers owned by a female religious house.[97] A more complex example is the *Seven Works of Mercy*, extant in three freestanding copies, but also within the second chapter of *Book to a Mother*, in a copy of *Pride, Wrath, and Envy*, and (heavily altered) in a form of confession.[98] Most complicated of all perhaps are the fortunes of the large

---

Readership, (eds.) Michael Van Dussen and Pavel Soukup (Turnhout, 2013), 71–104; on the six manners of consent see Somerset, *Feeling Like Saints*, 36–39.

[96] See Appleford, *Learning to Die*, 47; Somerset, *Feeling Like Saints*, 85–89.

[97] Mary Raschko, "Common Ground for Contrasting Ideologies: The Texts and Contexts of *A Schort Reule of Lif*," Viator 40 (2009): 387–410.

[98] Somerset, "Textual Transmission."

group of decalogue commentaries tracked by Judith Jefferson: twenty-seven versions, in sixty copies in all, depart from the opening claim that all should keep the commandments to provide widely differing expositions, drawn on in turn (or is it the other way around?) by other moralistic religious writings such as the *Pore Caitif*.[99]

4.3.2 Compilation-Texts

From another perspective, works like *Book to a Mother* or *Pore Caitif* may be viewed as compilation-texts, whose components might be omitted, or switched out for other material of the same kind, or altered as in the case of an individual text, as the preference or choices available to a given copyist might dictate. In fact no such omitting or switching took place in the textual tradition of *Book to a Mother*: the content of the four copies is remarkably stable, at least as stable as that of a canonical literary text copied with care and attention.[100] As in the early copying of the *English Wycliffite Sermons*, the fortunes of *Book to a Mother* suggest that in some circumstances, as for example when a text circulates only among a closed circle of like-minded readers, lollard book production was as carefully consistent as any could be. The *Pore Caitif* is another story however, so much so that the text's origins and contents across all of its copies are still poorly understood.[101] A somewhat simpler case is *Pride, Wrath, and Envy*, a composite text whose three parts circulated separately as well as together, and whose components—instruction on the seven deadly sins and their remedies, the five bodily and spiritual wits, the seven bodily and spiritual works of mercy, and the seven gifts of the holy spirit—were variously abbreviated, altered, switched for alternative expositions, or omitted.[102]

4.3.3 Manuscript Compilations

Manuscript compilations may gather contents of a desired sort according to a more or less fluid sense of what is needed to create a certain kind of book, creating combinations of mainstream and lollard materials whose ideological

---

99 Jefferson, "An Edition."
100 On consistent, accurate copying, see Daniel Wakelin, "Writing the Words," in *The Production of Books in England, 1350–1500*, (eds.) Alexandra Gillespie and Daniel Wakelin (Cambridge, 2011), 34–58.
101 Sr.M. Theresa Brady's work has yet to be superseded: see her edition, "The Pore Caitif, Edited from Harley 2336 with Introduction and Notes," (Ph.D. diss., Fordham University, 1954); "Lollard Sources of the *Pore Caitif*," and "Lollard Interpolations and Omissions in Manuscripts of The Pore Caitif," in *De Cella in Seculum: Religious and Secular Life and Devotion in Late Medieval England*, (ed.) Michael G. Sargent (Woodbridge, 1989), 183–203.
102 Russell and Newhauser, (eds.), *Pride, Wrath, and Envy*.

position may be difficult to discern—may indeed be less important to the compiler and his readers than the contents of the texts themselves. One fairly common impulse, for example, was to collect materials to cover the basics of pastoral instruction.[103] Another was to gather all available biblical materials, organized more or less in the order of the books of the Vulgate.[104] Another was to amass short texts of interest to the compiler (or subsequent readers) on blank folios left after copying the largest texts around which the volume was planned, and sometimes on added quires as well.[105]

One example of a compilation whose compilers' interest certainly included lollard writings, but also mainstream writings of a rigorist bent, will stand as a representative for the many manuscripts that might be discussed here. This is Cambridge University Library Ff.6.31, well known as one of a handful of examples of a "common-profit book," compiled using the resources of a bequest with the request of prayers for the departed's soul, to be passed on from reader to reader for the term of their lives and also loaned to other readers when not in use.[106] The manuscript as we now have it consists of two booklets, numbered separately; the first contains a short treatise on self will attributed (wrongly) to Walter Hilton, a fragment of a sermon, Richard Lavynham's treatise on the seven deadly sins, and a compilation of biblical quotations focused on following the commandments. The second contains the unique copy of the lollard *The Holi Prophet Dauid*; several long quotations from the *Glossed Gospels* roughly separated into separate tracts; three texts on discretion in meditation and prayer attributed to the *Cloud of Unknowing* author; the unique copy of an anonymous short text of spiritual advice about serving God rather than riches entitled *No Man May Serve Two Lords*; a pseudo-Hugh of St Victor treatise on temptations, *De pusillanimitate*, translated into English; and *Foure Errours Whiche Letten Þe Verrey Knowyng of Holy Writt*, a short unpublished text extant

---

103 On books of this kind and their range of audiences, see Margaret Connolly, "Books for the 'helpe of euery persoone þat þenkiþ to be saued': Six Devotional Anthologies from Fifteenth-Century London," *Yearbook of English Studies* 33 (2003): 170–81.

104 On this impulse see Ralph Hanna, "English Biblical Texts before Lollardy and Their Fate," in *Influence*, 141–53.

105 Hanna explains these tendencies in "Miscellaneity and Vernacularity" and "Booklets in Manuscripts."

106 Dove, *Earliest Advocates*, edits *The Holi Prophete Dauid*, 150–59. PR, 256 n. 153, details the sources of the *Glossed Gospel* quotations. For description of the contents see Connolly, *Manuscripts in the University Library, Cambridge*, 153–58. See also Wendy Scase, "Reginald Pecock, John Carpenter and John Colop's 'Common-Profit' Books: Aspects of Book Ownership and Circulation in Fifteenth-Century London," *Medium Aevum* 61.2 (1992): 261–74.

in ten manuscripts, some lollard affiliated. The *Cloud* author might seem an unlikely choice for inclusion alongside lollard contents, but he shows up as well among the items compiled in the lollard-interpolated *Pore Caitif* manuscript Oxford, Bodleian library MS 938, which contains a version of some chapters from the *Cloud of Unknowing*.

As in many such cases, it is clear that the interests of compiler and readers included lollard writings but were not limited to them—and indeed this is hardly surprising, in a reading milieu where a varied palette of expressions of intense piety and recommendations for religious practice for the laity were by now available. The extent to which one or another reader may have adopted the religious styles recommended by her or his reading, and if so for how long and in what ways, is beyond our knowing—except insofar as we can trace parallel paths through evidence from heresy trials. But that we can never know for certain what readers of these books may have thought and done seems a poor reason not to study them.

CHAPTER 5

Their Beliefs

In the Middle Ages, heresy was, first and foremost, a matter of belief. When Wyclif and those who followed in his footsteps were summoned to court, excommunicated, or burned at the stake, it was because they had believed that certain propositions about God, Christ, the sacraments, the church, or other theological matters which had been condemned as heterodox were instead true doctrine. In technical, canonical terms, they became guilty of heresy when they refused to accept the correction of ecclesiastical authorities, as we saw in Chapter 1. In reality, many were punished because prior to their encounter with church officials they had preached heterodox ideas, written or copied heterodox texts, or disseminated forbidden ideas to others.

In the last two chapters, we have been exploring the ways in which the study of lollard beliefs cannot be separated from the study of lollard practices, chief among them the practices of writing, translating, and reading devotional, theological, and biblical texts in the English vernacular. This chapter, by contrast, approaches lollardy through a more traditional, intellectual lens, that of theology. Here I seek to articulate, to the extent that the available evidence permits, what Wyclif and later lollards believed about many of the issues that caused controversy with their contemporaries. Before doing so, however, a few observations about the ways in which scholars have attempted to study lollards' beliefs, as well as about the limitations of the evidence, seem in order.

First, at a number of points over the past half-century, scholars have warned that studying the beliefs of lollards is akin to studying the beliefs of unicorns. If a thing does not exist in the first place, then how is it possible to analyze its attributes? The arguments against the existence of lollardy as a discrete historical phenomenon that we encountered in Chapter 1 have their logical corollaries in arguments, often advanced by the same scholars, that emphasize the futility of studying lollard theology.[1]

Others have stopped short of arguing against the existence of lollardy altogether, but still have objected to what they call the ahistorical, stereotyping tendencies of many published descriptions of lollard theology. These scholars have maintained that while there may have been lollards, in the sense that there were identifiable individuals, and possibly even groups of individuals,

---

1   See, for instance, R.N. Swanson, *Church and Society in Late Medieval England* (Oxford, 1989), 329–35; see below, 172, for discussion of Swanson's more recent, less sceptical work on lollardy.

whose beliefs caused them to be labeled as such by religious authorities in late medieval England, the beliefs of such individuals were so diverse as to render it impossible to describe them as a uniform or coherent system. In his 1975 doctoral thesis, for instance, Charles Kightly observed that "there was no real corpus of lollard beliefs, in the sense of a set of doctrines shared by all known lollards."[2] John Thomson, writing the previous decade, held a similar view: the beliefs of the heresy suspects whose trials he had studied varied "not only from group to group, but even from individual to individual within the same group."[3] Kightly and Thomson both grounded their arguments in the records of the trials of heresy suspects, but similar concerns about theological inconsistencies among lollards have also been set forth by scholars whose primary sources are literary. John Scattergood, analyzing the poem *Pierce the Ploughman's Crede*, noted that the text testifies to the existence of "a set of related problems which not only divided Lollards from the established church and the clergy, but divided one Lollard from another."[4]

Yet, if some have argued that lollardy was a phenomenon too religiously diverse to be said to have a characteristic theology, at the other end of the spectrum the coherence of lollards' beliefs has also been over-exaggerated. In the late nineteenth and early twentieth centuries, several of Wyclif's biographers assumed that all of the Oxford scholar's disciples, as they called them, must have thought just as he did about controverted theological issues. Gotthard Lechler, for instance, wrote about lollards as members of a cohesive religious group, noting that despite opposition they "remained firm, united, and progressive. They quitted the defensive attitude, and adopted active measures for the extension and consolidation of their body."[5] In an important sense, these scholars were echoing what they had read about lollards in medieval and early modern texts: Henry Knighton, the Augustinian canon who so vehemently chronicled the rise and fall of Wyclif and lollardy, and John Foxe, the Reformation propagandist, both observed that lollards spoke and wrote in

---

2   Charles Kightly, "The Early Lollards: A Survey of Popular Lollard Activity in England, 1382–1428," (Ph.D. diss., University of York, 1975), 576.
3   J.A.F. Thomson, *The Later Lollards: 1414–1520* (Oxford, 1965), 239.
4   V.J. Scattergood, "*Pierce the Ploughman's Crede*: Lollardy and Texts," in *Lollardy and Gentry*, 77–94, at 80.
5   Lechler, 480. As late as 1982, Margaret Aston maintained that there was a "comparative uniformity" of belief among the heresy suspects tried in Norwich in the late 1420s and 1430s. See Aston, "William White's Lollard Followers," *Catholic History Review* 48 (1982), 469–97, repr. in *Lollards and Reformers*, 71–100.

distinctive ways.[6] For Knighton and Foxe, as for their contemporaries, it was possible to mark someone out as a lollard by observing how that person deployed a specific set of theological arguments and rhetorical techniques. Knighton observed this about the preaching of early lollards:

> [T]hey carried an eloquent and mellifluous charm in their head, and venom in their tail. For in all their teaching their doctrine seemed at first devout and full of sweetness, and in its end withered in hateful cunning and disparagement. And even the newly-converted, or those most suddenly or briefly initiated into their sect at once began to speak in the same way, and to display a marvellous familiarity with their doctrines. And both men and women instantly became learned exponents of evangelical teaching in their mother tongue, as though they had been trained and taught in one school, and indeed instructed and raised up by a single master.[7]

Today, some scholars continue to be tempted by the prospect of finding even a modest level of coherence among the ideas propounded in lollard writings and the records of heresy trials. Andrew E. Larsen, for instance, proposed in a 2003 essay a list of beliefs that characterized lollards and distinguished them from their orthodox contemporaries.[8] And even though I argued strenuously against drawing up such lists of propositions in my 2010 book, *What Is a Lollard?*, I still catalogued eight features of lollard belief and practice that I claimed "seem likely to mark out an individual as a member of the lollard 'family.'"[9]

It is worth considering that the majority of arguments about the coherence or incoherence of lollard theology have implicitly relied on what we might call an inquisitorial paradigm, that is to say, the view that the most important facts about lollard beliefs have to do with whether lollards and suspected lollards might have endorsed a particular set of theological propositions. This paradigm has shaped arguments on both sides of the debate about the coherence of lollardy: for skeptics such as Kightly, the greatest challenge to thinking about

---

6   Knighton, 287, 303–7; *A&M*, 805. On the commonplace medieval and early modern theory that lollards all articulated the same beliefs, and in similar ways, see especially Anne Hudson, "A Lollard Sect Vocabulary?" in *So Meny People, Longages, and Tonges: Philological Essays in Scots and Mediaeval English Presented to Angus McIntosh*, (eds.) M. Benskin and M.L. Samuels (Edinburgh, 1981), 15–30, repr. in *Books*, 164–80.
7   Knighton, 303.
8   Andrew E. Larsen, "Are All Lollards Lollards?" in *Influence*, 59–72.
9   J. Patrick Hornbeck II, *What Is a Lollard? Dissent and Belief in Late Medieval England* (Oxford, 2010), 199.

lollard theology is that it is all but impossible to formulate a set of credal statements with which all lollards would have agreed, whereas for Knighton, Foxe, and more recently Larsen, what is crucial is that there are (at least a few) propositions that every lollard would have endorsed. However, a number of scholars in the last decade have proposed that this paradigm represents the wrong way to approach the study of lollard beliefs, because it is a way of proceeding that mimics the habits of medieval inquisitors and fails to get to the heart of the theological ideas that mattered most to lollards.

In his influential 2002 monograph *The Wycliffite Heresy*, Kantik Ghosh warned against accounts of lollardy that treat it as a specific doctrinal program. Instead, Ghosh argued, Wyclif and at least some of his early academic supporters saw their reform movement as being at least as much about a new form of biblical hermeneutics as the denial of traditional doctrines. Wyclif's goal was to reclaim scripture from "the threat of the realm of 'glossing' taking over the realm of the 'text'."[10] Indeed, Wyclif used the word "glossing" to refer disparagingly to the theological methods of his contemporaries who emphasized commentary on scholastic and patristic texts over the reading of scripture; he particularly associated these methods with theologians from the fraternal orders. Lollardy was thus "an intellectual heresy," concerned with the reformation of academic practice as well as of theology.[11] In his subsequent publications, Ghosh has continued to insist that lollardy was more a *mentalité* than a set of doctrines.[12] If Ghosh's approach framed Wyclif's ideas within the context of medieval debates about the interpretation of the Bible, Katherine C. Little's 2006 book on lollardy, confession, and the self has discerned in the study of lollard texts an important moment in the history of subjectivity: "This book argues that the Wycliffites and the controversy they engendered in the medieval period should be understood in terms of the history and the sources of the self." She proceeded to suggest that the Wycliffite movement "belong[s] not only to the history of dissent...but also to the history of the self."[13]

Beyond these broad arguments about the coherence (or incoherence) of lollardy, and about the risks of adopting the thought-patterns of inquisitors, there

10   Kantik Ghosh, *The Wycliffite Heresy: Authority and the Interpretation of Texts* (Cambridge, 2002), 7.
11   Ian Christopher Levy, reviewing Ghosh, *The Wycliffite Heresy*, in "The Fight for the Sacred Sense in Late Medieval England," *Anglican Theological Review* 85 (2003), 165–76.
12   See, for instance, "Reginald Bishop Pecock and the Idea of 'Lollardy,'" in *Text and Controversy*, 251–65.
13   Katherine C. Little, *Confession and Resistance: Defining the Self in Late Medieval England* (Notre Dame, Ind., 2006), 1, 3.

is a third caveat: that to reduce lollard beliefs to a set of contentious theological propositions carries with it the risk of overemphasizing certain aspects of lollard theology at the expense of others. For scholars who have perceived lollardy to comprise a tightly constructed theological system, the temptation to search for a belief or set of beliefs that constitutes the core of that system has been irresistible. However, such searches often say more about the theological preoccupations of the searcher than about lollardy itself. In particular, it may have been the central role that ideas about predestination and free will played in the vicissitudes of the sixteenth century reformations that vaulted Wyclif's ideas about the saved and the damned into a central place in many studies of his thought. As I observed in Chapter 2, for decades Wyclif's reputed predestinarianism has been thought to constitute the theological basis for his teachings as well as the beliefs of many of his followers.[14] The distinguished medieval historian Gordon Leff, for instance, argued that the effects of Wyclif's supposedly strict, almost Calvinist theology of salvation reverberate throughout his writings: "From the outset his metaphysical conception of the two bodies of Christ and Antichrist engendered an ambivalence to the church that became ultimately irreconcilable."[15] In this regard, Leff was echoing the early twentieth century Wyclif biographer H.B. Workman, who had maintained that for Wyclif, "the basis of the Church is the Divine election."[16]

Predestination has not, however, been the only doctrine thought to undergird Wyclif's and lollards' theological claims. Another prime candidate for the role of a central lollard teaching has been Wyclif's doctrine of dominion, according to which, as we have seen, claims to temporal or spiritual authority become null when a person falls into a state of sin; this is especially true of sinful lords, who thereby forfeit their claims to lordship. James Crompton put this case most clearly in one of the few book-length academic writings devoted solely to lollard theology: "The key then to Wyclif's theological system, which he himself provided, is the idea of Dominion, or Lordship."[17] Interest in Wyclif's ideas about lordship has persisted: as recently as 2009, Stephen E. Lahey has

---

14   See above, 30–35.
15   Gordon Leff, *Heresy in the Later Middle Ages: The Relation of Heterodoxy to Dissent, c. 1250–c. 1450*, 2 vols. (Manchester, 1967), 2:520; see also Leff, "The Place of Metaphysics in Wyclif's Theology," in *Ockham to Wyclif*, 217–32.
16   Workman, 2:9.
17   James Crompton, "Lollard Doctrine, With Special Reference to the Controversy over Image-Worship and Pilgrimages" (B.Litt. thesis, Oxford University, 1950), 11; note, however, that in much the same spirit as the present chapter, Crompton also cautioned that "it seemed dangerous to postulate anything like a body of doctrine common to the group of people encountered" in his research (p. 130).

pointed to Wyclif's *dominium* theory as the "foundation of Wyclif's political and ecclesiological vision."[18]

Dominium and predestination share a set of characteristics that make each of them an attractive starting-point for an account of lollard theology. Both are doctrines that have their tentacles in a wide range of theological and ecclesiological issues. What one believes about dominion, for instance, affects one's views about the legitimacy and powers of the pope, bishops, and temporal lords, as well as one's views about the validity of sacraments performed by sinful clerics. Likewise, what one believes about predestination informs one's perspective on the relationship between the material church on earth and the invisible church in heaven, on the authority of prelates and lords who are foreknown by God to damnation, and on the necessity of the sacraments for salvation. Nevertheless, in histories of Christianity it is often the case that doctrines which scholars and authorities perceive to be central to the theological vision of an individual or group are, instead, simply the doctrines that most clearly distinguish that writer or group from the mainstream.[19] A similar caution applies in the case of lollardy: before concluding that any particular belief is at the heart of lollard theology, one must consider the differences between the way in which an idea functioned in the writings of Wyclif and later lollards and the significance that that idea held in the minds of their persecutors.

Finally, the search for the heart of lollard theology, or indeed any investigation into the content of lollards' religious views, is bound to be handicapped by the limitations of the evidence.[20] Many of our extant sources are lists of condemned beliefs prepared by lollards' ecclesiastical opponents, including the 1377 bull that Pope Gregory XI issued to condemn Wyclif's *dominium* teaching, the proceedings of the 1382 council that met at the London house of the Blackfriars, the Wycliffite articles condemned by the Canterbury convocation in 1396, the 267 articles extracted from (some of) Wyclif's writings by an Oxford committee in 1411, and the two lists of beliefs anathematized at the Council of Constance in 1415.[21] Sources that likewise reflect hostile rather than sympathetic views of lollard beliefs also include the chronicles of Knighton, Thomas

---

18   Lahey, *Wyclif*, 199.
19   Rowan Williams makes this point about the relationship between the ideas of the fourth century priest Arius and the beliefs anathematized as "Arianism." See his *Arius: Heresy and Tradition*, 2nd ed. (London, 2001), 95.
20   On these limitations, see the extensive discussion in *PR*, Chapter 1.
21   For these documents, see Wilkins, 3:123, 157–58, 227–30, 339–49; and Tanner, *Decrees*, 1:411–13, 422–26. On the process that led to the condemnation of Wycliffite ideas at the Blackfriars council, see most recently Andrew Cole, *Literature and Heresy in the Age of Chaucer* (Cambridge, 2008), Chapter 1.

Walsingham, Adam of Usk, and others; the public declarations of royal and ecclesiastical officials; and the anti-Wycliffite sermons and writings of leading churchmen like Thomas Brinton, John Mirk, and Thomas Netter. Finally, the numerous records of the trials of suspected lollards contain literally thousands of propositions that these men and women were accused of or admitted to believing. Because they rarely convey unfiltered versions of the events they describe and because the process by which they were prepared was deeply indebted to the norms of the institutional church, trial records present a special set of challenges for modern scholars. I will explore the limitations of these fascinating documents at greater length in Chapter 7.

The four methodological challenges I have mentioned—the danger of subscribing to a kind of atomism that renders the category of lollard theology all but meaningless, the temptation to approach lollard beliefs as though they were reducible to a single set of theological propositions, the potential for limiting one's field of view by designating a particular doctrine as foundational to all others, and the inadequacy of the evidence—all these challenges present significant obstacles to the study of lollard theology. They do not, however, render totally opaque the beliefs that Wyclif and those who came after him held. This chapter seeks to marshal the available evidence for lollard views with regard to three broad categories of theological ideas: salvation and grace, the sacraments, and the church and mainstream religious practice.[22]

5.1   Salvation and Grace

Despite the risk of seeming to characterize any one doctrine as occupying a central place in the theological consciousness of lollards, an account of their theologies must start somewhere. And since for many years, it has been a scholarly commonplace to associate lollards with a doctrine of predestination that anticipated the teaching of John Calvin a century later, lollard views on salvation and grace provide one possible jumping-off point for our survey of the history and historiography of lollard thought.[23] Indeed, because lollard

---

22   For its discussions of lollard views on salvation and grace, the sacraments of the eucharist, marriage, and holy orders, and the papacy, the remainder of this chapter is greatly indebted to the findings of my *What Is a Lollard?*, Chapters 2–6.

23   For studies that place lollard ideas about salvation into dialogue with those of later reformers, see among others Lechler, 278; Robert Doyle, "The Death of Christ and the Doctrine of Grace in John Wycliffe," *Churchman* 99 (1985), 317–35, and O.T. Hargrave, "The Doctrine of Predestination in the English Reformation" (Ph.D. diss., Vanderbilt University, 1966).

beliefs have often been studied anachronistically, the theologies of salvation (in technical terms, soteriologies) that actually appear in lollard texts and trial records have been largely neglected by scholars in the nineteenth and twentieth centuries. More recent research has shown that rather than presupposing that God has divided human beings between the saved and the damned without regard to merit, Wyclif and many lollards instead developed theologies about salvation that stressed both the gratuity of God's grace and the significance of free will. Even though they frequently used some of the same terms that earlier predestinarian writers did (e.g., *predestinati* for those who will be saved and *praesciti* for those foreknown by God to be condemned), only in a few instances did lollards approach the rigor of Calvin's double predestinarianism. Likewise, only in a few instances did lollards write about those documents so despised by sixteenth-century reformers: indulgences.[24]

Salvation has long been a preoccupation of Christian believers, and there is not space here to describe in any depth the full range of ideas about salvation that historically have been developed and deployed.[25] Defining a few key terms, however, will help to orient our discussion. At one end of the spectrum are positions that downplay human agency and exalt divine power. "Single predestinarianism," or simply "predestinarianism," is the position that human beings can in no way merit salvation, which as a result is totally dependent on God's gratuitous choice or election. According to the strictest versions of this doctrine, the logic by which God makes salvific choices is inscrutable to us, and God's grace, when it is offered, is irresistible. "Double predestinarianism" goes beyond the claim that God chooses to elect some persons while passively allowing others to die without saving grace, and it maintains that God also actively chooses to condemn the damned. At the other end of the spectrum, "Pelagianism," a position associated by his opponents with the fifth-century monk Pelagius, holds that human persons can earn salvation on account of their freely chosen good deeds. Most soteriologies, however, fall somewhere between predestinarianism and Pelagianism. To the extent that a particular theology focuses on the sovereignty of God's grace, we can call it "grace-oriented," whereas to the extent that it focuses on human agency, we can call it "works-oriented."[26]

---

24 For Wyclif's and lollard views on indulgences, see Anne Hudson, "Dangerous Fictions: Indulgences in the Thought of Wyclif and His Followers," in *Promissory Notes on the Treasury of Merit: Indulgences in Late Medieval Europe*, (ed.) R.N. Swanson (Leiden, 2006), 197–214.

25 For a complete history of Western Christian attitudes about salvation, see Alister McGrath, *Iustitia Dei: A History of the Christian Doctrine of Justification*, 3rd ed. (Cambridge, 2005).

26 These categories exclude that of "semi-Pelagianism," a commonplace of many studies of late antique and medieval theologies of salvation. As Rebecca Harden Weaver has argued,

As we saw in Chapter 2, many scholars have identified Wyclif's philosophical realism, that is, his metaphysical commitments about the existence and significance of universals, as the ground of his philosophical and theological views.[27] Like these scholars, the churchmen who condemned Wyclif at the Council of Constance attributed his supposed predestinarianism to his ideas about universals, being, and necessity; they condemned, for instance, the thesis attributed to him that "all things that happen, happen from absolute necessity."[28] His medieval antagonists as well as many of his modern commentators have maintained that Wyclif's metaphysics required him to articulate a soteriology according to which God's foreknowledge necessitates double predestinarianism. On this account, the saved and the damned "represented two distinct modes of being...two universals which were eternally distinct from one another."[29]

It is not surprising that Wyclif was viewed as a proponent of predestination for more than six hundred years. His theology is reminiscent of and indebted to that of St. Augustine; he repeatedly defined the true church as "the congregation of the predestined"; and he regularly employed predestinarian imagery in his writings.[30] Nevertheless, in the late twentieth and twenty-first centuries, a chorus of critical voices has called for a reassessment of Wyclif's soteriology. Led by Ian Christopher Levy, these scholars have maintained that Wyclif used a philosophical concept, hypothetical necessity, to defend his view that God's omniscience does not entail that all events are predetermined.[31] According to these revisionists, Wyclif maintained that God's will is to save all people, that

---

there is a significant risk of anachronism to use this term outside of the fifth and sixth-century debates for which it was originally coined; even there, it is something of a misnomer. See Weaver, *Divine Grace and Human Agency: A Study of the Semi-Pelagian Controversy* (Macon, Ga., 1996), 40.

27   See above, 31–33.

28   Tanner, *Decrees*, 1:426.

29   John Stacey, "John Wyclif as Theologian," *Expository Times* 101 (1990), 134–41, at 138. Other scholars interpreting Wyclif along similar lines include J.A. Robson, *Wyclif and the Oxford Schools* (Cambridge, 1961); S.H. Thompson, "The Philosophical Basis of Wyclif's Theology," *Journal of Religion* 11 (1931), 86–116, at 113; and most influentially, Leff, *Heresy*, 2:517–44.

30   See, among other passages, *De ecclesia*, 2–3, 7, 37, 58; *De civili dominio*, 1:288, 358; and *Opera minora*, 176.

31   Ian Christopher Levy, "Grace and Freedom in the Soteriology of John Wyclif," *Traditio* 60 (2005), 279–337; and Lahey, *Wyclif*, 169–98. The trend toward perceiving Wyclif as something less than a strict predestinarian was begun two decades ago, in Anthony Kenny's slim monograph *Wyclif* (Oxford, 1985), 31–41.

God makes grace available to all, and that those who accept God's offer of grace are those who can rightly be called the predestined.

What did those of his sympathizers who came after Wyclif make of his soteriology? The evidence suggests that many lollards, not unlike Wyclif's opponents at the Council of Constance, may not fully have understood it. Some lollard writers took the predestinarian implications of Wyclif's language seriously and developed doctrines that rival Calvin's in their inflexibility; others maintained some version of Wyclif's balance between divine grace and human agency. To make this point more effectively, let us consider the soteriological leanings of three representative lollard texts. First, the long cycle of *English Wycliffite Sermons* contains a variety of doctrines of salvation. Some sermons incorporate what appear to be predestinarian references: for instance, one preacher maintains that "men seyn comunly þat þer ben here two manerys of chirches: holy chirche or chirche of God, þat on no maner may be dampnyd; and þe chirche of þe feend, þat for a tyme is good and lasteþ not, and þis was neuere holy chirche ne part þerof."[32] Others appropriate a version of the scholastic dictum *facere quod in se est*, which for a number of medieval theologians summed up the idea that God has graciously made a covenant with human beings so that those who "do what they can" or, literally, "do what is in one," can be saved. Thus, one sermon insists that "for do a man þat in hym is, and God is redy to his dedis," and another encourages, "Do we now þat in us is, and God wole haue us excusid."[33] A very few sermons seem to take the view that meritorious acts alone can earn one a place in heaven, including a sermon that Wyclif's biographer Workman mistakenly attributed to Wyclif himself: "for eche man þat schal be dampned, is dampned for his owne gylt, and eche man þat schal be saued, is saued by his owne meryȝt."[34]

Other lollard texts also betray ambivalence about salvation. In Chapter 4, we first encountered *The Lanterne of Liȝt*, a late compendium of lollard theology and ecclesiology. Its author defines the church in a number of ways, including "þe chosun noumbre of hem þat schullen be saued."[35] However, his soteriology is not strictly predestinarian. At the conclusion of the text, he asks his readers to take a moral inventory of their lives and proposes a remedy for those who find themselves wanting: "Neþeles assay [attempt] in þis lijf, if ȝe may leeue þe fendis chirche and brynge ȝoure silf boþe bodi and soule in to þe chirch of Iesu

---

32   *EWS*, 1:20/66–9.
33   *EWS*, 3:176/99–100; 3:229/47–48.
34   *EWS*, 2:100/82–84; see Workman, 2:9.
35   *The Lanterne of Liȝt*, (ed.) L.M. Swinburn (EETS o.s. 151, London, 1917), 23/3–4.

Crist while grace and mercy may be grauntid, axe [ask] of him þat offrid him silf...to saue vs alle whanne we were loost."³⁶ Such language is hardly compatible with a strict doctrine of predestination, since an individual irreversibly condemned to damnation would be unable, even through the grace and mercy of Christ, to bring herself or himself to leave the devil's church. Thus, the *Lanterne*'s position seems quite closely to resemble Wyclif's doctrine of salvation, where both God's grace and human choices are significant in determining one's status in the afterlife.

A third text, the poem *Pierce the Ploughman's Crede*, likewise runs counter to the stereotype that all lollards articulated predestinarian soteriologies. Indeed, the first half of the poem, in which the narrator meets members of the four fraternal orders and asks them to teach him the Creed, lacks any reference to predestination. In the second half, where the narrator encounters the destitute farmer of the poem's title, the comments made by the title character confirm that works have soteriological value. Peres the ploughman remarks that Christ "the clene hertes curtysliche blissed,/That coueten no katel but Cristes ful blisse,/That leeueth fulliche on God and lellyche thenketh/On his lore and his lawe and lyueth opon treweth."³⁷ The idea that Christ blesses Christians who believe fully, think loyally, and live truthfully is not likely to be of a piece with the idea that God is the arbitrary ruler of a predestinarian universe.

If these and other lollard authors did not articulate soteriologies reminiscent of the predestinarian position inaccurately imputed to Wyclif by many of his antagonists, did any heresy defendants do so? Again, here, the evidence is not uniform: while a few trial records do include language that seems to suggest that a particular defendant embraced a doctrine of predestination, the bulk of these documents do not. Those closer in time and space to Wyclif were more likely than others to use the vocabulary of predestinarianism, but like Wyclif's, their positions may have been caricatured by their opponents. The priest William Sawtre, tried in 1400, reportedly affirmed that he would rather show reverence to a predestined man than an angel, and John Purvey was charged with believing that any predestined man is a true priest.³⁸ Likewise, a letter sent by an anonymous lollard, possibly Walter Brut, to Wyclif's onetime Oxford colleague Nicholas Hereford includes predestinarian and deterministic language: "No peruersion of any reprobate is able to turne the congregation of

---

36   *Lanterne*, 136/13–17.
37   *Pierce the Ploughman's Crede*, in *The Piers Plowman Tradition*, (ed.) Helen Barr (London, 1993), lines 639–40.
38   FZ, 387.

the Elect from the fayth, because all thinges that shall come to passe, are eternallye in God."[39]

Nonetheless, in comparison to the many references to the sacraments and church hierarchy that can readily be found in the records of medieval English heresy trials, relatively few explicitly mention soteriology. Exceptions include the trial of the rebel Sir John Oldcastle, who apparently proclaimed in 1413 that "all tho that ben or shall be saued ben membres of this moste holy churche."[40] In 1415, the London leather-worker John Claydon, accused of having commissioned a copy of *The Lanterne of Liȝt*, was charged with believing that "no reprobate is a member of the church, but only such as be elected and predestined to salvation."[41] In the Norwich trials conducted by Bishop William Alnwick, the parchment-maker John Godesell confessed to believing that "the catholic church is the congregation of only those who are to be saved," a position that might, but does not necessarily, entail a strong doctrine of predestination.[42] Some decades later, in 1443, the clerk Thomas Bikenore, on trial in Salisbury diocese, abjured the belief that "holichirche catholike is a aggregacion of… men…[who] only shulbe saued."[43] Two defendants at the end of the fifteenth century, both in Coventry and Lichfield diocese, confessed that they had taught that all the works people accomplish in their lifetimes are soteriologically insignificant.[44]

Few if any of these individuals were asked specifically about their views on predestination, and the topic does not seem to have served as the same kind of litmus-test of orthodoxy as did the sacrament of the eucharist. The value of predestinarian belief as clear proof of lollardy seems to have declined over time in the minds of churchmen and inquisitors. While propositions thought to derive from Wyclif's doctrine of predestination appear prominently in lists of lollard errors published in 1382, 1388, 1396, and 1411, the documents of the 1415 Council of Constance mention soteriological themes only in passing, and a 1428 questionnaire to be administered to heresy suspects omits the predestinarian

---

39 *A&M*, 619. On Brut as the likely author of this letter, see Maureen Jurkowski, "Who Was Walter Brut?" *English Historical Review* 127 (2012), 285–302.
40 *The examinacion of Master William Thorpe…[and] The examinacion of the honorable Knyght syr Ihon Oldcastell Lorde Cobham* (n.p., 1530; STC 24045), 62.
41 *A&M*, 757–58.
42 *Norwich*, 61: "Ecclesia catholica est congregacio solum salvandorum."
43 Salisbury reg. Aiscough, 2: fol. 53r.
44 *Coventry*, 66, 70.

term *praesciti* (persons whose damnation God foreknows) in favor of the more general *mali* (evil persons).[45]

5.2 The Sacraments

If lollards—as well as those who have subsequently studied them—were not of the same mind with regard to the theology of salvation, we should not expect to find uniformity among them on other doctrinal questions. At the heart of most lollard objections to traditional religion lay the claim that the institutional church had perverted the meaning, the method of administration, or both, of the church's sacraments. In contrast with later reformers such as Martin Luther and John Calvin, lollards generally did not argue that the number of sacraments should be reduced from the seven commonly accepted by scholastic theologians such as Thomas Aquinas. Many lollards seem to have desired instead the purification of observances such as marriage, holy orders, and penance. Nevertheless, opinions about the sacraments varied widely among lollards and lollard communities.

5.2.1 *Sacraments of Initiation: Baptism and Confirmation*

Not unlike later reformers, Wyclif rejected few of the medieval church's teachings about baptism, the sacrament believed to initiate new members into the church and to cleanse them of the guilt of original sin.[46] In fact, for many years Wyclif and lollards were thought to be perfectly orthodox where this sacrament was concerned. For instance, the Methodist church historian Gordon Rupp, taking his cues from John Foxe, pronounced in 1966 that "there is no evidence that they denied Christian baptism or refused Christian burial."[47] However, the confidence that Rupp and earlier generations of scholars placed in Foxe has since proven to be unwarranted: just as Rupp's study was in press, another historian, John Thomson, was demonstrating conclusively that Foxe

---

45   *FZ*, 278; Knighton, 435–39; Wilkins, 3:229–30, 339–49; Anne Hudson, "The Examination of Lollards," *Bulletin of the Institute of Historical Research* 46 (1973), 145–59, repr. in *Books*, 124–40.

46   A lengthier analysis of Wyclif's and lollard ideas and texts about baptism and confirmation, as well as the references to these sacraments that appear in the records of late medieval English heresy trials, can be found in J. Patrick Hornbeck II, "'A Prophane and Heathyn Thing'? English Lollards on Baptism and Confirmation," *Mediaeval Studies* 74 (2012), 283–306.

47   E.G. Rupp, *Studies in the Making of the English Protestant Tradition* (Cambridge, 1966), 4.

had selectively constructed his accounts of some medieval heresy trials. In several cases, Thomson showed, "Foxe fails to note that a member of the accused denied the spiritual profit of baptism, an opinion which would have been considered heretical after the Reformation, and which in consequence would have spoiled the picture of the...Lollards as early protestants who suffered at the hands of a brutal persecuting Roman Church."[48]

As with any aspect of lollard belief, it is unsafe to venture generalizations about lollards' views on the sacrament of baptism. Wyclif discussed baptism over the course of several chapters of his late work *Trialogus*, as well as in a few other treatises, concluding that the sacrament was instituted by Christ and that it is "*necessary* to the wayfarer," a term that he and other medieval writers commonly used to describe the Christian making her way in the world.[49] But what, precisely, did Wyclif believe to be necessary? It was not simply immersion in water. As one of the characters in Wyclif's tract puts it: "It seems to diminish divine liberty or power, that God cannot, by interceding wholly on his own merit and by his passion, save an infant or adult member of the faithful" if such a person has failed for one reason or another to receive baptism in water according to the customs of the church.[50] Taking a position not unusual among theologians of his day, Wyclif distinguished between three kinds of baptism. Most people are baptized in water (*baptismus fluminis*), but some are baptized in blood (*baptismus sanguinis*) when they are martyred in the name of Christ, and some others are baptized in the Spirit (*baptismus flaminis*) when they die with the desire for baptism.[51] This last kind of baptism, Wyclif wrote, is the baptism of the Holy Spirit, "which is simply the more necessary to any person, if he is to be saved."[52]

Wyclif's distinctions between these types of baptism provided the foundation for at least one of the articles for which he was censured. In his Franciscan opponent William Woodford's list of Wyclif's errors, as well as in the lists of propositions condemned by the Canterbury convocation of 1396, the Oxford

48   J.A.F. Thomson, "John Foxe and Some Sources for Lollard History: Notes for a Critical Reappraisal," in *Studies in Church History* 2, (ed.) G.J. Cuming (London, 1965), 251–57, at 252. For further discussion of Foxe, see Chapter 8 below.
49   *Trialogus*, 281–82, original emphasis: "Hoc autem sacramentum est tam *necessarium viatori*."
50   *Trialogus*, 282: "Videtur enim derogare divinae libertati atque potentiae, quod Deus non posset intercedente toto merito suo atque passione salvare infantem vel adultum fidelem."
51   *Trialogus*, 285.
52   *Trialogus*, 285: "qui est simpliciter necessarius cuilibet homini, si salvetur." For the most recent critical analysis of Wyclif's theology of baptism, see Stephen Penn, "Wyclif and the Sacraments," in *Companion*, 241–90, at 273–74.

committee of 1411, and the Council of Constance in 1415, Wyclif was alleged to have taught that "they who do affirm that the infants of the faithful, departing without the sacrament of baptism, are not saved, are presumptuous and foolish."[53] Wyclif was also criticized by the Oxford committee for having taught that anointing with chrism is not a necessary part of the baptismal rite.

In contrast to Wyclif's relatively tame statements on baptism, many of the men and women tried for heresy in the decades after his death articulated more extreme views. Most prominent among the errors attributed to later lollards was the claim that if a child's parents were both baptized Christians, then the child does not need baptism herself; some lollards taught that a child is baptized directly in the mother's womb. Propositions of this sort first appear in a list of topics preached on Good Friday, 1382, by the peripatetic evangelist William Swinderby.[54] They recur in no fewer than eleven of the trials conducted in Norwich diocese under Bishop William Alnwick. As in the case of John Reve, these defendants were asked to abjure the belief that "the sacrament of Baptem done in water in fourme customed in the Churche is of non avail and not to be pondret if the fadir and modir of the childe be christened and of Christene beleve."[55] Other Norwich suspects were accused of or confessed to believing similar things, for instance that a person is "sufficiently baptized" by receiving Christ's law and commandments.[56] Elsewhere in the country, approximately half of the suspects whose trials include mention of baptism were accused of having taught that the child of baptized parents does not need baptism. A few suspects were accused of other errors, including that it is just as good to be baptized in a ditch as in a baptismal font, that baptism is simply unnecessary to salvation, and that baptism can be accomplished without a priest.[57] (It is worth noting that the institutional church itself embraced this last idea in the case of children who would otherwise die without baptism.)

Despite these interesting variations, baptism appears relatively rarely in the records of late medieval English heresy trials. Mention of the other sacrament of Christian initiation, confirmation, is even more rare. Wyclif devoted only a

---

53   *A&M*, 469; Wilkins, 3:227–30, no. 4, and 3:339–49, no. 124; and Tanner, *Decrees*, 1:422, no. 6, and 1:426, no. 57.

54   Thomas Walsingham, *The St. Alban's Chronicle: The Chronica Maiora of Thomas Walsingham*, 2 vols., (eds.) John Taylor, Wendy R. Childs, and Leslie Watkiss (Oxford, 2003–11), 1:588–60.

55   *Norwich*, 111.

56   *Norwich*, 121.

57   Hereford reg. Stanbury, 118–19; *Kent*, passim; Salisbury reg. Audley, fol. 160r.

few pages in his voluminous writings to this sacrament, declaring in *Trialogus* that there is no biblical precedent for confirmation, that it is not necessary for salvation, and that there is no scriptural reason for the church to restrict the administration of this sacrament only to bishops.[58] All of these points are accurately reported in the lists of articles prepared against Wyclif by his opponents.[59] One lollard text, "The Gret Sentence of Curs," echoes some of Wyclif's arguments in the course of criticizing the restrictions the church has placed on the sacraments more generally.[60] Finally, the view that confirmation is not necessary for salvation appears in the records of the few dozen heresy trials where confirmation was at issue, but the similarity of almost all such records to one another renders fruitless any further inquiry.[61]

5.2.2 *The Eucharist*

No sacrament evoked as much reverence in the middle ages, nor as much discussion in lollard texts and the records of heresy trials, as the eucharist. As Miri Rubin has argued, fourteenth century Christianity revolved around the sacrament of the altar: "at the centre of the whole religious system of the later Middle Ages lay a ritual which turned bread into flesh—a fragile, small, wheaten disc into God."[62] Undergirding medieval eucharistic practices was the doctrine of transubstantiation, which by the late fourteenth century was all but universally understood to mean that during the mass, at the words of consecration, the substances of bread and wine on the altar became the substances of Christ's body and blood, although the outward appearance of the consecrated elements (their "accidents") remained the same. It was Wyclif's views on the eucharist that led to the severing of his ties with the University of Oxford, and claims about the sacrament appear in nearly half of the extant trials of suspected lollards. Yet only a few scholars have studied in detail the eucharistic theologies that can be found in the writings of lollards and their antagonists: in 1991, Anne Hudson published an analysis of the relevant trial records; in 2004, David Aers surveyed the eucharistic views of Wyclif and two

---

58 *Trialogus*, 292–94; for analysis, see Penn, "Wyclif and the Sacraments," 275.
59 See, for instance, Wilkins, 3:227–30, no. 5; 3:339–49, nos. 125, 128.
60 "The Gret Sentence of Curs," in Arnold, 3:267–337, at 285.
61 See, for instance, the formulaic articles about confirmation abjured by more than a dozen suspects in each of the Norwich and Kent heresy persecutions: *Norwich* and *Kent*, passim.
62 Miri Rubin, *Corpus Christi: The Eucharist in Late Medieval Culture* (Cambridge, 1991), 1.

early lollards, Walter Brut and William Thorpe; and in 2010, my book *What Is a Lollard?* devoted a chapter to the sacrament.[63]

Among these and other scholars, a consensus has emerged that, for medieval inquisitors, the eucharist functioned as what modern political strategists might call a "wedge issue"—that is, a theological litmus-test that sharply distinguished the orthodox from the heterodox. The literary critic Paul Strohm has compellingly argued that the complicated, twisting terrain of eucharistic theology proved an easy hunting ground for error.[64] Defendants unable to articulate traditional yet subtle scholastic distinctions, such as that between the substance and accidents of the eucharistic elements, could easily be trapped by their own words. At the same time, the inquisitorial process also fit suspects' recorded statements on eucharistic topics into the thought-patterns of inquisitors. Yet to the extent that it is possible to glimpse lollards' views on the eucharist, it may be a valid assessment that most lollards tended to take one of two positions on the sacrament: either they argued that while Christ is spiritually present in the eucharist, so also are the material substances of bread and wine; or else they described the sacrament in figurative terms, stating that it merely commemorates the Last Supper.

Wyclif's position on the sacrament evolved over the course of his academic career. His opponent William Woodford claimed that Wyclif's views had careened from one extreme to the other, ranging from an orthodox account of transubstantiation to total agnosticism about what happens at the consecration.[65] It was, however, Wyclif's mature stance on the eucharist that earned him official condemnation. In *De eucharistia confessio*, a short text written in 1381 to defend his views on the sacrament, Wyclif begins by affirming Christ's presence in the consecrated bread and wine, affirming at the same time the presence of the substances of bread and wine themselves. Like Luther a century and a half later, Wyclif asserts that since Christ could not have told a lie, Christ's statement that he is present in the sacrament should be sufficient for any believer.[66] But for Wyclif, Christ is not present in the eucharist in the same

---

63 Anne Hudson, "The Mouse in the Pyx: Popular Heresy and the Eucharist," *Trivium* 26 (1991), 40–53; David Aers, *Sanctifying Signs: Making Christian Tradition in Late Medieval England* (Notre Dame, Ind., 2004), 53–98; and Hornbeck, *What Is a Lollard?* Chapter 3.

64 Paul Strohm, *England's Empty Throne: Usurpation and the Language of Legitimation, 1399–1422* (New Haven, Conn., 1998), 49.

65 Robson, *Wyclif*, 192–93; for additional views on Woodford, see Jeremy Catto, "William Woodford, O.F.M. (c.1330–c.1397)" (D.Phil. thesis, University of Oxford, 1969); and *PR*, 46–50.

66 *FZ*, 115; on this point, see Ian Christopher Levy, "*Christus Qui Mentiri Non Potest*: John Wyclif's Rejection of Transubstantiation," *Recherches de Théologie et Philosophie Médiévales* 66 (1999), 316–34.

way that he was present on earth or is now present in heaven; rather than being present "essentially, substantially, corporeally, or identically," Christ is in the eucharistic elements "virtually, spiritually, and sacramentally."[67] Thus, Christ's presence in the sacrament is spiritual, but it is no less real than the medieval church claimed; it is instead the *mode* of Christ's presence about which Wyclif believes the institutional church to be mistaken. Wyclif turns to the incarnation of Christ as an analogy for his teaching on the eucharist: just as two natures are there joined in a single person, so also are two substances, Christ's body and bread, both present in the consecrated host.[68]

For decades, scholars have debated what provoked Wyclif's departure from the eucharistic orthodoxy of his day. Some, like his early-twentieth-century biographer Workman, along with Workman's near-contemporary John Thomas McNeill, argued that Wyclif's theology of the eucharist, like his supposed predestinarianism, was a necessary outgrowth of his metaphysics. Since Wyclif's theories about being and universals did not permit the possibility that the substances of bread and wine could be annihilated, Wyclif had no choice but to reject the doctrine of transubstantiation. As Workman put it, "[A]bove all else, Wyclif was a metaphysician. He approached the eucharist from the standpoint not of abuses, but of a metaphysical system."[69] Others, however, have argued that Wyclif's philosophical qualms about transubstantiation were outweighed by his fear of the idolatries that he perceived to be wrapped up in popular eucharistic devotions.[70] It is perhaps not surprising that the kinds of training that scholars have brought to this question have shaped their responses: with some notable exceptions, philosophers and theologians have emphasized the incongruities between transubstantiation and Wyclif's metaphysical system,

---

[67] *FZ*, 115; see also *De blasphemia*, 22; *Trialogus*, 248, 278; *De eucharistia*, 11–13, 84–86.

[68] *FZ*, 122. For a different kind of philosophical analysis of Wyclif's theology of the eucharist, see Heather Phillips, "John Wyclif and the Optics of the Eucharist," in *Ockham to Wyclif*, 245–58.

[69] Workman, *Wyclif*, 2:30; McNeill, "Some Emphases," 447–66.

[70] Gordon Leff, "Ockham and Wyclif on the Eucharist," *Reading Medieval Studies* 2 (1976), 1–13; Jeremy Catto, "John Wyclif and the Cult of the Eucharist," in *The Bible in the Medieval World: Essays in Memory of Beryl Smalley*, (eds.) K. Walsh and D. Wood, Studies in Church History, Subsidia 4 (Oxford, 1985), 269–86; Maurice Keen, "Wyclif, the Bible, and Transubstantiation," in Anthony Kenny, (ed.), *Wyclif in His Times* (Oxford, 1986), 1–17; and Dallas G. Denery II, "From Sacred Mystery to Divine Deception: Robert Holkot, John Wyclif, and the Transformation of Fourteenth-Century Eucharistic Discourse," *Journal of Religious History* 29 (2005), 129–44.

whereas historians have pointed to Wyclif's concerns about popular practice. However, in the end no doubt Wyclif's intentions were multifaceted.[71]

Regardless of Wyclif's motivation, it is clear that sometime around 1379, he publicly rejected transubstantiation, the central doctrine of the medieval sacramental system. While the surviving evidence reveals that most of those who followed in Wyclif's footsteps did the same, it also witnesses to the diverse range of eucharistic theologies that lollards articulated. Many texts produced soon after Wyclif's death take a stance similar to his: for instance, a majority of the *English Wycliffite Sermons* adopt the position that in the eucharistic elements there are both bread and Christ's body and wine and Christ's blood. One representative text puts it this way: "þanne men schulden here Godis word gladly, and dispuyse fablis, and erre not in þis sacrud oost but graunte þat it is two þingis, boþe bred and Godus body, but principally Godus body."[72] A few sermons do, however, teach that the eucharist is Christ's body in only a figurative sense. John the Baptist is not Elijah personally, one of these texts argues, but is Elijah figuratively, "[a]nd riȝt so þe sacrid oost is uery bred kyndely ant Goddis body figuraly, riȝt as Crist hymsilf seiþ."[73] A majority of other lollard writings, including the long treatise *Tractatus de oblacione iugis sacrificii*, which ostensibly is dedicated to the sacrament of the altar but in fact addresses a whole range of issues that its author perceives to stem from the abuse of ecclesiastical authority, take positions similar to Wyclif's. According to the *Tractatus*, the sacrament cannot simply consist of accidents without their subject, as Wyclif and many lollard writers caricatured the doctrine of transubstantiation, but instead "is not after þe consecracioun only brede but olso verri Cristis bodi."[74]

Only one major lollard text—in fact, one dating from the final years of lollard literary production—articulates a fully figurative or commemorative theology of the eucharist, in contrast both to transubstantiation and to Wyclif's views. *Wycklyffes Wycket* objects that a human being cannot claim to make God; it also offers a sophisticated reinterpretation of the scriptural passages on which others have based their claims about Christ's presence. When Christ took bread and blessed it, "it semeth more that he blyssed hys disciples and apostles, whom he had ordained witnesses of his passion...He sayd not this

---

71 As Ian Christopher Levy has persuasively argued, in *John Wyclif: Scriptural Logic, Real Presence, and the Parameters of Orthodoxy* (Milwaukee, Wisc., 2003), esp. 220.
72 *EWS*, 1:E17/70–73.
73 *EWS*, 3:125/39–41.
74 *Tractatus de oblacione iugis sacrificii*, in Anne Hudson, (ed.), *The Works of a Lollard Preacher* (EETS o.s. 317, 2001), lines 513–15.

bread is my body or that the brede shuld be geuen for the lyfe of the world."[75] As a result, the sacrament does not make Christ present on the altar but simply commemorates Christ in his absence; it is "but a sygne or mynde of a thyng passed or a thynge to come."[76]

Whereas Wyclif and the authors of lollard texts had the opportunity to articulate at some length the nuances of their eucharistic views, the same cannot be said for most heresy defendants, who as we have already seen were often pressed into making Latinate, scholastic distinctions for which they had neither the training nor, likely, the interest. It is impossible to categorize easily the more than 200 defendants whose trials involved questions about the eucharist. In most cases, the articles that they abjured admit of multiple interpretations: they could reflect either Wyclif's view or a figurative theology of the sacrament akin to that of *Wycklyffes Wycket*. Nevertheless, to the extent that the records permit us to establish, the question about the eucharist most frequently asked in the trials of heresy suspects was whether the eucharistic elements remain bread and wine in substance after the words of consecration have been spoken. Prominent among these defendants were John Purvey, Wyclif's onetime student or colleague; William Thorpe, who as we know wrote an account of his examination by Archbishop Arundel; and Sir John Oldcastle, the knight who after his escape from custody led a revolt against King Henry V. Thorpe and Oldcastle both maintained at their trials that since the gospel does not use terms such as "material bread" or "substance," nor should latter-day Christians; the gospel, as Thorpe put it, "suffisiþ in þis mater."[77]

It would be tedious to recount in detail every case in which a defendant confessed to believing that the substances of bread and wine remain in the consecrated elements. A significant minority of cases, however, did involve figurative or commemorative theologies of the sacrament. The first of these was the trial in Lincoln diocese of John Seynon ("John who says no") in 1400; the next, in the same diocese, was the trial of John Qwyrk in 1463.[78] Later, in Salisbury and Winchester dioceses, commemorative theologies of the sacrament became relatively prominent. Between 1491 and 1512, no fewer than fifteen defendants in those dioceses described the eucharist, as one of them put

---

75 *Wycklyffes Wycket* (London, 1546; STC 25590), A9v–A10v.
76 *Wycklyffes Wycket*, B6r.
77 *The Testimony of William Thorpe*, in Anne Hudson, (ed.), *Two Wycliffite Texts* (EETS o.s. 301, 1993), 53; Oldcastle, n.p. On Thorpe and Oldcastle, see further below, 167–171.
78 I am grateful to Maureen Jurkowski for drawing my attention to the pun embedded in Seynon's surname.

it, as "cristes body in a figure and not the veray body."[79] Intriguingly, at least several of these individuals demonstrably had access to the text *Wycklyffes Wycket*, and it stands to reason that they learned their somewhat idiosyncratic eucharistic views from that tract.[80]

5.2.3   *Penance*

Scholastic theology and popular religious practice both juxtaposed the sacraments of the eucharist and penance. The Fourth Lateran Council, meeting in 1215, had decreed that every Christian was to make a private confession to her or his parish priest at least once a year; since the sacramental absolution that followed confession was believed to restore the penitent to the state of grace necessary to approach the eucharist, it was considered advisable for people to confess shortly before receiving their annual communion at Eastertide. Stephen Penn has shown that Wyclif, following in the same vein, also treated penance in conjunction with the eucharist.[81] However, the views on penance that Wyclif set forth in late works such as *De eucharistia*, *De blasphemia*, and *Trialogus* were not as extreme as his antagonists claimed. He rejected the standard medieval definition of the sacrament as having three parts—contrition, confession, and satisfaction—arguing that since these three things belong to different categories, they cannot together comprise a single sacrament. Wyclif agreed with the church that sinners should have contrition for their sins—in fact, they *must* feel contrition if those sins are to be forgiven—but he disagreed that oral confession to a priest is a necessary element of penance. Christ's apostles and many saints of the early church had lived and died without confessing their sins to priests, Wyclif argued, and when Peter at Pentecost urged the crowds to repent, he did not specify oral confession as the sole means for them to do so.[82] Nonetheless, even as he focused his treatment of penance on the contrition that an individual should feel in the sight of God, Wyclif also believed that a faithful priest might help that individual to come to contrition and, thus, to God's forgiveness.[83]

A majority of the extant lollard texts that discuss the sacrament of penance take a position similar to Wyclif's: confession to a priest may be helpful—indeed, some tracts go so far as to concede that priests have the power to

---

79   Winchester reg. Fox, 3: fols. 69–70.
80   J. Patrick Hornbeck II, "*Wycklyffes Wycket* and Eucharistic Heresy: Two Series of Cases from Sixteenth-Century Winchester," in *Wycliffite Controversies*, 279–94.
81   Penn, "Wyclif and the Sacraments," 283–84.
82   *Trialogus*, 327.
83   Penn, "Wyclif and the Sacraments," 287.

pronounce absolution—but in the final analysis it is God, not the church or a priest, who ultimately forgives a person's sins. The vernacular tract "De Pontificum Romanorum Schismate" also follows Wyclif's lead in arguing that in the time of the apostles, people made their confessions to one another, seeking out priests only as counselors. The text charges Pope Innocent III, who convoked the Fourth Lateran Council, with perverting the church's time-honored tradition of mutual confession.[84] Other texts point to the many contemporary abuses of the sacrament of penance: some priests accept money in exchange for absolution, while for others, hearing the confession of a woman who has committed sexual sins incites them to desire sexual contact with her. Since most lollard authors believed that contrition alone, rather than oral confession, can merit God's forgiveness, they also expressed skepticism about the practice of popes and bishops granting indulgences in return for monetary gifts or religious works.[85]

Similar ideas dominate the discussions of penance to be found in the records of heresy trials. After the eucharist, penance was the sacrament second most often at issue in proceedings against suspected lollards: more than 120 cases involve controverted statements about it. One article commonly abjured was that confession to a priest is unnecessary, since confession is just as valid if made to one's fellow believers; in some cases suspects are recorded as saying that confessing to "a faithful person of their sect" is best of all.[86] A few specifically denied that priests have the power of absolution and cannot, as three suspects in Winchester diocese put it, "cause a man's soul to come to heaven, be he in or out of sin, for he has no power from almighty God to absolve a man from his sins."[87] Others denied the necessity for confession to anyone at all, maintaining that contrition alone is necessary to obtain forgiveness.[88]

5.2.4   Sacraments for States of Life: Marriage and Holy Orders

Nearly all medieval Europeans expected that their lives would be shaped by one of the two sacraments of Christian living, marriage or holy orders. For most, marriage (in one's late teens or early twenties) represented a personal

---

84   "De Pontificum Romanorum Schismate," in Arnold, 3:242–66 at 254–55.
85   See, for instance, "On the Twenty-Five Articles," in Arnold, 3:454–96 at 459–61. For further discussion of lollard ideas about confession, see Little, *Confession and Resistance*.
86   See, for instance, the cases of three defendants tried in Ely diocese in 1457: Ely reg. Gray, fol. 130b.
87   Winchester reg. Fox, 3: fols. 73v, 75r, 75v; these records are translated in *Wycliffite Spirituality*, 356 et al.
88   See, e.g., the case of Thomas Taylor, Worcester reg. Carpenter, 1:133.

commitment as well as a public contract, an agreement with economic and legal as well as sexual consequences.[89] For a smaller number of individuals, all men, the successive stages of holy orders marked the trajectory of a career in the service of Christ and the church.[90] Women of course were barred from ordination, and a few people—nuns, religious brothers, and single women and men—lived and died without receiving either sacrament. Such exceptions aside, these two sacraments established and reinforced familial and ecclesial expectations for people at all levels of the social hierarchy.

Scholarship on lollard attitudes toward marriage has been relatively scarce. A number of studies have focused on lollard views about clerical marriage, an emphasis perhaps best explained by the visibility of married clergy in the reformations of the sixteenth century, as well as by the extravagance of some lollards' positions on the question.[91] Far more often, as we saw in Chapter 2, scholars whose work has touched on the subject of marriage have been primarily interested in lollard views about women.[92] While some scholars maintain that lollardy provided religious opportunities to women, others have argued instead that lollard communities were for the most part as patriarchal as the institutional church. In one of the most recent studies of gender and sexuality in lollardy, Elizabeth Schirmer has employed a theoretically inflected approach to argue that the language about sexuality used in lollard texts implicitly raises marriage above virginity, partly by correlating improper uses of sexuality with improper readings of scripture. It is significant, Schirmer suggests, that the presumed asexuality of medieval clergymen was for some lollards a misappropriation or misuse of authentic masculinity.[93]

---

89 Valuable introductory surveys of the medieval theory and practice of Christian marriage are Christopher N.L. Brooke, *The Medieval Idea of Marriage* (Oxford, 1994); Peter Coleman, *Christian Attitudes to Marriage* (London, 2004); and Conor McCarthy, *Marriage in Medieval England* (Woodbridge, 2004). For the average age of marriage, see Peter Fleming, *Family and Household in Medieval England* (Basingstoke, 2001), 19–23.

90 A valuable study of the development of the sacrament of orders is Aidan Nichols, *Holy Order: The Apostolic Ministry from the New Testament to the Second Vatican Council* (Dublin, 1990).

91 See, for instance, Henry Hargreaves, "Sir John Oldcastle and Wycliffite Views on Clerical Marriage," *Medium Aevum* 42 (1973), 141–46; Dyan Elliott, "Lollardy and the Integrity of Marriage and the Family," in *The Medieval Marriage Scene*, (eds.) Sherry Roush and Cristelle L. Baskins (Tempe, Ariz., 2005), 37–53; and *PR*, 292, 357–58.

92 See discussion in Chapter 2, 54–57 above.

93 Elizabeth Schirmer, "'Trewe Men': Pastoral Masculinity in Lollard Polemic," in *Masculinities and Femininities in the Middle Ages and the Renaissance*, (ed.) Fred Kiefer (Turnhout, 2009), 117–30.

To return to the medieval sources, let us first note that Wyclif broke little new ground in his writings on marriage, which figures only rarely in his voluminous output. It was only late in his career that he set forth his views on marriage systematically. In *Opus evangelicum*, like many other medieval theologians and canonists, he held up the ostensibly chaste marriage of Mary and Joseph as a model, asserting that a marriage in which the partners help each other toward blessedness is preferable to a marriage contracted for the sake of procreation or the release of libido.[94] Nevertheless, Wyclif acknowledged that not all have the capacity for lifelong celibacy. Accordingly, he believed that Christ instituted marriage as a vehicle for what St. Augustine had famously called its three goods: *fides* (the commitment of the partners to one another), *proles* (their offspring), and *sacramentum* (the blessing of marriage by God and the church).[95] All this was orthodox enough, but Wyclif rejected as unscriptural many of the ways in which the medieval church sought to regulate marriage, including the church's emphasis on the verbal, rather than the mental, consent of the partners; the practice of divorce; and the tightening of consanguinity laws.[96] For similar reasons, he neither specifically endorsed nor rejected outright the possibility of clerical marriage, on the one hand writing that enforced celibacy is often the cause of sexual vice and that church history supports the practice of clerical marriage, but on the other hand averring that just because something is possible does not mean that it is appropriate.[97]

Like Wyclif, only a few lollard texts address the sacrament of marriage directly. Where they do, they tend to adopt views of marriage and sexuality more pessimistic than Wyclif's, except with regard to clerical marriage. For instance, the preacher of the *Lollard Sermons* joins Wyclif in arguing that the marriage of Mary and Joseph should be taken as a model. Marriages need not be consummated, and the spiritual marriage of two chaste people is the best of all possible unions.[98] Although sexual acts are not always sinful, they are nevertheless to be avoided. Likewise, the prose text *Of Weddid Men and Wifis*, perhaps the only surviving lollard writing dedicated primarily to marriage and child-rearing, praises virginity more highly than marriage and declares that sexual activity should take place within marriage only to procreate or to keep

---

94   *Opus evangelicum*, 1:169. On the marriage of Mary and Joseph, see Irvin M. Resnick, "Marriage in Medieval Culture: Consent Theory and the Case of Joseph and Mary," *Church History* 69 (2000), 350–71.

95   *Trialogus*, 317.

96   For these and other objections, see *Trialogus*, 322–24; *Opus evangelicum*, 175–77.

97   See *Opus evangelicum*, 40–41; *Trialogus*, 206; *De officio regis*, 29; *De ecclesia*, 365.

98   *Lollard Sermons*, (ed.) Gloria Cigman (EETS O.S. 294, 1989), sermon 5.

oneself or one's spouse from sinning sexually with others.[99] About clerical marriage, the text makes the point that Christ did not prohibit his disciples from marrying or from having sexual intercourse, and in this, it joins a wide range of lollard writings in arguing for the legitimacy, or in some cases even the necessity, of clerical marriage.[100]

A number of heresy trials involved contested statements about marriage and sexuality, with at least four dozen defendants abjuring the proposition that a couple can marry without solemnizing their union before a priest; incidentally, the medieval church did hold such "clandestine" marriages to be valid, if not licit.[101] William Mundy, tried in 1412 in Salisbury diocese, confessed to believing that a married person is equal in status to a priest.[102] Seven defendants in Norwich diocese, inspired perhaps by the preaching of William White, abjured the belief that marriage is permissible for priests and nuns; a number of later suspects did the same.[103] A few outlandish claims about marriage are simply roguish, such as William Colyn's assertion in 1429 that marriage should be abolished and all women held in common.[104]

It is unsurprising that few lollards contested the intrinsic value of marriage, but their equally conventional views on the second sacrament of Christian life, holy orders, may be more difficult to reconcile with the longstanding stereotype of lollards as iconoclastic and anti-authoritarian. Indeed, until the mid-1980s, the dominant historiography of the Middle Ages and Reformation in England took as one of its foundational categories that of "anticlericalism."[105] More recently, however, revisionist scholars have argued that anticlericalism is both anachronistic and too capacious a term to provide a viable explanation for the origins of English Protestantism. They have observed that most of the cases in which medieval people expressed opposition to the clergy had more to

---

99   *Of Weddid Men and Wifis*, in Arnold, 3:188–201.

100 For lollard discussion of clerical marriage, see for instance "Twelve Conclusions of the Lollards," in *Selections*, 25–28; "Of Prelates," in Matthew, 100; and "Of the Leaven of Pharisees," in Matthew, 6. For commentary, see Emma Lipton, *Affections of the Mind: The Politics of Sacramental Marriage in Late Medieval English Literature* (Notre Dame, Ind., 2007), 7–8, 111–16.

101 The majority of these defendants were caught up in the persecutions of Bishop Alnwick in Norwich diocese and of Archbishop Warham in Canterbury diocese; each group of abjurations appears to have been based on a formula. See *Norwich* and *Kent*, passim.

102 Salisbury reg. Hallum, no. 1142.

103 See, e.g., *Norwich*, 73. White's examination appears in FZ, 420–25.

104 *Norwich*, 91.

105 For one representative of this phase of historiography, see, e.g., G.G. Coulton, *Ten Medieval Studies* (Cambridge, 1930).

do with the perceived misbehavior of individual priests than with the prerogatives of the clerical estate as a whole.[106] As I argued in 2010, many late medieval Englishpeople were not so much anticlerical as "hyperclerical," subscribing to traditional theologies of priesthood but desiring the restoration of ideal standards of clerical behavior.[107]

The majority of lollards whose views we can ascertain likewise seem to have been more hyperclerical than anticlerical. Wyclif himself endorsed the sacrament of orders, defining it as the power given by God in order that a clergyman might minister in the church.[108] Like his orthodox contemporaries, he affirmed the notion that in the sacrament of orders a man receives a character that sets him apart from the laity. But Wyclif strongly rejected the idea that it is the ordination rite itself, however faithfully performed, that makes a man a priest. Sacramental grace, according to Wyclif, is not given by the minister but by God, and thus not every humanly ordained priest is in God's eyes a true priest.[109] This view runs contrary to that ascribed to Wyclif by many of his early biographers, including Lechler and Workman, who argued that Wyclif, anticipating Luther, had articulated a doctrine of the universal priesthood of the predestined.[110]

Not unlike Wyclif, a majority of lollard writers affirmed the standard medieval distinction between clerics and laypeople, and many of their arguments against the behavior of corrupt clergymen depended for their logical and rhetorical force on the existence of a distinct clerical estate. Also like Wyclif, they rejected the novelties they believed the institutional church had introduced into the sacrament of orders, such as gaudy ordination rituals. True priests, following in the footsteps of Christ and his apostles, are those who "sheewe to the puple ensaumple of holi lyuynge, and…preche truli the gospel bi werke and word."[111] Later in this chapter, we will see how claims such as these motivated lollard writers to criticize aspects of the governance and financial management of the church.

---

106   Important contributions on this point are those of Christopher Haigh, "Anticlericalism and the English Reformation," repr. in *The English Reformation Revised* (Cambridge, 1987), 56–74; and R.N. Swanson, "Problems of the Priesthood in Pre-Reformation England," *English Historical Review* 105 (1990), 846–69. A response by A.G. Dickens, a proponent of the earlier terminology, is "The Shape of Anticlericalism and the English Reformation," in *Late Monasticism and the Reformation* (London, 1994).
107   Hornbeck, *What Is a Lollard?* 144.
108   *Trialogus*, 295.
109   *Trialogus*, 296; *De ecclesia*, 515.
110   Lechler, 335–37; Workman, 2:13.
111   *Remonstrance against Romish Corruptions in the Church*, (ed.) Josiah Forshall (London, 1851), 4.

It is not until we turn to the records of heresy trials that we can find evidence for the view that orders are altogether superfluous. A few English heresy defendants moved beyond the view that the clergy needs to be purified, arguing instead that all Christians are already priests, or that the sacrament of orders conveys no special character, or both. The claim that "any just man, whatever his learning, is a priest" first enters the extant records in 1389, in the case of eight Leicester townspeople tried by the visiting Archbishop of Canterbury.[112] Similar views were attributed in the early fifteenth century to Wyclif's associate John Purvey, who was said by one of his opponents to have taught that every good Christian is a true priest, ordained by God in order to offer up the body of Christ.[113] Likewise, at least six defendants in the trials conducted by Bishop Alnwick of Norwich articulated the view that all good Christians, including in some cases women, have the capacity to exercise priestly powers; just as with regard to the sacrament of marriage, these defendants' views may have been shaped by the teaching of William White, who at his second trial was accused of teaching "that any faithful person in Jesus Christ is a priest elected for the church of God."[114] Heterodox views on the sacrament of orders appeared in only a few other trials, almost all from the late fifteenth and early sixteenth centuries.

5.2.5 *Extreme Unction*

Earlier in this chapter, I described the wide spectrum of lollard views about salvation and grace. For Wyclif and at least some later lollards, salvation comes about neither as a result of an inscrutable process of divine predestination, nor as a result of receiving the sacraments, but rather from a person's ongoing decision to accept God's grace. It should therefore not be surprising that the last sacrament, extreme unction, administered to Christians at the point of death, does not figure at all prominently in Wyclif's theology or the writings of later lollards. Wyclif dedicated only a few paragraphs to the sacrament of unction in his systematic treatise *Trialogus*, where he argued that the passage in the letter of James on which the institutional church had based its ideas about unction is not weighty enough to justify the inclusion of this ritual among the sacraments. "If this bodily anointing were a sacrament," Wyclif continued, "Christ

---

112 J.H. Dahmus, (ed.), *The Metropolitan Visitations of William Courtenay, Archbishop of Canterbury, 1381–1396* (Urbana, Ill., 1950), 164.

113 *FZ*, 387; see Anne Hudson, "John Purvey: A Reconsideration of the Evidence for His Life and Writings," *Viator* 12 (1981), 355–80, repr. in *Books*, 85–110, at 357–58.

114 See, e.g., the trial of Margery Baxter, in *Norwich*, 42. The quotation from the record of White's trial is at *FZ*, 423.

and his apostles would not have been silent about the need for preaching or performing it."[115] He concluded that it would be against the faith to conclude that salvation was impossible without this sacrament.

If Wyclif had little to say about extreme unction, later lollards were even less interested in the topic. It appears only in passing in their writings, and fewer than twenty-five heresy defendants between the end of the fourteenth century and the beginning of the sixteenth are recorded to have mentioned it.[116] Those who did described unction as an unnecessary ritual; thus Hawisia Mone, tried in Norwich diocese in 1430, abjured the view that "it is but a trufle [i.e., a trifle] to enoynt a seke man with material oyle consecrat be a bisshop, for it sufficeth every man at hys last ende oonly to have mende of God."[117] Three other Norwich defendants were accused of believing that unction is superfluous, as were four defendants in Ely diocese, one each in Winchester and London dioceses, and a group of lollards detained in Scotland in 1494.[118] Unction plays an appreciable role in only one extant set of records, namely, the proceedings undertaken by Archbishop Warham against Kentish lollards in 1511 and 1512; there, eleven defendants all abjured an identical article: "the sacrament of extreme unction is neither useful nor necessary to the salvation of the soul."[119]

5.3 The Church and Mainstream Religious Practice

Just as lollards took different positions on the sacraments, so also they advanced a range of sometimes conflicting proposals for the reform of the church, its structures, and its traditions. As "hyperclericalists," as I have been calling a majority of lollard writers and heresy defendants, most lollards sought the renovation, rather than the outright abolition, of the ecclesiastical structures of their day. And for most lollards, like other reformers throughout the history of Christianity, "renovation" meant a return to the presumed purity of the apostolic era.

---

115 *Trialogus*, 334: "Si enim ista corporalis unctio foret sacramentum...Christi et ejus apostoli ejus promulgationem et executionem debitam non tacerent."
116 For one of the very few mentions of this sacrament in lollard writings, see "The Gret Sentence of Curs," in Arnold, 3:285.
117 *Norwich*, 141.
118 *Norwich*, 33, 147, 153; Ely reg. Gray, fol. 130b; Winchester reg. Courtenay, fol. 26; *A&M*, 980; John Knox, *The Historie of the Reformation of the Church of Scotland* (London, 1644), 2–3.
119 *Kent*, passim.

When lollards thought about the church, many seem to have had in mind something different from and greater than the official ecclesiastical hierarchy. Indeed, definitions of the church offered in lollard texts most commonly resemble that of *The Lanterne of Liȝt*: the church is the congregation of those who will be saved. A communitarian ecclesiology, stressing the spiritual bonds that unite Christ's faithful, in contrast to the emphasis placed on institutional continuity by many of their antagonists, informed in significant ways their attitudes toward such practices and structures as the papacy, the exercise of authority by bishops and other prelates, ecclesiastical finance, and the relationship between church and crown.[120]

Wyclif and later lollards have often been called antipapal, and it is certainly true that many of their writings name the pope and his curia as Antichrist. Nevertheless, just as we have seen that lollard views on the clerical estate and the sacrament of holy orders cannot easily be pigeonholed, neither can lollards' ideas about the papacy. Wyclif's views on the pope changed significantly over the course of his career and in response to the outbreak and development of the western schism, and in his most polemical moments he seems to have dismissed the papacy altogether.[121] His final position, however, seems to have entailed at least three interrelated claims: that the pope cannot be the head of the whole church, since the church has no head apart from Christ; that notwithstanding this, the pope can be the head of what Wyclif called a "particular" church, namely, the church whose seat is at Rome; and that the pope can rightly exercise his jurisdiction only if he governs the church in accordance with the law of Christ, as revealed in scripture. In short, the mature Wyclif argued that only those popes who successfully imitate the role that Peter played in the early church can rightly claim a place of primacy among Christ's people; this place of primacy, moreover, Wyclif preferred to describe in terms of captaincy rather than headship.[122]

---

120 This distinction between "institutional" and "communitarian" ecclesiologies draws on the theoretical framework of Avery Dulles's work *Models of the Church*, exp. edn. (New York, 1987).

121 On Wyclif's views on the schism, see Margaret Harvey, *Solutions to the Schism: A Study of Some English Attitudes, 1378–1409* (St. Ottilien, 1983).

122 For recent discussions of Wyclif's view of the papacy, see Takashi Shogimen, "Wyclif's Ecclesiology and Political Thought," in *Companion*, 199–240; Ian Christopher Levy, "John Wyclif and the Primitive Papacy," *Viator* 38 (2007), 159–89, and Levy, "John Wyclif on Papal Election, Correction, and Deposition," *Mediaeval Studies* 69 (2007), 141–85; Michael Wilks, "The *Apostolicus* and the Bishop of Rome," 2 parts, *Journal of Theological Studies* n.s. 13 (1962), 290–317, and n.s. 14 (1963), 311–54; and Hornbeck, *What Is A Lollard?*, Chapter 6.

Lollard writings about the papacy join Wyclif in urging that the pope should return to a simpler, biblical style of governance. The long vernacular sermon *Of Mynystris in þe Chirche*, for instance, borrows a metaphor from Wyclif in declaring that "Petre was not heed of the chyrche but a capteyn of þe chyrche. And certis werriours wolon scorne þis resoun þat ȝif a man be capteyn he is heed."[123] In addition, the sermon continues, Peter was not the *only* captain of the church; each apostle had authority over the church in his particular region of the world. Other texts likewise seek to place constraints on the exercise of papal authority; thus the *Thirty-Seven Conclusions* declare that the pope is to be obeyed only insofar as he commands things which are lawful and helpful to salvation, while the Middle English translation of the *Rosarium* warns its readers to beware that not every pope is a truly holy man.[124]

Hardly any lollard text can be said with certainty to have repudiated the institution of the papacy altogether, but a number of heresy defendants were accused of having called the pope Antichrist. Among them was the itinerant preacher William Swinderby, whom we met in Chapter 2; he argued that "[g]if Crist then came to saufe men and nohte to slee hem, who that doith the reverse hereoffe is ageyn Crist, and then he ys Anticrist."[125] Thomas Bikenore, tried in Salisbury diocese in 1442, likened each element of the papal court to an aspect of the beast of the biblical apocalypse: "the Pope of Rome ys antecriste and like to the hede of a dragon...Bisshopes and other astatis of the churche ar...like to the body of the seide dragon...Religious men as monkys chanons freris and suche other be the tayle of that dragon."[126] For most such defendants, the records preserve only their most extreme statements, often without describing the context within which those statements were made. In other cases, the records preserve the qualifications that defendants hedged around their views of the papacy; for instance, six of the defendants tried before Bishop Alnwick in Norwich diocese said that the pope can enjoy the powers that Peter received from Christ, but only if he follows Peter's example.[127]

The logic that many lollards applied to the papacy—namely, that the pope is capable of exercising authority only if he does so in accordance with Christ's law—is of a piece with many of the other elements of lollard theology we have been examining. It is not a bishop's hands but God's election that ordains a

---

123 *EWS*, 2:MC/654–58.
124 *Remonstrance against Romish Corruption*, 47; Christina von Nolcken, (ed.), *The Middle English Translation of the Rosarium Theologie* (Heidelberg, 1979), 79.
125 Hereford reg. Trefnant, 269.
126 Salisbury reg. Aiscough, fol. 53r.
127 *Norwich*, 108, 116, 122, 127, 135, 170.

man, not a papal document but God's law that invalidates a marriage, not an ecclesiastical decree but divine censure that renders someone excommunicate.[128] At the root of these and other issues was a profound concern on many lollards' part for the proper exercise of authority in the church. Who rightly wields authority, in what ways, and under what conditions were questions that Wyclif addressed in his complex theories of *dominium*, as we observed in Chapter 2. Later lollards likewise engaged with questions about ecclesiastical authority in their own writings.

The vernacular *Tractatus de oblacione iugis sacrificii*, for instance, is on its face a tract about the eucharist. Its author does indeed investigate the subtleties of eucharistic theology, framing his own interpretations of the words of consecration and condemning the belief, which he ascribes to the friars, that the sacrament consists of "accidents without a subject."[129] Nonetheless, the tract is equally, if not more, about authority in the church. It does not mention the eucharist in its first two hundred lines, which are instead given over to a wholesale condemnation of the presumptuousness, hypocrisy, and desire to win the obedience of all people that the author attributes to Antichrist. Only after treating such topics as the endowment of the clergy does the author identify as one of Antichrist's greatest transgressions the perversion of authentic eucharistic theology. The tract's initial preoccupation is thus not with theological minutiae concerning the eucharist but rather with the right exercise of ecclesiastical authority. Similar claims might be made about other lollard texts as well, especially *The Testimony of William Thorpe, The Lanterne of Liȝt*, and the Upland series.[130]

Questions about authority also shaped lollard discussions of the church's financial arrangements and religious orders. Joining a long line of medieval reformers, Wyclif and many later lollards traced much of the church's decadence back to the Donation of Constantine, the purported fourth-century document in which the emperor granted to the papacy universal jurisdiction over the western Roman empire.[131] Wyclif did not live to see the Donation proved a forgery by Lorenzo Valla in 1440, but his discontent with it was

---

128 On early Wycliffite views of excommunication, see Ian Forrest, "William Swinderby and the Wycliffite Attitude to Excommunication," *Journal of Ecclesiastical History* 60 (2009), 246–69.

129 *Tractatus de oblacione iugis sacrificii*, lines 402–03.

130 On Thorpe's *Testimony*, see especially Anne Hudson, "William Thorpe and the Question of Authority," in *Christian Authority: Essays in Honour of Henry Chadwick*, (ed.) G.R. Evans (Oxford, 1988), 127–37.

131 As did many of their contemporaries, including the poet William Langland. See David Aers, "Langland on the Church and the End of the Cardinal Virtues," *Journal of Medieval and Early Modern Studies* 42 (2012), 59–81, at 71–72.

foundational to his criticisms of ecclesiastical endowments. It is worth emphasizing that amid his often strident criticisms, Wyclif did allow that some financial privileges can benefit the church: "To put it briefly, the administration of temporal goods is not a privilege for the clergy, except insofar as it stimulates [them] to follow Christ in his behavior and to seek out the privilege of his love."[132] But in Wyclif's view, the medieval church far overstepped its bounds in its entanglements with material goods. He proposed that clergymen should seek temporary, rather than perpetual, alms; that lords should step in to take endowements away from those priests who abuse their privileges; and that laypeople should withhold their tithes from clerics who fail to perform their duties.[133] Thus, on Wyclif's account, all clerics should be content to live by whatever tithes and alms that they receive as free gifts. If these prove insufficient, then they should follow the example of the apostle Paul, who worked as a tentmaker, by taking on manual labor, teaching, or other paid work.[134]

Later lollards also criticized the Donation of Constantine and sought to rein in what they perceived to be clerics' abuse of their financial privileges. In their sermons and tracts, many urged that clergymen not be permitted to exercise worldly lordship nor to take positions of secular authority. Lollard writers linked the argument that churchmen are distracted from their spiritual duties by their involvement in temporal politics with their concerns about the church's excessive wealth. The remedies that they proposed included the withdrawal of tithes from sinful clergymen. William Thorpe justified this proposal theologically by pointing out that although tithes may have been commanded in the Old Testament, neither Christ nor his apostles took tithes or commanded that they should be paid. Instead, "Crist tauȝte þe peple to do almes, þat is werkis of mercy, to pore nedi men of þe surpluys of her temperal goodis."[135] Other lollard texts also argued that tithes should only be paid to clergymen who properly perform the duties of their office. The English tract *De Officio Pastorali*, for instance, argues that to give money to evil churchmen is to contribute to the devil's war against Christ; the tract's author also attempts to hoist the clergy by its own petard by arguing that canon law already requires laypeople to avoid the services of priests who are known to keep concubines.[136]

---

132   *De ecclesia*, 190–91: "Et breviter ministracio temporalium non est clero in privilegium, nisi de quanto promovet ad sequentum Christum in moribus et inpetrandum privilegium amoris sui."
133   *De ecclesia*, 274, 329; *De veritate sacrae scripturae*, 3:3.
134   *Dialogus*, 51.
135   *Thorpe*, 67–68.
136   *De Officio Pastorali*, in Matthew, 405–57, at 418.

Most lollards were content to advocate the removal of tithes and temporal goods from corrupt clergymen, but others took the more radical step of claiming that ecclesiastical endowments are inherently sinful.[137] Most famously, the "Lollard Disendowment Bill," supposedly presented to Parliament in either 1407 or 1410, calculates in detail the income the king would gain if the temporalities of bishops, abbots, priors, and other churchmen were confiscated; it puts the total at £143,734 10s. 4d., a massive sum in the late fourteenth century.[138] Less ambitious proposals can be found in the tract "Of Poor Preaching Priests," which suggests that religious endowments should be spent on the "defence of þe rewme, and releuynge of þe pore comouns," as well as in one of Nicholas Hereford's sermons, where he argued that seizing the possessions of the religious orders would enable the king not to have to tax the poor.[139]

How did lollards propose to support the clergy once it had been disendowed? The answer is unclear, since most lollard writers did not propose an alternative model for financing a reformed clerical estate. Some, like the author of the *Tractatus de oblacione*, urged churchmen to adopt the model of Christ's apostles, who worked for their living with their hands; others expressed confidence that clergymen who fulfill the responsibilities of their office will receive sufficient alms from their parishioners to sustain a modest lifestyle.

All these criticisms—that the church had departed from the gospel, that churchmen had become too comfortable with temporal wealth and especially with landed endowments, that members of the clergy were not willing to work for their own sustenance—were also part of the vitriolic attacks that Wyclif and later lollards launched against the religious orders. In doing so, they were participating in a tradition of antifraternal writing that can be traced on the continent back to the thirteenth century and that emerged in England in the 1350s, not more than two decades before Wyclif's rise to notoriety.[140] Many of the complaints that lollards raised against the friars, whom they styled with the disparaging biblical acronym CAIM (for Carmelites, Augustinians, Iacobites or Dominicans, and Minorites or Franciscans), appeared as well in other, non-lollard writings such as William Langland's *Piers Plowman*.[141] The relationship

---

137 See, for instance, *Church Temporalities*, in Arnold, 3:213–18; "Dialogue between a Knight and a Clerk," in *Selections*, 132–33.
138 *Selections*, 137.
139 *Of Poor Preaching Priests*, in Matthew, 275–80, at 279; Simon Forde, "Nicholas Hereford's Ascension Day Sermon, 1382," *Mediaeval Studies* 51 (1989), 205–41, at 240.
140 Penn R. Szittya, *The Antifraternal Tradition in Medieval Literature* (Princeton, N.J., 1986).
141 For the acronym, see Margaret Aston, "'Caim's Castles': Poverty, Politics, and Disendowment," in *Church, Politics, and Patronage in the Fifteenth Century*, (ed.) B. Dobson (New York, 1984), 45–81, repr. in Aston, *Faith and Fire*, 95–132. The relationship between Langland and

between followers of Wyclif and the friars appears to have disintegrated over time: while it is possible that some early Wycliffite texts were copied at the Franciscan convent in Oxford, Wyclif's late writings refer to the "private religions" in the most unflattering of terms, and many surviving lollard texts pull no punches in their criticism of friars, monks, and secular canons.[142] Lollard writers charge that Christ never established religious orders and that their vows are against Christ's law, that friars should not have university degrees, that God made marriage but not religious orders, that friars are contemporary Pharisees, and that many friars have abandoned the mission of preaching that justified the founding of their orders.[143] As with lollard views on the papacy, these authors appear divided as to whether the religious orders were once good and fell into sin over time or whether the concept of "private religions" is intrinsically contrary to the gospel.[144] Either way, there is near-consensus among extant lollard texts that the religious are chiefly responsible for the perversion of the gospel in the present day.

5.3.1 Devotions and Other Religious Practices

For many lollards, critiques of the practices that characterized late medieval Christianity went hand-in-hand with critiques of mainstream theology. Among the traditions that lollard texts and heresy suspects objected to were fasts and feast days, tithing, preaching that was not grounded in the text of the Bible, oath-taking, and prayers to the saints.[145] Especially prominent sites of contestation,

---

lollardy has a long and contested history: among other studies see Pamela Gradon, "Langland and the Ideology of Dissent," *Proceedings of the British Academy* 66 (1980), 179–205; David Lawton, "Lollardy and the *Piers Plowman* Tradition," *Modern Language Review* 76 (1981), 780–93; and J. Patrick Hornbeck II, "Barn of Unity or the Devil's Church? Salvation and Ecclesiology in Langland and the Wycliffites," in Seeta Chaganti, (ed.), *Medieval Poetics and Social Practice: Reflections on Penn Szittya's Work* (Bronx, 2012), 33–52.

142 On the copying of Wycliffite texts at Greyfriars, Oxford, see Anne Hudson, "Five Problems in Wycliffite Texts and a Suggestion," *Medium Aevum* 80 (2011), 301–24 at 312.

143 For these criticisms, see J.H. Todd, (ed.), *Apology for Lollard Doctrines* Camden Society (London, 1842), 100; the long sermon "The Church and Her Members" in *EWS*; *De Officio Pastorali*, 428, 447; *Lanterne*, Chapter 6; *Of Weddid Men and Wifis*, 189; *Tractatus de Pseudo-Freris*, in Matthew, 294–324; and *Fifty Heresies and Errors of Friars*, in Arnold, 3:367–401.

144 For instance, "The Church and Her Members" holds that the original members of religious orders were praiseworthy, but that their ideals have since been corrupted, whereas *De Officio Pastorali* claims that religious orders are altogether against the law of Christ.

145 Examples of these and other objections are too numerous to list here, but see, for instance, the cases of John Belgrave (fasting and tithing; Lincoln Diocesan Records Vj/0, fol. 10); Robert Spycer (preaching; Lincoln reg. Chedworth, fol. 61v); Richard Fleccher

throughout the period from Wyclif's death until the Henrician Reformation, were the practices of undertaking pilgrimages to holy sites and of showing reverence to religious images, whether of the Trinity, Christ, Mary, or other saints.

There is not space here to address each of these topics in detail, but a short overview of lollard views on the adoration of images may provide some insight into the ways in which lollards constructed their arguments about traditional devotional practices. Indeed, for several decades, ideas about images have been "regarded as one of the most consistent features of the Lollard heresy...a criterion for distinguishing its adherents at the beginning of the movement and its end." Margaret Aston, whose work on iconoclasm in late medieval England has provided a model for many later scholars, proposed in 1984 that views on images both served as a litmus-test for lollardy in the late Middle Ages, and in the early modern period provided evangelicals with an important reason to describe lollardy as the forerunner of their religious movement.[146]

As with virtually every topic this chapter has considered, lollard views on images were by no means uniform. On Aston's account, though Wyclif "did not deny the value and legitimacy of images" and in fact endorsed the traditional medieval view of them as books for laypeople, he also worried that the uneducated might mistake images for the holy people they signified.[147] In one of his sermons, Wyclif linked this concern with his objection to popular eucharistic devotions: he charged that many "stupid people" violate the first commandment by adoring both images and the consecrated host, and for him these two transgressions against the commandment are often entangled with one another.[148] Some later lollards, however, moved beyond Wyclif's relatively moderate position to call for the total elimination of images, arguing that to use images as aids in prayer entails too great a risk that reverence will be rendered to "dead" objects made of wood and stone, rather than to human persons made in the image of God.[149] A typical article was that abjured by thirty-seven

(oath-taking; *Norwich*, 84–89); and Isabel Dort (prayers to saints, Salisbury reg. Langton, 82–3, nos. 503–4).

146 Margaret Aston, *England's Iconoclasts: Volume I: Laws against Images* (Oxford, 1998); and "Lollards and Images," in *Lollards and Reformers*, 135–92, quote at 136. In many ways similar to Aston's essay, but far less influential among scholars, is W.R. Jones, "Lollards and Images: The Defense of Religious Art in Later Medieval England," *Journal of the History of Ideas* 34 (1973), 27–50.

147 On the trope of images as books for the laity, see Ann Eljenholm Nichols, "Books-for-Laymen: The Demise of a Commonplace," *Church History* 56 (1987), 457–73.

148 *Sermones*, 1:90.

149 Kathleen Kamerick, *Popular Piety and Art in the Late Middle Ages: Image Worship and Idolatry in England, 1350–1500* (London, 2002), 15.

of the defendants tried by Archbishop William Warham in Canterbury diocese in 1511 and 1512: "that images of the holy cross and crucifix and the blessed virgin Mary and other saints are in no way to be venerated, and those who venerate such images commit idolatry."[150] Other lollards objected only to the employment of especially elaborate images, just as they objected to the use of ornate reliquaries rather than to the retention and veneration of relics more generally.[151] In this vein, the author of the *Lanterne of Liȝt* wrote:

> þe peyntour makiþ an ymage forgid wiþ diuerse colours, til it seme in foolis iȝen as a lyueli creature. þis is sett in þe chirche, in a solempne place, fast bounden wiþ boondis for it schulde not falle. Prestis of þe temple bigilen þe peple wiþ þe foule synne of Balaam in her open preching.... [W]hi gedre ȝe prestos richesses bi ȝoure peyntid ymages to make ȝoure silf worldly riche in spoiling of þe peple?[152]

While some heresy suspects urged the wholesale destruction of images, in only a few cases is there evidence that they put their beliefs into practice.[153]

The survey of lollard views on images that Aston published in 1984 remains influential, but in a recent study, Shannon Gayk has proposed a different reading of the evidence.[154] Rather than always preferring written texts to images, Gayk has argued, some lollards suggested that discerning readers of texts could acquire the skill of distinguishing true images from false ones. Some lollard writings, such as the cycle of *Lollard Sermons*, point for Gayk to the existence of a "distinctive, morally inflected Lollard iconography, an appropriation of visual mode and imagery...a medium for the critique of devotional images."[155]

---

150 *Kent*, passim.
151 On Wycliffite views of relics and reliquaries, see the important argument of Robyn Malo, "Behaving Paradoxically? Wycliffites, Shrines, and Relics," in *Wycliffite Controversies*, 199–210.
152 *Lanterne*, 84/28–85/4, quoted in Aston, "Lollards and Images," 151.
153 Of the few medieval documents those that charge lollards with actually destroying images, Henry Knighton's tale of two lollards who chopped up and burned an image of St. Katherine in order to add fuel to their cooking fire is surely the best known. For discussion, see Aston, "Lollards and Images," 167–74; Sarah Stanbury, "The Vivacity of Images: St. Katherine, Knighton's Lollards, and the Breaking of Idols," in *Images, Idolatry, and Iconoclasm in Medieval England: Textuality and the Visible Image*, (eds.) Jeremy Dimmick, James Simpson, and Nicole Zeeman (Oxford, 2002), 131–50.
154 For evidence of Aston's ongoing influence, cf. Kamerick, *Popular Piety*, 22–42.
155 Shannon Gayk, *Image, Text, and Religious Reform in Fifteenth-Century England* (Cambridge, 2010), 15–44, quote at 17.

On her revisionist account, it is overly simplistic to perceive lollards as merely opposed to images, without considering which images lollards rejected and which they embraced; some even went so far as to include in their writings detailed descriptions (*ekphrasis*) of devotional images, buildings, and other religious objects.[156] Clearly, as with regard to their opinions on other devotions, lollards' views of and practices concerning the adoration of images await further study.[157]

5.4 Conclusions

This chapter's investigations into the beliefs that lollards held on a variety of theological issues reveal that while they sometimes articulated an intellectual and theological consensus that can be traced back to John Wyclif's ideas, lollards just as often differed sharply with Wyclif and one another. Contrary to older ideas about the development of lollard beliefs, dissenting views did not simply migrate from the academic to the popular context, becoming more simplified and less sophisticated along the way. Nor did they remain constant, as Knighton, Foxe, and others proposed.

Do any themes, however, emerge from the portrait of lollard beliefs that I have been sketching in this chapter? Some pages ago, I criticized those scholarly approaches that have sought to view lollard theological positions through the prism of a single, all-important doctrine; likewise I also cautioned against the assembly of lists of propositions thought to characterize the essence of lollardy. Those caveats notwithstanding, there are a few characteristics that seem to mark the beliefs that a majority of lollards seems to have held on a majority of contested theological topics. In *What Is a Lollard?*, I listed eight "attributes" that, when viewed not as essential tenets but rather as the most common methodological moves of lollard theology, frequently characterize lollard writings and heresy suspects: (1) locating theological authority not in institutional structures but rather in scripture rightly interpreted; (2) avoiding the improper entanglement of what we might call the "spiritual" and the "secular"; (3) expressing concern about unscriptural ecclesiastical regulations; (4) using apocalyptic and, in some cases, predestinarian imagery to bifurcate

---

156 On this point, see also Bruce Holsinger, "Lollard Ekphrasis: Situated Aesthetics and Literary History," *Journal of Medieval and Early Modern Studies* 35 (2005), 67–90.

157 Most recently, see James Simpson, "Orthodoxy's Image Trouble: Images in and after Arundel's Constitutions," in *After Arundel: Religious Writing in Fifteenth-Century England*, (eds.) Vincent Gillespie and Kantik Ghosh (Turnhout, 2011), 91–113.

the world into those with them and those against them; (5) rejecting the doctrine of transubstantiation; (6) employing and exploring the theological resources of the English language; (7) knowing and collaborating with other lollards; and (8) being excluded from full membership in the institutional church.[158] A ninth might be added, namely, opposition to monks and friars, the "private religious" so often condemned in lollard writings.[159] These attributes are neither distinctive nor exclusive markers of lollardy, and it should not be the case that an individual must be found to demonstrate a certain number of them in order to rightly be considered a lollard. They do, however, reflect in broad terms the theological principles that many lollards brought to a variety of issues.

Lollards' beliefs varied substantially across time, geography, and educational background. Several patterns of variation appear in the sources cited in this chapter. First, there is variation over time: for instance, predestinarian beliefs, which were more common among Wyclif's early followers, appeared less and less frequently as the decades went by. It may not have been that lollards made conscious decisions to abandon doctrines of predestination, but rather that a decline in the number of lollard evangelists who preached predestination and the cumulative background influence of the largely works-oriented culture of traditional medieval religion together rendered predestinarianism less attractive. Second, there is variation over space: to take one example, we have observed that especially in the late fifteenth and early sixteenth centuries, specific sets of views on the eucharist were concentrated in particular places, with inquisitors in Salisbury, Winchester, and Coventry and Lichfield dioceses encountering far more proponents of commemorative or figurative theologies of the sacrament than their counterparts elsewhere. This may have had to do with the circulation of particular preachers and texts, especially *Wycklyffes Wycket*, among members of those communities. Finally, there is variation by learning: defendants with formal theological training often put that knowledge to work in their preaching, writing, and testimony. The rhetorical moves that William Thorpe made in discussing the doctrine of transubstantiation as well as those of John Purvey on the adoration of angels versus predestinate men, to take but two examples, reveal levels of theological sophistication that many non-academic defendants were unable to match.

The history of lollard beliefs is one of variation and flux rather than consistency and continuity. Sometimes variations occurred along broadly identifiable lines, as in the instances just rehearsed, but in other cases they were highly

---

158   Hornbeck, *What Is a Lollard?* conclusion.
159   I am indebted for this point to the anonymous reader for the press.

random. It is therefore largely impossible, in the absence of specific evidence, to predict what any lollard writer or heresy defendant may have thought about a given theological issue. That fact did not stop medieval church authorities, nor has it stopped some later scholars, from pigeonholing lollards and their beliefs. Scholarly investigations into the beliefs that lollards held and for which they occasionally died are ongoing, but we must turn our attention now to those who censured such beliefs. The next two chapters will profile the most prominent opponents of lollardy and chronicle the trials of suspected lollards.

CHAPTER 6

Their Opponents

Mishtooni Bose

In the sequence of scholastic texts produced by William Woodford, O.F.M., in the 1380s and 1390s, Wyclif was the chief, but not quite the sole, target: the colophon of one of Woodford's later works describes it as *Responsiones contra Wiclevum et Lollardos* (1395), acknowledging that Wyclif had followers, and that the *responsiones* are directed at one such *discipulus*. However, in this particular case, it was clear that "[i]n replying to the disciple Woodford was also answering the master."[1] By the time that the extensive *Doctrinale* was produced by Thomas Netter, O. Carm., in the 1420s, the target had broadened well beyond Wyclif to include those whom Netter called the *Wiclevistae*, and whose reputed machinations are vividly evoked throughout the work, as in his warning to the faithful ("Christifideles") to resist the Wycliffites' inducements to read their books, in which a faithful person might, like a hapless bird, be caught in a subtle net ("quando provocant vos ad legendum suos libros, in quibus capiendi estis sicut in impercepto rete avis incauta").[2]

Netter could segue fluently between preoccupation with Wyclif and a broader perspective that kept in view the image of his followers as numerous and insidious. But in the *Liber Veritatum*, compiled during the first half of the fifteenth century by the Oxford theologian Thomas Gascoigne, a different, and provocative, perspective emerges. Gascoigne castigates a previous archbishop of Canterbury, Thomas Arundel, for the first of his *Provincial Constitutions* (1407–09), which restricted the office of preaching to those who had obtained a licence from a bishop. After having constricted the word of God in this way— at least in Gascoigne's view—the archbishop suffered a horribly appropriate form of retribution, developing an obstruction in the throat that prevented him from speaking and eating, leading to his death in 1414. Gascoigne goes on to claim that men believed that God had bound up Arundel's tongue because "he had bound up the tongues of practically all preachers on account of a few heretics" ("ligavit linguas quasi omnium praedicatorum propter paucos haereticos").[3]

---

1 Eric Doyle, O.F.M., "William Woodford, O.F.M. (c. 1330–c.1400): His Life and Works Together With a Study and Edition of His 'Responsiones Contra Wiclevum et Lollardos,'" *Franciscan Studies* 43 (1983), 17–187 (p. 63).
2 Netter, *Doctrinale*, I: 19B.
3 *Loci e Libro Veritatum*, (ed.) James E. Thorold Rogers (Oxford, 1881), 35.

Gascoigne's distinction between what he regarded as the "handful" of heretics ("pauci haeretici") that were Arundel's immediate target and the much larger number of blameless preachers ("quasi omnes praedicatores") who suffered under what he regarded as crude and disproportionate legislation deserves prominence in an account of the opponents of lollardy, because it is an uncompromising expression of a late-medieval mentality that the burgeoning of "lollard studies" is in danger of minimizing: that is (and as I have expressed it elsewhere), for some thinkers during the decades of the Wycliffite controversies, religious reform may have been the big picture, and heresy the detail.[4] Particularly in as complex a historiographical narrative as that of opposition to lollardy must be, Gascoigne's *Liber* is a powerful and provocative witness to the variety of religious attitudes that persisted in England during the early decades of the fifteenth century. His prejudices make the *Liber Veritatum* a book of essentially subjective truths; in its fixation on the shortcomings of bishops, for example, it is tonally very distant from the kind of anti-heretical stance adopted by Netter, whom Gascoigne nevertheless greatly respected. But the example of Gascoigne's complex, peculiar set of allegiances and grievances warns us against seeing opposition to lollardy as an homogeneous, univocal phenomenon. The *Liber* valuably documents the fact that it remained possible for one English theologian vehemently to criticize the institutional church while leaving his reader in no doubt about his acceptance of its fundamental authority, thereby guaranteeing his freedom from any taint of heresy. Gascoigne is a witness, as Thomas Brinton, O.S.B., had been in an earlier generation, to the extent to which the noisome phenomenon of lollardy risked diverting attention from the ideas of those sympathetic to ecclesiastical reform but prepared to negotiate from within.[5]

I have previously written an account of Wyclif's opponents, considering in particular elements of contact and distance between discursive and legislative responses to the challenges posed by his ideas; some of the literary strategies used by the avowedly orthodox; the extent to which some of Wyclif's opponents fashioned themselves as public intellectuals and the overlapping of the intramural and extramural spheres in which the Wycliffite controversies played out; and the important differences between heresy and reformist thought during a period coterminous with the Great Schism.[6] I draw on some

---

4 "Intellectual Life in Fifteenth-Century England," *New Medieval Literatures* 12 (2010), 333–70 (p. 351).
5 *The Sermons of Thomas Brinton, Bishop of Rochester, 1373–1389*, (ed.) M.A. Devlin, 2 vols., Camden Society 3rd ser. 85–86 (1954).
6 "The Opponents of John Wyclif," in *A Companion to John Wyclif. Late Medieval Theologian*, (ed.) Ian Christopher Levy (Leiden, 2006), 407–55.

of that material here, particularly in a condensed version of the chronological narrative of opposition to lollardy, in an attempt to help readers new to this material to begin to find their way through this complex historiographical terrain. I do not address elements of the opposition to lollardy, such as heresy trials, that are discussed elsewhere in this volume. Likewise, I omit consideration of the debates that Wyclif had with Ralph Strode and John Kynyngham earlier in the 1370s: significant as they undoubtedly are for medieval intellectual history, they are not as central to the present volume's concerns as is the 1377 condemnation by Pope Gregory XI, which could be said to have inaugurated the complex history of opposition to lollardy.[7] Instead, having outlined the chronology of this opposition, I reflect on the ways in which it reflected, and sometimes became caught up in, broader intellectual and institutional currents. It has been claimed that, challenging as the emergence of Wyclif was in late-medieval England, the fear of dissidence did not coalesce around one individual, but rather that "[he] was followed by a generation of unrestrained preachers and publicists urging every point of view."[8] The picture of discursive energy and diversity evoked the phrase "every point of view" is a vivid and apt context for consideration of the different forms taken by opposition to lollardy from the 1380s to the 1450s. While not seeking to minimize awareness of the constraints and challenges to intellectual debate that anti-heretical legislation and censure sought to impose, the present account allows for the emergence of a mixed picture in which profound and sustained challenges to scholastic liberties were balanced by individual acts of discursive resourcefulness and imagination. It thereby corroborates the resistance to a grand narrative articulated at the beginning of this volume, maintaining that what is true of the history of lollardy in that respect is equally true of the history of opposition to it.

6.1 Chronology[9]

1377: Gregory XI takes issue with Wyclif's ideas about dominion, as expressed in the treatise *De civili dominio*. Wyclif incorporated in this text responses to two of his opponents: the Cistercian Henry Crump (who was later accused of sympathizing with Wyclif's views) and arguably Wyclif's most prominent and

---

7 For discussion of the debate with Kynyngham, see my "The Opponents of John Wyclif," 429–36.
8 Jeremy Catto, "The King's Government and the Fall of Pecock, 1457–58," in *Rulers and Ruled in Late Medieval England. Essays Presented to Gerald Harriss*, (eds.) R.E. Archer and Simon Walker (London, 1995), 201–22 (p. 201).
9 See also "The Opponents of John Wyclif," 418–29.

intellectually distinguished opponent, the Franciscan William Woodford. The second book was written in response to Crump, and two chapters of the third book were written in response to the first thirty arguments of Woodford's *De dominio civili clericorum*.

Adam Easton, O.S.B. writes against Wyclif in the *Defensorium ecclesiasticae potestatis*.

c. 1377–78: Wyclif's response to William Binham, O.S.B., regarding the right of the clergy to exercise civil dominion.

c. 1378: Nicholas Radcliff, O.S.B., writes six Latin dialogues, still unedited, in the course of which, and most explicitly in the sixth dialogue, Wyclif's ideas are interrogated. The dialogues focus chiefly on the subject of dominion, with the sixth dialogue laying out ten arguments *contra* Wyclif, drawing on a variety of perspectives in order to defend the right of the clergy to exercise civil dominion. The dialogues have been preserved in London, British Library, MS Royal 6.D.X., which also contains several other works by Radcliff on controversial topics such as the Eucharist and images.

1380–81: William Barton, chancellor of Oxford, convenes a group of theologians and canon lawyers to condemn two propositions based on Wyclif's arguments concerning the Eucharist, without naming Wyclif himself. Significantly for the history of opposition to lollardy, rather than simply to Wyclif, Barton condemns a group of "malign spirits" ("maligni spiritus") who teach publicly, not only within but also outside the schools ("tam in ista universitate, quam extra, publice dogmatizant"). Barton's charges are, first, that the substance of the bread and wine remain after consecration; and second, that Christ is only present figuratively in the sacrament.[10] The text known as Wyclif's *De eucharistia minor confessio* is provoked by this condemnation, and gives rise in turn to two responses: the *Confessio* by John Tyssyngton, O.F.M., and the *Absolutio* by Thomas Winterton, O.E.S.A., both of which closely scrutinize Wyclif's interpretation of the Latin formulae associated with transubstantiation.[11]

1382: opposition to Wyclif comes to a head at the Canterbury session of the Blackfriars Council, resulting in the condemnation of ten heresies and fourteen errors. Again, Wyclif is not named; instead, Courtenay directs his opprobrium at a vividly-evoked group of unlicensed preachers, spreading heresies through his province.[12] Of the ten heresies, three concern the Eucharist: first, that the substance of bread and wine remain after the words of consecration

---

10   *FZ*, 110.

11   *FZ*, 133–80 and 181–238 respectively.

12   *FZ*, 275. For a provocative reading of the possible motives behind Courtenay's vivid evocation of a group of dissident preachers, see Andrew Cole, *Literature and Heresy in the Age of Chaucer* (Cambridge, 2008), 1–22.

had been uttered; secondly, that an accident cannot remain without a subject after consecration; and thirdly, that Christ is not corporeally present in the sacrament. The fourth heresy asserts that sacraments can be vitiated if performed by a priest in a state of mortal sin. The fifth asserts that oral confession is superfluous in the case of a truly contrite person. The sixth asserts that the scriptures have not established that Christ had instituted the Mass. The seventh asserts that God should obey the devil. The eighth asserts that a pope in a state of mortal sin has no power over the faithful. The ninth asserts that after the time of Urban the sixth, churches should be independent of papal power. The tenth asserts that churchmen should not have temporal possessions. The fourteen errors consist of arguments about excommunication, unlicensed preaching, mortal sin, church property, special prayers and the religious orders. Wyclif's opponents on this occasion include William Barton and Henry Crump, the Benedictines John Wells and Nicholas Radcliff and the Carmelite Peter Stokes.

5 June (Corpus Christi): Robert Rygge, Chancellor of the University of Oxford, resists Peter Stokes' attempts to have the Blackfriars condemnation of Wyclif's views pronounced before Philip Repingdon, one of Wyclif's supporters at this time, preached.

William Courtenay, archbishop of Canterbury, calls into question the immunity of the University of Oxford from ecclesiastical jurisdiction over the question of the public condemnation of Wyclif's views.

c. 1380–84: exchange between Wyclif and the Cistercian, William Rymington: Rymington, *Quadraginta quinque Conclusiones;* Wyclif, *Responsiones*; Rymington, *Dialogus inter catholicam veritatem et haereticam pravitatem.*

1383: William Woodford writes anti-Wycliffite treatise on the Eucharist, the *Septuaginta duae quaestiones de sacramento altaris.*

1384: death of Wyclif.

1389–90: Woodford writes *Quatuor determinationes in materia de religione* against Wyclif.

1390–92: disputation of the anti-Wycliffite Richard Maidstone, O.Carm., against John Ashwardby.

1395: Woodford's anti-Wycliffite *Responsiones*; Roger Dymoke, O.P., responds to the posting of the lollard *Twelve Conclusions* in his *Liber contra xii errores et hereses Lollardorum.*

1397: At the instigation of certain members of the University of Oxford, a Synod in London condemns eighteen erroneous propositions derived from Wyclif's *Trialogus* and *Supplementum Trialogi.*[13] Archbishop Thomas Arundel

---

13   Doyle, "Responsiones," 50.

commissions Woodford to produce a refutation of the same views in *De causis condempnationis articulorum 18 damnatorum Joannis Wyclif*. The list of articles condemned comprises three items on the Eucharist; several on some of the other sacraments (baptism, confirmation, extreme unction); articles on marriage and divorce; one concerning the sufficiency of the orders of priests and deacons; several condemning temporal possessions for the clergy; the assertion that everything that happens, happens of necessity; and one on the necessity for the Pope and his cardinals to base their pronouncements on the words of scripture.[14]

Late 1390s: writings by John Deveros, Thomas Palmer, O.P., and Robert Alyngton, focusing on the defence of pilgrimages and the veneration of images.

1401: statute *Contra Lollardos*, authorizing the burning of those convicted of heresy in cases where the individual does not recant, or is convicted a second time even if recanting; Richard Ullerston writes *Defensorium dotacionis ecclesie*, a relatively late contribution to the arguments against Wyclif's views concerning dominion.

1407–09: Thomas Arundel's *Provincial Constitutions*.

By 1410: the Carthusian Nicholas Love's translation, *The Mirror of the Blessed Life of Jesus Christ* and his *Treatise on the Sacrament*.

1410–11: eighteen conclusions and 267 propositions derived from Wyclif's works drawn up and condemned in Oxford, then forwarded to Arundel, who also condemned them before forwarding them to John XXIII.[15]

1411: Archbishop Arundel's visitation of the University of Oxford to investigate cases of heresy.[16]

1413: Sir John Oldcastle tried for heresy and imprisoned, subsequently escaping from the Tower of London.

1414: death of Thomas Arundel. Henry Chichele becomes archbishop of Canterbury. Council of Constance begins. The Oldcastle revolt.

1415: articles derived from Wyclif's works condemned at the Council of Constance.

Oldcastle rising.

1417: Oldcastle recaptured and executed for heresy.

---

14   *Fasciculus rerum expetendarum ac fugiendarum*, (ed.) Edward Brown, vol. 1 (London, 1737), 191–265 (p. 191).
15   *Snappe's Formulary And Other Records*, (ed.) H.E. Salter (Oxford, 1924), 90–135; Anne Hudson, "Notes of an Early Fifteenth-Century Research Assistant, and the Emergence of the 267 Articles against Wyclif," *English Historical Review* 118 (2003), 685–97.
16   *Snappe's Formulary*, 156–75; Jeremy Catto, "Wyclif and Wycliffism," in *The History of the University of Oxford*, vol. 2, (eds.) J.I. Catto and R. Evans (Oxford, 1992), 175–261 (pp. 248–52).

1418: Conclusion of the Council of Constance. Election of Martin V.

1420s: Thomas Netter, O.Carm., produces his comprehensive treatise, the *Doctrinale antiquitatum fidei ecclesiae*, dedicated to Pope Martin V and secondarily addressed to his fellow Carmelites. Woodford was the most prominent and intellectually distinguished Ricardian anti-Wycliffite theologian; Netter assumed this role under the Lancastrian regime.

1428: Wyclif's body belatedly exhumed and burned in line with a decree made at Constance; ashes discarded in the River Swift.

1436: revision of the first part of the *Boke* of Margery Kempe, detailing her travels through England in the 1410s and her tense but ultimately sympathetic encounters with a diverse group of prominent English clergymen, including Thomas Arundel, Philip Repingdon and Henry Bowet, who had, earlier in their respective careers, occupied very different points on a notional spectrum of attitudes towards Wycliffism.

1430s–50s: vernacular writings of Reginald Pecock, written with the "lay partie" in mind and consistently showing knowledge of, and respect for, a critical and spiritually ambitious laity. Thomas Gascoigne's *Liber Veritatum*, which contains criticisms of Arundel and Pecock as well as of heretics.

As may be seen from this chronology, early preoccupation with Wyclif's views about civil dominion and ecclesiastical temporalities quickly expanded to include concern with his later views concerning Eucharistic metaphysics, and was accompanied by consideration of attacks on pilgrimages and image veneration, as these had been expressed, for example, in the *Twelve Conclusions* of Wyclif's supporters. There were many constant or recurring features in these polemical engagements. As Dymoke focused on lollard opposition to some of the sacraments in 1395, so Netter in the 1420s would comprehensively engage with all aspects of sacraments and sacramentals in the *Doctrinale*, having first attacked Wyclif's metaphysics. In the lists of condemned ideas, the Eucharist and civil dominion would remain central. Another consistent feature of such opposition is the longevity of disputative manoeuvres grounded in assumptions about the defensibility of an orthodox hermeneutics.[17] Redolent of such an approach is the tactic, employed by several opponents from different generations, of asserting that dissenting ideas and theological methods were at variance with an authoritative *consensus fidelium* that extended diachronically from the Church Fathers to much later masters. Such an approach would form the backbone of Netter's *Doctrinale*, but it may also be seen much earlier in the work of Wyclif's hostile contemporaries, such as John Tyssyngton, O.F.M., who

---

17   Kantik Ghosh, *The Wycliffite Heresy. Authority and the Interpretation of Texts* (Cambridge, 2002).

not only took issue with Wyclif's metaphysics directly in his *Confessio*, but also appealed to a tradition of interpretation going back to Pseudo-Dionysius, St. Augustine, St. Ambrose and St. Jerome, and including Lanfranc and Robert Grosseteste. Likewise, Thomas Winterton draws in his *Absolucio* on the work of a canon of doctors whose authority Wyclif recognizes; and even when arguing against Wyclif using reason (*rationes*), Winterton seeks to rescue the authorities whom Wyclif uses by showing how his own position might be upheld on the basis of the same *auctoritates* used by his opponent.[18] He thus gets drawn into the scholastic game of glossing and counter-glossing that a much later opponent, such as Pecock, would attempt to sidestep altogether.[19]

It may already be clear from these remarks that the history of opposition to Wyclif and his supporters was closely enmeshed with the unfolding of broader intellectual issues. Prominent amongst these was the recurrence of challenges to scholastic liberties, as enacted in the relationship between the University of Oxford and the ecclesiastical authorities; and in the context of that particular engagement, it could not be taken for granted that lollards and their opponents were necessarily on different sides. Anthony Kenny has observed that it was not Thomas Netter's "scholarship and sensitivity" that shaped reaction to Wyclif but "the crude anathemas of 1415."[20] This precisely captures a fundamental tension in opposition to lollardy between the intellectual vitality and originality of some of the discursive responses listed above, not only in the work of Netter but also in that of Woodford and Pecock, and the necessary stifling of such vitality in the lists of condemned errors and heresies that were repeatedly compiled from 1382 to 1415. For the Blackfriars Council in May 1382, the target of censure was a set of ideas.[21] By the time of Arundel's *Provincial Constitutions* in 1407–09, attention had turned from heretical or erroneous ideas to a range of academic practices that might generate or disseminate such ideas. These included preaching without a license; straying, when preaching on potentially controversial topics, beyond the teachings of the church; including potentially complex theological material in the basic instruction of children; the reading of Wyclif's works without prior approval; unauthorized translation of scripture into the vernacular, or the reading of such translations;

---

18   *FZ*, 218.
19   I discuss Pecock's anti-patristic manouevres in "Vernacular Philosophy and the Making of Orthodoxy in the Fifteenth Century," *New Medieval Literatures* 7 (2005), 73–99.
20   "The Accursed Memory: The Counter-Reformation Reputation of John Wyclif," in *Wyclif in His Times*, (ed.) Anthony Kenny (Oxford, 1986), 147–68 (p. 157).
21   The heresies and errors are listed in *FZ*, 277–82, as promulgated in Courtenay's letter to Peter Stokes, O.Carm., at Oxford.

the inclusion of abstruse philosophical terms in scholastic disputations or conclusions; and the use of authoritative literature such as decretals and constitutions as material for disputation.[22] This legislation, therefore, makes explicit Arundel's understanding of orthodox clergy as "custodians of a discourse" (a phrase originally used by Terry Eagleton to describe modern literary critics, but singularly apt in this context).[23] It could be seen as the culmination of a process that had begun with William Courtenay's contempt, over two decades previously, for what he insisted was not the work of a single rogue scholar, John Wyclif, but a group of unlicensed preachers disseminating heresies throughout his province. Arundel's legislation is also an important event in the sequence of challenges to academic freedom mounted as part of ecclesiastical opposition to the dissemination of lollard ideas.[24] That Arundel's actions were understood in this way is made clear by the reported words of John Birch, an Oxford proctor elected in 1411, in the wake of both the promulgation of the *Constitutions* and the consequent establishment at Oxford of a committee of twelve theologians charged with the task of investigation into Wyclif's writings. Birch, it is recorded, urged resistance to Arundel's measures and argued "that the faculty of arts should be free to hold probable opinions as in the past."[25] If these were indeed the words he used, they are an extremely important and precise articulation of what some scholars thought was at stake: not merely the curtailment of heresy, but also a radical threat to a far wider spectrum of modes of uncertain knowledge. It is in the context of such a fraught relationship between the archbishop and the University, as extensively documented in *Snappe's Formulary*, that H.E. Salter could interpret the reason for the repetition of the

---

22 Wilkins, 3: 315–19.
23 Terry Eagleton, *Literary Theory: An Introduction* (Oxford, 1983), 201. For further nuanced situation of the possible impact and intellectual context of some of the *Constitutions*, see Rita Copeland, *Pedagogy, Intellectuals, and Dissent in Late Medieval England. Lollardy and Ideas of Learning* (Cambridge, 2004), 119–25.
24 This narrative can be traced through Catto, "Wyclif and Wycliffism," and through the documents collected in *Snappe's Formulary*.
25 Catto, "Wyclif and Wycliffism," 234–39. The view imputed to Birch in the document concerning an inquisition at Oriel College is that "facultas artium staret libera in suis opinionibus probabilibus sicut olym": *Snappe's Formulary*, 198. On the vulnerability of uncertain knowledge in this period, see Kantik Ghosh, "Logic, Scepticism and 'Heresy' in Early Fifteenth-Century Europe: Oxford, Vienna, Constance," in *Uncertain Knowledge. Scepticism, Relativism and Doubt in the Middle Ages*, (eds.) Dallas G. Denery II, Kantik Ghosh and Nicolette Zeeman (Turnhout, 2014), 261–83.

Constitutions in 1409 as simply the fact that "so little had been done" in the two years since they had been first formulated.[26]

It has been observed that Arundel's visitation in 1411 had the power to bring "the 'radical chic' of Lollardy to heel" while leaving the "settled convictions" of as resourceful a Wycliffite sympathizer as Peter Payne untouched.[27] Two implications emerge from this. First, the phrase "radical chic" acknowledges the shifting allegiances among reformist clergy during the early phase of the Wycliffite controversies. It has been demonstrated that many early adherents of Wyclif's ideas were successfully reabsorbed into the institutional hierarchy of the church, where they found different outlets for their reformist energies.[28] A late literary witness to the consequences of this process is the *Boke* of Margery Kempe, which may be read not only as the authorized biography of Kempe herself, but also as the unauthorized biography of this phase of English church history, purporting as it does to record her encounters with a broad array of clergymen.[29] When read in this way, the text can be seen to do justice to the imaginative capacity of the institutional Church through whose provinces Kempe made her picaresque way in the politically sensitive, Oldcastle-haunted 1410s. But the phrase "radical chic" also acknowledges that open sympathy with Wycliffite views was only temporarily possible, a fleeting phenomenon that had burned out in England by the time of Arundel's death and the opening of the Council of Constance. In order to test this claim, it is only necessary to think back to the 1390s and the "Dialogue between a Friar and a Secular" in which Thomas, duke of Gloucester is a possible addressee, and to acknowledge that even a textual event such as this, in which an aristocrat can be imagined presiding over and protecting a discursive arena in which dissenting ideas could be subject to deliberation rather than automatic censure, had become unimaginable by 1414.[30] There may thus be some justification for dividing the history of opposition to lollardy into "Ricardian" (that is to say, relatively open) and "Lancastrian" (that is, relatively closed) phases.

---

26   *Snappe's Formulary*, 99.
27   "Wyclif and Wycliffism," 252.
28   Jeremy Catto, "Fellows and Helpers: The Religious Identity of the Followers of Wyclif," in *The Medieval Church: Universities, Heresy and the Religious Life. Essays in Honour of Gordon Leff*, (eds.) Peter Biller and R.B. Dobson, Studies in Church History, Subsidia 11 (Woodbridge, 1999), 141–61.
29   Sarah Rees Jones, "'A Peler of Holy Cherch': Margery Kempe and the Bishops," in *Medieval Women: Texts and Contexts in Late Medieval Britain: Essays for Felicity Riddy*, (eds.) Jocelyn Wogan-Browne and others (Turnhout, 2000), 377–91.
30   *Four Wycliffite Dialogues*, (ed.) Fiona Somerset, Early English Text Society o.s. 333 (Oxford, 2009), xlvii–xlix.

Another way of testing this hypothesis is through attentiveness to the extent to which degrees of discursive openness and closure might be tracked through the dialogues generated by the controversies. As a recent repertorium of Latin dialogues from the thirteenth and fourteenth centuries shows, the Wycliffite controversies played a respectable part in the evolution of the dialogue as a genre that could cross the boundaries between intra- and extramural worlds.[31] From Wyclif's *Dialogus* and *Trialogus* onwards, the polyvocal text was a particularly important genre in the unfolding history of lollard and counter-lollard literature: the desire for "dialogazacioun" expressed by so late an opponent as Pecock can be situated in a long lineage of opposition to Wyclif's ideas, with Radcliff's dialogues as one of the earliest examples.[32] Dialogue, it might be argued, offers at least the possibility of a reflexive way of accommodating one's frank imaginings about the mentality of an opponent. But even in the Ricardian period, when only one contributor's writings survive (as in the case of the Maidstone-Ashwardby confrontation), the voice and character of the other interlocutor's rhetoric and preoccupations can sometimes only be guessed at.[33] And it is striking that the major texts generated by opponents of lollardy during the Lancastrian years—Netter in Latin, Pecock in English—are largely one-sided. Netter's *Doctrinale* does contain an embedded dialogue between a friar and a secular priest in which each interlocutor competes to praise his opponent, but the imperatives behind this dialogue are hardly drawn from the Wycliffite controversies alone.[34] As the existence of the *English Wycliffite Sermons* and the *Works of a Lollard Preacher* show, distinctive, stylistically and intellectually resourceful lollard voices did not disappear entirely, but texts in which both pro- and anti-lollard positions could co-exist, each functioning autonomously in an experimental scholastic arena, were less likely to be written as the controversies wore on.

Even though the kinds of dialogues mentioned here fell far short of Socratic opennesss, at the opposite end of the discursive range were narratives in which lollards would be reduced to little more than objects in the mind of their opponent. And for the modern reader, one of the most seductive and problematic

---

31 C. Cardelle de Hartmann, *Lateinische Dialoge 1200–1400: Literaturhistorische Studie und Repertorium* (Leiden, 2007).

32 *Reginald Pecock's Book of Faith: a Fifteenth-Century Tractate*, (ed.) J.L. Morison (Glasgow, 1909), 122.

33 Valerie Edden, "The Debate between Richard Maidstone and the Lollard Ashwardby," *Carmelus* 34 (1987), 113–34.

34 I discuss this dialogue further in "Writing, Heresy and the Anticlerical Muse," in *The Oxford Handbook of Medieval Literature*, (eds.) Greg Walker and Elaine Treharne (Oxford, 2010), 276–93 (pp. 285–87).

aspects of the historiography of lollardy is how easily serious engagement with dissenting ideas can give way to the easier and more polemically rewarding task of channelling perceptions of dissenters, whether real or imagined. This is vividly shown in an episode in the *Boke* of Margery Kempe in which the monks of Canterbury feel free to call Margery a "false lollare," threatening to burn her without anything approaching due process.[35] Whether or not such threats were actually made, or took precisely the form that the *Boke* ascribes to them, it is significant enough that such a scene could be imagined at all. Similarly, mobility of voice and perspective in John Audelay's early fifteenth-century poem "Marcolf and Solomon," written by 1426, dramatize the extent to which perception and hearsay had become dominant features of the response to lollardy:[36]

> The prophecy of the prophetus (*prophets*), ale nowe hit (*it*) doth apere (*appear*),
> That sumtyme was sayd be (*concerning*) the clergy:
> That leud men, the laue of God that schuld love and lere,
> Fore curatis fore here covetyse, wold count noght therby,
> Bot to talke of here teythys, Y tel you treuly.
> And yif the secular say a soth, anon thai bene eschent,
> And lyen apon the leud men and sayn, "Hit is Lollere!"
> Thus the pepul and the prestis beth of one asent; (*in agreement*)
> Thai dare no noder do, (*dare not do otherwise*)
> Fore (*because*) dred of the clergé,
> Wold dampnen (*damn*) hem unlaufully (*illegally*)
> To preche (*preach*) apon the peleré, (*pillory*)
> And bren (*burn*) hem after too. (ll. 664–676)[37]

It is significant that lines 666–670 require wholesale translation by their editor, Susanna Fein: "That common people, who should love and learn the law of God, / Shall be wholly disregarded by curates, who, on account of their avarice, / Preach only about their tithes, I tell you truly. / And if the laity speak the truth

---

35 *The Book of Margery Kempe*, (eds.) Sanford Brown Meech and Hope Emily Allen, Early English Text Society o.s. 212 (Oxford, 1940), 28.

36 John the Blind Audelay, *Poems and Carols* (Oxford, Bodleian Library MS Douce 302), (ed.) Susanna Fein (Kalamazoo, Michigan, 2009). I discuss this poem further in "Useless Mouths: Reformist Poetics in Audelay and Skelton," in *Form and Reform: Reading Across the Fifteenth Century*, (eds.) Shannon Gayk and Kathleen Tonry (Columbus, Ohio, 2011), 159–79.

37 *Poems and Carols*, 52–53. Glosses are my own.

(i.e., in criticism of the clergy), they are disgraced straightway, / And [the clergy] lie to the common people and say, 'It is Lollardy!'"[38] Editorial translation has been necessitated by the elliptical syntax that has put the full grammatical sense of the lines at risk of being lost. It is mimetic of the stanza's subject matter in which speech is muffled through dread: the lines swallow themselves as some of the relationships between pronouns and antecedents become unclear and one verb loses its subject. There is quite a distance between the plethora of anxieties and incompatible perspectives voiced in this poem and the intramural precision that had marked earlier phases of opposition such as Woodford's engagement with Wyclif's ideas, or even, from a period contemporary with Audelay, the extramural flamboyance of Netter's virtuoso assault on *Wiclevistae*. Outside the relatively protected environment of the schools, lollardy flourished as an *imaginaire*. Heretics were a gift to chroniclers because they provided fodder for that essential narrative component, the anecdote, as in the case of the Augustinian Henry Knighton's account of the desecration of an image of St. Katherine.[39] Just as egregious in this context is the negative *exemplum* concerning the heretic John Badby's encounter, during this second trial, with a large spider that he was unable to remove from his mouth.[40] Janette Dillon's focus on performance in relation to this narrative helpfully foregrounds the extent to which many of these narratives of opposition, this time in chronicles, were driven precisely by the need to perform the act of opposing rather than solely by the need to refute particular theses: and it is not, after all, unexpected that in the history of opposition to lollardy, extramural gestures would often come to supplant esoteric argumentation.

But resistance to caricature is not necessarily hard to find. Pecock's description of his readership as the "lay partie" may at first appear willfully to obscure its possible referents. This lexical choice is, however, a nuanced evocation of his imagined, and desired, readership, which included heretics and the faithful, both of whom might be characterized by spiritual curiosity. His use of the phrase reflects his ability to generate keywords that were reflective and accommodating towards the heterogeneity of his imagined readership, and this in turn signals the important fact, acknowledged in different ways by Allan Westphall and Kirsty Campbell, that Pecock's writings were usually driven by the need to educate the faithful rather than simply the imperative of combating

---

38 Ibid., 53.

39 See the discussion in Sarah Stanbury, *The Visual Object of Desire in Late Medieval England* (Philadelphia, 2011), 33–75.

40 Janette Dillon, *The Language of Space in Court Performance, 1400–1625* (Cambridge, 2010), 161–62.

heresy.[41] In this, he was typical of several other importance opponents of lollardy, such as Netter, who had even broader concerns than simply the desire to refute heretical beliefs.[42] But I wish to conclude by briefly discussing yet another of the best-known anti-Wycliffite writers, Nicholas Love. I have previously acknowledged the obvious contrasts between the intellectual temperaments of Love and Pecock, suggesting that Love's affective orthodoxy was precisely what Pecock's syllogistically-driven approach was designed to resist.[43] But these grounds for contrast, however justifiable, should not be taken to imply that Love's repertoire of responses to lollardy is intellectually undernourished. Both the *Mirror of the Blessed Life of Jesus Christ* and Love's *Treatise on the Sacrament* are important witnesses for the present discussion not least because, by contrast even with a later writer such as Netter, Love leaves Wyclif behind and concentrates squarely on writing *contra lollardos*, as marginal notes to the *Mirror* regularly testify, or "in confusion of alle fals lollardes," as a passage at the end of his translation of the *Mirror* would confirm. Even when calling into question the remit of "kyndely (*natural*) reson" where the miracle of transubstantiation is concerned in the *Treatise on the Sacrament*, Love argues his case strenuously, scrutinizing different ways of thinking and arguing erroneously in a discourse that does not absolutely pre-empt close scrutiny of the metaphysical complexities being broached.[44] And when discussing in the *Mirror* itself ways in which the nature of this sacrament might legitimately be apprehended, Love adroitly marginalizes evidence provided by the "bodily wittes" (*senses*) in favour of a process of "sensible felyng" and the witness provided by a "merueylose wirching & felyng aboue comune kynde (*common nature*) of manne."[45] This requires Love to draw some nuanced distinctions between different kinds of bodily testimony, and the result is an anti-heretical discourse in which a shift towards modes of sensory experience offers the

---

41 *The Reule of Crysten Religioun*, (ed.) William Cabell Greet, Early English Text Society, o.s. 171 (London, 1927), 19. Allan Westphall, "Reconstructing the Mixed Life in Reginald Pecock's *Reule of Crysten Religioun*," in *After Arundel: Religious Writing in Fifteenth-Century England*, (eds.) V. Gillespie and K. Ghosh (Turnhout, 2011), 267–84; Kirsty Campbell, *The Call to Read: Reginald Pecock's Books and Textual Communities* (Notre Dame, 2010).

42 Kevin Alban, O.Carm., *The Teaching and Impact of the Doctrinale of Thomas Netter of Walden (c.1374–1430)* (Turnhout, 2010).

43 See my "Reversing the Life of Christ: Dissent, Orthodoxy, and Affectivity in Late Medieval England," in *The Pseudo-Bonaventuran Lives of Christ. Exploring the Middle English Tradition*, (eds.) Ian Johnson and Allan F. Westphall (Turnhout, 2013), 55–77.

44 *The Mirror of the Blessed Life of Jesus Christ: A Full Critical Edition*, (ed.) Michael Sargent (Exeter, 2005), 225.

45 Ibid., 152.

possibility of sidestepping the closed circuit of the kind of scholastic game in which Tyssyngton and Winterton had earlier become embroiled.[46]

In the foregoing narrative, no less than in the case of any other aerial view of complex terrain, the map cannot constitute the whole territory. One important point remains to be made where this particular body of material is concerned. Wycliffite literary culture has benefited immeasurably from the attention of assiduous editors; to date, its opponents have not been nearly as fortunate. An edition of Nicholas Radcliff's dialogues would give him a far more secure foothold in this narrative as well as enriching our understanding of the Benedictine literary culture within which those dialogues took shape.[47] Other promising texts for editing are the various treatises on images, the works of John Deveros, and even the *Fasciculi Zizaniorum*, which would benefit from presentation in a modern scholarly edition, as an invaluable record not only of the unfolding of the controversies but also of the processes by which opponents of lollardy sought to achieve some control over the official narratives about heretics. It could also be regarded as a milestone in the intellectual history of the English Carmelites. Above all, a collected edition of William Woodford's various responses to Wyclif would enable us not only the better to appreciate the Franciscan's intellectual finesse, but also possibly to challenge Netter's current prominence in the history of anti-Wycliffism. Editions of these and other texts would also serve the intellectual history of the medieval period by enabling a wider range of readers to judge for themselves the extent to which opposition to heresy often functioned as one point of departure for a series of broader engagements with ecclesiastical and intellectual concerns.

---

46 But see also the different account in Ghosh, *The Wycliffite Heresy*, 147–73.

47 On this culture, see James G. Clark, *A Monastic Renaissance at St. Albans: Thomas Walsingham and his Circle, c. 1350–1440* (Oxford, 2004).

CHAPTER 7

Their Trials

We do not know what Margery Baxter was doing when she was summoned to court by the bishop of Norwich's officers. The wife of a reasonably prosperous wright (what today we would call a carpenter), William Baxter, Margery lived in the Norfolk village of Martham, just under twenty miles from the bishop's seat.[1] We do know that on October 8, 1428, Margery appeared on suspicion of heresy before a tribunal of ecclesiastical judges that included the bishop, William Alnwick, three theologians, and two canon lawyers.[2] This was a deadly serious occasion: a trial for heresy that, like the hundreds of other such trials that took place in late medieval England, was a matter of life and death. The bishop and his officials required Margery to swear on a book of the gospels to tell the truth, and then they questioned her about her interactions with a notorious lollard preacher, William White, who had been executed for heresy earlier the same year.

Margery told her judges much of what they wanted to hear. According to the surviving records of her interrogation, she admitted that she had allowed White to hide in her home, where she "for five consecutive days protected and concealed and sheltered him; and…she gave and supplied to the same William counsel, help, and favor, to the degree that she was able; and…she secretly transported the books of the said William White from the village of Yarmouth to the village of Martham and hid them."[3] Margery also acknowledged that White had taught her several points of heresy, which she had begun to believe. Among them were the ideas that oral confession to priests was unnecessary; that pilgrimages should not be made nor images of the saints adored; and that "every good person is a priest, and that no person will finally come to heaven unless he or she is a priest."[4] The records indicate that Margery told her judges

---

1 On the socioeconomic standing of Margery and her fellow heresy defendants in Norwich diocese, see Maureen Jurkowski, "Lollardy and Social Status in East Anglia," *Speculum* 82 (2007), 120–52. An earlier study, Derek Plumb, "The Social and Economic Spread of Rural Lollardy: A Reappraisal," in W.J. Sheils and Diana Wood, (eds.), *Voluntary Religion*, Studies in Church History 23 (Oxford, 1986), 111–29, makes a similar point with regard to lollardy throughout England.
2 The record of Margery's trial is preserved in a fifteenth-century manuscript, London, Westminster Diocesan Archives, B.2, 219–20, 273–78, and printed in *Norwich*, 41–51. A modern English translation of the proceedings is printed in *Wycliffite Spirituality*, 327–36.
3 *Wycliffite Spirituality*, 327–28.
4 *Wycliffite Spirituality*, 328.

that she wished to renounce these heresies, and she swore a second oath on the gospels to that effect. She also pledged to accept the punishment that the bishop was about to assign her. The sentence meted out was that Margery would be flogged around the parish church in Martham on four separate occasions; would be flogged in the nearby town of Acle twice; and would appear at the cathedral in Norwich the following Ash Wednesday and Holy Thursday, where she would do further penance for her crimes.

For most heresy defendants, abjuring and pledging upon pain of death not to offend again would have marked the end of their interaction with the ecclesiastical justice system. Most defendants appear in the court records for only one set of proceedings, and most renounced their beliefs rather than suffer the ultimate punishment. Though Margery Baxter confessed, she also seems to have continued to stir up trouble: the bishop of Norwich's records reveal that three of her fellow villagers testified against her in the spring of the following year. Joan Clifland, one of Margery's sewing partners, informed the bishop's court that Margery had spoken out against oaths, against showing reverence to the crucifix and the images of the saints, and against orthodox understandings of the sacraments of baptism, marriage, and the eucharist. Margery had said that the pope, cardinals, and bishops were deceiving the people and killing "the most holy sons and teachers of God," including William White. Going further than this, Margery also declared that she prayed every day to White, whom she said she regarded as "a great saint in heaven and a most holy teacher ordained and sent by God."[5] Clifland testified that Margery had invited her and her servant to join Margery and her husband in reading at night from an unnamed book, one that likely contained what were feared to be unauthorized English translations of the scriptures. Finally, Clifland accused Margery of threatening to defame her to her neighbors if she revealed Margery's beliefs to the bishop. Indeed, Margery bragged that she had already publicly blackened the name of a Carmelite friar who had accused her of heresy. Two of Clifland's servants, Agnes Bethom and Joan Grymle, also testified that they had heard Margery make heterodox statements, as well as that when Clifland sent them to Margery's house on an errand, they had discovered her cooking pork in the fasting season of Lent. All this testimony was recorded for use if Margery were tried again in the future, when a conviction would have rendered her a relapsed heretic and sent her to the stake. As far as we know (and the Norwich records from this period are among the most complete), such an eventuality never happened.

---

5 *Wycliffite Spirituality*, 332.

The case of Margery Baxter features elements typical of heresy trials as they made their way through England's ecclesiastical courts: a list of charges, an abjuration, a penance to be performed. Yet as H.A. Kelly has shown, Margery's trial broke a few of the church's procedural rules, which English ecclesiastical courts generally followed to the letter.[6] Her case also differs from others insofar as it provides us with a bevy of details usually absent from the records of such proceedings: the specific beliefs she was accused of and confessed to holding, the names of the witnesses who testified against her, and the content of their testimony. As we will see in this chapter, Baxter's case was both ordinary and extraordinary. The records of proceedings like hers comprise a rich trove of information for scholars seeking to reconstruct what may actually have transpired in the ecclesiastical courtrooms of late medieval England.

7.1   The Inquisitorial Process

The time-honored portrait of lollards as the spiritually bereft, carping critics of traditional religion was painted early on, in the records of their trials before diocesan bishops and their associates.[7] It was these records that both evangelical propagandists like John Foxe and Catholic writers such as Nicholas Harpsfield used, abridged, and amended as they constructed their reformation-era histories of lollardy and lollard belief.[8] That trial records could be used in this fashion is anything but surprising. Since they rarely convey the fullness either of lollard theology and spirituality or of the exchanges between heresy suspects and inquisitors, these records tend to portray suspects' religious claims in negative terms: one person denied this doctrine, another refused to take part in that practice. Limited and biased though they may be, however, the records of heresy trials sit alongside the texts written by Wyclif and his followers as a second crucial corpus of evidence for what late medieval women and men believed, what they valued, and how they practiced their religion. It is helpful to note in this connection that, in contrast to the case of other

---

6 H.A. Kelly, "Inquisitorial Due Process and Secret Crimes," in *Inquisitions and Other Trial Procedures in the Medieval West* (London, 2001), item II, 425–26, esp. n. 63.

7 In Chapter 3, I described how recent work on lollard spirituality and religious practice is helping to shed new light on the theological and spiritual affirmations that made lollard versions of Christianity appealing to their practitioners. Much of the impetus for this movement has come from the editing and translation of lollard devotional writings. Parts of the following section of the present chapter are drawn from my contributions to the introduction to a volume of such writings (*Wycliffite Spirituality*).

8 Nicholas Harpsfield, *Historia Anglicana ecclesiastica* (Douai, 1622), 661–711.

medieval heresies such as the so-called "Cathars" of Italy and southern France and the so-called "heretics of the Free Spirit" of the Low Countries, where there are few extant texts written by those subject to persecution, the volume of information available in the records of English lollard dissenters' trials can be compared with the equally extensive volume of information that can be gleaned from their own writings.[9]

Before turning to the content of the records, though, a brief overview of the inquisitorial process is in order. Speaking in broad terms, in late medieval England there existed two parallel sets of courts: civil courts, which handled offenses against the crown, secular criminal matters, and many civil disputes; and church or ecclesiastical courts, which dealt with a range of matters judged to be spiritual.[10] Defamation, for instance, was prosecuted as a spiritual crime, since it involved the bearing of false witness and, therefore, the breaking of one of the Ten Commandments; petitions for divorce (technically, annulment) also came through ecclesiastical rather than civil courts, since marriage ranked among the sacraments of the church. Heresy (technically, "the crime of heretical depravity") ranked among the gravest of spiritual offenses, and as a result, heresy suspects almost always appeared before ecclesiastical judges.[11] Since heresy was a high-profile matter, the venue for heresy trials was usually the court of the diocesan bishop, who either presided himself or delegated his authority to a senior aide; far less regularly, heresy cases were heard in the consistory court of the diocese or in the court of an archdeacon. Heresy investigations usually entailed four phases: detection, arrest, trial, and punishment.[12]

---

9   As recent work on "Cathar" and "Free Spirit" heretics has noted, the relative dearth of texts written by the proponents of these movements makes it more likely that the preconceptions and biases of inquisitors will survive in modern scholarship. John H. Arnold, in "Lollard Trials and Inquisitorial Discourse," in *Fourteenth Century England 11*, (ed.) Christopher Given-Wilson (Woodbridge, 2002), 81–94, discusses the ways in which students of English and continental heresies can learn from each other's methods.

10 For more extensive accounts of late medieval courts and inquisitorial practices, see Richard M. Wunderli, *London Church Courts and Society on the Eve of the Reformation* (Cambridge, Mass., 1981); Ralph A. Houlbrooke, *Church Courts and the People during the English Reformation* (Oxford, 1979); Ian Forrest, *The Detection of Heresy in Late Medieval England* (Oxford, 2005); and Kathleen Kamerick, "Shaping Superstition in Late Medieval England," *Magic, Ritual and Witchcraft* 3 (2008), 29–53.

11 There were, of course, exceptions. Individuals caught up in rebellions against royal authority who also were suspected of heresy were often tried and sentenced by civil courts, including for instance the participants in Sir John Oldcastle's abortive rebellion of 1414. On this point, see J.A.F. Thomson, *The Later Lollards: 1414–1520* (Oxford, 1965), 5–19.

12 Forrest, *Detection*, 32.

Responsibility for these phases usually alternated between church and crown, with secular authorities arresting and punishing defendants who had been identified and tried by the church.

Unlike in the modern world, where the term "detection" carries the sense of an investigation by a professional police force, in the middle ages the word signified the process of reporting or informing on a suspect. People were "detected to" church authorities for a range of reasons, not all of them religious: as R.I. Moore has observed, "political rivalry and personal enmity were probably always the commonest source of heresy investigations."[13] The procedure that church officials employed in proceeding against heresy suspects was known as inquisition, and it was a procedure that was not new in fifteenth- and sixteenth-century England, having been honed in the church's decades of experience with heretics on the continent.[14] Widespread stereotypes about later inquisitions, such as that of early modern Spain, make it necessary for us to remember that inquisition in late medieval England was a procedure rather than an organization.[15] Ian Forrest has explained in his study *The Detection of Heresy in Late Medieval England* that "the detection of heresy in England was carried out by bishops with the assistance of specially delegated inquisitors, who might be bishops themselves, but were sometimes diocesan officials or heads of religious houses."[16] While a few heresy trials involved intentional or unintentional violations of established legal procedures, the expertise of these officials meant that the majority of trials were conducted according to established norms.[17]

The dominant role that bishops played in the inquisitorial process goes a long way toward explaining why the frequency and intensity of heresy investigations

---

13   R.I. Moore, "The War against Heresy in Medieval Europe," *Historical Research* 81 (2008), 189–210, at 194.

14   H.A. Kelly, "Inquisition, Public Fame, and Confession: General Rules and English Practice," in *The Culture of Inquisition in England, 1215–1515*, (eds.) Mary C. Flannery and Katie Walter (Woodbridge, 2013), 8–29.

15   Richard Kieckhefer, *The Repression of Heresy in Medieval Germany* (Philadelphia, 1979), 5. On the development of some bureaucratic structures among inquisitors, see Kieckhefer, "The Office of Inquisition and Medieval Heresy: The Transition from Personal to Institutional Jurisdiction," *Journal of Ecclesiastical History* 46 (1995), 36–61.

16   Forrest, *Detection*, 58.

17   H.A. Kelly has done more than any other scholar to rehabilitate the reputations of bishops and inquisitors in the face of early claims about the ruthlessness of such officials. See among his many other publications *Inquisitions and Other Trial Procedures in the Medieval West* (Aldershot, 2001), especially items v and vi, and "Thomas More on Inquisitorial Due Process," *English Historical Review* 123 (2008), 845–94.

varied significantly across time and place. As we will see below in surveying the extant records of English heresy trials, external events, such as the recently crowned King Henry VIII's desire for England to be seen as an active force in the fight against heresy at the time of the convocation of the Fifth Lateran Council, might accelerate the volume or speed of heresy investigations; the same effect might be caused by the personal dispositions of particular bishops.[18] Other events, such as the outbreak of the Wars of the Roses, might divert the attention of bishops and royal officials. During the period from Wyclif's exile from Oxford in 1381 through Henry's reformation of the 1530s, a number of bishops initiated large-scale heresy investigations. Others allowed years or decades to elapse between heresy trials, undertaking prosecutions only in response to external stimuli.

However he or she (in what follows, I will use "she" for convenience) came to trial, an accused person was usually presented with a list of the charges against her, along with a crucial choice: should she admit that she had taught or done certain erroneous things, though she now regretted doing so; should she deny the charges; or should she admit that the charges were true, yet maintain that she still believed in what she had said or done? In some cases, defendants were interrogated by church officials on a range of theological and religious questions. Some sets of such questions were assembled into formal questionnaires beginning in the 1420s; these were then administered to each heresy suspect who later appeared in a particular court. Anne Hudson's research has unearthed evidence of questionnaires being used in the dioceses of Canterbury, Worcester, Bath and Wells, and Salisbury; below we shall explore the significance of these documents for the evidentiary value of the extant trial records.[19]

We learned in Chapter 1 that, in technical theological terms, the crime of heresy did not entail only the holding of a heterodox belief; to commit heresy,

18 Heresy prosecutions were not, of course, the only means by which early Henrician church leaders sought reform: consider, for instance, the famous 1512 convocation sermon of John Colet, Dean of St. Paul's. On Colet, see most recently Andrew Hope, "Conformed and Reformed: John Colet and His Reformation Reputation," in Linda Clark, Maureen Jurkowski, and Colin Richmond, (eds.), *Image, Text, and Church: Essays for Margaret Aston* (Toronto, 2009), 214–38.

19 Anne Hudson, "The Examination of Lollards," *Bulletin of the Institute of Historical Research* 46 (1973), 145–59, repr. in *Books*, 124–40. To the contrary, H.A. Kelly finds only one case where such a list of questions was explicitly employed, but he appears to have looked only for direct evidence of the use of questionnaires, rather than indirect signs of their use in similar patterns of questions and answers. "Lollard Inquisitions: Due and Undue Process," in Kelly, *Inquisitions*, item VI, 302.

a person must also refuse to return to the orthodox position when apprised of her error by a church official.[20] Thus, the moment at which a defendant was presented with the choice whether or not to abjure her erroneous teachings or practices was also the moment at which, formally speaking, she could commit the crime of heresy. However, in the practice of church courts, these technicalities were honored more in the breach than in the observance. Defendants who were found to have engaged in activities redolent of heresy were convicted and given the choice to abjure or to be burned.

If a defendant chose to abjure, the usual procedure was for her to list and forswear his erroneous teachings, using a formula prepared (and sometimes even read aloud) for her by court officials. This formal abjuration was often performed publicly, in order to demonstrate publicly the heretic's "schism with the church, his symbolic reconciliation, and the unity of his prosecutors as representatives of orthodoxy."[21] Whether public or private, the abjuration was then entered into the record of the trial, with a copy sometimes made for the defendant to take away with her. The bishop or other presiding official would assign her a penance, ranging from public acts of penitence in her home parish to restrictions on her liberty or temporary or permanent incarceration. It was not uncommon for heretics who had admitted their crime to be required to carry some marker of the event on either their clothes or their bodies: some bishops mandated that abjured heretics sew a badge depicting burning wood onto their clothes, while at least one other bishop ordered the abjured to be branded on the cheek with the letter *H*.[22] These markers were especially significant for the future, since if an individual who had abjured heresy was later found to have offended again, the penalty for relapse was death at the stake.

If, on the other hand, a defendant chose to contest the charges against her, church officials would seek her conviction by producing documents or witnesses; when the evidence was insufficient to demonstrate the defendant's guilt, she was sometimes acquitted outright or, more frequently, required to produce a set number of witnesses called compurgators (literally, "fellow-purgers"). These witnesses were local residents of good character, ideally of high standing in church and society, who would testify to the moral character of the defendant and put their own reputations behind her claim to innocence.

---

20 See 19–21 above.

21 Ian Forrest, "The Dangers of Diversity: Heresy and Authority in the 1405 Case of John Edward," in *Studies in Church History* 43 (2007), 230–40, at 231.

22 For the wearing of faggot badges, see the case of John Brewster of Colchester, later burned as a relapsed heretic: *A&M*, 929–30. For branding, see the Coventry and Lichfield diocese case of Joan Warde *alias* Wasshingburn: *Coventry*, 239.

If a sufficient number of such witnesses came forward, the case against the defendant would be dismissed.

Most heresy trials in late medieval England ended either with the abjuration of the defendant or with the appearance of enough compurgators to assure the court of the defendant's reputation.[23] Nevertheless, the stake cast its shadow across all heresy proceedings, even those that did not result in the condemnation of the suspect. Heresy defendants were sentenced to death for two reasons: relapse into heresy, in the case of those who had previously abjured but were found to have again endorsed or disseminated heterodox ideas, and obstinacy, in the case of those who even on their first appearance refused to abjure. In either case, the presiding official would, in the language of the records, "relinquish" the defendant "to the secular arm" for burning. Canon law provided that no cleric could shed blood, so death sentences against relapsed or contumacious heretics were carried out by secular officials rather than ecclesiastical ones.

Late medieval heresy trials thus produced a variety of outcomes. In most cases, suspects abjured and were assigned penances. Less frequently, when the charges against them could not be proven, suspects found the requisite number of compurgators, as a result of whose testimony the case was dismissed. Less frequently still, when suspects refused to abjure or were found guilty of relapse into heresy, they were "relinquished" to secular officials for execution. (In a few cases, of course, trials were dissolved because the defendant had fled or died.) No matter the outcome, however, a heresy trial generated the production of documents. As in the case of Margery Baxter, the testimony of accusers and witnesses was sometimes written down, as (more often) were abjurations made by defendants who chose to admit their guilt. A scribe or registrar was present for each stage of the proceedings and was responsible for entering the facts of the case into the court's records. Whether they took the form of items in a bishop's register, court roll, or dedicated heresy court-book, these records may have included information on the charges against the defendant, the defendant's replies to those charges, the statements of witnesses, the verdict of the court, the names of the presiding judge and his assistants, and the date and location of the trial. Many of the surviving records also include what purport

---

23   This fact may come as a surprise to those accustomed to thinking of medieval heresy defendants as religious freedom-fighters. The gap between the extant recantations and the stereotype of religious enthusiasts willing "to withstand the bitterest persecution and the most repulsive forms of death" was noted late in the nineteenth century by Edward P. Cheyney, "The Recantations of the Early Lollards," *American Historical Review* 4 (1899), 423–35, at 432.

to be verbatim, first-person abjurations by defendants and verbatim sentences by their judges.

7.2   The Making of Records

Yet these records are not as transparent as at first they might seem; they are certainly not the equivalent of modern court transcripts. Nor are they the only texts that purport to document the proceedings of church courts against suspected heretics. As we have already seen, a few English heresy suspects produced their own accounts of their trials and hearings before ecclesiastical judges. Before turning to the records kept by church authorities, then, it will be helpful to consider briefly some of these alternative narratives.

Of the texts produced by defendants in medieval English heresy proceedings, perhaps none is as well known, or as memorable, as the *Testimony of William Thorpe*. Thorpe, whom we first met in Chapter 2, was an early follower of Wyclif's who had at some point been investigated for heresy by Bishop Robert Braybrooke of London; he was accused of teaching that a priest in mortal sin could not consecrate the eucharist and that it was right for laypeople to withhold their tithes from sinful clergy.[24] Many details about Thorpe's life remain vague, including whether he ever formally appeared on heresy charges before either Bishop Braybrooke or Archbishop of Canterbury Thomas Arundel, but the text ascribed to his name claims to be a first-person account of a conversation between Thorpe and Arundel on August 7, 1407.[25] At the time, Thorpe was a prisoner in Arundel's castle of Saltwood, in Kent; as we learned, the text reports that Arundel ordered Thorpe back to prison at the conclusion of the conversation it narrates.

Thorpe's *Testimony* survives in three medieval manuscripts and an early printed version.[26] Though the relationships between these witnesses are complex, and thus the origin of the text difficult to ascertain, scholarly judgments have tended to come down on the side of Thorpe's historicity: Anne Hudson,

---

[24]   See above, 40–41.
[25]   The text is printed by Anne Hudson in *Two Wycliffite Texts* (EETS o.s. 301, 1993), where Hudson's introduction provides helpful biographical and bibliographical details. For further information on Thorpe's case, see among others Jurkowski, "Arrest of William Thorpe," 273–95.
[26]   The manuscripts, Oxford, Bodleian Library Rawlinson C.208; Vienna, Österreichische Nationalbibliothek 3936; and Prague, Metropolitan Chapter Library O.29, and the early modern edition, STC 24045, are described by Hudson in *Two Wycliffite Texts*, xxvi–xxx.

for instance, has observed that "on almost every issue where Thorpe can be checked...he can be shown to be reasonably reliable."[27] That Thorpe may have had a conversation with Archbishop Arundel and that his text contains historically verifiable details, however, do not mean that the encounter took place just as Thorpe narrated it.[28] His *Testimony* divides itself into two sections: a prologue, where Thorpe explains his reasons for writing the text (because his friends asked him to; because his interrogation revealed the truth of his beliefs and the error of the archbishop's; because he wished to provide an account of his beliefs to his readers; and because he desired to encourage others who were being persecuted), and an account of the examination itself. Thorpe claims that Arundel interrogated him about five theological issues on which Thorpe's public preaching had stirred up controversy: the eucharist, the adoration of images, pilgrimage, the withholding of tithes from the clergy, and oath-taking. On each of these issues, even as he employs the vocabulary and rhetorical techniques of formal academic disputation, Thorpe portrays himself as a defender of the biblically grounded orthodoxy of the apostolic church; he depicts Arundel as insisting that Christians believe things not required by the gospel.[29] As Hudson has argued, in Thorpe's telling the discussion between him and Arundel ultimately boils down to a debate about the locus of authority in the church.[30] Take, for instance, an exchange between the two men about the eucharist. Thorpe declares to Arundel that he believes that the eucharist is "verri Cristis fleisch and his blood in forme of breed and wyne." Arundel, unsatisfied, presses as to whether the sacrament is "in *fourme* of breed" or "in

---

27   Hudson, (ed.), *Two Wycliffite Texts*, lii. John Fines, "William Thorpe: An Early Lollard," *History Today* 18 (1968), 495–503, at 498–503, takes Thorpe's claims at face value.

28   For excellent analysis of the ways to which Thorpe's use of narrative in his *Testimony* reflected his intention to use narrative, rather than outright polemic, as a way to "sidestep...the textual strategies that had come to define both sides in the Lollard controversy, expanding the discursive territory of vernacular Wycliffism," see Elizabeth Schirmer, "William Thorpe's Narrative Theology," *Studies in the Age of Chaucer* 31 (2009), 267–99.

29   On Thorpe's use of academic discourse, see Fiona Somerset, "Vernacular Argumentation in the *Testimony of William Thorpe*," *Mediaeval Studies* 58 (1996), 207–41.

30   Anne Hudson, "William Thorpe and the Question of Authority," in *Christian Authority: Essays in Honour of Henry Chadwick*, (ed.) G.R. Evans (Oxford, 1988), 127–37; for related studies see David Aers, *Sanctifying Signs: Making Christian Tradition in Late Medieval England* (Notre Dame, Ind., 2004), Chapter 4, and Aers, "The *Testimony of William Thorpe*: Reflections on Self, Sin, and Salvation," in *Studies in Late Medieval and Early Renaissance Texts in Honour of John Scattergood*, (eds.) Anne Marie D'Arcy and Alan J. Fletcher (Dublin, 2005), 21–34.

substance of breed"; and Thorpe finally responds that this and other theological questions are "scole-mater aboute whiche I neuer bisied me for to knowe in," superfluities which distract from true faith in Christ and the sacrament.[31]

Did Thorpe and Arundel really have the conversations reported in Thorpe's *Testimony*? We will never know, and as Fiona Somerset has observed, "patently the text's value is not as a record of actual procedure but a representation of ideal, even exemplary, steadfastness in adversity."[32] On the one hand, since the topics that Thorpe claims he discussed with Arundel did figure prominently in the theological and ecclesiological controversies of the early fifteenth century, it is possible that Thorpe captured with some accuracy the content of his encounter with the archbishop. On the other hand, since Thorpe so consistently portrays himself as an eloquent, indeed intellectually victorious, champion of the gospel, and to the contrary portrays Arundel as an often angry, sometimes incoherent authoritarian figure, our suspicion must be strong that Thorpe's agenda drove the structure and content of his narrative.

The same can be said of another Wycliffite prison writing, the one penned by Richard Wyche in a 1401 letter to an anonymous Bohemian correspondent.[33] Wyche, whom we also encountered in Chapter 2, was a priest who, after his release from prison, was later associated with both Sir John Oldcastle and Jan Hus. Burned on Tower Hill in 1140, Wyche had previously been tried for heresy before Bishop Walter Skirlaw of Durham.[34] His letter, written in Latin, includes an account of his examination that, like Thorpe's *Testimony*, purports to include verbatim quotations from Wyche and his inquisitors. The theological topics at issue closely mirror those featured in Thorpe's examination, though in some ways Wyche was closer to the theological mainstream; at two points in Wyche's text, he appears to endorse the necessity of oral confession for salvation.[35] Also as in the case of Thorpe, the dialogue between Wyche and his inquisitors turns on issues of ecclesiastical authority. For instance, at one point one of Wyche's examiners declares, "You say that Christ said, 'This is my body'; therefore it is necessary to believe that this is only his body and not any bread."

---

31 *The Testimony of William Thorpe*, in Hudson, (ed.), *Two Wycliffite Texts*, lines 968–69, 970, 1030–31; emphasis mine.
32 Somerset, "Vernacular Argumentation," 210.
33 Detailed, comparative analysis of the trials and self-portraits of Thorpe and Wyche can be found in Joanna Summers, *Late-Medieval Prison Writings and the Politics of Autobiography* (Oxford, 2004), Chapter 4.
34 See the official record of Wyche's trial printed in Matthew, "Trial of Richard Wyche."
35 Christina von Nolcken, "Richard Wyche, a Certain Knight, and the Beginning of the End," in *Lollardy and Gentry*, 127–54.

Wyche responds, "It suffices for any faithful person to believe as Christ says, not adding to his words."[36]

Issues of authority recur yet again in our third and final narrative of a heresy examination that was written from the perspective of the defense rather than the prosecution. In Chapter 2, I described John Oldcastle's abortive revolt against King Henry V and mentioned that in 1413, prior to the rebellion, Oldcastle had appeared before an ecclesiastical court on suspicion of holding and teaching lollard beliefs.[37] An unsigned text that purports to be an account of the proceedings undertaken against him at that time was printed first by William Tyndale in Antwerp in 1530 and then again by John Bale, also in Antwerp, in 1544.[38] Like Thorpe and Wyche, many of the questions put to Oldcastle concerned his beliefs about the eucharist; also like his predecessors, Oldcastle used such questions as a segue into a discussion of what Christians must believe, as opposed to what he accused the institutional church of compelling Christians to believe. Asked about the remanence of material bread after the words of consecration, for example, Oldcastle allegedly responded: "The scriptus maketh no mecion of this woorde materyal: and therfore my faith hath nothing to do therwith. But thys I say and beleue it, that it is Cristes bodye and bread."[39] Unsurprisingly, this answer proved unsatisfactory to his inquisitors, who exhorted him to believe as the church had determined. He responded that his inquisitors "be no part of crists holy churche, as your ope[n] dedes doth shew." For Oldcastle, the church is instead "the number of them which shalbe saued of whom Christ is the head."[40]

The texts concerning the trials of Wyche and Oldcastle present different interpretive challenges. For Wyche's letter, the key issue is similar to the one we

---

36 Matthew, "Trial of Richard Wyche," 537: "Tu dicis quod Christus dicit: Hoc est corpus meum; ideo oportet se credere quod hoc est nisi corpus suum et sic non panis. Sufficit, dixi, cuilibet fideli credere sicut Christus dicit, non addendo verbis eius." For additional discussion of Wyche, see Chapter 2, 42, above.

37 Kelly, "Lollard Inquisitions," 289. The only article-length biography of Oldcastle, apart from the entry by John A.F. Thomson in the *Oxford Dictionary of National Biography*, is W.T. Waugh's 1905 article "Sir John Oldcastle," *English Historical Review* 20 (1905), 434–56, 637–58. A new, compelling examination of the evidence for Oldcastle's trial and its communication to broad publics is Diane Vincent, "The Contest over the Public Imagination of Inquisition, 1380–1430," in *The Culture of Inquisition in England, 1215–1515*, (eds.) Mary C. Flannery and Katie L. Walter (Woodbridge, 2013), 60–76.

38 The early printed texts are STC 24045 and 1276, respectively.

39 John Bale, *A brefe chronycle concernynge the examinacyon…of syr Iohan Oldcastell the lorde Cobham* (Antwerp, 1544), Diiii v.

40 Bale, *Brefe chronicle*, Dv v; Dvi r.

encountered in Thorpe's case: can a heresy defendant be expected to portray his inquisitors as well as his responses to them accurately? For the account of Oldcastle's interrogation, the fact that neither Tyndale nor Bale named the source for the text that they printed should raise an additional eyebrow. It may not be coincidental that Tyndale printed his version of Oldcastle's examination in the same pamphlet as his edition of Thorpe's *Testimony*; they are similarly structured enough that some borrowing of one text from the other is possible.

It should be apparent from even this cursory summary of texts by or about Thorpe, Wyche, and Oldcastle that narratives produced by suspects in heresy investigations are unlikely to meet modern standards of reportorial accuracy. Not only did heresy suspects not have access to writing materials, but they also had every reason to recount the stories of their trials in ways that emphasize the theological themes that they believed differentiated them from their inquisitors. Yet if it is not wise to trust that heresy suspects recorded "the truth, the whole truth, and nothing but the truth" about their trials, then it is equally foolish to trust the veracity of the records produced by the courts that tried them. Suspicions about the motives of ecclesiastical judges can be traced back at least as far as the time of John Foxe, and starting in the late nineteenth century, a number of historians and literary scholars have leveled substantial critiques at the accuracy of trial records and the methods of those historians who have used them too naively.[41] These critiques become all the more forceful when one considers that the records of many heresy trials are no longer extant in their original form; instead, their contents are available to scholars only through the published writings and unpublished notebooks of Reformation-era propagandists like Foxe, or through the surviving, often abridged, copies of the records made by later church officials.

Broadly speaking, modern scholars have advanced four sets of arguments against uncritical readings of the trial records. The first of these is that the procedures that governed the trials and sentencing of defendants may have resulted in oversimplifications of their views. In both early and later periods of the campaign against lollardy, bishops and inquisitors came to believe that a lollard would possess a certain set of theological views. If they agreed with Henry Knighton that lollards spoke "according to a single common idiom," then the easiest way for judges to determine who was and who was not a lollard was to ask each suspect about the most controversial issues of the day: the

---

41 The traditional account of the late medieval inquisition as a bloodthirsty and ruthless organization can be found in Henry Charles Lea, *A History of the Inquisition in the Middle Ages*, 3 vols. (London, 1888), vol. 1.

presence of Christ in the eucharist, the validity of the other sacraments, and the authority of the pope and church hierarchy.[42] As a result, especially once inquisitors began to make use of formal questionnaires, the range of topics that an individual heresy trial covered narrowed quite sharply; the use of standardized interrogation techniques also made it more likely that those defendants who abjured did so in roughly consistent language. The repetition of many of the same articles in surviving abjurations suggests that the preconceptions of inquisitors and the conveniences entailed in using formulae to capture defendants' beliefs shaped the manner in which those beliefs were recorded for posterity. Thus, scholars such as R.N. Swanson, Paul Strohm, Norman Tanner, and Shannon McSheffrey have argued that the extant records of heresy trials permit us to access only what inquisitors thought about heretics, rather than what heretics thought about themselves.[43] In a recent study, Swanson has gone further, claiming that orthodox attention to lollardy may have given it "more coherence as a programme and movement than it actually possessed, and thus stimulated a more coherent, comprehensive and anxious institutional response."[44]

A second set of objections has to do with the chronological and documentary gaps between the original proceedings of a heresy trial and the manner in which those proceedings were recorded. As Leonard Boyle and others have pointed out with regard to the analogous case of "Cathar" heretics in the Languedoc, most records extant today are at a remove of several degrees from the events that they document.[45] The scribe recording a particular proceeding may have transformed a defendant's English words (only a few heresy defendants in late

---

42   Knighton, 302. See further comments on the concept of a lollard "sect vocabulary" at 73–74 and 106–107 above.

43   For these critiques, see R.N. Swanson, *Church and Society in Late Medieval England* (Oxford, 1989); Paul Strohm, "Counterfeiters, Lollards, and Lancastrian Unease," in *New Medieval Literatures*, (eds.) Wendy Scase, Rita Copeland, and David Lawton, vol. 1 (Oxford, 1997), 31–58; *Coventry*, 14. Swanson has recently softened his views in this area: see "'…Et examinatus dicit…': Oral and Personal History in the Records of English Ecclesiastical Courts," in *Voices from the Bench: The Narratives of Lesser Folk in Medieval Trials*, (ed.) Michael Goodich (New York, 2005), 203–25.

44   R.N. Swanson, "'Lollardy,' 'Orthodoxy,' and 'Resistance' in Pre-Reformation England," *Theological Journal* (Tartu, Estonia) 64:1 (2003), 12–26.

45   Leonard E. Boyle, "Montaillou Revisited: Mentalité and Methodology," in *Pathways to Medieval Peasants*, (ed.) J. Raftis (Toronto, 1981), 119–40; see also Peter Biller, "'Deep Is the Heart of Man, and Inscrutable': Signs of Heresy in Medieval Languedoc," in *Text and Controversy*, 267–80; and Margaret Aston, "Bishops and Heresy: The Defence of the Faith," in *Faith and Fire*, 73–94.

THEIR TRIALS   173

medieval England were able to speak—much less to write—Latin) into a series of formal Latin articles and then later may have used those articles to compose an abjuration in the vernacular for the defendant to read and sign. These transitions from English to Latin and back to English again would on their own have made it likely that some defendants' thoughts were garbled by scribes, and the often significant differences in defendants' and scribes' levels of theological knowledge and education most certainly did not help.[46] In addition, the bishops' registers and heresy court-books available to modern historians are not always the original records of the trials they document. For instance, in the case of Margery Baxter, the original minutes of the proceedings, which are no longer extant, were recopied shortly after the trials took place; the twentieth-century editor of these records has speculated that Bishop Alnwick ordered the production of the manuscript copy in order to have a complete record of the trials available for later reference.[47] This process may have resulted in a summary, rather than a verbatim transcript, of the original material, though in cases where the original documents have not survived, it is impossible to know with certainty. Margaret Aston has pursued this line of argumentation with perhaps the greatest vigor, adding that the records of heresy trials may in some cases have influenced one another. Since many bishops and inquisitors believed that all lollards thought alike, these churchmen sometimes circulated among themselves the records of heresy trials under their jurisdiction. A defendant, therefore, might well have been asked about unusual or unexpected ideas that had surfaced in trials that had taken place elsewhere in his diocese or even in other dioceses around England.[48]

In other cases, the instability of the records may have less to do with the ordinary chance events that affect the survival of all types of medieval records than with the possibility of deliberate tampering. John Thomson and Thomas Freeman have both pointed out that Reformation martyrologists such as John Foxe likely removed from the records those claims made by heresy defendants that would have revealed, in theological terms, that they were something other

---

46   In one of the more fanciful, yet fascinating, contributions to the literature on the trials of lollards, Steven Justice has argued that John Exeter, the scribe of the Norwich court that tried Margery Baxter, recorded some of the defendants' words in English simply because he was bored and found them interesting in the middle of a long day of inquisitorial activity. See Justice, "Inquisition, Speech, and Writing: A Case from Late Medieval Norwich," *Representations* 48 (1994), 1–29. There is, of course, no way to prove or disprove Justice's hypothesis, but as I discuss below, Exeter's scribal habits may provide us with important reasons to trust the registrars of heresy proceedings.

47   *Norwich*, 5.

48   Margaret Aston, "Bishops and Heresy," 73–80.

than the forerunners of sixteenth-century English evangelicals.[49] For instance, as we saw in Chapter 5, Foxe neglected to mention that several dozen lollards had denied the necessity of baptism, with some arguing that a child born to baptized Christians had already been baptized in her mother's womb.[50]

A third set of arguments against the utility of trial records rests on the possibility that some defendants lied to inquisitors, or at the very least massaged their testimony, thus rendering the documents an uncertain source of knowledge for what heresy suspects actually believed. In the early fourteenth century, the Dominican friar Bernard Gui, who was then leading the inquisition into heresy in the south of France, wrote in his book *Practica inquisitionis hereticae pravitatis* (*Practices of the Inquisition into Heretical Depravity*) that heresy suspects not only lied but also agreed among one another on a tale to tell the church's representatives.[51] It is possible that some English lollards did the same: at least one lollard text, titled by its editor "Sixteen Points on Which the Bishops Accuse Lollards," provides a set of ready-made responses to questions often asked about the eucharist, the papacy, and other doctrines.[52] If Wycliffites advised one another on how to respond to their inquisitors, then it cannot be taken for granted that their answers (and, hence, the reporting of their answers in trial records) reflected their deepest personal beliefs.

Finally, also taking their methodological cues from the study of medieval heresy in the south of France, some scholars have recently begun to consider the effect that the vast power differentials between suspects and inquisitors had on the records of heresy proceedings. Historians of the religious phenomenon commonly known as Catharism have drawn upon critical theorist Michel Foucault's perspective on the relationship between inquisitor and accused. Among the more successful of studies in this vein has been John Arnold's *Inquisition and* Power, which argues that much of what appears in the records of heresy trials reflects the power of inquisitors to determine what theological topics were and were not worthy of discussion. Arnold also claims that despite this form of theological colonization, some of the defendants' own concerns

---

49 J.A.F. Thomson, "John Foxe and Some Sources for Lollard History: Notes for a Critical Reappraisal," in *Studies in Church History* 2, (ed.) G.J. Cuming (London, 1965), 251–57. Thomas Freeman, "Texts, Lies, and Microfilm: Reading and Misreading Foxe's 'Book of Martyrs," *Sixteenth Century Journal* 30 (1999), 23–46, points out that some of Foxe's Victorian editors attempted clumsily to hide Foxe's omissions, in the process introducing additional instabilities into his text.

50 See 117–20 above.

51 Translated in *Heresies of the High Middle Ages*, (eds. and trans.) Walter L. Wakefield and Austin Evans (New York, 1991), esp. 397–402.

52 Printed in *Selections*, 19–24.

do surface in the records.[53] The most recent application of this line of thought to the trials of suspected lollards appears in the work of Genelle Gertz, who has argued that "the fact that the court required abjurations to be written in English, drafted in the first-person voice, and signed by the accused merely reinforced the problem of their authenticity. The abjuration appeared to represent the individual voice of the person on trial, but when it actually supplied that face one heard only ventriloquism—it was the court's confession, after all, and not the defendant's."[54]

Scholars working in this vein have also borrowed from insights from the study of heresy in other periods of the history of Christianity. For instance, as Rowan Williams argued in his study of fourth- and fifth-century "Arian" beliefs, the frequency with which particular topics appear in the records of church authorities does not necessarily correlate with the importance that those topics held for the women and men who spoke about them.[55] The nature of a heresy trial was such that, in most records, a suspect's beliefs appear not in the order and to the extent that he chose, but rather in the order and to the extent that inquisitors and scribes wished them to appear. If he were able to utter them at all, a suspect's statements about the meaning for him of lollard forms of Christianity could all but disappear under the weight of negative claims about which aspects of traditional religion he did or did not reject. As we saw in Chapter 3, the scanty evidence for lollards' spiritual and religious practices, or for the appeal of lollardy as a religious system, may the result of this tendency. Especially when these practices were neither controversial nor heterodox in and of themselves, it is unlikely that a defendant's explanation of them would have been significant enough to inquisitors for it to appear in the distilled account of her trial preserved in a bishop's register.

Each of these four sets of arguments should, in its own way, give pause to those who would too quickly read the records of medieval heresy trials as if

---

53 Arnold, *Inquistion and Power: Catharism and the Confessing Subject in Medieval Languedoc* (Philadelphia, 2011). Arnold's approach is not without its critics, however. Mark Gregory Pegg has claimed that Arnold's method, far from uncovering the dynamics of representation in Cathar trial records, reinscribes old assumptions about "the Inquisition" and "the Cathars." See his review of Arnold, *Speculum* 79 (2004), 123–25. For a summary of his own position, as well as for passing comments on the study of English lollardy, see Mark Gregory Pegg, "Albigenses and the Antipodes: An Australian and the Cathars," *Journal of Religious History* 35 (2011), 577–600.

54 Genelle Gertz, "Heresy Inquisition and Authorship, 1400–1560," in *The Culture of Inquisition in England, 1215–1515*, (eds.) Mary C. Flannery and Katie L. Walter (Woodbridge, 2013), 130–45. See also Moore, "War against Heresy," 191.

55 Rowan Williams, *Arius: Heresy and Tradition*, 2nd ed. (London, 2001), 95.

they were the transcripts of Congressional hearings or court proceedings today. In the 1990s and early 2000s, as scholars began to take more seriously the possibility that "lollardy" designated less an organized, coherent religious movement and more the politically charged construct of ecclesiastical and civil authorities, skepticism about the usefulness of trial records as sources for the beliefs of late medieval heresy defendants reached its peak.[56] The concerns of these historians catalyzed a re-evaluation of the evidentiary value of such sources, and it has only been in recent years that trial records have once again been used prominently in the study of heresy in late medieval England. For instance, Michael Goodich has observed that despite the obvious limitations of these documents, "the probing questions of the court officials may allow us to recreate the lost private worlds of a host of otherwise silent denizens of our historical imagination."[57]

Likewise, in my 2010 book, *What Is a Lollard?*, I argued that critics have sometimes exaggerated the limitations of trial records.[58] To illustrate my point, I turned to the case of William Masse of Earsham, who was tried in 1431 by the same bishop of Norwich who had brought Margery Baxter to court. I observed that in producing the surviving copy of the record of Masse's trial, the scribe John Exeter crossed out with his pen one of the eight heterodox claims that Masse was accused of affirming.[59] It is not difficult to conclude that this particular article, which accused Masse of denying the doctrine of transubstantiation, had been included in the original record mistakenly. Perhaps as a result of the effects of inquisitorial questionnaires, at least thirty-four other defendants who appeared before Bishop Alnwick were charged with the same heresy, but it seems that Masse was not. It is harder, however, to explain why Exeter crossed out the mistaken article. If medieval inquisitors were as keen to stereotype heresy defendants as some critics have suggested, then Exeter would have had no reason to regret, much less to correct, his error. There was little propaganda value in ensuring that the record of Masse's trial was accurate, because he prepared his court-book only for the internal use of the bishop and his colleagues. And from a legal point of view, the specific heresies that Masse had abjured were irrelevant: if he had been tried again at some later date, then conviction

---

56   In this regard, see especially McSheffrey's and Tanner's preface to their edition of trial records from Coventry and Lichfield diocese: *Coventry*, 14.

57   Michael Goodich, introduction to *Voices from the Bench: The Narratives of Lesser Folk in Medieval Trials* (New York, 2005), 2–3.

58   J. Patrick Hornbeck II, *What Is a Lollard? Dissent and Belief in Late Medieval England* (Oxford, 2010), xi–xviii.

59   London, Westminster Diocesan Archives, B.2, 250.

on any count of heresy would have constituted relapse. The most likely explanation, therefore, is that Exeter was a conscientious scribe and was genuinely concerned for the accuracy of his record.

I also used Exeter's Norwich court-book to argue that while documents of its sort often betray the traces of inquisitorial formulae, they sometimes do reveal what may actually have been said in the ecclesiastical courtrooms of the later Middle Ages. In fact, one of the most intriguing features of Exeter's manuscript is the way in which it breaks down the boundaries between Latin and vernacular discourses. In recording the 1429 trial of John Burell, for example, Exeter notes that the defendant

> dicit...quod quidam sutor, famulus Thome Mone, docuit...quod nullus homo tenetur ieiunare diebus Quadragesimalibus nec sextis feriis nec vigiliis apostolorum, quia talia ieiunia nunquam erant instituta ex precepto divino sed tantum ex ordinacione presbiterorum, for every Fryday is fre day.[60]
>
> [said that a certain cobbler, a servant of Thomas Mone, taught that no man is obligated to fast on the days of Lent, or on Fridays or on the vigils of the apostles, for no fast was instituted by divine command, but rather by the commandment of the priests, for every Friday is a free day.]

In the original record, which I have transcribed verbatim here, Exeter slides without comment from judicial Latin into vernacular English, recording Burell's pun on the words *Friday/free day*. In other dioceses as well, scribes preserved defendants' English words not in their abjurations, which as we have already seen ecclesiastical officials usually prepared for them, but instead in the surviving depositions of witnesses. Thus, the Coventry tailor Roger Landesdale's vernacular explication of the eucharist as a memorial of Jesus' death appears in the testimony of his fellow suspect Thomas Abell. The Coventry lollards' passwords ("May we all drinke of a cuppe" and "God kepe you and God blesse you"), by which they allegedly identified themselves to one another, were disclosed in Landesdale's own testimony.[61]

I continue to believe that cases like Masse's and Burell's demonstrate that at least some of the individuals involved in the prosecution of heresy in the later Middle Ages were conscientious enough not to tar all heretics with the same broad brush. As I look back on my earlier argument, though, I wonder if I perhaps pressed the point too strongly: could it be that the instances in which trial

---

60   London, Westminster Diocesan Archives, B.2, 234; see also the printed edition in *Norwich*, 74.
61   *Coventry*, 117.

records mostly accurately reflect the content of late medieval court proceedings are significantly outnumbered by the instances in which they are simply too formulaic to be useful? The only way to answer this question will be to review the records themselves.

7.3   A Survey of the Extant Records

Documents that record the trials of heresy suspects survive in the archives of many English dioceses and in local record offices, as well as in other repositories such as The National Archives and in the printed works of medieval chroniclers and early modern historians.[62] The earliest of these documents, which notes the appearance of Wyclif's immediate followers Nicholas Hereford, Philip Repingdon, and John Aston before the Blackfriars Council, dates from 1382.[63] Between that year and 1517, when Martin Luther fatefully posted his theses on the door of the Wittenberg castle church and after which, as a result, the possibility of overlap between Lutheran and native English lollard beliefs makes the nature of suspects' views progressively more difficult to distinguish, records survive for more than 650 individuals who were formally charged with the crime of heresy. In the case of approximately two-thirds, or roughly 420, of these defendants, information is also preserved about the specific beliefs that they were accused of holding. The quality of the physical evidence—which takes the form of bishops' registers, court-books, letter rolls, and other documents—ranges widely, as does the level of detail recorded for each defendant.

The number of trials conducted during each year of this approximately 140-year period varied substantially. Indeed, the prosecution of heresy was neither as continuous nor as intense as evangelical propagandists charged a century

---

[62]   Details of the whereabouts of specific documents may be found via the Access to Archives project of The National Archives: www.nationalarchives.gov.uk/a2a, accessed 10 July 2014. For bishops' registers, detailed tables of contents have been compiled by David Smith in his excellent *Guide to Bishops' Registers of England and Wales: A Survey from the Middle Ages to the Abolition of Episcopacy in 1646* (London, 1981), and its supplement (London, 2004).

[63]   A number of recent studies have emphasized that the charges against Wyclif's followers were not the first accusations of heresy made in medieval England. Andrew E. Larsen's book *The School of Heretics: Academic Condemnation at the University of Oxford, 1277–1409* (Leiden, 2011) examines in detail practices of intramural censure at Oxford, and Kathryn Kerby-Fulton, in *Books under Suspicion: Censorship and Tolerance of Revelatory Writing in Late Medieval England* (South Bend, Ind., 2006), has likewise catalogued a series of heresy proceedings unrelated to Wyclif and his views.

later; in fact, most years saw only a few heresy trials take place anywhere in England, and a number of years witnessed not a single trial. It was only toward the end of the fifteenth century, starting in the late 1480s, that heresy prosecutions became a regular feature of English church life; in the early years of the sixteenth century, they intensified further still.

What might account for these dramatic variations in the number of heresy trials conducted each year? A facile explanation might be that the appeal of lollardy waxed and waned a number of times over the course of the decades; another alternative might be that lollards' willingness to express their convictions publicly likewise changed. No doubt both of these hypotheses carry some truth, but it is unlikely that the number of heresy trials in any given year is directly proportionate to the number of people who held heterodox beliefs at that point in time. Instead, we must look to a series of other factors, both internal and external to the church, that shaped the institutional response to lollardy. On the one hand, some bishops valued the prosecution of heresy more highly than others; thus, for instance, Lincoln bishop Philip Repingdon (r. 1405–1419), himself a former follower of Wyclif's, tried fewer cases over the fifteen years of his episcopacy than the later bishop of Lincoln John Chedworth (r. 1451–71) did in the single year 1467. When bishops conducted visitations of their dioceses, they were more likely to encounter accusations of heresy than when they remained at their residences or served at the royal court. Absentee bishops, such as those who resided in London while they discharged their duties as officers of state, were on the whole less likely to pursue heresy prosecutions than resident bishops. At the same time, English bishops may have occasionally felt pressure from the wider church to demonstrate that the country which had given birth to John Wyclif was responding well to the threat posed by lollardy. It is for this reason, some have argued, that many of the years with the largest numbers of heresy prosecutions coincided with the impending convocation of church councils, including the Council of Basel in 1431 and the Fifth Lateran Council in 1512.[64] On the other hand, the century after Wyclif's emergence into prominence witnessed a series of seismic events in English politics, not least the internecine struggles known to history as the Wars of the Roses. Bishops, too, were involved in these conflicts, and the relative dearth of heresy prosecutions in wartime may testify to the fact that many bishops were focusing their energies elsewhere. Likewise, both the accession of Henry Tudor in 1485 and the coronation of the second Tudor monarch, Henry VIII, in 1509

---

64 On this point, see *Norwich*, 7–8; *Coventry*, 4; John Fines, "Heresy Trials in the Diocese of Coventry and Lichfield," *Journal of Ecclesiastical History* 14 (1963), 160–174 at 160.

may have provided the impetus for renewed anti-heresy proceedings on the part of bishops who wished to endear themselves to the Crown.

Whatever the reasons, it is clear that the prosecution of heresy in late medieval England moved in fits and starts. It is impossible to describe in detail the whole of the church's anti-heresy initiatives, but in what follows, I will survey a number of the most energetic campaigns against lollardy undertaken by the English episcopate.[65] I have already described the trials of several prominent lollards, including William Swinderby, Walter Brut, William Sawtre, and William White, in Chapter 2.

In 1389, Archbishop William Courtenay undertook a massive visitation of all the dioceses in Canterbury province, an action that was not well received by some of his suffragan bishops. At Ramsey Abbey, in Cambridgeshire, the archbishop encountered a monk who "had become tainted with Wyclyf's teachings and for a long time had refused to say mass or receive communion."[66] Courtenay convinced the errant monk to abjure and ordered that he be reported if he said mass fewer than twice each week. In the town of Leicester, in Lincoln diocese, the archbishop encountered a group of eight lollards, among them a chaplain, Richard Waystathe. They were charged with a series of articles concerning the eucharist, penance, holy orders, the power of the church over excommunication, and the adoration of images, including the crucifix. Initially, the archbishop placed under interdict any church that the defendants might enter; later in the course of his visitation, he received four of the suspects back into communion and assigned them penances.[67]

Heresy was not, of course, so easily eliminated from Lincoln diocese, where both the University of Oxford and Wyclif's parish of Lutterworth were situated. In 1413, Philip Repingdon, formerly canon and abbot of Leicester Abbey and now bishop of Lincoln, carried out a visitation of his diocese's archdeaconry of Leicester, uncovering a total of more than seven hundred crimes and other faults committed by 575 defendants.[68] Among them, seven defendants were charged with heresy, and one was accused of preaching without holding a license from the relevant parish priest. Three defendants, William Tryvet, John

---

65   A highly detailed account of English heresy trials in the period after Oldcastle's revolt can be found in J.A.F. Thomson's classic study, *Later Lollards*.

66   J.H. Dahmus, (ed.), *The Metropolitan Visitations of William Courtenay, Archbishop of Canterbury, 1381–1396* (Urbana, Ill., 1950), 45, 156–57; see also Dahmus, *William Courtenay, Archbishop of Canterbury, 1381–1396* (University Park, Pa., 1966).

67   Dahmus, (ed.), *Metropolitan Visitations*, 48–50, 164–72.

68   Forrest, *Detection*, 208; an earlier study of some of these proceedings appears in Crompton, "Leicestershire Lollards," 11–44. The original record of the proceedings appears in Lincoln, Lincolnshire Archives, Vj/0.

Belgrave, and John Anneys, were charged with preaching in local taverns; three others, John Hutte junior, Peter Herrick, and William Smith were in possession of "suspect English books" and had allegedly been declaring publicly that priests could preach anywhere, the requirements of Archbishop Arundel's constitutions notwithstanding. A majority of the suspects were prominent and prosperous members of the local community, a fact that in at least a few of their cases may have made convictions harder for Repingdon to obtain.[69]

Sir John Oldcastle's abortive revolt of 1414 led to the arrest and prosecution of a number of his followers; the primary charge against them, however, was sedition rather than heresy, and the records of proceedings against them accordingly survive in secular rather than ecclesiastical archives.[70]

It was not until the late 1420s that an extensive series of heresy cases was again pursued by a single bishop. Archbishop Henry Chichele, Arundel's successor in Canterbury, had conducted heresy trials throughout his episcopacy, but in the provincial convocation of 1428, he charged approximately two dozen suspects with a range of heretical views. Other bishops likewise followed suit.

The year that saw the greatest number of heresy trials under Archbishop Chichele also witnessed the beginning of one of the series of investigations for which the most detailed evidence survives. Beginning on September 2, 1428, and continuing through March 1431, Bishop William Alnwick of Norwich summoned at least sixty heresy defendants to appear before him. Most of the trials took place at Alnwick's palace in Norwich or at his manor-house at Thorpe, just outside the city; either Alnwick himself or his vicar-general, William Bernham, presided at almost all of the trials. John Exeter, the scribe about whose activities we have been learning, recorded almost all of the minutes; they were later compiled, likely also by Exeter, into one of the few court-books from late medieval England dedicated solely to heresy proceedings. The book is now part of a manuscript in the keeping of the Roman Catholic archbishop of Westminster.

Far from being localized in a single place, the defendants whom Alnwick tried hailed from a number of small towns and villages in the diocese of Norwich; most came from Norfolk and northern Suffolk localities near to Norwich, but very few from the city itself. Small groups of defendants reported that they knew one another, but the Norwich defendants as a whole seem not to have formed a cohesive community. Instead, local leaders such as Thomas and Hawisia Mone in Loddon and John and Sybil Godsell in Ditchingham seem to have provided space for nearby associates to meet in their homes; in these

---

69   Forrest, *Detection*, 213–19.
70   See, for instance, *Calendar of Patent Rolls* (London, 1901), 1413–16: 157, 162, 175, 200, and *Calendar of Close Rolls* (London, 1900), 1413–19: 109–10, 114–15, 176–77, 428, 434–35.

"scoles of heresie," as Hawisia Mone's abjuration called them, group members almost certainly heard readings from forbidden books written in the vernacular tongue.

The beliefs the Norwich defendants confessed to holding and teaching ran the gamut from the commonplace to the outlandish. Ideas about the sacraments predominated, with refusal to engage in traditional devotional practices like fasting and reverencing images of the saints running a close second. In Exeter's manuscript, many charges—such as belief in the remanance of material bread in the sacrament of the eucharist, the redundancy of baptism when a child's parents were themselves baptized, and the superfluity of the sacrament of confirmation—recur verbatim in one trial after another, and it must remain unclear to what extent any of the defendants involved would have formulated her opinions in these terms.[71] Some defendants' views, such as those of William Colyn, were truly idiosyncratic: in addition to confessing that he had said that he would rather touch a woman's genitals than the eucharistic host, he also admitted to believing that the sacrament of marriage had been annulled and that all women were to be held in common.[72] In other cases, as I mentioned above, Exeter recorded puns and other exclamations that were likely the defendants' original English words: the record for the trial of Margery Baxter, for instance, interrupts a Latin sentence to record Baxter's comparison of prelates to "that cursed Thomma of Canterbury, for thay falsly and cursedly desseyve the puple with thair false mawentryes and lawes."[73]

None of the Norwich defendants was sent to the stake, and some escaped penance by purging themselves through the assistance of witnesses. On those who confessed to holding heterodox beliefs, Alnwick imposed a range of penances, including flogging, fasts of various lengths, and public penance either before the bishop or before a local parish community for a certain number of days or years. The punishments of being branded or wearing a badge on one's outer garments were not employed in the Norwich trials, nor were most defendants restricted from moving freely around the diocese and the countryside.

---

71   For instance, at least a dozen defendants in the Norwich trials abjured nearly identical articles concerning the necessity of baptism, both in Latin and in English: "quod sacramentum Baptismi, factum in aqua in forma in Ecclesia communiter usitata, parum vel modicum est ponderandum si parentes infantis nati sint Christiani"; "that the sacrament of Baptem done in water in fourme customed in the Churche is of non avail and not to be pondret if the fadir and modir of the childe be christened and of Cristene beleve" (*Norwich*, 107, 111; cp. 46, 52, 56, 60, 66, 95, 126, 134, 157, 165, 196). See above, 119–20.
72   *Norwich*, 91.
73   *Norwich*, 45.

Alnwick's trials represented the final large-scale persecution of suspected lollards that took place during the lifetimes of Wyclif's known associates. Thereafter, it was not for more than another three decades that a bishop was to try more than a few defendants at a time. In the mid- to late 1460s, John Chedworth, then bishop of Lincoln, prosecuted nearly fifty suspects for heresy. In comparison to Alnwick's court-book, his register unfortunately records few details about the beliefs of most of these defendants. One of them, John Qwyrk, declared that he believed the eucharist to be merely a memorial of Christ's sacrifice, a position that, as we saw in Chapter 5, was shared by few of his contemporaries.[74] Another, William Apleward, had previously been arrested on charges of sorcery and now returned to Chedworth's court to answer the accusation that he had made heterodox and blasphemous statements about the eucharist, baptism, penance, the pope, and the important English relic the Blood of Hailes.[75] A number of Chedworth's defendants also admitted to possessing English books, whether translations of the gospels, sermons, portions of Chaucer's *Canterbury Tales*, or other vernacular works.[76]

Like Chedworth's register, the extant records for the series of trials conducted by John Stanbury, bishop of Hereford, and Robert Stillington, bishop of Bath and Wells, reveal little about the thirteen and six defendants that they prosecuted, respectively, in the 1470s.

The reigns of Henry VII and Henry VIII both saw renewed interest among English bishops in prosecuting heresy suspects. In the elder Henry's case, his accession to the throne coincided with the first of two major initiatives against heresy in the diocese of Coventry and Lichfield, to which we shall return momentarily. Later in his reign, prosecutions took place in Norwich diocese under Bishop Richard Nykke; in Salisbury diocese under two successive bishops, Thomas Langton and John Blythe; and in Bath and Wells diocese under Bishop Oliver King.[77] Both the Salisbury and the Bath and Wells cases revolved primarily around defendants' beliefs about the eucharist, with heterodox statements about the adoration of images and pilgrimage also appearing regularly. Two Salisbury defendants, Thomas Tailour and Augustine Sterne, dubbed the pope a "panyer maker," which may have been a reference to the burdens that these defendants believed the pope had placed on the backs of true

---

[74] Lincoln reg. Chedworth, fols. 59v–60; see 124 above for further discussion of Qwyrk's case and its place in the history of lollard ideas about the eucharist.

[75] Lincoln reg. Chedworth, fol. 61–61v.

[76] See, for instance, the case of John Baron: Lincoln reg. Chedworth, fol. 62v.

[77] On Norwich, see R.A. Houlbrooke, "Persecution of Heresy and Protestantism in the Diocese of Norwich under Henry VIII," *Norfolk Archaelogy* 35 (1973), 308–26.

Christians. A few such defendants made unusual statements: the record of the Salisbury case of Richard Hyllyng notes his prophecy that "within [ten] yere space ther shalbe one folde and one sheppard meanyng herby that all heretikis and lollardis the which have receyved grace shall preche openly and no man shall dare say agayn theim."[78] One of the Bath and Wells defendants, John Walsh, declared that there are three gods.[79]

Just as happened around the time of his father's accession, the arrival of Henry VIII on the English throne coincided with a rise in episcopal interest in heresy. Within a few years of the younger Henry's coronation, no fewer than five dioceses had undertaken substantial anti-heresy campaigns; these may have been timed to coincide with the convocation of Lateran V, at which the English delegation was under pressure to demonstrate that the island nation had responded adequately to the danger of false belief. Bishops Edmund Audley of Salisbury, Richard Fitzjames of London, Richard Fox of Winchester, and Geoffrey Blythe of Coventry and Lichfield, along with Archbishop William Warham, together tried no fewer than 165 defendants in the period from 1509 to 1516. In Canterbury, Warham summoned to trial fifty-three men and women from a variety of Kentish villages; the greatest numbers of suspects came from Tenterden, Maidstone, and Cranbrook.[80] Of these defendants, he sent five to the stake; one of them, John Browne, was a relapsed heretic who had previously abjured under Archbishop John Morton.[81] Since the records of Warham's trials are even more formulaic than usual, it is likely that he relied on questionnaires in examining his defendants. The evidentiary value of his register therefore lies not so much in what it can disclose about lollard belief as in what it reveals about the archbishop's sentencing practices; as Norman Tanner has shown, Warham tailored the penances he assigned each defendant to fit the crimes of which she was accused.[82]

---

78 Salisbury reg. Langton, 75–6, nos. 488–94.
79 Bath and Wells reg. King, 40–1, no. 239.
80 Both Tenterden and Cranbrook were sites of long-term episcopal interest in heresy, with cases involving the two villages dating from the 1420s through the later Reformation in England. See, on Tenterden, Robert Lutton, *Lollardy and Orthodox Religion in Pre-Reformation England: Reconstructing Piety* (London, 2006), and on Cranbrook, Patrick Collinson, "Cranbrook and the Fletchers: Popular and Unpopular Religion in the Kentish Weald," in *Reformation Principle and Practice: Essays Presented to A.G. Dickens*, (ed.) P.N. Brooks (London, 1980), 173–202.
81 *Kent*, 43–49.
82 Tanner, "Penances Imposed." Kirsti Norris, in her unpublished paper "Authors of Fate: Episcopal Voices in Lollard Trials," delivered at the International Medieval Congress, Leeds, 13 July 2009, proposed that the educational backgrounds of bishops—whether

Bishop Blythe's investigations in Coventry and Lichfield diocese were just beginning as Warham's trials in Kent were winding down. The diocese had not been immune from heresy in recent times, and among older citizens, the memory may have lingered of the trials and abjurations of eight heresy defendants under Bishop John Hales in March 1486. A few isolated cases were heard during the intervening years, but beginning in October 1511, Blythe proceeded against nearly seventy named defendants. While only one of them, Joan Warde *alias* Wasshingburn, was condemned to the stake, seven of the defendants from 1511 relapsed into heresy and were burned following a subsequent series of trials that took place in 1520 and 1522. As in the case of Bishop Alnwick's trials in Norwich, the proceedings against the latter groups of Coventry and Lichfield defendants were recorded in a dedicated court-book, now known as the Lichfield Court Book and preserved in the Lichfield Record Office, as well as in the registers of Bishops Hales and Blythe.[83]

The Lichfield Court Book records that the defendants who appeared before the bishops of Coventry and Lichfield articulated the full range of opinions associated with lollardy: in particular, Bishop Blythe seems to have been interested in his defendants' views on the eucharist, pilgrimage, and images, as well as in the books that defendants possessed and the people with whom they associated. As in Norwich, some defendants' beliefs fell well outside the bounds of what their inquisitors expected to hear: in 1490, for instance, Robert Clerke asserted that "he knew how to make people speak with God face to face."[84] Apart from those sentenced to relaxation to the secular arm for execution, the other defendants for whom a sentence was recorded were ordered to undergo public penance, with some required to walk at the head of a church procession, carrying a bundle of wood.

Heresy trials did not end in England for many centuries to come, but the final series of sustained heresy prosecutions that I have space to review here is the one that was conducted in 1511 and 1512 in Winchester diocese, under Bishop Richard Fox. During these years, Fox put on trial eleven defendants who represented two distinct communities of lollards. One group, centered on what is now the London borough of Kingston-upon-Thames, consisted of a relapsed heretic, Thomas Denys, several other longstanding religious dissenters who had been trained by heretics from other regions of the country, and a few local townspeople. Distinctively among later lollard communities, almost

---

they were, for instance, theologians or canon lawyers—shaped the matter in which they assigned penances to heresy defendants.

83   *Coventry*, 49.
84   *Coventry*, 95.

all of the defendants articulated a commemorative or figurative theology of the eucharist, according to which the sacrament is simply a way for Christians to remember Christ's sacrifice.[85] Similar statements about the eucharist also appeared among the second group of defendants, who lived in a cluster of villages near the country town of Farnham; as one of them, Elizabeth Swaffer, put it, "the body of almighty god in heven cannot be in flesh and blode in forme of brede in the Auter, for that thing that is doen there by the preest at the altar is doon in signification of the passion of Criste, and it is noen oder thing."[86] In addition to their claims about the eucharist, both groups of suspects abjured articles about confession, holy orders, the papacy, images, and pilgrimages; several defendants also confessed to owning or destroying forbidden vernacular texts. All but Denys escaped with a penance; he, however, was burned on March 6, 1512.

7.4 Conclusions

Our survey of the surviving records of the English bishops' major anti-heresy initiatives calls to mind several of the themes I identified earlier in this chapter. First, while extant documents such as bishops' registers and court-books can reveal important details about a heresy defendant's beliefs, they nevertheless cannot tell the full story. Whether because of the inherently adversarial nature of discourse between a suspect and an inquisitor, because anything less than a verbatim transcript is likely to distort the content of a trial, or because inquisitors used standard formulae and questionnaires in their investigations, crucial questions about many of the heresy trials I have been describing will always remain unanswered. Nevertheless, as we have seen, especially in the Norwich, Coventry, and Winchester records, some of the defendants' original statements and distinctive theological views can still be discerned in the pages of the documents prepared by their clerical antagonists.

Second, whether a bishop chose to proceed against one, two, a dozen, or more heresy suspects in his diocese was, in most cases, a decision largely

---

85 For additional discussion of these defendants, see Clayton J. Drees, *Authority and Dissent in the English Church: The Prosecution of Heresy and Religious Non-Conformity in the Diocese of Winchester, 1380–1547* (Lewiston, 1997), 76–83; J. Patrick Hornbeck II, "*Wycklyffes Wycket* and Eucharistic Heresy: Two Series of Cases from Sixteenth-Century Winchester," in *Wycliffite Controversies*, 279–94; and 124–25 above.

86 Winchester reg. Fox, 3: fol. 75v; the modern English translation in *Wycliffite Spirituality* is at 362–63.

dependent upon factors external to the lollard communities under persecution. The impending convocation of a church council or regional meeting of clergy, the accession to the throne of a new monarch, or the outbreak of civil war all affected the speed and vigor with which bishops pursued heresy suspects, as did other factors, local, national, and international. It is therefore unsafe to conclude from the number of trials conducted that lollardy attracted progressively larger numbers of adherents from the fifteenth through the early sixteenth centuries. I will be exploring the relevance of this fact to the history of lollardy's role in the Henrician Reformation in the next chapter.

Finally, it is worth noting that church officials, by and large, observed established procedures for the detection, investigation, and sentencing of heresy defendants. Scholars of lollardy are continuing to explore the extent to which English churchmen imported these procedures from continental Europe, but whatever their origin, they varied little from diocese to diocese and decade to decade. A few bishops and inquisitors may well have brought to their task nothing less than a hatred of heresy and its practitioners, but contrary to much earlier historiography, most were conscientious bureaucrats doing what many modern people would consider distasteful and discriminatory work. The hearings they conducted and the records they left behind testify to the seriousness with which the persecutors of lollardy approached their task, the presuppositions and stereotypes they formed about the individuals they judged, and, at the same time, the wide variety of beliefs and practices they encountered.

CHAPTER 8

Their Afterlife

Although Wyclif died in 1384, and many of his closest Oxford associates returned to the fold of the church around the turn of the fifteenth century, "lollardy" remained a word to conjure with for decades to come. Royal letters called for the expulsion of lollards from Oxford and their arrest by local bishops, and rewards were offered to those who identified lollards in hiding.[1] Suspects in cases of heresy and sedition were warned not to hold heretical opinions, nor assist lollards, "nor shew or procure them favour."[2] The stigma of lollardy reached beyond the circle of those inspired by Wyclif: without any discernible connection to the Oxford scholar or his reform movement, Margery Kempe, a mystic who fell into uncontrollable fits of tears when she recollected the passion of Christ, was reportedly called a "loller" and a heretic by the people of Yorkshire.[3] And as we saw in Chapter 1, later writers made much of lollardy for their own political and theological purposes; at least one strand of historiography since the mid-sixteenth century has held Wyclif's heresy to be a proximate cause of the English Reformation.

But what actually happened to lollards and to lollardy? This chapter surveys the range of arguments about lollardy's longevity, its influence on later events in England and on the continent, and its impact on the development of a distinctively English variety of Protestantism. In doing so, the chapter attempts to distinguish, to the greatest extent possible, between the kind of afterlife that lollard communities may actually have enjoyed in late medieval and early modern England and the kind of afterlife that historians and propagandists have *believed* that they enjoyed. This distinction will be especially important as we consider the possibility of a causal relationship between later lollardy and the English Reformation; as Peter Marshall has argued, the controversy about the nature of that relationship "is a problem as old as the Reformation itself."[4] We will begin by discussing the evidence for the survival of lollard communities from the fourteenth and fifteenth through the sixteenth centuries, as

---

1   *Calendar of Patent Rolls, 1413–1416, Henry V*, vol. 1 (London, 1910), 157.
2   *Calendar of Close Rolls, 1422–1429, Henry VI*, vol. 1 (London, 1933), 201.
3   *The Book of Margery Kempe*, (ed.) Lynn Staley (Kalamazoo, Mich., 1996), Chapters 52–53. For analysis of what Kempe's antagonists may have had in mind in denouncing her as a "loller," see Andrew Cole, *Literature and Heresy in the Age of Chaucer* (Cambridge, 2008), 156–81.
4   Peter Marshall, "Lollards and Protestants Revisited," in *Wycliffite Controversies*, pp. 295–318 at 295.

well as by investigating the transmission of lollard texts from England to Bohemia and the formative influence that lollard ideas had on several early evangelical reformers. Next, we will consider the ways in which some of the first Reformation historiographers, John Bale and John Foxe, cast lollardy in a vital supporting role in their narratives of the religious changes of the sixteenth century. The chapter will conclude with a brief survey of later accounts of the place of lollardy in the genesis and success of the English Reformation.

8.1   Lollards and Lollard Communities in the Sixteenth Century

Toward the end of the previous chapter, we discovered that the first two decades of the sixteenth century witnessed a number of major anti-heresy initiatives being carried out by English bishops. Some such efforts, such as the trials conducted by Archbishop William Warham in Canterbury diocese, Bishop Richard Fox in Winchester diocese, and Bishop Geoffrey Blythe in Coventry and Lichfield diocese, involved dozens of defendants. A substantial majority of the views that these defendants abjured resembled the doctrines that earlier generations of inquisitors had associated with Wyclif and lollardy. However, as we also learned in Chapter 7, doctrinal similarity does not necessarily nor decisively imply the influence of one individual or group on another. So, can we say that these sixteenth century defendants owed their beliefs to Wyclif and his long-dead followers?

It would be a mistake to assume that all the defendants caught up in the anti-heresy prosecutions of the early sixteenth century were members of discrete, self-identified communities, whether or not they called themselves lollards. In some instances, these individuals certainly were: many of the defendants in Bishop Blythe's trials, for instance, reported knowing and interacting with one another. Likewise, two distinct cells of defendants emerged from the trials that Bishop Fox held in two separate locations in Winchester diocese: some suspects were from what is now the London borough of Kingston-upon-Thames, while others came from a collection of villages in the Hampshire countryside. But while the members of each cell admitted to learning from one another and meeting in one another's homes, the two *groups* may have been connected only at a distance, perhaps through wandering preachers who had known each other years earlier.[5]

---

5   See above, 185–86. For an argument skeptical of the existence (let alone persistence) of relationships between sixteenth century lollards in different areas of England, see Derek Plumb, "A Gathered Church? Lollards and Their Society," in Margaret Spufford, (ed.), *The World of Rural Dissenters, 1520–1575* (Cambridge, 1995), 132–63.

Factors such as these make the nature of the relationships between communities of lollards rarely easy to ascertain; the origins of those communities that that can be identified are equally murky, if not in fact more so. In a few locations, such as the Weald of Kent, it is possible to demonstrate that communities that considered themselves to be outside the ecclesiastical mainstream existed, with a reasonable degree degree of continuity, from the early fifteenth to the early sixteenth centuries. Patrick Collinson, for instance, has established that the Kentish village of Cranbrook, which supplied four defendants in Warham's investigations of 1511 and 1512, was one such location, hosting a tradition of "anti-Catholic and specifically anti-sacramentarian sentiment" from at least 1428 through 1511.[6] Likewise, heresy prosecutions remained a regular, if not especially frequent, part of church life in Norwich diocese from the time of Bishop William Alnwick's trials of 1428–31 through the 1520s; the same is also true of other localities in Hampshire, Buckinghamshire, and the West Midlands.[7] In some counties, Reformation-era evangelicals came from the same places that had produced suspected lollards, whereas in other places, such as Scotland, lollard ideas seem to have appeared for the first time late in the fifteenth century.[8] Yet even where there appear to be continuities, these may be deceptive: long gaps between the appearance of heresy suspects in the records may mean that a group had managed to evade detection for a period of some years, but those same gaps may just as well point to the arrival of new individuals in a region known for its relative toleration of heterodox views.

6 Patrick Collinson, "Cranbrook and the Fletchers: Popular and Unpopular Religion in the Kentish Weald," in Patrick Collinson, (ed.), *Godly People: Essays on English Protestantism and Puritanism* (London, 1984), 399–428; on Kent, see also Christopher Hill, "From Lollards to Levellers," in Maurice Cornforth, (ed.), *Rebels and Their Causes: Essays in Honour of A.L. Morton* (London, 1978), 49–67.

7 R.A. Houlbrooke, "Persecution of Heresy and Protestantism in the Diocese of Norwich under Henry VIII," *Norfolk Archaeology* 35 (1973), 308–26.

8 On the first claim here, see Diarmaid MacCulloch, *Tudor Church Militant* (London, 2000), 109–14; see also Nesta Evans, "The Descent of Dissenters in the Chiltern Hundreds," in Margaret Spufford, (ed.), *The World of Rural Dissenters* (Cambridge, 1995), 288–308; C.J. Clement, *Religious Radicalism in England* (Lewiston, 1994), 338–39. On lollardy in Scotland, see T.M.A. McNab, "The Beginnings of Lollardy in Scotland," *Records of the Scottish Church History Society* 11 (1953), 254–60; W. Stanford Reid, "The Lollards in Pre-Reformation Scotland," *Church History* 11 (1942), 269–83; and Martin Holt Dotterweich, "A Book for Lollards and Protestants: Mudroch Nisbet's New Testament," in *Literature and the Scottish Reformation*, (eds.) Crawford Gribben and David George Mullan (Farnham, 2009), 233–45. In contrast, James McGoldrick, *Luther's Scottish Connection* (Rutherford, N.J., 1989), holds that lollardy was a part of the Scottish religious scene fairly consistently from the beginning of the fifteenth century onward (p. 16), although McGoldrick's evidence is not fully persuasive.

The emergence in the late 1510s of a new brand of religious reform, that associated with the German Augustinian friar Martin Luther, complicates still further the task of ascertaining the persistence of lollard ideas in England. The first public burning of Luther's books on May 12, 1521, was followed by other book burnings, anti-Lutheran sermons, and ultimately the publication of King Henry VIII's *Assertio septem sacramentorum* in response to Luther's treatise on the sacraments. All these endeavors demonstrate the extent to which the English church and crown made opposition to Lutheranism a public priority. Heresy trials continued, reaching a point of greatest intensity in the so-called *magna abjurata* of 1528, which targeted Lutheran as well as lollard suspects. However, evidence for the circulation of Luther's writings in England in the *early* 1520s is scarce: his German compositions had not yet widely been translated into English, and his Latin texts had not yet attracted the interest that English scholars were to pay them in subsequent years. Perhaps as a result, only a minority of those individuals brought to trial for heresy in this period, and only in a few localities, were specifically asked about or testified in support of Luther's ideas.[9] Concerning those bishops who did undertake anti-Lutheran campaigns, Craig D'Alton has noted that their motives were often more about propaganda than about actual cohorts of Lutherans: "the English could rightly claim that the number of heretics was few, that once detected those of more educated opinions could always be persuaded to recant, and that the Lutheran cause was so weak that no-one had been found who was so enamoured of it that she or he was willing to be pronounced contumacious."[10]

These caveats notwithstanding, it cannot be denied that Luther's views did eventually make their way to England. Their gradual impact, as well as the importation and translation of Luther's writings, both make it difficult, after

---

[9] The most prominent exception to this claim is the series of investigations undertaken in the 1520s by Bishop John Longland of Lincoln diocese. On Longland's prosecutions, omitted from the previous chapter's survey because they took place after Lutheran ideas had arrived in England, see especially Margaret Bowker, *The Henrician Reformation: The Diocese of Lincoln under John Longland, 1521–1547* (Cambridge, 1981). Unfortunately, the records of these trials are no longer extant, although a summary (albeit of debatable accuracy) survives in Foxe's *Actes and Monuments*.

[10] Craig D'Alton, "The Suppression of Heresy in Early Henrician England" (Ph.D. diss., University of Melbourne, 1999), provides excellent analysis of the Henrician government's campaign against heresy, taking early Henrician policy on its own terms rather than insisting upon reading it through the lens of the Reformation (quote here at 180). While the bulk of this research remains unpublished, some of D'Alton's findings appear in his article "The Suppression of Lutheran Heretics in England, 1526–1529," *Journal of Ecclesiastical History* 54 (2003), 228–53.

the first few years of the 1520s, to identify with a high degree of precision the sources of heterodox views that were expressed in heresy trials and reformist writings. As Collinson has written, "Catholic bishops…found it difficult and perhaps unnecessary to distinguish between old Lollards and new Protestants and continued to burn both kinds of heretics for the selfsame beliefs (above all denial of the miracle of transubstantiation in the sacrament of the altar) which Lollards had held long before Martin Luther invented Protestantism."[11]

Not only did churchmen not yet have the experience with Lutheran ideas that they had with lollard ones, but some of the most prominent men who were drawn to Luther's ideas lived in places with longstanding traditions of religious radicalism. Of these, some can even be shown to have interacted with lollard writings. The evangelical polemicist and biblical translator William Tyndale, for instance, was likely born in 1494, on the border between Wales and Gloucestershire, to the west of the river Severn, in a region where "there is evidence of the presence of a number of individuals holding Lollard beliefs, toward the end of the fifteenth and…the beginning of the sixteenth century."[12] Indeed, heresy trials took place near Tyndale's birthplace as late as 1511, and the *Oxford Dictionary of National Biography* asserts that even in the 1530s, Tyndale "appears to have been in demand…as a preacher" in part as a result of "the strong commitment to Lollardy in the county." Certainly his work as a tutor for his first patron, Sir John Walsh of Little Sodbury Manor in Gloucestershire, was of a reforming bent, including his translation of Erasmus's *Enchiridion militis Christiani* for the Walsh family.[13]

The similarities between Tyndale's theological views and those of lollards have been the subject of a cottage industry among some scholars, with Donald Dean Smeeton's 1986 monograph putting most staunchly the case for the influence of lollardy on Tyndale.[14] Among the points of similarity between Tyndale and lollards that Smeeton identified are their shared use of terms such as "known men," their concern with civic and social morality, and their emphasis, following Augustine, on the theological distinction between visible and invisible churches. According to Smeeton, Tyndale followed lollards in

---

11 Patrick Collinson, "England," in *The Reformation in National Context*, (eds.) B. Scribner, R. Porter, and M. Teich (Cambridge, 1994), 80–94 at 85.

12 Andrew J. Brown, *William Tyndale on Priests and Preachers: With New Light on His Early Career* (London, 1996), 22; see also Carl Trueman, *Luther's Legacy: Salvation and English Reformers, 1525–1556* (Oxford, 1994), 10–11.

13 David Daniell, "Tyndale, William," *Oxford Dictionary of National Biography* (Oxford, 2004), http://www.oxforddnb.com/view/article/29747, accessed 14 September 2014.

14 Donald Dean Smeeton, *Lollard Themes in the Reformation Theology of William Tyndale* (Kirksville, Mo., 1986).

creating space for women's participation in religion, in highlighting complaints about clerical misconduct, and in rejecting elaborate church music. Some of these similarities are more apparent than real, however: as we have learned earlier in this volume, not all scholars agree that lollards either rejected works-oriented theologies of salvation or provided greater opportunities for women than did the established church.[15] However, despite ongoing disagreements about Tyndale's acquaintance with lollard thought early in his career, it seems clear that he did contribute to the publication of some lollard texts, including the *Testimony of William Thorpe*.[16]

Just as Tyndale hailed from a lollard-leaning region of Gloucestershire, so also was another sixteenth-century reformer, John Frith, born in an area of Kent where heresy prosecutions continued throughout his childhood, culminating in the trials of 1511–12 under Archbishop Warham.[17] Originally a university student at Cambridge, Frith moved to Oxford in the mid-1520s at the behest of Cardinal Thomas Wolsey, who saw promise in the young theologian. However, as Foxe tells the story, Frith and several other junior scholars of a reformist mindset ran into trouble at Wolsey's new foundation, Cardinal College: "conferring together vpon the abuses of Religion being at that time crept into þe Church, were therefor accused of heresie vnto the Cardinall, & cast into a prison, within a deepe caue vnder þe ground, of the same Colledge, where their saltfishe was layde, so that through the filthy stinch therof, they were all infected."[18] Released and expelled from Oxford, Frith made his way to the Low Countries, where he joined Tyndale and contributed to the production

---

15   See 54–56, 111–17 above. Michael S. Whiting, *Luther in English: The Influence of His Theology of Law and Gospel on Early English Evangelicals*, Princeton Theological Monographs Series 142 (Eugene, Ore., 2010), is a fervent opponent of Smeeton's thesis. Other works relevant to this debate include William A. Clebsch, *England's Earliest Protestants* (New Haven, Conn., 1964), 136–99, 308; W.D.J. Cargill Thompson, "The Two Regiments: The Continental Setting of William Tyndale's Political Thought," in Derek Baker, (ed.), *Reform and Reformation: England and the Continent, c. 1500–c. 1750* (Oxford, 1979), 17–33; Michael McGiffert, "William Tyndale's Conception of Covenant," *Journal of Ecclesiastical History* 32 (1981), 167–84; and Marvin W. Anderson, "William Tyndale: A Martyr for All Seasons," *Sixteenth Century Journal* 17:3 (1986), 338–40.

16   Smeeton, *Lollard Themes*, 257. On the relationship between lollardy and Tyndale, see further Gordon Rupp, *Studies in the Making of the English Protestant Tradition* (Cambridge, 1966), esp. Chapter 1.

17   Trueman, *Luther's Legacy*, 14–15.

18   *A&M*, 1213. On Frith, see also David Daniell, "Frith, John," in *Oxford Dictionary of National Biography* (Oxford, 2004), http://www.oxforddnb.com/view/article/10188, accessed 14 September 2014. See also Clebsch, 79–136. For further details on the theological climate prevailing in Oxford in the 1520s, see Guy Fitch Lytle, "John Wyclif, Martin Luther and

of English reforming literature there. He was arrested on a visit to England in 1531, imprisoned in the Tower of London, and eventually executed in 1533, after refusing to recant his beliefs about the eucharist and purgatory.[19] As with Tyndale, it is uncertain to what extent Frith was influenced by specifically lollard ideas, although his "emphasis upon conscientious adherence to biblical doctrine alone" and his differences with Luther on "such matters as justification, predestination, election, church, and vocation" have been held up as evidence for the native English sources of his reforming beliefs. It is possible, as well, that Frith's thinking was shaped by his knowledge of lollard writings; several elements of what Hudson has called the lollard sect-vocabulary appear in his works.[20]

Robert Barnes, a third reformer, developed a theology that was largely Lutheran in tone and content, although the ways in which he differed from Luther may point to the influence of lollard ideas. Like Tyndale and Frith, Barnes came from an area with a history of lollardy, in his case the town of Bishop's Lynn in Norfolk.[21] As a student and later regent master at the University of Cambridge, Barnes criticized the clergy for venality and corruption; later, even while under arrest in the Augustinian friary in London, he helped to coordinate the dissemination of Tyndale's translation of the New Testament. Carl Trueman has argued that documents that establish connections between Barnes and late lollards such as John Tyball also prove that Barnes was himself influenced by lollardy, but this may push the evidence too far.[22] More convincing may be William Clebsch's observation that Barnes chose not to follow Luther in his near-rejection of the epistle of James, a favorite lollard text, as well as Clebsch's argument that Barnes formulated a definition of the church more reminiscent of Wyclif's than of Luther's.[23]

Edward Powell: Heresy and the Oxford Theology Faculty at the Beginning of the Reformation," in *Ockham to Wyclif*, 465–79.

19 For analysis of the specific points of disagreement between Frith and his opponents, whose views were articulated by Thomas More in repeated polemics, see Walter M. Gordon, "A Scholastic Problem in Thomas More's Controversy with John Frith," *Harvard Theological Review* 69:1–2 (1976), 131–49. Trueman, *Luther's Legacy*, 43, holds that Frith, in contrast to lollards of his time, developed a sophisticated theology of the eucharist, albeit one less philosophical than Wyclif's.

20 Clebsch, *England's Earliest*, 79; quotes at 136, 134.

21 Trueman, *Luther's Legacy*, 17.

22 Carl R. Trueman, "Barnes, Robert," in *Oxford Dictionary of National Biography* (Oxford, 2004), http://www.oxforddnb.com/view/article/1472, accessed 14 September 2014.

23 Clebsch, *England's Earliest*, 70–71; Margaret Aston, "Lollardy and the Reformation: Survival or Revival," repr. in *Lollards and Reformers*, 219–42 at 231. On Barnes, see also

Further examples could be multiplied, but that the lives of Tyndale, Frith, and Barnes may have intersected with those of lollards provides corroboration, even if not definite proof, about the origins of their reforming views. In other cases, however, similarities between typical lollard beliefs and an individual's views do not conclusively establish lollard influence. For instance, the ideas about pilgrimage and the adoration of images articulated by Thomas Bilney, an evangelical scholar from Cambridge who was burned in Norwich in 1531, have often been thought to point to lollardy as a source for his theology, but his story is surely more complex. Unlike Wyclif and most English heresy suspects, Bilney affirmed transubstantiation, claimed that the church is both a visible institution and "the whole congregation of the elect," and did not openly repudiate the pope.[24]

Hence it is likely that in the first quarter of the sixteenth century, there were a variety of ways in which individuals and communities in England deviated from orthodoxy. A few, it seems, were the descendants of earlier groups of lollards. At the other end of the spectrum, individuals such as those who gathered around the Scottish reformer Mudroch Nisbet seem to have had little to do with lollardy, being formed instead by the new theology of Luther.[25] Still others, like Thomas Batman, charged with holding both lollard and Lutheran heresies in Canterbury diocese in 1524, may have held some combination of views, including ideas specific neither to Lutheranism nor to lollardy; in these cases, the evidence simply does not permit us to distinguish between them further.[26]

However, the many ambiguities of the extant records have not stopped some historians from attempting one way or another to characterize the status of English lollardy in the first few decades of the sixteenth century. Margaret Aston and A.G. Dickens both employed subterranean metaphors for later lollardy, describing it, respectively, as occupying a "dark uncertain underground" and as being a "deep, murky, and quiet" river that "ran underground and seldom

---

Korey Maas, *The Reformation and Robert Barnes: History, Theology, and Polemic in Early Modern England* (Woodbridge, 2010).

24 P.R.N. Carter, "Bilney, Thomas," in *Oxford Dictionary of National Biography* (Oxford, 2004), http://www.oxforddnb.com/view/article/2400, accessed 7 July 2014, makes the point about Bilney's beliefs on images and pilgrimage. Greg Walker, "Saint or Schemer? The 1527 Heresy Trial of Thomas Bilney Reconsidered," *Journal of Ecclesiastical History* 40 (1989), 219–38 (quote at 231); J.F. Davis, "The Trials of Thomas Bylney and the English Reformation," *Historical Journal* 24 (1981), 775–90; and Whiting, *Luther in English*, 151, are all more skeptical about the relationship between Bilney and lollardy.

25 Dotterweich, "Book for Lollards," 237–44.

26 John F. Davis, *Heresy and Reformation in the South-East of England* (London, 1983), 41.

emerged before reaching the lake."[27] On their account, to the extent that lollardy existed on the eve of the Henrician Reformation, it did so in the background, creating at most an intellectual and religious climate receptive to reform. J.F. Davis has argued that lollardy was more lively, describing it as a decisive source for Henrician religion and claiming that "Tudor Lollardy" discernibly existed through the middle of the sixteenth century.[28] To the contrary, Andrew Hope has called later lollardy "insubstantial," unable to make new converts and virtually nonexistent outside a few gentry families.[29] We will return to this debate toward the end of this chapter, when we consider the ways in which writers since the Tudor period have characterized the relationship between lollardy and the English Reformation.

8.2 England and Bohemia

If it remains an open question to what extent lollardy persisted in early sixteenth-century England, there is little debate about the formative role that Wyclif's ideas played in the Hussite reform movement of fifteenth-century Bohemia. Jan Hus, noted scholar and preacher at the Bethlehem Chapel in Prague, was ultimately condemned and burned at the stake by order of the Council of Constance in 1415, but as early as 1405 his writings and public preaching reveal traces of Wyclfi's influence. Even though Hus far from slavishly copied Wyclif's ideas—he never denied transubstantiation, for instance—sixteenth-century historians and artists regularly depicted him as the link between Wycliffite reformers on the one hand and Luther and the Protestant Reformation on the other. No doubt, much historiography of this sort has been spurred on by Luther's famous remark to Georg Spalatin in 1520: "In short, unawares, we are all Hussites."[30] While it is all but impossible that Luther knowingly drew upon the ideas of Wyclif and Hus as he developed the distinctive themes of his own

---

27 Aston, "Lollardy and the Reformation," 239; A.G. Dickens, *Lollards and Protestants in the Diocese of York* (London, 1982), 252.

28 John Davis, "Joan of Kent, Lollardy, and the English Reformation," *Journal of Ecclesiastical History* 33 (1982), 225–33 at 225.

29 Andrew Hope, "Lollardy: The Stone the Builders Rejected," in *Protestantism and the National Church in Sixteenth Century England*, (eds.) P. Lake and M. Dowling (London, 1987), 1–35.

30 Quoted in Martin Brecht, *Martin Luther: His Road to Reformation, 1483–1521* (Philadelphia, 1985), 332. On Hus's selective borrowing from and nuancing of Wyclif's views on ecclesiology, for instance, see Matthew Spinka, *John Hus' Concept of the Church* (Princeton, 1966).

theology, there is far more evidence for the existence of scholarly and textual exchanges between England and Bohemia in the early fifteenth century.

Limitations of space prohibit an extensive discussion of the relationship between lollardy and Hussitism here, but some of the best recent work in this area has been done by the literary historian Michael Van Dussen.[31] He has conclusively argued that the ground for cultural connections between England and Bohemia had been prepared separately from the emergence of the Wycliffite controversies, in the 1382 marriage of Anne of Bohemia to King Richard II as well as in the extension and development of the Anglo-Bohemian alliance in the early Lancastrian period, when England and the Holy Roman Empire found themselves on the same side of the western schism.[32] Van Dussen's research has freed Queen Anne herself from suspicion of heterodoxy, but he has shown that some of the travelers who came from Prague to London during and after her lifetime were not so innocent. In particular, two students from Bohemia, Mikuláš Faulfiš and Jiri of Knêhnice, were in England in 1406 and 1407, when they copied several of Wyclif's works, including *De dominio divino*, *De ecclesia*, and *De veritate sacrae scripturae*.[33] (It is clear that Faulfiš returned to England a second time, and he may have been attempting a third trip at the time of his death.) Some of Wyclif's writings were destined to be translated into Czech in the first two decades of the fifteenth century; the labors of travelers and translators, combined with the attempts of English authorities to destroy Wyclif manuscripts in Oxford and elsewhere, are to be counted among the reasons that more copies of Wyclif's writings are extant today in central Europe than in the United Kingdom. But Faulfiš and Knêhnice did not only copy Wyclif's works; they also brought back to Bohemia in 1407 a

---

31 Especially Michael Van Dussen, *From England to Bohemia: Heresy and Communication in the Later Middle Ages* (Cambridge, 2012). For an older, but still in many ways helpful, biography of Hus, see Matthew Spinka, *John Hus: A Biography* (Princeton, 1979). A more recent study of Hus's legal battles, Thomas A. Fudge, *The Trial of Jan Hus* (Oxford, 2013), is useful for details of his trials both before and at the Council of Constance, even if Fudge employs anachronistic categories to find Hus guilty of heresy. See further many of the papers in Anne Hudson's collection, *Studies in the Transmission of Wyclif's Writings*.

32 Van Dussen, *England to Bohemia*, 1.

33 Van Dussen, *England to Bohemia*, 61. In addition to Faulfiš and Knêhnice, at least one other reforming Bohemian academic, Paul Kravar, crossed the English Channel, arriving in Scotland in 1433, where he was arrested and burned at St. Andrew's (p. 67). English and Scottish preachers, among them Richard Wyche and Quentin Folkhyrde, corresponded with Hus and other Bohemians. On Kravar, see further Matthew Spinka, "Paul Kravar and the Lollard-Hussite Relations," *Church History* 25 (1956), 16–26; and McGoldrick, *Luther's Scottish Connection*, 18. On Wyche, see above, 169–70.

document, purporting to have been authorized by the chancellor of Oxford, which claimed "that Wyclif was upstanding, that he was a most accomplished scholar and teacher of Scripture and that he had never been condemned or posthumously burned as a heretic."[34] Regardless of how the letter was obtained—suggestions have ranged from outright theft of the chancellor's seal to academics' displeasure about Oxford University's ongoing conflict over academic freedom with Archbishop Arundel—the document was used by Hus, his ally Jerome of Prague, and others to establish Wyclif's theological *bona fides*, as well as by extension the legitimacy of their own theological views. In addition, other researchers have explored dimensions of the relationship between English and Bohemian heresy. Marcela K. Perett has shown that Wyclif's ideas about the eucharist had a warm reception in Bohemia, where they were brought by Peter Payne.[35] Pavlina Cermanová has demonstrated connections between English and Bohemian apocalyptic writing, Luigi Campi has done the same with regard to philosophical tracts on determinism, and Ota Pavlicek has explored the influence of Wyclif on the Bohemian master Jerome of Prague.[36] It is clear that the theological, political, and literary interchanges between England and Bohemia deserve substantial further study.

8.3 Lollard Literature and the New Reforms

We have been exploring some of the ways in which lollardy may have shaped the course of the Hussite and Henrician reformations. But it is important to remember that not only living people, but also written texts, can exert influence. So even though there were few individuals who played roles in the Henrician reformation and who can be unambiguously identified as lollards, the lollard past certainly did shape the religious history of sixteenth-century England through the printing of lollard texts by latter-day reformers. Anne Hudson has produced a catalogue of the lollard writings printed in the 1530s and 1540s, including the *Lanterne of Liȝt*, *Jack Upland*, portions of the General Prologue to the Wycliffite Bible, and *Wycklyffes Wycket*. Some of these, she has found, were edited to bring them into line with the new evangelical theology, but most editions were transparent about their lollard origins, even though

---

34   Van Dussen, *England to Bohemia*, 71; see also 89.
35   Perett, "A Neglected Eucharistic Controversy: The Afterlife of John Wyclif's Eucharistic Thought in Bohemia in the Early Fifteenth Century," *Church History* 84 (2015), 64–89.
36   See each of their contributions to the forthcoming collection *Europe after Wyclif*, (eds.) J. Patrick Hornbeck II and Michael Van Dussen (New York, 2016).

lollard manuscripts had still been prohibited only a few years earlier.[37] Indeed, in some cases texts that did not emerge from lollard milieux, such as *Piers Plowman*, were given lollard pedigrees by their printers and editors.[38]

Perhaps no reformer did more to contribute to the survival and retrieval of lollard writings than did John Bale, a former Carmelite whose antiquarian activities have been invaluable to scholars in reconstructing the literary world of the late middle ages. Born in 1495 in Suffolk and a contemporary at Cambridge of Thomas Cranmer's and Robert Barnes's, Bale converted to evangelicalism well before he discovered a passion for lollardy. Indeed, as late as 1536, Bale was still openly critical of lollards and referred to Wyclif as a heretic; Bale's teachers were his Cambridge dons and fellow students, not lollard evangelists; and his theological positions, for instance on the eucharist, were more Swiss than they were Lutheran or lollard.[39]

Despite not being sympathetic toward lollardy, Bale was aware of it from early in his career; as Leslie Fairfield has noted, "on at least one occasion during the early 1520s he visited his home convent at Norwich and copied some material from a manuscript there about Carmelite opponents of John Wyclif."[40] He later rescued that manuscript upon the convent's dissolution and took it into exile with him in 1540, when Henry VIII enacted the conservative Act of Six Articles. Under the title *Fasciculi Zizaniorum*, Bale's manuscript has since been an invaluable resource for scholars of Wyclif and lollardy.[41] More famously, Bale compiled several catalogues of English authors' writings and in 1545 produced *The Image of Bothe Churches*, an extensive commentary on the book of

---

37 Anne Hudson, "'No Newe Thyng': The Printing of Medieval Texts in the Early Reformation Period," repr. in *Books*, 227–48; David Loades, "Books and the English Reformation prior to 1558," in Karin Maag and Jean-Francis Gilmont, (eds.) and trans., *The Reformation and the Book*, 2nd ed. (Aldershot, 1998), 264–91. For further information on the sixteenth century printings of one of these texts, see Matti Peikola, "'Innumerable and Shameful Errors': Some Textual Observations on *Wycklyffes Wycket*," in *Language and Beyond*, (eds.) Mayumi Sawada, Larry Walker, and Shizuya Tara (Tokyo, 2007), 73–95.

38 Hudson, "No Newe Thyng," 247; see also John N. King, *English Reformation Literature: The Tudor Origins of the Protestant Tradition* (Princeton, 1986), 4, and Seymour Baker House, "Literature, Drama, and Politics," in *The Reign of Henry VIII: Politics, Policy, and Piety*, (ed.) Diarmaid MacCulloch (London, 1995), 181–201.

39 Peter Happé, *John Bale* (New York, 1996), 28; Richard Rex, "John Bale, Geoffrey Downes, and Jesus College," *Journal of Ecclesiastical History* 49 (1998), 486–93.

40 Leslie P. Fairfield, *John Bale: Mythmaker for the English Reformation* (West Lafayette, Ind., 1976), 9.

41 James Crompton, "*Fasciculi Zizaniorum*," *Journal of Ecclesiastical History* 12 (1961), 35–45, 155–66, provides a history of this fascinating text and reminds us that the printed edition of *FZ* contains less than half of the original.

Revelation that shaped the annotations of the 1560 Geneva Bible.[42] Like many of Bale's writings, *Image* is apocalyptic in tone; more than anyone else, he was responsible for importing into English reformist historiography the apocalyptic-prophetic framework of the medieval writer Joachim of Fiore.[43] Bale also produced a biography of Sir John Oldcastle, borrowing in its composition from Tyndale's editions of the trials of Thorpe and Oldcastle.[44] Bale's attention to Wyclif and lollard figures contributed significantly to the roles that they have subsequently held in the history of English literature: as John King has argued, "[i]n Bale's history, John Wyclif emerges as the central English author. Aside from the dedicatory portraits of Bale himself, the woodcut of Wyclif is the only image of a British author in *Summarium* [one of Bale's catalogues]. Both Wyclif and Bale are seen in the evangelical pose with book in hand."[45] Bale never completed his planned edition of *Fasciculi Zizaniorum*, which he intended to entitle *The battayle of John Wycleff*, but perhaps no phrase of his has had a longer life than the epithet that he applied to Wyclif in *Image*: morning star (*stella matutina*) of the Reformation.[46] In total, Bale cited as many as twenty of Wyclif's works across his writings.[47]

However, after the close of the sixteenth century, Bale has rarely if ever been a household name. William Haller has put it in stark terms: "Most historians who have given any attention at all to Bale have been so repelled by his extraordinary virtuosity in the art of verbal abuse that they have been unable or unwilling to assess his very real historical importance."[48] Instead, it has been Bale's good friend and fellow evangelical writer John Foxe who has gone down in history as the greatest propagandist of English Protestantism. As Katharine Firth has neatly summarized it, "When Foxe undertook his great work [i.e., the *Actes and monuments*], he answered Bale's wish that some learned Englishman should write the true history of the Church."[49] Foxe and Bale lived as near

---

42   On *Image*, see Happé, *John Bale*, 50–51; Fairfield, *John Bale*, 59–85.
43   Katharine R. Firth, *The Apocalyptic Tradition in Reformation Britain, 1530–1645* (Oxford, 1979), 41.
44   Annabel Patterson, "Sir John Oldcastle as Symbol of Reformation Historiography," in *Religion, Literature, and Politics in Post-Reformation England, 1540–1688*, (eds.) Donna B. Hamilton and Richard Strier (Cambridge, 1996), 6–26.
45   King, *English Reformation Literature*, 70.
46   Fairfield, *John Bale*, 203, n. 38; *John Bale*, Happé, 62.
47   Richard Bauckham, *Tudor Apocalypse: Sixteenth Century Apocalypticism, Millennarianism, and the English Reformation: From John Bale to John Foxe and Thomas Brightman* (Oxford, 1978), 23.
48   William Haller, *Foxe's Book of Martyrs and the Elect Nation* (London, 1963).
49   Firth, *Apocalyptic Tradition*, 68.

neighbors in the Swiss city of Basle in the mid-1550s, as well as earlier in England in the house of Marie, Duchess of Richmond, and Bale's researches into the documentary remains of lollardy provided much fodder for Foxe's two histories, his Latin *Rerum in ecclesia gestarum* and his far more successful English *Actes and monuments*, known to later generations as Foxe's *Book of Martyrs*.[50] No doubt as a result of Bale's influence, Foxe's books accorded to Wyclif and his followers a leading role in preserving the gospel despite persecution from the institutional church.[51]

Space does not permit a thorough analysis of the writings of Bale, Foxe, and other evangelical writers, but among the other features they share in common, these texts often take an apocalyptic perspective on the events of their day. Of course, apocalyptic writing has been part of Christianity's quest for self-understanding from the very beginning; for instance, the Donatist writer Tyconius's reading of the biblical book of the Apocalypse influenced such orthodox giants as Augustine, Bede, and Richard of St. Victor.[52] Some lollard writings, too, employ apocalyptic imagery: we have seen that Wyclif himself gradually came to identify the papacy with Antichrist, that lollard texts like the *Tractatus de oblacione iugis sacrificii* did the same, and that at least one lollard writer produced, in Latin, a full Apocalypse commentary, *Opus arduum*.[53] *Opus arduum*, in particular, seems to have exerted influence on Bale: like that earlier lollard text, and in keeping more with medieval commentators like Rupert of Deutz and Joachim of Fiore than with sixteenth-century reformers like Luther, Bale's *Image* relied upon the division of history into seven periods.[54]

According to Paul Christianson, Bale's commentary on the Apocalypse "seems to have acted as a paradigm" for his contemporaries and successors and subsequently shaped English interpretations of the Church of England's break

---

50   Haller, *Foxe's*, 71; see also Jesse W. Harris, *John Bale: A Study of the Minor Literature of the Reformation* (Urbana, Ill., 1940), 108; and Jane Facey, "John Foxe and the Defence of the English Church," in Peter Lake and Maria Dowling, (eds.), *Protestantism and the National Church* (London, 1987), 162–92.

51   The literature on Foxe and his leading role in the writing of English religious history from an evangelical perspective is enormous. See for instance Haller, *Foxe's*; J.A.F. Thomson, "John Foxe and Some Sources for Lollard History: Notes for a Critical Appraisal," in *Studies in Church History* 2, (ed.) G.J. Cumming (London, 1965), 251–257; and Thomas Freeman, "Texts, Lies, and Microfilm: Reading and Misreading Foxe's 'Book of Martyrs,'" *Sixteenth Century Journal* 30 (1999), 23–46.

52   Curtis V. Bostick, *The Antichrist and the Lollards: Apocalypticism in Late Medieval and Reformation England* (Leiden, 1998), 20.

53   See above, 90–92.

54   Bostick, *Antichrist*, 81; see also Bauckham, *Tudor Apocalypse*, 31.

from Rome.⁵⁵ Christianson has identified three characteristics of Christian apocalyptic thought that Bale shaped into a nationalistic tradition whose key feature, above all, was the rejection of "popery": "a polarized view of the universe, a catastrophic explanation of events, and a firm concern with prophecy and its fulfilment."⁵⁶ Thus, while it is never easy to trace the precise influence of one writer or text upon another, it is not at all unlikely that the distinctively English apocalypticism—nationalistic, patriotic, vigorously antipapal—that was well established by the end of the sixteenth century owed something to the survival and reprinting of lollard texts. From Foxe's history back through Bale's *Image*, *Opus arduum*, and other lollard texts, both Latin and vernacular, runs a thread of consistency that can be pursued even as far as earlier writers such as Joachim. Much as lollards and later reformers would have been aghast to discover it, medieval apocalpyticism contributed much to the shape of English reformist historiography. And at the same time, the reprinting and rereading of lollard texts of all stripes in the sixteenth century helped to establish Wyclif and his purported followers as progenitors of English literature and culture more broadly.

8.4 Historiography and Lollardy

The evidence we reviewed at the beginning of this chapter makes it seem reasonable to assert that by the year 1534, when Henry VIII's parliament passed the Act of Supremacy and thus confirmed the king in his newly assumed role of supreme head on earth of the Church of England, there were few individuals who could straightforwardly be identified as lollards. Few communities survived the multiple rounds of official persecution that occurred over the course of more than a century and a half; those that did became gradually less distinct from newer groups favoring Lutheran or Swiss approaches to ecclesiastical reform.

But the story of lollardy does not end with the passing out of existence of readily discernible lollards. Rather, as we have just been seeing in the works of Reformation writers like Bale and Foxe, lollardy continued to play a role—namely, the role that historically minded writers and theologians assigned to it in their accounts of the English Reformation. Over the past five centuries, for historians whose work was bound up with the Christian denominations that emerged from the Reformation, lollardy has provided an answer to the

---

55 Paul Christianson, *Reformers and Babylon: English Apocalyptic Visions from the Reformation to the Eve of the Civil War* (Toronto, 1978), 9.

56 Christianson, *Reformers*, 5; Facey, "John Foxe," 172.

question that Protestants have so frequently faced from their Catholic antagonists: "Where was your church before Luther?"[57] From a Bohemian psalter printed in 1572 through a brief article that H.B. Workman published in 1926, and beyond, those working in this vein have taken Wyclif to have struck the spark of reform with which Hus and Luther subsequently lit up Europe.[58] Much to the contrary, for Catholic intellectuals, the story of lollardy—or, more precisely, of the medieval church's response to it—points to the vitality of traditional religion, a vitality demonstrated by the vigorous (and mostly successful) persecution of lollards, as well as by the failure of lollard ideas to establish themselves permanently.

The debate over the place of lollardy in the English Reformation is one that has already stretched over more than four centuries. Several phases of the debate have received extensive scholarly attention, indeed attention so detailed that any remarks here can barely scratch the surface. Most recently, Susan Royal has explored the ways in which lollardy appeared in late sixteenth- and seventeenth-century Protestant histories of the Reformation, while Rosemary O'Day and Peter Marshall have traced the fate of lollardy in twentieth- and twenty-first-century historiography.[59] According to Marshall, by the end of the Victorian period, a combination of "Protestant triumphalism" and "nationalistic pride"—both elements that we have encountered in our survey of lollard and Tudor apocalypticism—led lollardy to be seen as a key element in the "march of national progress," progress, that is, from popery to Protestantism and ultimately empire.[60] Dissenting voices of the 1900s and 1910s, such as those of the English cardinal Francis Aidan Gasquet and the historian James Gairdner, both of whom saw lollardy as marginal (at best) to the trajectory of the English Reformation, raised some doubts about the validity of this nationalistically inclined story, but despite these critics, the traditional historiography was once again ascendant by the conclusion of the Second World War.[61]

---

57 Anthony Milton, *Catholic and Reformed: The Roman and Protestant Churches in English Protestant Thought, 1600–1640* (Cambridge, 1995).
58 H.B. Workman, "Wyclif, Hus, Luther, Wesley," *Proceedings of the Wesley Historical Society* 15 (1926), 141–46.
59 Susan Royal, "John Foxe's *Acts and Monuments* and the Lollard Legacy in the Long Reformation" (Ph.D. diss., University of Durham, 2013); Rosemary O'Day, *The Debate on the English Reformation* (London, 1986), esp. 137–54; Marshall, "Lollards and Protestants Revisited."
60 Marshall, "Lollards and Protestants Revisited," 296–97.
61 Marshall, "Lollards and Protestants Revisited," 307. Consider, for instance, this characteristic statement of Gairdner's: "[T]he candid student of pre-Reformation history will hardly be of opinion that Lollardy was productive of skilled dialecticians capable of overthrowing in logical combat the positions which had been established by the great divines

Indeed, even today many of the assertions about the relationship between lollardy and the Reformation that were first made by John Foxe and echoed for generations thereafter remain entrenched in popular, if not academic, historical writing. In the 1960s and for at least the following two decades, A.G. Dickens's classic study *The English Reformation* reigned almost supreme as the authoritative account of its subject.[62] It provided an influential narrative, familiar especially to the English secondary school students who encountered it at A-level, of a medieval English public dissatisfied with traditional religion, of a corrupt church and clergy, and of a speedy reformation driven in large part by public sentiment. Both in this work and in his earlier book *Lollards and Protestants in the Diocese of York*, Dickens conceived of lollardy as a "still vital force" in English religious affairs that provided the basis for the swift reception of Lutheran and Swiss ideas in localities such as the Weald of Kent.[63] Lollards both directly and indirectly shaped the course of the Reformation, Dickens argued: on the one hand, there simply were more lollards than earlier historians had acknowledged, and on the other, lollard sentiments comprised a "deep, murky river" of religious dissent that contributed to the collection of circumstances that made possible a popularly accepted reformation.[64]

Dickens was not alone in making arguments such as these. Two decades later, J.F. Davis argued in a series of publications for the direct influence of lollardy on reformers like Bilney, Batman, and Joan Bocher, the so-called Maid of Kent. As we have already seen in Chapter 7, Davis also took forward Dickens's observation that many lollards in Yorkshire were part of weaving communities and argued that there was an almost innate link between lollardy and the textile trade.[65] In some ways, the arguments of Dickens, Davis, and historians of their ilk represented a modern reinscription of the narratives of Foxe, Bale, and their fellow evangelical writers. Both argued for the substantial, if not widespread, survival of lollardy into the Reformation period; both also claimed that without lollardy, the English Reformation would have looked substantially different.

---

and schoolmen of past ages." *Lollardy and the Reformation in England: An Historical Survey*, 4 vols. (London, 1908–1913), i.66.

62   For a helpful introduction to Dickens's telling of the Reformation, as well as the critical reception of it by Eamon Duffy and Diarmaid MacCulloch, see Ian Hugh Clary, "Backgrounds to the English Reformation: Three Views," *Mid-America Journal of Theology* 22 (2011), 77–87.

63   Dickens, *Lollards and Protestants*, 8.

64   Dickens, *Lollards and Protestants*, 252.

65   Davis, "Trials of Thomas Bylney"; *Heresy and Reformation*; "Joan of Kent." On Bocher, see also Clement, *Religious Radicalism in England*, 64–65.

However, in the last quarter of the twentieth century, a variety of revisionist and post-revisionist approaches to the study of the English Reformations—now often written in the plural—have prompted reassessments of traditional accounts of lollardy and its influence. For instance, while in her 1964 study "Lollardy and the Reformation" Margaret Aston proposed that evangelical reformers read lollard texts and appropriated lollard arguments for their own, she also claimed that they did so without necessarily knowing any living lollards. While Aston allowed that some lollard communities did survive into the Tudor period, on her account their activities were at best limited in scope.[66] Other historians have joined Aston in placing emphasis on the ways in which medieval lollard texts, rather than sixteenth century lollards, shaped the intellectual environment of the English Reformation. For William Clebsch, John King, Andrew Hope, and others, "certain cherished religious and theological ideas of these Lollards shaped the content of many a Protestant paragraph."[67]

Stronger critiques of Dickens came from several schools of historians who sought to challenge his portrayal of a corrupt church unbeloved by its members, as well as his account of a so-called "rapid reformation from below." Eamon Duffy's landmark 1992 study, *The Stripping of the Altars*, characterized traditional religion on the eve of the Reformation as vibrant rather than worn-out, the clergy as mostly attentive rather than mostly corrupt, and the Reformation itself as an unwelcome imposition by the state rather than a result desired by the people. Lollardy barely made an appearance in the first edition of Duffy's book; in the second edition, in response to criticism he received from those who believed that Wyclif and lollardy deserved more attention, Duffy responded forcefully and unapologetically:

> [I]f we are to believe the surviving visitations and court records, fifteenth-century Lollardy seems to have been less of an irritant to most diocesan authorities than local cunning-men or womanising priests, and there is no convincing evidence that it served as *the* shaping factor in any of the major developments of late medieval English piety.... I am suggesting that there was something religiously—by which I suppose I mean imaginatively—sterile about Lollardy.[68]

---

66 Margaret Aston, "Lollardy and the Reformation: Survival or Revival?" *History* 49 (1964), 149–70, repr. in *Lollards and Reformers*, 219–42.

67 Clebsch, *England's Earliest Protestants*, 4. See also King, *English Reformation Literature*; Hope, "Lollardy."

68 Eamon Duffy, *The Stripping of the Altars: Traditional Religion in England, 1400–1580*, 2nd ed. (New Haven, 2005), xxii–xxiii, xxvii.

A decade later, Duffy's junior colleague Richard Rex published a slim work that, among other iconoclastic claims, sought to call into question the possibility that lollardy had exerted any meaningful influence on the English Reformation. Rex allowed that lollardy provided evangelicals with an answer to Catholic skepticism about the legitimacy of their reforms, as well as that the threat that lollardy posed to the medieval church did produce such innovations as new catechetical efforts and restrictions on vernacular scripture. Yet for Rex, lollardy did not exert a significant enough influence in the sixteenth century to justify the place that it has traditionally held in histories of the Tudor period.[69]

Other developments in English Reformation research, especially the production of many local and regional studies from the 1970s onward, simultaneously militated against the traditional account of lollardy and its influence. Marshall has noted that studies of counties like Lincolnshire and Lancashire revealed that lollardy was by no means a widespread phenomenon in sixteenth-century England, and these new social histories of the Tudor reformations produced conclusions such as that of J.J. Scarisbrick: "[O]n the whole, English men and women did not want the Reformation and most of them were slow to accept it when it came."[70] The subsequent work of scholars like Christopher Haigh, whose 1993 textbook on the Reformation, like Duffy's monograph, assigned neither a dedicated chapter nor a substantial place to lollardy, created an alternative narrative about the relationship between lollardy and the Reformation at least as widely accepted as Dickens's.[71] Still other scholars have attempted to bridge the gap between the traditional and revisionist historiographies, for instance arguing that in some regions, the remnants of lollardy may have been a factor in the speedy reception of the Reformation, while in other regions the Reformation was indeed imposed as an act of state.[72]

As Marshall has observed, revisionist work on the English Reformation—and on the early Henrician Reformation in particular—has taken the study of lollardy "a long way from the image of a close-knit club of spiritual travellers

---

69 Rex, *The Lollards*, 138–48.

70 J.J. Scarisbrick, *The Reformation and the English People* (Oxford, 1984), 1, quoted in Marshall, "Lollards and Protestants Revisited," 310.

71 See for instance Christopher Haigh, *English Reformations: Religion, Politics, and Society under the Tudors* (Oxford, 1993); Haigh, (ed.), *The English Reformation Revised* (Cambridge, 1987).

72 This is for instance the view of Diarmaid MacCulloch, *Tudor Church Militant*, 114; see also MacCulloch, "Can the English Think for Themselves? The Roots of English Protestantism," *Harvard Divinity Bulletin* 30 (2001), 17–20. For discussion of other, similar writers, see Marshall, "Lollards and Protestants Revisited," 313–15.

anxiously checking their watches for the arrival of the 15:17 from Wittenberg."[73] Yet while historians will continue to debate the extent to which lollardy was present in and shaped the religious dynamics of sixteenth-century England, it is all but indisputable that many sixteenth-century Englishpeople *thought* that lollards, and lollardy, remained at large. Scholars of the Reformation will continue to assess the role that lollardy played in the events of their period, but those interested in lollardy itself can take from the many controversies about its afterlife a sense of healthy skepticism. Whenever the story of lollardy has been told, that story has been shaped, in some ways decisively, by the prevailing historical, theological, and intellectual climate. Perhaps this is true of all kinds of historical writing, but if this chapter has served to reveal the contingency of many long-standing assertions about lollardy and its afterlife, then it will have served its purpose.

---

73   Marshall, "Lollards and Protestants Revisited," 318.

Conclusion

It has been nearly five hundred years since the last heresy trials that involved distinctively lollard opinions took place. Across the intervening centuries, lollardy has played a variety of roles in historical and theological writing on the Middle Ages and the early modern period. The legacy of lollardy has transformed John Wyclif, an Oxford academic whose intellectual interests were similar to those of most scholars of his day, into an evangelical reformer who was radically committed to making the Bible available to his countrymen. Lollardy has served as a point of entry for studies of the contested religious and literary scene of late-fourteenth-, fifteenth-, and early sixteenth-century England, in the process spawning an academic subfield of its own. Perhaps more than anything else, lollardy has been used to provide an explanation for the success of the English Reformation—either because lollards kept alive the reformist ideas of Wyclif until such a time as they could find ready hearers at the court of King Henry VIII, or because reformers near the king reached back into history and claimed lollardy as a precedent for their actions.

This book has sought to demonstrate that lollardy was all of these things—and also none of them. From Henry Knighton and his fellow chroniclers, who picked up their pens to caricature Wyclif as a heresiarch who was walking in the footsteps of notorious heretics down the centuries, to John Foxe and his fellow evangelicals, who lauded Wyclif and his disciples for bearing witness to the gospel in a time of decadence and corruption, to modern scholars, some of whom have continued to read Wyclif through the lens of their own religious commitments, writers about lollardy has never been free of presuppositions. Only in the last several decades has it become commonplace for scholars to attempt with a greater degree of neutrality "to appreciate what lollardy was and what it meant to its adherents and its opponents."[1] The result of their work has been a more nuanced understanding of why those whom the medieval world denounced as lollards believed what they did, how they sought to practice Christianity, how they related to their neighbors, and how they responded to the anti-heresy initiatives of the institutional church.

In the past decade in particular, as the trend toward taking lollardy on its own terms has accelerated, scholars have adjusted their focus in at least three ways. First, although much of the textual evidence for lollard beliefs and lollard practices that remains extant to us is written from the perspective of those who persecuted lollards as heretics, concerted efforts have been made to identify

---

1 Richard Rex, *The Lollards* (Basingstoke, 2002), 149.

the positive characteristics of the spirituality that inspired lollards to risk their lives in rejecting the ecclesiastical consensus of their day. Studies such as Somerset's recent book *Feeling Like Saints* have revealed that lollards were first and foremost Christians—Christians who, not unlike their less controversial contemporaries, sought to live out and to spread the gospel.[2] Lollards did not think of themselves as heretics, and in the few instances when they took on that label, they wore it as a badge of pride—remembering Christ, who, they said, was "the most blessed loller that ever was or shall be."[3] Second, while indeed lollardy remained a name to conjure with at the time of King Henry's reformation, and while perhaps there even remained some lollard communities that could trace their origin back to the time of Wyclif, scholars have recently begun to interpret lollardy other than teleologically, that is, other than as a factor in the genesis and unfolding of the English Reformation. Rather than seeking to demonstrate whether lollards did (or did not) affect the shape of the Reformation, many studies have now aimed to situate individuals and communities within what we know was the diverse and thriving context of late medieval Christianity—a context in which lollards were not the only ones to incur suspicion. Finally, while it remains true that lollardy was in many ways "the English heresy," in the sense both of a heresy that emerged in England and of one that prized the use of the English language for religious purposes, recent work has set English lollards and their persecutors in a pan-European context, exploring for instance how inquisitorial techniques that were first developed in France might have affected proceedings in England, how dissenting ideas were disseminated from England to Bohemia as well as vice versa, and how the anti-Wycliffite measures of the Council of Constance were implemented for a European, rather than solely an English, audience.[4]

All of these trajectories in recent scholarship have revealed lollardy to have been a multifaceted and a dynamic religious phenomenon. Freed from the presuppositions of earlier Protestant as well as Catholic scholarship, lollardy now appears to be one among many religious subcultures in late medieval England. It was a subculture that, as we have seen in this book, had its own practices (especially the reading and discussion of texts—resolutely orthodox, clearly heterodox, and all shades of gray in between), moral commitments (especially concerning the welfare of the community, the support of the poor,

---

2 Fiona Somerset, *Feeling Like Saints: Lollard Writings after Wyclif* (Ithaca, N.Y., 2014).
3 See above, 72.
4 Michael Van Dussen, *From England to Bohemia: Heresy and Communication in the Later Middle Ages* (Cambridge, 2012); J. Patrick Hornbeck II and Michael Van Dussen, (eds.), *Europe After Wyclif* (New York, forthcoming 2016).

and the recognition of the image of God in all people), doctrines (especially an insistence on the capacity of God to act independently of the dictates and regulations of the institutional church), and leaders (Wyclif, his first Oxford associates, and the diverse cast of preachers and teachers who sustained lollard communities over the years). While neither an alternative church in the manner envisioned by its medieval antagonists, nor a sect in the terms proposed by modern sociology, lollardy attracted those who continued to attend the services of the institutional church as well as those who deliberately and self-consciously rejected traditional religion, denouncing it for having been infected by Antichrist. It is therefore difficult to pigeonhole lollards and lollard communities, a fact that, as we have seen, continues to make our language about them imperfect at best.

At the same time that lollardy appears to have been more complex than earlier scholars may have allowed, it also seems to have been less static. As with other instances of resistance to a socially privileged *status quo*, lollardy took different forms at different places and times.[5] Efforts aimed at suppressing lollardy sometimes had the effect of changing how lollards behaved, what and how they read, with whom they associated, and what beliefs they sought to pass on. For example, the production of new lollard texts declined substantially after the enactment of Archbishop Arundel's stringent constitutions of 1409, and the members of some later lollard communities appear to have owned only unauthorized translations of the scriptures—incriminatory material, to be sure, but less so than tracts that condemned the pope and friars. Likewise, we have encountered evidence of groups of lollards who ceased to communicate about controversial matters when they were joined by those not of their number, as well as of particular theological ideas being emphasized by some peripatetic preachers but not others.

Taken together, all this evidence demonstrates that many of Christianity's traditional presuppositions about heresy are not always borne out by the facts—at least not in late medieval England. From the trinitarian and christological controversies of the fourth and fifth centuries, the rich discourse about heresy that church leaders and theologians have developed has included a number of sweeping assumptions: that heresies are generally led or instigated by a single individual, that they seek to replicate in their own perverse terms the structures of the true church, that members of heretical groups are trained to believe precisely the same things, and that heresies do not change over time but only grow stagnant. As we have seen, none of these assumptions is true of

---

5 R.N. Swanson, "'Lollardy,' 'Orthodoxy,' and 'Resistance' in Pre-Reformation England," *Theological Journal* (Tartu, Estonia) 64:1 (2003), 12–26.

lollardy. Certainly John Wyclif played a leading role in formulating a set of ideas that went against the teachings of the institutional church, but there is little evidence that he organized a cohesive movement of dissent, let alone personally supervised the production of such texts as the Wycliffite Bible. In Chapter 3, in particular, we discovered that few lollard communities had recognizable structures; fewer still organized themselves into anything that we might identify as a hierarchy. Finally, in Chapter 5, we explored the diversity of lollard theology, with many lollard writings and heresy defendants propounding different views on key theological topics. We also learned that lollard communities were shaped by the particular sets of circumstances within which they existed: which texts may have been available, which wandering preacher they came into contact with, which doctrines a local bishop may have wished to emphasize as orthodox.

Thus, to tell the story of lollardy in the second decade of the twenty-first century is to do so with a set of tools and categories that were not available to earlier generations. As of this writing, lollardy appears to have been less a heretical movement—whatever that word might mean in this context—than one among a number of forms of Christianity current in late medieval England. Lollards certainly did find themselves running afoul of the institutional church, but as we have seen, they thought of themselves as true Christians and held that it was the official church that had departed from the teachings of Christ and the example of the apostolic age. As scholars continue to investigate the ideas and values that made lollardy attractive to its practitioners, we will surely continue to deepen our understanding of why lollards were prepared to be labeled heretics and to face the ultimate penalty for their beliefs.[6] However, in recent years we have already learned that lollardy was not incompatible with service in minor or even major orders, with a range of orthodox devotions, and with practices and ideas that are normally associated with the medieval cult of the saints.[7]

---

6 The question of lollardy's appeal to those who risked life and limb to adopt its teachings and practices is one that has recently been receiving greater scholarly attention, though it is far from being answered. Chapters 3 and 5 above have sought to identify some of lollardy's intellectual and spiritual attractions. For the suggestion that "its creed of self-reliance" made it appealing to a rising class of burgesses and yeomen, see Jurkowski, "Lollardy and Social Status," 152. More broadly, on questions of belief and doubt in the late middle ages, see John H. Arnold, *Belief and Unbelief in Medieval Europe* (London, 2005).

7 See, for instance, Robert Lutton, *Lollardy and Orthodox Religion in Pre-Reformation England: Reconstructing Piety* (London, 2006); Robyn Malo, "Behaving Paradoxically? Wycliffites, Shrines, and Relics," in *Wycliffite Controversies*, 199–210.

The full story of lollardy has of course not yet been told. Due to the destruction of evidence—both intentional, for instance on the part of those who did not wish their beliefs and practices to be visible to potential persecutors, and collateral, for instance in the bombing of many English archives during World War II—as well as to the sheer absence of evidence that comes along with the clandestine nature of illegal activities, there are some questions about lollardy that we will never be able to answer. Others, however, await further research and investigation. Texts such as *Opus arduum* remain to be edited, printed, and translated. Texts already in print, such as the *English Wycliffite Sermons*, remain to be re-read and reinterpreted in the light of new findings about the relationship between lollardy and medieval orthodoxy. Perhaps still other texts remain to be discovered—in miscellanies and commonplace books, for instance, as well as in church court records that have not yet been fully analyzed. The relationship between lollardy and other medieval religious phenomena, such as the apocalyptic forms of spirituality and spiritual writing that Kathryn Kerby-Fulton has investigated, remains to be more fully studied, as does the relationship between those charged in England as lollards and those contemporaneously charged elsewhere in Europe with other forms of heresy.[8] Finally, although it may well be argued that too much scholarly ink has already been spilled tracing the relationship between lollardy and the Reformation, perhaps further studies of Henrician texts will reveal how lollard ideas remained in circulation during the religious changes of the sixteenth century. Both interdisciplinary and discipline-specific methods, borrowing from each other's findings, will help to answer these and other questions.

In the end, to appreciate lollardy on its own terms is to immerse ourselves in the religious world of late medieval England—a world in which long-held certainties were being challenged by more than one new form of religious enthusiasm. Many of the women and men who held beliefs and participated in practices reviled by the institutional church demonstrated courage, even if a majority of them also demonstrated that they were all too human, abjuring their beliefs when summoned to court. Church leaders, too, brought to the persecution of heresy their own deeply held convictions about Christian truth and the need to defend it against those they perceived to be the agents of the devil. In some respects, lollardy was new: it certainly deserves its place in English literary history as the context for the production of some of the first large-scale vernacular religious works, and in places John Wyclif's theology was a daring synthesis of controversial scholarly claims. In other respects, lollardy was a

---

8   Kathryn Kerby-Fulton, *Books under Suspicion: Censorship and Tolerance of Revelatory Writing in Late Medieval England* (South Bend, Ind., 2006).

CONCLUSION

manifestation of some of the oldest reformist energies in the history of Christianity: a desire to return to the supposedly pristine practices of the apostolic church, a frustration with the accretions of later years and later traditions. However, lollardy was a product of its place and time—an English phenomenon, employing the resources of the English language, helping to craft distinctively English attitudes toward religious difference, and long after its heyday finding itself enshrined in the pantheon of English Protestantism. Perhaps, in the end, this is legacy enough.

Bibliography

Manuscripts, Episcopal Registers, and Other Ecclesiastical Documents

Bath and Wells diocese, register of Oliver King (r. 1496–1503): H.C. Maxwell Lyte (ed.), *The Registers of Oliver King, Bishop of Bath and Wells, 1496–1503, and Hadrian de Castello, Bishop of Bath and Wells, 1503–1518* (London, 1939).

Canon Law Society of America, *Code of Canon Law, Latin-English Edition, New English Translation* (Washington, 1999).

Ely diocese, register of William Grey (r. 1454–78): Cambridge, Cambridge University Library, Ely Diocesan Records MS G/1/5.

Hereford diocese, register of John Trefnant (r. 1389–1404): W.W. Capes (ed.), *The Register of John Trefnant, Bishop of Hereford, A.D. 1389–1404* (Hereford, 1914).

Hereford diocese, register of John Stanbury (r. 1453–74): Joseph H. Parry and A.T. Bannister (eds.), *The Register of John Stanbury, Bishop of Hereford 1453–1474* (Hereford, 1918).

Lincoln Diocesan Records Vj/0.

Lincoln diocese, register of John Chedworth (r. 1452–71): Lincoln, Lincoln Archive Office, Episcopal Register XX.

London, Westminster Diocesan Archives, B.2.

Oxford, Bodleian Library MS Douce 369.1.

Salisbury diocese, register of Robert Hallum (r. 1407–17): J.M. Horn (ed.), *The Register of Robert Hallum, Bishop of Salisbury 1407–1417* (Canterbury and York Society 72, 1982).

Salisbury diocese, register of William Aiscough (r. 1438–50): Chippenham, Wiltshire and Swindon History Centre, D1/2/10.

Salisbury diocese, register of Thomas Langton (r. 1485–93): Chippenham, Wiltshire and Swindon History Centre, D1/2/12.

Salisbury diocese, register of Edmund Audley (r. 1502–24): Chippenham, Wiltshire and Swindon History Centre, D1/2/14.

Winchester diocese, register of Peter Courtenay (r. 1487–92): Winchester, Hampshire Record Office, A1/15.

Winchester diocese, register of Richard Foxe (r. 1501–28): Winchester, Hampshire Record Office, A1/17-20.

Worcester diocese, register of John Carpenter (r. 1444–76): Hereford and Worcester Record Office, b 716.093-BA.2648/6(ii).

Printed Primary Sources

Arnold, Thomas (ed.), *Select English Works of John Wycliffe*, 3 vols. (Oxford, 1869–71).

Audelay, John the Blind, *Poems and Carols (Oxford, Bodleian Library MS Douce 302)*, ed. Susanna Fein (Kalamazoo, Michigan, 2009).

Augustine of Hippo, *Heresies*, in *Arianism and Other Heresies*, ed. John E. Rotelle, trans. Roland J. Teske (Hyde Park, N.Y., 1995).

Bale, John, *A brefe chronycle concernynge the examinacyon...of syr Iohan Oldecastell the lorde Cobham* (Antwerp, 1544).

———, *Illustrium maioris Britanniae scriptorum...summarium* ([Wesel], 1548).

Barr, Helen (ed.), *The Piers Plowman Tradition* (London, 1993).

The Book of Margery Kempe, ed. Lynn Staley (Kalamazoo, Mich., 1996).

Book to a Mother, ed. A.J. McCarthy (Salzburg, 1981).

Bradley, Christopher G., ed. and trans., "The Letter of Richard Wyche: An Interrogation Narrative," *PMLA* 127 (2012), 626–42.

Brinton, Thomas, *The Sermons of Thomas Brinton, Bishop of Rochester, 1373–1389*, ed. M.A. Devlin, 2 vols., Camden Society 3rd ser. 85–86 (1954).

Calendar of Close Rolls (London, 1900).

Calendar of Close Rolls, 1422–1429, Henry VI, vol. 1 (London, 1933).

Calendar of Patent Rolls (London, 1901).

Calendar of Patent Rolls, 1413–1416, Henry V, vol. 1 (London, 1910).

Cigman, Gloria (ed.), *Lollard Sermons* (EETS o.s. 294, 1989).

Clanvowe, John, *The Two Ways*, in *The Works of John Clanvowe*, ed. V.J. Scattergood (Cambridge, 1967), 57–80.

Compston, H.F.B. (ed.), "The Thirty-Seven Conclusions of the Lollards," *English Historical Review* 26 (1911): 738–49.

Connelly, Margaret, *The Index of Middle English Prose, Handlist XIX: Manuscripts in the University Library, Cambridge (Dd-Oo)* (Cambridge, 2009).

Dahmus, J.H. (ed.), *The Metropolitan Visitations of William Courtenay, Archbishop of Canterbury, 1381–1396* (Urbana, Ill., 1950).

Dean, James M. (ed.), *Six Ecclesiastical Satires*, TEAMS Middle English Texts (Kalamazoo, MI, 1991).

——— (ed.), *Medieval English Political Writings*, TEAMS Middle English Texts (Kalamazoo, MI, 1996).

Dove, Mary (ed.), *The Earliest Advocates of the English Bible: The Texts of the Medieval Debate* (Exeter, 2010).

Embree, Dan (ed.), *The Chronicles of Rome: The Chronicle of Popes and Emperors and The Lollard Chronicle* (Woodbridge, 1999).

Epiphanius of Salamis, *The Panarion of Epiphanius of Salamis*, trans. Frank Williams, 2 vols. (Leiden, 1987–94).

The examinacion of Master William Thorpe... [and] The examinacion of the honorable Knyght syr Ihon Oldcastell Lorde Cobham (n.p., 1530; STC 24045).

Fasciculus rerum expetendarum ac fugiendarum, ed. Edward Brown, vol. I (London, 1737).

Forshall, Josiah (ed.), *Remonstrance against Romish Corruptions in the Church* (London, 1851).
Forshall, Josiah, and F. Madden (eds.), *The Holy Bible... [made] by John Wycliffe and His Followers*, 4 vols. (Oxford, 1850).
Foxe, John, *The... Ecclesiasticall History Contaynyng the Actes and Monuments* (London, 1570).
Francis, W. Nelson (ed.), *The Book of Vices and Virtues*, EETS, o.s. 217 (London, 1942).
Gascoigne, Thomas, *Loci e Libro Veritatum*, ed. James E. Thorold Rogers (Oxford, 1881).
Genet, J.P. (ed.), *Four English Political Tracts of the Later Middle Ages*, Camden Society, fourth series, vol. 18 (London, 1977).
Hanna, Ralph, *Index of Middle English Prose Handlist XII: Smaller Bodleian Collections* (Cambridge, 1997).
Harpsfield, Nicholas, *Historia Anglicana ecclesiastica* (Douai, 1622).
Hornbeck, J. Patrick II, Stephen E. Lahey, and Fiona Somerset (eds. and trans.), *Wycliffite Spirituality* (Mahwah, N.J., 2013).
Hudson, Anne (ed.), *Two Wycliffite Texts* (EETS o.s. 301, 1993).
——— (ed.), *Selections from English Wycliffite Writings*, rev. edn. (Toronto, 1997).
——— (ed.), *The Works of a Lollard Preacher* (EETS o.s. 317, 2001).
——— (ed.), *Two Revisions of Rolle's English Psalter Commentary and the Related Canticles*, 3 vols., EETS o.s. 340, 341, and 343 (2012–14).
——— (ed.), *Doctors in English: A Study of the Wycliffite Gospel Commentaries* (Liverpool, 2015).
Hudson, Anne, and Pamela Gradon (eds.), *English Wycliffite Sermons*, 5 vols. (Oxford, 1983–97).
A Kempis, Thomas, *The Imitation of Christ*, trans. E.M. Blaiklock (London, 2009).
Knighton, Henry, *Chronica de eventibus Angliae a tempore regis Edgari usque mortem regis Richardi Secundi*, ed. and trans. Geoffrey H. Martin (Oxford, 1995).
Knox, John, *The Historie of the Reformation of the Church of Scotland* (London, 1644).
The Lanterne of Liȝt, ed. L.M. Swinburn (EETS o.s. 151, London, 1917).
Matthew, F.D., "The Trial of Richard Wyche," *English Historical Review* 5 (1890), 530–44.
——— (ed.), *The English Works of Wyclif Hitherto Unprinted*, rev. edn. (EETS o.s. 74, 1902).
McSheffrey, Shannon, and Norman Tanner (eds. and trans.), *Lollards of Coventry, 1486–1522* (Camden Fifth Series 23, 2003).
Meech, Sanford Brown, and Hope Emily Ellen (eds.), *The Book of Margery Kempe*, Early English Text Society o.s. 212 (Oxford, 1940).
More, Thomas, *The Confutation of Tyndale's Answer*, in *The Complete Works of St Thomas More*, ed. Louis A. Schuster, Richard C. Marius, et al., vol. 8 (New Haven, Conn., 1973).
Netter, Thomas, *Doctrinale antiquitatum fidei Catholicae ecclesiae*, ed. B. Blanciotti, 3 vols. (Venice, 1757–59).

Pecock, Reginald, *Reginald Pecock's Book of Faith: A Fifteenth-Century Tractate*, ed. J.L. Morison (Glasgow, 1909).

———, *The Reule of Crysten Religioun*, ed. William Cabell Greet, Early English Text Society, o.s. 171 (London, 1927).

Sargent, Michael (ed.), *The Mirror of the Blessed Life of Jesus Christ: A Full Critical Edition* (Exeter, 2005).

Scattergood, John, "*The Two Ways*—An Unpublished Religious Treatise by Sir John Clanvowe," *English Philological Studies* 10 (1967), 33–56.

Schaffner, Paul F. (ed. and trans.), *Life of Soul*, in *Cultures of Piety: Medieval English Devotional Literature in Translation*, ed. Anne Clark Bartlett and Thomas Howard Bestul (Ithaca, N.Y., 1999), 118–40.

Shirley, W.W. (ed.), *Fasciculi zizaniorum* (Rolls Series, 1858).

Snappe's Formulary and Other Records, ed. H.E. Salter (Oxford, 1924).

Somerset, Fiona (ed.), *Four Wycliffite Dialogues*, EETS 333 (2009).

Talbert, Ernest W., and S. Harrison Thomson, "Wyclyf and His Followers," in *A Manual of the Writings in Middle English 1050–1500*, vol. 2, ed. J. Burke Severs (Hamden, CT, 1970).

Tanner, Norman P. (ed.), *Heresy Trials in the Diocese of Norwich, 1428–1431* (London, 1977).

——— (ed.), *Decrees of the Ecumenical Councils*, 2 vols. (Washington, 1990).

——— (ed.), *Kent Heresy Proceedings, 1511–12* (Kent Records 26, 1997).

Todd, J.H. (ed.), *Apology for Lollard Doctrines*, Camden Society (London, 1842).

Vergil, Polydore, *Anglicae historiae*, 2 vols. (Ghent, 1556–58).

Von Nolcken, Christina (ed.), *The Middle English Translation of the Rosarium Theologie* (Heidelberg, 1979).

Wakefield, Walter L., and Austin Evans (eds. and trans.), *Heresies of the High Middle Ages* (New York, 1991).

Walsingham, Thomas, *The St. Albans Chronicle: The Chronica Maiora of Thomas Walsingham*, 2 vols., ed. John Taylor, Wendy R. Childs, and Leslie Watkiss (Oxford, 2003–11).

Wenzel, Siegfried, *Latin Sermon Collections from Later Medieval England* (Cambridge, 2005).

Wilkins, David (ed.), *Concilia Magnae Brittaniae et Hiberniae*, 4 vols. (1737, repr. Brussels, 1964).

Wycklyffes Wycket (London, 1546).

Wyclif, John, *Trialogus cum supplemento trialogi*, ed. G. Lechler (Oxford, 1869).

———, *De civili dominio*, ed. R.L. Poole and J. Loserth, 4 vols. (London, 1885–1904).

———, *De ecclesia*, ed. J. Loserth (London, 1886a).

———, *Dialogus sive speculum ecclesie militantis*, ed. A.W. Pollard (London, 1886b).

———, *Sermones*, ed. J. Loserth, 4 vols. (London, 1886–89).

———, *De officio regis*, ed. Alfred W. Pollard and Charles Sayle (London, 1887).
———, *Opus evangelicum*, ed. J. Loserth, 2 vols. (London, 1895).
———, *De veritate sacrae scripturae*, ed. R. Buddensieg, 3 vols. (London, 1906), trans. as *On the Truth of Holy Scripture*, trans. Ian Christopher Levy (Kalamazoo, Mich., 2001).
———, *Opera minora*, ed. J. Loserth (London, 1913).

Secondary Sources

Aers, David, "Altars of Power: Reflection on Eamon Duffy's *The Stripping of the Altars*," *Literature and History* 3rd ser. 3 (1994), 90–105.
———, "John Wyclif's Understanding of Christian Discipleship," in *Faith, Ethics, and Church: Writing in England, 1360–1409* (Woodbridge, 2000), 119–48.
———, *Sanctifying Signs: Making Christian Tradition in Late Medieval England* (Notre Dame, Ind., 2004).
———, "The *Testimony of William Thorpe*: Reflections on Self, Sin, and Salvation," in *Studies in Late Medieval and Early Renaissance Texts in Honour of John Scattergood*, ed. Anne Marie D'Arcy and Alan J. Fletcher (Dublin, 2005), 21–34.
———, "Langland on the Church and the End of the Cardinal Virtues," *Journal of Medieval and Early Modern Studies* 42 (2012), 59–81.
Alban, Kevin, *The Teaching and Impact of the Doctrinale of Thomas Netter of Walden (c. 1374–1430)* (Turnhout, 2010).
Anderson, Marvin W., "William Tyndale: A Martyr for All Seasons," *Sixteenth Century Journal* 17:3 (1986), 338–40.
Appleford, Amy, *Learning to Die in London* (Philadelphia, forthcoming 2015).
Archer, M., "Philip Repingdon, Bishop of Lincoln, and His Cathedral Chapter," *University of Birmingham Historical Journal* 4 (1954), 81–97.
Arnold, John H., *Inquisition and Power: Catharism and the Confessing Subject in Medieval Languedoc* (Philadelphia, 2001).
———, "Lollard Trials and Inquisitorial Discourse," in *Fourteenth Century England II*, ed. Christopher Given-Wilson (Woodbridge, 2002), 81–94.
———, "Inquisition, Texts, and Discourse," in *Texts and the Repression of Medieval Heresy*, ed. Caterina Bruschi and Peter Biller (Woodbridge, 2003), 63–80.
———, *Belief and Unbelief in Medieval Europe* (London, 2005).
———, "The Materiality of Unbelief in Late Medieval England," in *The Unorthodox Imagination in Late Medieval Britain*, ed. Sophie Page (Manchester, 2010), 65–95.
Aston, Margaret, "Bishops and Heresy: The Defence of the Faith," in *Faith and Fire* (1993), 73–94.
———, "Lollardy and Sedition," *Past and Present* 17 (1960), 1–44, repr. in *Lollards and Reformers*, 1–47.
———, "John Wycliffe's Reformation Reputation," *Past and Present* 30 (Apr., 1965), 23–51.

———, "Lollard Women Priests?" *Journal of Ecclesiastical History* 31 (1980), 441–62, repr. in *Lollards and Reformers*, 49–70.

———, "William White's Lollard Followers," *Catholic History Review* 48 (1982), 469–97, repr. in *Lollards and Reformers*, 71–100.

———, "'Caim's Castles': Poverty, Politics, and Disendowment," in *Church, Politics, and Patronage in the Fifteenth Century*, ed. B. Dobson (New York, 1984a), 45–81, repr. in Aston, *Faith and Fire*, 95–132.

———, *Lollards and Reformers: Images and Literacy in Late Medieval Religion* (London, 1984b).

———, "Corpus Christi and Corpus Regni: Heresy and the Peasants' Revolt," *Past and Present* 143 (1993a), 3–47.

———, *Faith and Fire: Popular and Unpopular Religion, 1350–1600* (London, 1993b).

———, *England's Iconoclasts: Volume I: Laws against Images* (Oxford, 1998).

———, "Lollards and Images," in *Lollards and Reformers* (1984b), 135–92.

———, "Lollardy and the Reformation: Survival or Revival?" repr. in *Lollards and Reformers* (1984b), 219–42.

———, "Were the Lollards a Sect?" in *The Medieval Church: Universities, Heresy, and the Religious Life: Essays in Honour of Gordon Leff*, ed. Peter Biller and R.B. Dobson, Studies in Church History, Subsidia 11 (Oxford, 1999), 163–91.

———, "Wyclif and the Vernacular," in *Ockham to Wyclif* (1987), 281–330.

Aston, Margaret, and Colin Richmond (eds.), *Lollardy and the Gentry in the Later Middle Ages* (Sutton, 1997).

Barr, Helen, and Ann M. Hutchinson (eds.), *Text and Controversy from Wyclif to Bale: Essays in Honour of Anne Hudson* (Turnhout, 2005).

Bauckham, Richard, *Tudor Apocalypse: Sixteenth Century Apocalypticism, Millennarianism, and the English Reformation: From John Bale to John Foxe and Thomas Brightman* (Oxford, 1978).

Bergstrom-Allen, Johan, and Richard Copsey (eds.), *Thomas Netter of Walden: Carmelite, Diplomat and Theologian (c.1372–1430)* (Faversham, Eng., 2009).

Biller, Peter, "'Deep is the Heart of Man, and Inscrutable': Signs of Heresy in Medieval Languedoc," in *Text and Controversy*, 267–80.

Bose, Mishtooni, "Vernacular Philosophy and the Making of Orthodoxy in the Fifteenth Century", *New Medieval Literatures* 7 (2005), 73–99.

———, "The Opponents of John Wyclif," in *A Companion to John Wyclif. Late Medieval Theologian*, ed. Ian Christopher Levy (Leiden, 2006), 407–55.

———, "Intellectual Life in Fifteenth-Century England," *New Medieval Literatures* 12 (2010a), 333–370.

———, "Writing, Heresy and the Anticlerical Muse," in *The Oxford Handbook of Medieval Literature*, ed. Greg Walker and Elaine Treharne (Oxford, 2010b), 276–93.

———, "Useless Mouths: Reformist Poetics in Audelay and Skelton," in *Form and Reform. Reading across the Fifteenth Century*, ed. Shannon Gayk and Kathleen Tonry (Columbus, Ohio, 2011), 159–79.

———, "Reversing the Life of Christ: Dissent, Orthodoxy, and Affectivity in Late Medieval England," in *The Pseudo-Bonaventuran Lives of Christ. Exploring the Middle English Tradition*, ed. Ian Johnson and Allan F. Westphall (Turnhout, 2013), 55–77.

Bose, Mishtooni, and J. Patrick Hornbeck II (eds.), *Wycliffite Controversies* (Turnhout, 2012).

Bostick, Curtis V., *The Antichrist and the Lollards: Apocalypticism in Late Medieval and Reformation England* (Leiden, 1998).

Bowker, Margaret, *The Henrician Reformation: The Diocese of Lincoln under John Longland, 1521–1547* (Cambridge, 1981).

Boyarin, Daniel, *Border Lines: The Partition of Judaeo-Christianity* (Philadelphia, 2004).

Boyle, Leonard E., "Montaillou Revisited: Mentalité and Methodology," in *Pathways to Medieval Peasants*, ed. J. Raftis (Toronto, 1981), 119–40.

Brady, M. Theresa, "Lollard Sources of the Pore Caitif," *Traditio* 44 (1988): 389–418.

———, "Lollard Interpolations and Omissions in Manuscripts of the Pore Caitif," in *De Cella in Seculum: Religious and Secular Life and Devotion in Late Medieval England*, ed. Michael G. Sargent (Woodbridge, 1989), 183–203.

Brecht, Martin, *Martin Luther: His Road to Reformation, 1483–1521* (Philadelphia, 1985).

Brooke, Christopher N.L., *The Medieval Idea of Marriage* (Oxford, 1994).

Brown, Andrew, *Popular Piety in Late Medieval England: The Diocese of Salisbury, 1250–1550* (Oxford, 1995).

Brown, Andrew J., *William Tyndale on Priests and Preachers: With New Light on His Early Career* (London, 1996).

Burgess, Clive, "A Hotbed of Heresy? Fifteenth Century Bristol and Lollardy Reconsidered," in *Authority and Subversion*, ed. Linda Clark (Woodbridge, 2003), 43–62.

Campbell, Kirsty, *The Call to Read: Reginald Pecock's Books and Textual Communities* (Notre Dame, 2010).

Cannon, H.L., "The Poor Priests: A Study in the Rise of English Lollardry," in *Annual Report of the American Historical Association for the Year 1899*, 2 vols. (Washington, 1900), 1:451–82.

Cardelle de Hartmann, C., *Lateinische Dialoge 1200–1400: Literaturhistorische Studie und Repertorium* (Leiden, 2007).

Cargill Thompson, W.D.J., "The Two Regiments: The Continental Setting of William Tyndale's Political Thought," in Derek Baker (ed.), *Reform and Reformation: England and the Continent, c. 1500–c. 1750* (Oxford, 1979), 17–33.

Carpenter, Christine, "Gentry and Community in Medieval England," *Journal of British Studies* 33 (1994), 340–80.

Carter, P.R.N., "Bilney, Thomas," in *Oxford Dictionary of National Biography* (Oxford, 2004).

Catto, Jeremy, "John Wyclif and the Cult of the Eucharist," in *The Bible in the Medieval World: Essays in Memory of Beryl Smalley*, ed. K. Walsh and D. Wood, Studies in Church History, Subsidia 4 (Oxford, 1985a), 269–86.

———, "Religious Change under Henry V," in *Henry V: The Practice of Kingship*, ed. G.L. Harriss (Oxford, 1985b), 97–115.

———, "Theology after Wycliffism," in *The History of the University of Oxford*, Volume 2: Late Medieval Oxford, ed. J.I. Catto and Ralph Evans (Oxford, 1992a), 263–80.

———, "Wyclif and Wycliffism at Oxford, 1356–1430," in *The History of the University of Oxford*, Volume 2: Late Medieval Oxford, ed. J.I. Catto and Ralph Evans (Oxford, 1992b), 175–261.

———, "The King's Government and the Fall of Pecock, 1457–58," in *Rulers and Ruled in Late Medieval England. Essays Presented to Gerald Harriss*, ed. R.E. Archer and Simon Walker (London, 1995), 201–22.

———, "Fellows and Helpers: The Religious Identity of the Followers of Wyclif," in *The Medieval Church: Universities, Heresy, and the Religious Life: Essays in Honour of Gordon Leff*, ed. Peter Biller and R.B. Dobson, Studies in Church History, Subsidia 11 (Oxford, 1999), 141–61.

Chenu, M.-D., "Orthodoxie et hérésie: le point de vue du théologien," in *Hérésies et sociétés dans l'Europe pré-industrielle* (Paris, 1968), 9–17.

Cheyney, Edward P., "The Recantations of the Early Lollards," *American Historical Review* 4 (1899), 423–35.

Christianson, Paul, *Reformers and Babylon: English Apocalyptic Visions from the Reformation to the Eve of the Civil War* (Toronto, 1978).

Clark, James G., *A Monastic Renaissance at St. Albans: Thomas Walsingham and his Circle, c. 1350–1440* (Oxford, 2004).

Clary, Ian Hugh, "Backgrounds to the English Reformation: Three Views," *Mid-America Journal of Theology* 22 (2011), 77–87.

Clebsch, William A., *England's Earliest Protestants* (New Haven, Conn., 1964).

Clement, C.J., *Religious Radicalism in England* (Lewiston, 1994).

Clopper, Lawrence, "Is the *Tretise of Miraclis Pleyinge* a Lollard Tract against Devotional Drama?" *Viator* 34 (2003): 229–71.

Cole, Andrew, *Literature and Heresy in the Age of Chaucer* (Cambridge, 2008).

———, "William Langland and the Invention of Lollardy," in *Influence* (2003), 37–58.

Coleman, Peter, *Christian Attitudes to Marriage* (London, 2004).

Collinson, Patrick, "Cranbrook and the Fletchers: Popular and Unpopular Religion in the Kentish Weald," in *Reformation Principle and Practice: Essays Presented to A.G. Dickens*, ed. P.N. Brooks (London, 1980), 173–202, repr. in Patrick Collinson (ed.), *Godly People: Essays on English Protestantism and Puritanism* (London, 1984), 399–428.

———, "A Chosen People? The English Church and the Reformation," *History Today* 36 (March 1986a), 14–20.

———, "The English Conventicle," in W.J. Sheils and Diana Wood (eds.), *Voluntary Religion*, Studies in Church History 23 (Oxford, 1986b), 223–59.

———, "England," in *The Reformation in National Context*, ed. B. Scribner, R. Porter, and M. Teich (Cambridge, 1994), 80–94.

Connolly, Margaret, "Books for the 'helpe of euery persoone þat þenkiþ to be saued': Six Devotional Anthologies from Fifteenth-Century London," *Yearbook of English Studies* 33 (2003): 170–81.

———, "Preaching by Numbers: The 'Seven Gifts of the Holy Ghost' in Late Middle English Sermons and Works of Religious Instruction," In *Preaching the Word in Manuscript and Print in Late Medieval England: Essays in Honour of Susan Powell*, ed. Martha W. Driver and Veronica O'Mara (Turnhout, 2013), 83–100.

Copeland, Rita, *Pedagogy, Intellectuals, and Dissent in the Later Middle Ages* (Cambridge, 2001).

———, "Lollard Instruction," in Miri Rubin (ed.), *Medieval Christianity in Practice* (Princeton, N.J., 2009), 27–32.

Coulton, G.G., *Ten Medieval Studies* (Cambridge, 1930).

Courtenay, William J., "The Bible in the Fourteenth Century: Some Observations," *Church History* 54 (1985), 176–87.

Crompton, James, "*Fasciculi Zizaniorum*," *Journal of Ecclesiastical History* 12 (1961), 35–45, 155–66.

———, "John Wyclif: A Study in Mythology," *Transactions of the Leicestershire Archaeological and Historical Society* 42 (1966–67), 6–34.

———, "Leicestershire Lollards," *Transactions of the Leicestershire Archaeological and Historical Society* 44 (1968–69), 11–44.

Cross, Claire, "'Great Reasoners in Scripture': The Activities of Women Lollards 1380–1530," in *Medieval Women*, ed. Derek Baker, Studies in Church History, Subsidia 1 (Oxford, 1978), 359–80.

Dahmus, Joseph H., *The Prosecution of John Wyclyf* (New Haven, 1952).

———, "Wyclyf was a Negligent Pluralist," *Speculum* 28 (1953), 378–81.

———, *William Courtenay, Archbishop of Canterbury, 1381–1396* (University Park, Pa., 1966).

D'Alton, Craig, "The Suppression of Lutheran Heretics in England, 1526–1529," *Journal of Ecclesiastical History* 54 (2003), 228–53.

Daly, Lowrie, *The Political Theory of John Wyclif* (Chicago, 1962).

———, "Wyclif's Political Theory: A Century of Study," *Medievalia et humanistica* 4 (1973), 177–89.

Daniell, David, "Frith, John," in *Oxford Dictionary of National Biography* (Oxford, 2004a).

———, "Tyndale, William," in *Oxford Dictionary of National Biography* (Oxford, 2004b).

Davies, Richard, "Lollardy and Locality," *Transactions of the Royal Historical Society*, 6th ser., 1 (1991), 191–212.

Davis, John F., "Lollard Survival and the Textile Industry in the Southeast of England," in *Studies in Church History* 3, ed. G.J. Cuming (Oxford, 1966), 191–201.

———, "The Trials of Thomas Bylney and the English Reformation," *Historical Journal* 24 (1981), 775–90.

———, "Joan of Kent, Lollardy, and the English Reformation," *Journal of Ecclesiastical History* 33 (1982), 225–33.

———, *Heresy and Reformation in the South-East of England, 1520–1559* (London, 1983).

De Certeau, Michel, *The Practice of Everyday Life* (repr. Berkeley, 2011).

Denery, Dallas G. II, "From Sacred Mystery to Divine Deception: Robert Holkot, John Wyclif, and the Transformation of Fourteenth-Century Eucharistic Discourse," *Journal of Religious History* 29 (2005), 129–44.

Dickens, A.G., "Heresy and the Origins of English Protestantism," repr. in *Reformation Studies* (London, 1982a), 363–82.

———, *Lollards and Protestants in the Diocese of York* (London, 1982b).

———, "The Shape of Anticlericalism and the English Reformation," in *Late Monasticism and the Reformation* (London, 1994).

Dillon, Janette, *The Language of Space in Court Performance, 1400–1625* (Cambridge, 2010).

Dotterweich, Martin Holt, "A Book for Lollards and Protestants: Mudroch Nisbet's New Testament," in *Literature and the Scottish Reformation*, ed. Crawford Gribben and David George Mullan (Farnham, 2009), 233–45.

Dove, Mary, *The First English Bible* (Cambridge, 2007).

Doyle, Eric, "William Woodford, O.F.M. (c. 1330–c.1400): His Life and Works Together with a Study and Edition of His 'Responsiones Contra Wiclevum et Lollardos'," *Franciscan Studies* 43 (1983), 17–187.

Doyle, Robert, "The Death of Christ and the Doctrine of Grace in John Wycliffe," *Churchman* 99 (1985), 317–35.

Drees, Clayton J., *Authority and Dissent in the English Church: The Prosecution of Heresy and Religious Non-conformity in the Diocese of Winchester, 1380–1547* (Lewiston, 1997).

Duffy, Eamon, *The Stripping of the Altars: Traditional Religion in England, c. 1400–c. 1580*, 2nd ed. (New Haven, Conn., 2005).

———, *Marking the Hours: English People and Their Prayers, 1240–1570* (New Haven, Conn., 2011).

Dulles, Avery, *Models of the Church*, exp. ed. (New York, 1987).

Dupuis, Jacques, *Toward a Christian Theology of Religious Pluralism* (Maryknoll, N.Y., 1999).

Dutton, Elisabeth, "Textual Disunities and Ambiguities of Mise-en-Page in the Manuscripts Containing *Book to a Mother*," *Journal of the Early Book Society* 6 (2003): 140–59.

Eagleton, Terry, *Literary Theory: An Introduction* (Oxford, 1983).

Edden, Valerie, "The Debate between Richard Maidstone and the Lollard Ashwardby," *Carmelus* 34 (1987), 113–34.

Elliott, Dyan, "Lollardy and the Integrity of Marriage and the Family," in *The Medieval Marriage Scene*, ed. Sherry Roush and Cristelle L. Baskins (Tempe, Ariz., 2005), 37–53.

Emden, A.B., *A Biographical Register of the University of Oxford to AD 1500*, 3 vols. (Oxford, 1957–59).

———, *An Oxford Hall in Medieval Times: Being the Early History of St Edmund Hall*, rev. ed. (Oxford, 1968).

Evans, Gillian R., *John Wyclif: Myth and Reality* (Downer's Grove, Ill., 2006).

Evans, Nesta, "The Descent of Dissenters in the Chiltern Hundreds," in Margaret Spufford (ed.), *The World of Rural Dissenters* (Cambridge, 1995), 288–308.

Facey, Jane, "John Foxe and the Defence of the English Church," in Peter Lake and Maria Dowling (eds.), *Protestantism and the National Church* (London, 1987), 162–92.

Fairfield, Leslie P., *John Bale: Mythmaker for the English Reformation* (West Lafayette, Ind., 1976).

Fines, John, "Heresy Trials in the Diocese of Coventry and Lichfield," *Journal of Ecclesiastical History* 14 (1963), 160–74

———, "William Thorpe: An Early Lollard," *History Today* 18 (1968), 495–503.

Firth, Katharine R., *The Apocalyptic Tradition in Reformation Britain, 1530–1645* (Oxford, 1979).

Flannery, Mary C. and Katie L. Walter (eds.), *The Culture of Inquisition in England, 1215–1515* (Woodbridge, 2013).

Fleming, Peter, *Family and Household in Medieval England* (Basingstoke, 2001).

Forde, Simon, "Nicholas Hereford's Ascension Day Sermon, 1382," *Mediaeval Studies* 51 (1989), 205–41.

———, "Lay Preaching and the Lollards of Norwich Diocese, 1428–1431," *Leeds Studies in English* 29 (1998), 109–26.

———, "Hereford, Nicholas," in *Oxford Dictionary of National Biography* (Oxford, 2008a).

———, "Repyndon, Philip," in *Oxford Dictionary of National Biography* (Oxford, 2008b).

———, "Theological Sources Cited by Two Canons of Repton: Philip Repyngdon and John Eyton," in *Ockham to Wyclif* (1987), 419–28.

Forrest, Ian, *The Detection of Heresy in Late Medieval England* (Oxford, 2005).

———, "The Dangers of Diversity: Heresy and Authority in the 1405 Case of John Edward," in *Studies in Church History* 43 (2007), 230–40.

———, "William Swinderby and the Wycliffite Attitude to Excommunication," *Journal of Ecclesiastical History* 60 (2009), 246–69.

———, "English Provincial Constitutions and Inquisition into Lollardy," in *The Culture of Inquisition in England, 1215–1515*, ed. Mary C. Flannery and Katie L. Walter (Woodbridge, 2013), 45–59.

———, "Lollardy and Late Medieval History," in *Wycliffite Controversies* (2012), 121–34.
Freeman, Thomas, "Texts, Lies, and Microfilm: Reading and Misreading Foxe's 'Book of Martyrs,'" *Sixteenth Century Journal* 30 (1999), 23–46.
Fudge, Thomas A., *The Trial of Jan Hus* (Oxford, 2013).
Gayk, Shannon, *Image, Text, and Religious Reform in Fifteenth-Century England* (Cambridge, 2010).
———, "Lollard Writings, Literary Criticism, and the Meaningfulness of Form," in *Wycliffite Controversies* (2012), 135–52.
Gertz, Genelle, "Heresy Inquisition and Authorship, 1400–1560," in *The Culture of Inquisition in England, 1215–1515*, ed. Mary C. Flannery and Katie L. Walter (Woodbridge, 2013), 130–45.
Ghosh, Kantik, *The Wycliffite Heresy: Authority and the Interpretation of Texts* (Cambridge, 2002).
———, "Logic, Scepticism and 'Heresy' in Early Fifteenth-Century Europe: Oxford, Vienna, Constance," in *Uncertain Knowledge. Scepticism, Relativism and Doubt in the Middle Ages*, ed. Dallas G. Denery II, Kantik Ghosh and Nicolette Zeeman (Turnhout, 2014), 261–83.
———, "Reginald Bishop Pecock and the Idea of 'Lollardy,'" in *Text and Controversy* (2005), 251–65.
———, "Wycliffite 'Affiliations': Some Intellectual-Historical Perspectives," in *Wycliffite Controversies* (2012), 13–32.
Gillespie, Vincent, "Vernacular Books of Religion," in Jeremy Griffiths and Derek Pearsall (eds.), *Book Production and Publishing in Britain 1375–1475* (Cambridge, 1989), 317–44.
Given, James B., *Inquisition and Medieval Society: Power, Discipline and Resistance in Languedoc* (Ithaca, N.Y., 2001).
Goodich, Michael (ed.), *Voices from the Bench: The Narratives of Lesser Folk in Medieval Trials* (New York, 2005).
Gordon, Walter M., "A Scholastic Problem in Thomas More's Controversy with John Frith," *Harvard Theological Review* 69:1–2 (1976), 131–49.
Grundmann, Herbert, "Hérésies savantes et heresies populaires au moyen age," in *Hérésies et sociétés dans l'Europe pré-industrielle, 11e–18e siècles*, ed. J. Le Goff (Paris, 1968), 212–13.
Haigh, Christopher, "Anticlericalism and the English Reformation," repr. in *The English Reformation Revised* (Cambridge, 1987a), 56–74.
——— (ed.), *The English Reformation Revised* (Cambridge, 1987b).
———, *English Reformations: Religion, Politics, and Society under the Tudors* (Oxford, 1993).
Haller, William, *Foxe's Book of Martyrs and the Elect Nation* (London, 1963).

Hanna, Ralph, "Booklets in Manuscripts: Further Considerations," rev. and repr. in *Pursuing History: Middle English Manuscripts and their Texts* (Stanford, 1996a), 21–34

———, "English Biblical Texts before Lollardy and Their Fate," in *Influence* (2003), 141–53.

———, "Miscellaneity and Vernacularity: Conditions of Literary Production in Late Medieval England," in *The Whole Book: Cultural Perspectives on the Medieval Miscellany*, ed. Stephen G. Nicholas and Siegfried Wenzel (Philadelphia, 1996b), 37–51.

Happé, Peter, *John Bale* (New York, 1996).

Hargreaves, Henry, "Sir John Oldcastle and Wycliffite Views on Clerical Marriage," *Medium Aevum* 42 (1973), 141–46.

———, "Popularising Biblical Scholarship: The Role of the Wycliffite Glossed Gospels," in *The Bible and Medieval Culture*, ed. W. Lourdaux and D. Verhelst (Leuven, 1979), 171–89.

———, "The Wycliffite *Glossed Gospels* as Source: Further Evidence," *Traditio* 48 (1993): 247–51.

Harris, Jesse W., *John Bale: A Study of the Minor Literature of the Reformation* (Urbana, Ill., 1940).

Harvey, Margaret, *Solutions to the Schism: A Study of Some English Attitudes, 1378–1409* (St. Ottilien, 1983).

Havens, Jill C., "Shading the Grey Area: Determining Heresy in Middle English Texts," in *Text and Controversy*, 337–52.

Hendrix, Scott H., "In Quest of the Vera Ecclesia: The Crises of Late Medieval Ecclesiology," *Viator* 8 (1977), 347–69.

Hill, Christopher, "From Lollards to Levellers," in Maurice Cornforth (ed.), *Rebels and Their Causes: Essays in Honour of A.L. Morton* (London, 1978), 49–67.

Holsinger, Bruce, "Lollard Ekphrasis: Situated Aesthetics and Literary History," *Journal of Medieval and Early Modern Studies* 35 (2005), 67–90.

Hope, Andrew, "Lollardy: The Stone the Builders Rejected?" in *Protestantism and the National Church in Sixteenth Century England*, ed. P. Lake and M. Dowling (London, 1987), 1–35.

———, "Conformed and Reformed: John Colet and His Reformation Reputation," in Linda Clark, Maureen Jurkowski, and Colin Richmond (eds.), *Image, Text, and Church: Essays for Margaret Aston* (Toronto, 2009), 214–38.

Hornbeck, J. Patrick II, "*Lollard* Sermons? Soteriology and Late Medieval Dissent," *Notes and Queries* 53 (Mar. 2006), 26–30.

———, *What is a Lollard? Dissent and Belief in Late Medieval England* (Oxford, 2010).

———, "'A Prophane and Heathyn Thing?' English Lollards on Baptism and Confirmation," *Medieval Studies* 74 (2012), 283–306.

———, "A Most Stupid Scoundrel: Some Early English Responses to Luther," in John Edwards and Edward Wesley (eds.), *Literatures of Luther* (Eugene, Ore., 2014), 1–25.

———, "*Wycklyffes Wycket* and Eucharistic Heresy: Two Series of Cases from Sixteenth-Century Winchester," in *Wycliffite Controversies* (2012), 279–94.

Hornbeck, J. Patrick II, and Michael Van Dussen (eds.), *Europe after Wyclif* (New York, forthcoming 2016).

Houlbrooke, Ralph A., *Church Courts and the People during the English Reformation* (Oxford, 1979).

———, "Persecution of Heresy and Protestantism in the Diocese of Norwich under Henry VIII," *Norfolk Archaeology* 35 (1973), 308–26.

House, Seymour Baker, "Literature, Drama, and Politics," in *The Reign of Henry VIII: Politics, Policy, and Piety*, ed. Diarmaid MacCulloch (London, 1995), 181–201.

Hudson, Anne, "Additions and Modifications to a Bibliography of English Wycliffite Writings," in *Books* (1985), 249–52.

———, "Contributions to a History of Wycliffite Writings," in *Books* (1985), 1–12.

———, "The Expurgation of a Lollard Sermon Cycle," *Journal of Theological Studies* n.s. 22 (1971): 435–42, repr. in *Books*, 201–15.

———, "A Lollard Compilation and the Dissemination of Wycliffite Thought," *Journal of Theological Studies* n.s. 23 (1972a), 65–81, repr. in *Books*, 13–29.

———, "A Lollard Mass," *Journal of Theological Studies* n.s. 23 (1972b): 407–19, repr. in *Books*, 111–23.

———, "The Examination of Lollards," *Bulletin of the Institute of Historical Research* 46 (1973), 145–59, repr. in *Books*, 124–40.

———, "A Lollard Compilation in England and Bohemia," *Journal of Theological Studies* n.s. 25 (1974): 129–40, repr. in *Books*, 30–42.

———, "Middle English," in *Editing Medieval Texts: English, French, and Latin Written in England; Papers Given at the Twelfth Annual Conference on Editorial Problems, University of Toronto*, ed. A.G. Rigg (Toronto, 1977), 34–57.

———, "A Neglected Wycliffite Text," *Journal of Ecclesiastical History* 29 (1978): 257–79.

———, "John Purvey: A Reconsideration of the Evidence for His Life and Writings," *Viator* 12 (1981a), 355–80, repr. in *Books*, 85–110.

———, "A Lollard Sect Vocabulary?" in *So Meny People, Longages, and Tonges: Philological Essays in Scots and Mediaeval English Presented to Angus McIntosh*, ed. M. Benskin and M.L. Samuels (Edinburgh, 1981b), 15–30, repr. in *Books*, 164–80.

———, *Lollards and Their Books* (London, 1985).

———, "The Lay Folk's Catechism: A Postscript," *Viator* 18 (1988a): 307–09.

———, *The Premature Reformation: Wycliffite Texts and Lollard History* (Oxford, 1988b).

———, "William Thorpe and the Question of Authority," in *Christian Authority: Essays in Honour of Henry Chadwick*, ed. G.R. Evans (Oxford, 1988c), 127–37.

———, "The Mouse in the Pyx: Popular Heresy and the Eucharist," *Trivium* 26 (1991), 40–53.

———, "*Laicus Litteratus*: The Paradox of Lollardy," in *Heresy and Literacy, 1000–1530*, ed. Peter Biller and Anne Hudson (Cambridge, 1994), 222–36.

———, "William Taylor's 1406 Sermon: A Postscript," *Medium Aevum* 64:1 (1995): 100–06.

———, "Which Wyche? The Framing of the Lollard Heretic and/or Saint," in *Texts and the Repression of Medieval Heresy*, ed. Caterina Bruschi and Peter Biller (Woodbridge, 2002), 221–37.

———, "Notes of an Early Fifteenth-Century Research Assistant, and the Emergence of the 267 Articles against Wyclif," *English Historical Review* 118 (2003), 685–97.

———, "Swinderby, William," in *Oxford Dictionary of National Biography* (Oxford, 2004a).

———, "Wycliffite Prose," in *Middle English Prose: A Critical Guide to Major Authors and Genres*, ed. A.S.G. Edwards (Woodbridge, 2004b), 195–214.

———, "The Problems of Scribes: The Trial Records of William Swinderby and Walter Brut," *Nottingham Mediaeval Studies* 49 (2005): 80–104.

———, "Dangerous Fictions: Indulgences in the Thought of Wyclif and His Followers," in *Promissory Notes on the Treasury of Merit: Indulgences in Late Medieval Europe*, ed. R.N. Swanson (Leiden, 2006), 197–214.

———, "Purvey, John," in *Oxford Dictionary of National Biography* (Oxford, 2008a).

———, *Studies in the Transmission of Wyclif's Writings* (Aldershot, 2008b).

———, "Thorpe, William," in *Oxford Dictionary of National Biography* (Oxford, 2008c).

———, "Five Problems in Wycliffite Texts and a Suggestion," *Medium Aevum* 80 (2011), 301–24.

———, "Lollard Book Production," in *Book Production*, ed. Griffiths and Pearsall (1989), 125–42.

———, "'No Newe Thyng': The Printing of Medieval Texts in the Early Reformation Period," repr. in *Books* (1985), 227–48.

Hudson, Anne, and Michael Wilks (eds.), *From Ockham to Wyclif*, Studies in Church History Subsidia 5 (Oxford, 1987).

Jones, W.R., "Lollards and Images: The Defense of Religious Art in Later Medieval England," *Journal of the History of Ideas* 34 (1973), 27–50.

Jurkowski, Maureen, "New Light on John Purvey," *English Historical Review* 110 (1995), 1180–90.

———, "Heresy and Factionalism at Merton College in the Early Fifteenth Century," *Journal of Ecclesiastical History* 48 (1997), 658–81.

———, "The Arrest of William Thorpe in Shrewsbury and the Anti-Lollard Statute of 1406," *Historical Research* 75 (2002), 273–95.

———, "Lollardy and Social Status in East Anglia," *Speculum* 82 (2007), 120–52.

―――, "Aston, John," in *Oxford Dictionary of National Biography* (Oxford, 2008).

―――, "Lollard Networks," in *Wycliffite Controversies* (2012), 261–78.

―――, "Lollardy in Oxfordshire and Northamptonshire: The Two Thomas Compworths," in *Influence* (2003), 73–95.

―――, "Who was Walter Brut?" *English Historical Review* 127 (2012), 285–302.

Justice, Steven, "Inquisition, Speech, and Writing: A Case from Late Medieval Norwich," *Representations* 48 (1994a), 1–29.

―――, *Writing and Rebellion: England in 1381* (Berkeley, 1994b).

Kamerick, Kathleen, *Popular Piety and Art in the Late Middle Ages: Image Worship and Idolatry in England, 1350–1500* (London, 2002).

―――, "Shaping Superstition in Late Medieval England," *Magic, Ritual and Witchcraft* 3 (2008), 29–53.

Keen, Maurice, "Wyclif, the Bible, and Transubstantiation," in Anthony Kenny (ed.), *Wyclif in His Times* (Oxford, 1986), 1–17.

Kelly, H.A., *Inquisitions and Other Trial Procedures in the Medieval West* (Aldershot, 2001).

―――, "Thomas More on Inquisitorial Due Process," *English Historical Review* 123 (2008), 845–94.

―――, "Inquisition, Public Fame, and Confession: General Rules and English Practice," in *The Culture of Inquisition in England, 1215–1515*, ed. Mary C. Flannery and Katie L. Walter (Woodbridge, 2013), 8–29.

―――, "Inquisitorial Due Process and Secret Crimes," in Kelly, *Inquisitions and Other Trial Procedures*, item II (2001).

―――, "Lollard Inquisitions: Due and Undue Process," in Kelly, *Inquisitions and Other Trial Procedures*, item VI (2001).

―――, *The Middle English Bible: A Reassessment* (1987).

Kennedy, K.E., *The Courtly and Commercial Art of the Wycliffite Bible* (Turnhout, 2014a).

―――, "Reintroducing the English Books of Hours, or 'English Primers,'" *Speculum* 89 (2014b): 693–723.

Kenny, Anthony, *Wyclif* (Oxford, 1985).

――― (ed.), *Wyclif in His Times* (Oxford, 1986a).

―――, "The Accursed Memory: The Counter-Reformation Reputation of John Wyclif," in *Wyclif in His Times*, ed. Anthony Kenny (Oxford, 1986b), 147–68.

―――, "Realism and Determinism in the Early Wyclif," in *Ockham to Wyclif*, (1987), 165–78.

Kerby-Fulton, Kathryn, "*Eciam Lollardi*: Some Further Thoughts on Fiona Somerset's '*Eciam Mulier*: Women in Lollardy and the Problem of Sources,'" in *Voices in Dialogue: Reading Women in the Middle Ages*, ed. Linda Olson and Kerby-Fulton (Notre Dame, Ind., 2005), 261–68.

―――, *Books under Suspicion: Censorship and Tolerance of Revelatory Writing in Late Medieval England* (South Bend, Ind., 2006).

Kieckhefer, Richard, *The Repression of Heresy in Medieval Germany* (Philadelphia, 1979).

———, "The Office of Inquisition and Medieval Heresy: The Transition from Personal to Institutional Jurisdiction," *Journal of Ecclesiastical History* 46 (1995), 36–61.

Kightly, Charles, "Lollard knights (*act. c.*1380–*c.*1414)," in *Oxford Dictionary of National Biography* (Oxford, 2008).

King, John N., *English Reformation Literature: The Tudor Origins of the Protestant Tradition* (Princeton, 1986).

King, Karen L., *What is Gnosticism?* (Cambridge, Mass., 2005).

Kuhn, S.M., "The Preface to a Fifteenth-Century Concordance," *Speculum* 43 (1968): 258–73.

Lahey, Stephen E., *Philosophy and Politics in the Thought of John Wyclif* (Cambridge, 2003).

———, *John Wyclif* (Oxford, 2008).

Lambert, Malcolm, *Medieval Heresy: Popular Movements from the Gregorian Reform to the Reformation*, 2nd ed. (Oxford, 1992).

Larsen, Andrew E., "Are All Lollards Lollards?" in *Influence* (2003), 59–72.

———, "John Wyclif, c. 1331–1384," in *Companion* (2006), 1–65.

———, *The School of Heretics: Academic Condemnation at the University of Oxford, 1277–1409* (Leiden, 2011).

Lavinsky, David, "'Knowynge Cristes speche': Gender and Interpretive Authority in the Wycliffite Sermon Cycle," *Journal of Medieval Religious Cultures* 38 (2012), 60–83.

Le Boulluec, Alain, *La notion d'hérésie dans la literature grecque*, 2 vols. (Paris, 1985).

Lea, Henry Charles, *A History of the Inquisition in the Middle Ages*, 3 vols. (London, 1888).

Lechler, Gotthard Victor, *John Wycliffe and His English Precursors*, trans. P. Lorimer (London, 1884), 439.

Leff, Gordon, *Heresy in the Later Middle Ages: The Relation of Heterodoxy to Dissent, c. 1250–c. 1450*, 2 vols. (Manchester, 1967).

———, "Ockham and Wyclif on the Eucharist," *Reading Medieval Studies* 2 (1976), 1–13.

———, "The Place of Metaphysics in Wyclif's Theology," in *Ockham to Wyclif* (1987), 217–32.

Levy, Ian Christopher, "A Contextualized Wyclif—*Magister Sacrae Paginae*," in *Wycliffite Controversies* (2012), 33–57.

———, "John Wyclif and Augustinian Realism," *Augustiniana* 48 (1998), 87–106.

———, "*Christus Qui Mentiri Non Potest*: John Wyclif's Rejection of Transubstantiation," *Recherches de Théologie et Philosophie Médiévales* 66 (1999), 316–34.

———, "Was John Wyclif's Theology of the Eucharist Donatistic?" *Scottish Journal of Theology* 53 (2000), 137–53.

———, "The Fight for the Sacred Sense in Late Medieval England," *Anglican Theological Review* 85 (2003a), 165–76.

——, *John Wyclif: Scriptural Logic, Real Presence, and the Parameters of Orthodoxy* (Milwaukee, Wisc., 2003b).

——, "Grace and Freedom in the Soteriology of John Wyclif," *Traditio* 60 (2005), 279–337.

—— (ed.), *A Companion to John Wyclif: Late Medieval Theologian* (Leiden, 2006).

——, "John Wyclif and the Primitive Papacy," *Viator* 38 (2007a), 159–89.

——, "John Wyclif on Papal Election, Correction, and Deposition," *Mediaeval Studies* 69 (2007b), 141–85.

——, *Holy Scripture and the Quest for Authority at the End of the Middle Ages* (Notre Dame, Ind., 2012).

Lewis, Anna, "Rethinking the Lollardy of the *Lucidarie*: The Middle English Version of the Elucidarium and Religious Thought in Late Medieval England," *Florilegium* 27 (2010): 209–36.

Lewis, John, *A Complete History of the Several Translations of the Holy Bible, and New Testament, into English, both in MS and in Print: And of the Most Remarkable Editions of Them since the Invention of Printing* (London, 1739).

Lipton, Emma, *Affections of the Mind: The Politics of Sacramental Marriage in Late Medieval English Literature* (Notre Dame, Ind., 2007).

Little, Katherine C., *Confession and Resistance: Defining the Self in Late Medieval England* (Notre Dame, Ind., 2006).

Lloyd, M.E.H., "John Wyclif and the Prebend of Lincoln," *English Historical Review* 61 (1946), 388–94.

Loades, David, "Books and the English Reformation prior to 1558," in Karin Maag and Jean-Francis Gilmont (eds.) and trans., *The Reformation and the Book*, 2nd ed. (Aldershot, 1998), 264–91.

Lollard Society, "Bibliography of Secondary Sources," http://lollardsociety.org/?page_id=10.

Lowe, Ben, *Commonwealth and the English Reformation: Protestantism and the Politics of Religious Change in the Gloucester Vale* (Farnham, 2010).

Lutton, Robert, "Godparenthood, Kinship, and Piety in Tenterden, England, 1449–1537," in *Love, Marriage, and Family Ties in the Middle Ages*, ed. I. Davis, M. Muller, and S. Rees Jones (Turnhout, 2003), 217–34.

——, *Lollardy and Orthodox Religion in Pre-reformation England: Reconstructing Piety* (London, 2006).

——, "Geographies and Materialities of Piety: Reconciling Competing Narratives of Religious Change in Pre-reformation and Reformation England," in *Pieties in Transition: Religious Practices and Experiences, c.1400–1640*, ed. Robert Lutton and Elisabeth Salter (Aldershot, 2007), 11–39.

Lyman, Rebecca, "A Topography of Heresy: Mapping the Rhetorical Creation of Arianism," in *Arianism after Arius: Essays on the Development of the Fourth-Century Trinitarian Conflicts*, ed. M.R. Barnes and D.H. Williams (Edinburgh, 1993), 45–62.

———, "Heresiology: The Invention of 'Heresy' and 'Schism'," in *The Cambridge History of Christianity, Volume 2: Constantine to c. 600*, ed. Augustine Casiday and Frederick W. Norris (Cambridge, 2007), 296–313.

Lytle, Guy Fitch, "John Wyclif, Martin Luther and Edward Powell: Heresy and the Oxford Theology Faculty at the Beginning of the Reformation," in *Ockham to Wyclif*, 465–79.

Maas, Korey, *The Reformation and Robert Barnes: History, Theology, and Polemic in Early Modern England* (Woodbridge, 2010).

MacCulloch, Diarmaid, *Tudor Church Militant* (London, 2000).

———, "Can the English Think for Themselves? The Roots of English Protestantism," *Harvard Divinity Bulletin* 30 (2001), 17–20.

———, *Reformation: Europe's House Divided* (London, 2003).

Macy, Gary, *The Theologies of the Eucharist in the Early Scholastic Period: A Study of the Salvific Function of the Sacrament according to the Theologians* (Oxford, 1984).

Malo, Robyn, "Behaving Paradoxically? Wycliffites, Shrines, and Relics," in *Wycliffite Controversies*, 199–210.

Marshall, Peter, "Lollards and Protestants Revisited," in *Wycliffite Controversies* (2012), 295–318.

———, "(Re)defining the English Reformation," *Journal of British Studies* 48 (2009), 564–86.

Martin, Geoffrey, "Wyclif, Lollards, and Historians, 1384–1984," in *Influence*, 237–50.

Maxfield, Ezra Kempton, "Chaucer and Religious Reform," *PMLA* 39 (1924), 64–74.

McCarthy, Conor, *Marriage in Medieval England* (Woodbridge, 2004).

McFarlane, K.B., *John Wycliffe and the Beginnings of English Nonconformity* (London, 1952).

———, *Lancastrian Kings and Lollard Knights* (Oxford, 1972).

McGiffert, Michael, "William Tyndale's Conception of Covenant," *Journal of Ecclesiastical History* 32 (1981), 167–84.

McGoldrick, James, *Luther's Scottish Connection* (Rutherford, N.J., 1989).

McGrade, A.S., "The Medieval Idea of Heresy: What are We To Make of It?" in *The Medieval Church: Universities, Heresy, and the Religious Life: Essays in Honour of Gordon Leff*, ed. Peter Biller and R.B. Dobson, Studies in Church History, Subsidia 11 (Oxford, 1999), 111–39.

McGrath, Alister, *Iustitia Dei: A History of the Christian Doctrine of Justification*, 3rd ed. (Cambridge, 2005).

McHardy, A.K., "*De heretico comburendo*, 1401," in *Lollardy and Gentry* (1997), 112–26.

———, "The Dissemination of Wyclif's Ideas," in *Ockham to Wyclif* (1987), 361–68.

McNab, T.M.A., "The Beginnings of Lollardy in Scotland," *Records of the Scottish Church History Society* 11 (1953), 254–60.

McNeill, John Thomas, "Some Emphases in Wyclif's Teaching," *Journal of Religion* 7 (1927), 447–66.

McNiven, Peter, *Heresy and Politics in the Reign of Henry IV* (Woodbridge, 1987).

McSheffrey, Shannon, *Gender and Heresy: Women and Men in Lollard Communities 1420–1530* (Philadelphia, 1995).

———, "Heresy, Orthodoxy, and English Vernacular Religion 1480–1525," *Past and Present* 186.1 (2005), 47–80.

Miller-McLemore, Bonnie J. (ed.), *The Wiley-Blackwell Companion to Practical Theology* (Oxford, 2012).

Milton, Anthony, *Catholic and Reformed: The Roman and Protestant Churches in English Protestant Thought, 1600–1640* (Cambridge, 1995).

Minnis, Alastair, "Making Bodies: Confection and Conception in Walter Brut's 'Vernacular Theology,'" in *The Medieval Translator: The Theory and Practice of Translation in the Middle Ages*, ed. Rosalynn Voaden, René Tixier, et al. (Turnhout, 2003), 1–16.

———, "'Respondet Walterus Bryth…': Walter Brut in Debate on Women Priests," in *Text and Controversy* (2005), 229–49.

———, "Wyclif's Eden: Sex, Death, and Dominion," in *Wycliffite Controversies* (2012), 59–78.

Moore, R.I., "The War against Heresy in Medieval Europe," *Historical Research* 81 (2008), 189–210

Nichols, Aidan, *Holy Order: The Apostolic Ministry from the New Testament to the Second Vatican Council* (Dublin, 1990).

Nichols, Ann Eljenholm, "Books-for-Laymen: The Demise of a Commonplace," *Church History* 56 (1987), 457–73.

Nisse, Ruth, "Reversing Discipline: *The Tretise of Miraclis Pleyinge*, Lollard Exegesis, and the Failure of Representation," *Yearbook of Langland Studies* 11 (1997): 163–94.

———, "Prophetic Nations," *New Medieval Literatures* 4 (2001): 95–115.

Ocker, Christopher, *Biblical Poetics before Humanism and Reformation* (Cambridge, 2002).

O'Day, Rosemary, *The Debate on the English Reformation* (London, 1986).

Anonymous (Ogle, Arthur), "Dr. Gasquet and the Old English Bible," *Church Quarterly Review* 51 (1901), 138–46.

Orme, Nicholas, "John Wycliffe and the Prebend of Aust," *Journal of Ecclesiastical History* 61 (2010), 144–52.

Osmer, Richard, *Practical Theology: An Introduction* (Grand Rapids, Mich., 2008).

Pantin, W.A., "The *Defensorium* of Adam Easton," *English Historical Review* 51 (1936), 675–80.

Patterson, Annabel, "Sir John Oldcastle as Symbol of Reformation Historiography," in *Religion, Literature, and Politics in Post-reformation England, 1540–1688*, ed. Donna B. Hamilton and Richard Strier (Cambridge, 1996), 6–26.

Pearsall, Derek, "The Whole Book: Late Medieval English Manuscript Miscellanies and their Modern Interpreters," in *Imagining the Book*, ed. Stephen Kelly and John J. Thompson (Turnhout, 2005), 17–29.

Pegg, Mark Gregory, *The Corruption of Angels: The Great Inquisition of 1245–1246* (Princeton, N.J., 2001).
———, *A Most Holy War: The Albigensian Crusade and the Battle for Christendom* (New York, 2008).
———, "Albigenses and the Antipodes: An Australian and the Cathars," *Journal of Religious History* 35 (2011), 577–600.
Peikola, Matti, *Congregation of the Elect: Patterns of Self-fashioning in English Lollard Writings* (Turku, Finland, 2000).
———, "'Innumerable and Shameful Errors': Some Textual Observations on *Wycklyffes Wycket*," in *Language and Beyond*, ed. Mayumi Sawada, Larry Walker, and Shizuya Tara (Tokyo, 2007), 73–95.
Penn, Stephen, "Wyclif and the Sacraments," in *Companion*, 241–90.
Phillips, Heather, "John Wyclif and the Optics of the Eucharist," in *Ockham to Wyclif*, 245–58.
Plumb, Derek, "The Social and Economic Spread of Rural Lollardy: A Reappraisal," in W.J. Sheils and Diana Wood (eds.), *Voluntary Religion*, Studies in Church History 23 (Oxford, 1986), 111–29.
———, "A Gathered Church? Lollards and Their Society," in Margaret Spufford (ed.), *The World of Rural Dissenters, 1520–1575* (Cambridge, 1995), 132–63.
Preston, Joseph H., "English Ecclesiastical Historians and the Problem of Bias, 1559–1742," *Journal of the History of Ideas* 32 (1971), 203–20.
Raschko, Mary, "Common Ground for Contrasting Ideologies: The Texts and Contexts of *A Schort Reule of Lif*," *Viator* 40 (2009): 387–410
———, "Oon of Foure: Harmonizing Wycliffite and Pseudo-Bonaventuran Approaches to the Life of Christ," in *The Pseudo-Bonaventuran Lives of Christ: Exploring the Middle English Tradition*, ed. Ian Johnson and Allan F. Westphall (Turnhout: Brepols, 2013), 341–373.
Rees Jones, Sarah, "'A Peler of Holy Cherch': Margery Kempe and the Bishops," in *Medieval Women: Texts and Contexts in Late Medieval Britain: Essays for Felicity Riddy*, ed. by Jocelyn Wogan-Browne and others (Turnhout, 2000), 377–391.
Reid, Eleanor J.B., "Lollards at Colchester in 1414," *English Historical Review* 20 (1914), 101–04.
Reid, W. Stanford, "The Lollards in Pre-reformation Scotland," *Church History* 11 (1942), 269–83.
Resnick, Irvin M., "Marriage in Medieval Culture: Consent Theory and the Case of Joseph and Mary," *Church History* 69 (2000), 350–71.
Rex, Richard, "John Bale, Geoffrey Downes, and Jesus College," *Journal of Ecclesiastical History* 49 (1998), 486–493.
———, "Not a Lollard Mass After All?" *Journal of Theological Studies* n.s. 62 (2001): 207–17.

———, *The Lollards* (Basingstoke, 2002).
———, "Thorpe's Testament: A Conjectural Emendation," *Medium Aevum* 75 (2005), 109–13.
———, "'Which is Wyche?' Lollardy and Sanctity in Lancastrian London," in *Martyrs and Martyrdom in England, c. 1400–1700*, ed. Thomas Freedman and Thomas Maye (Woodbridge, 2007), 88–106.
Rice, Nicole, *Lay Piety and Religious Discipline in Middle English Literature* (Cambridge, 2008).
Ridgard, John, "From the Rising of 1381 in Suffolk to the Lollards," in *Religious Dissent in East Anglia*, ed. David Chadd (Norwich, 1996), 9–28.
Rigg, A.G., "Two Latin Poems against the Friars," *Mediaeval Studies* 30 (1968): 106–18.
———, *Anglo-Latin Literature* (Cambridge, 1992).
Robson, J.A., *Wyclif and the Oxford Schools* (Cambridge, 1961).
Rubin, Miri, *Corpus Christi: The Eucharist in Late Medieval Culture* (Cambridge, 1991).
Rupp, E.G., *Studies in the Making of the English Protestant Tradition* (Cambridge, 1966).
Sargent, Michael G., "Censorship or Cultural Change? Reformation and Renaissance in the Spirituality of Late Medieval England," in *After Arundel: Religious Writing in Fifteenth-Century England*, ed. Vincent Gillespie and Kantik Ghosh (Turnhout, 2011), 55–72.
Scarisbrick, J.J., *The Reformation and the English People* (Oxford, 1984).
Scase, Wendy, "'Heu! quanta desolatio Angliae praestatur': A Wycliffite Libel and the Naming of Heretics, Oxford 1382," in *Influence* (2003), 19–36.
———, *'Piers Plowman' and the New Anti-clericalism* (Cambridge, 1989).
———, "Reginald Pecock, John Carpenter and John Colop's 'Common-Profit' Books: Aspects of Book Ownership and Circulation in Fifteenth-Century London," *Medium Aevum* 61.2 (1992): 261–74.
Scattergood, John, "The Date of Sir John Clanvowe's *The Two Ways* and the 'Reinvention' of Lollardy," *Medium Aevum* 79 (2010), 116–20.
———, "*Pierce the Ploughman's Crede*: Lollardy and Texts," in *Lollardy and Gentry* (1997), 77–94.
Schirmer, Elizabeth, "'Trewe Men': Pastoral Masculinity in Lollard Polemic," in *Masculinities and Femininities in the Middle Ages and the Renaissance*, ed. Fred Kiefer (Turnhout, 2009a), 117–30.
———, "William Thorpe's Narrative Theology," *Studies in the Age of Chaucer* 31 (2009b), 267–99.
Shklar, Ruth, "Cobham's Daughter: *The Book of Margery Kempe* and the Power of Heterodox Thinking," *Modern Language Quarterly* 56 (1995), 277–304.
Shogimen, Takashi, "Wyclif's Ecclesiology and Political Thought," in *Companion*, 199–240.

Simpson, James, "Orthodoxy's Image Trouble: Images in and after Arundel's Constitutions," in *After Arundel: Religious Writing in Fifteenth-Century England*, ed. Vincent Gillespie and Kantik Ghosh (Turnhout, 2011), 91–113.

Šmahel, F., "Payne, Peter," in *Oxford Dictionary of National Biography* (Oxford, 2004).

Smalley, Beryl, "John Wyclif's *Postilla super totam bibliam*," *Bodleian Library Record* 4 (1953), 185–205.

———, "The Bible and Eternity: John Wyclif's Dilemma," *Journal of the Warburg and Courtauld Institutes* 27 (1964), 73–89, repr. in Smalley (ed.), *Studies in Medieval Thought and Learning from Abelard to Wyclif* (London, 1981), 399–415.

Smeeton, Donald Dean, *Lollard Themes in the Reformation Theology of William Tyndale* (Kirksville, Mo., 1986).

Smith, David, *Guide to Bishops' Registers of England and Wales: A Survey from the Middle Ages to the Abolition of Episcopacy in 1646* (London, 1981); see also its supplement (London, 2004).

Somerset, Fiona, "Vernacular Argumentation in the *Testimony of William Thorpe*," *Mediaeval Studies* 58 (1996), 207–41.

———, *Clerical Discourse and Lay Audience in Late Medieval England* (Cambridge: Cambridge University Press, 1998).

———, "Professionalizing Translation at the Turn of the Fifteenth Century: Ullerston's *Determinacio*, Arundel's *Constitutiones*," in *The Vulgar Tongue: Medieval and Postmedieval Vernacularity*, ed. Fiona Somerset and Nicholas Watson (University Park, Penn., 2003), 145–57.

———, "Wycliffite Prose," in *Middle English Prose: A Critical Guide to Major Authors and Genres*, ed. A.S.G. Edwards (Woodbridge, 2004), 195–214.

———, "Eciam Mulier: Women in Lollardy and the Problem of Sources," in *Voices in Dialogue: Reading Women in the Middle Ages*, ed. Linda Olsen and Kathryn Kerby-Fulton (Notre Dame, Ind., 2005), 245–60.

———, "Textual Transmission, Variance, and Religious Identity," in *Religious Controversy in Europe, 1378–1536: Textual Transmission and Networks of Readership*, ed. Michael Van Dussen and Pavel Soukup (Turnhout, 2013), 71–104.

———, *Feeling Like Saints: Lollard Writings after Wyclif* (Ithaca, N.Y., 2014).

———, "Before and After Wyclif: Consent to Another's Sin in Medieval Europe," in J. Patrick Hornbeck II and Michael Van Dussen (eds.), *Europe after Wyclif* (New York, forthcoming 2016).

———, "Wycliffite Spirituality," in *Text and Controversy* (2005), 375–86.

Somerset, Fiona, Jill C. Havens, and Derrick Pitard (eds.), *Lollards and Their Influence in Late Medieval England* (Woodbridge, 2003).

Spencer, H. Leith, "The Fortunes of a Lollard Sermon Cycle in the Later Fifteenth Century," *Mediaeval Studies* 48 (1986): 352–396.

———, *English Preaching in the Late Middle Ages* (Oxford, 1993).

Spiegel, Gabrielle M., "The Task of the Historian," *American Historical Review* 114 (2009), 1–15.
Spinka, Matthew, "Paul Kravar and the Lollard-Hussite Relations," *Church History* 25 (1956), 16–26.
——, *John Hus' Concept of the Church* (Princeton, 1966).
——, *John Hus: A Biography* (Princeton, 1979).
Stacey, John, *John Wyclif and Reform* (London, 1964).
——, "John Wyclif as Theologian," *Expository Times* 101 (1990), 134–41.
Stanbury, Sarah, "The Vivacity of Images: St. Katherine, Knighton's Lollards, and the Breaking of Idols," in *Images, Idolatry, and Iconoclasm in Medieval England: Textuality and the Visible Image*, ed. Jeremy Dimmick, James Simpson, and Nicole Zeeman (Oxford, 2002), 131–50.
——, *The Visual Object of Desire in Late Medieval England* (Philadelphia, 2011).
Stock, Brian, *The Implications of Literacy* (Princeton, N.J., 1987).
——, *Listening for the Text: On the Uses of the Past* (Philadelphia. 1997).
Strohm, Paul, "The Trouble with Richard: The Reburial of Richard II and Lancastrian Symbolic Strategy," *Speculum* 71 (1996), 87–111.
——, "Counterfeiters, Lollards, and Lancastrian Unease," in *New Medieval Literatures*, ed. Wendy Scase, Rita Copeland, and David Lawton, vol. 1 (Oxford, 1997), 31–58.
——, *England's Empty Throne: Usurpation and the Language of Legitimation, 1399–1422* (New Haven, Conn., 1998).
Summers, Joanna, *Late-Medieval Prison Writings and the Politics of Autobiography* (Oxford, 2004).
Swanson, R.N., *Church and Society in Late Medieval England* (Oxford, 1989).
——, "Problems of the Priesthood in Pre-reformation England," *English Historical Review* 105 (1990), 846–69.
——, "Literacy, Heresy, History and Orthodoxy: Perspectives and Permutations for the Late Middle Ages," in *Heresy and Literacy, 1000–1530*, ed. Peter Biller and Anne Hudson (Cambridge, 1994), 279–93.
——, "'Lollardy', 'Orthodoxy', and 'Resistance' in Pre-Reformation England," *Theological Journal* (Tartu, Estonia) 64:1 (2003), 12–26.
——, "'…Et examinatus dicit…': Oral and Personal History in the Records of English Ecclesiastical Courts," in *Voices from the Bench: The Narratives of Lesser Folk in Medieval Trials*, ed. Michael Goodich (New York, 2005), 203–25.
Szittya, Penn R., "'Sedens super flumina': A Fourteenth-Century Poem against the Friars," *Mediaeval Studies* 41 (1979): 30–43.
Tanner, Norman P., "Penances Imposed on Kentish Lollards by Archbishop Warham, 1511–12," in *Lollardy and Gentry*, 229–49.
Taylor, Claire, *Heresy, Crusade and Inquisition in Medieval Quercy* (York, 2011).

Taylor, Jamie K., *Fictions of Evidence: Witnessing, Literature, and Community in the Late Middle Ages* (Columbus, Ohio, 2013).

Thomas, John A.F., "Wyche, Richard," in *Oxford Dictionary of National Biography* (Oxford, 2008).

Thompson, Samuel Harrison, "The Philosophical Basis of Wyclif's Theology," *Journal of Religion* 11 (1931), 86–116.

Thompson, W.D.J. Cargill, "The Two Regiments: The Continental Setting of William Tyndale's Political Thought," in Derek Baker (ed.), *Reform and Reformation: England and the Continent, c. 1500–c. 1750* (Oxford, 1979), 17–33.

Thomson, J. Radford, *The Life and Work of John Wyclif* (London, n.d.).

Thomson, J.A.F., "John Foxe and Some Sources for Lollard History: Notes for a Critical Reappraisal," in *Studies in Church History* 2, ed. G.J. Cuming (London, 1965a), 251–57.

———, *The Later Lollards: 1414–1520* (Oxford, 1965b).

———, "Oldcastle, John," in *Oxford Dictionary of National Biography* (Oxford, 2008a).

———, "Perkins, William," in *Oxford Dictionary of National Biography* (Oxford, 2008b).

———, "Wyche, Richard," in *Oxford Dictionary of National Biography* (Oxford, 2008c).

Trevelyan, G.M., *England in the Age of Wycliffe*, 4th edn. (London, 1909).

Troeltsch, Ernst, "Stoic-Christian Natural Law and Modern Secular Natural Law," in *Religion in History*, trans. James Luther Adams and Walter F. Bense (Minneapolis, 1991), 321–42.

Trueman, Carl, *Luther's Legacy: Salvation and English Reformers, 1525–1556* (Oxford, 1994).

———, "Barnes, Robert," in *Oxford Dictionary of National Biography* (Oxford, 2004).

Van Dussen, Michael, "Conveying Heresy: 'A Certayne Student' and the Lollard-Hussite Fellowship," *Viator* 38 (2007), 217–34.

———, *From England to Bohemia: Heresy and Communication in the Later Middle Ages* (Cambridge, 2012).

Van Engen, John, *Sisters and Brothers of the Common Life: The Devotio Moderna and the World of the Later Middle Ages* (Philadelphia, 2008).

———, "A World Astir: Europe and Religion in the Early Fifteenth Century," in *Europe after Wyclif*, ed. J. Patrick Hornbeck II and Michael Van Dussen (New York, forthcoming 2016).

Vincent, Diane, "The Contest over the Public Imagination of Inquisition, 1380–1430," in *The Culture of Inquisition in England, 1215–1515*, ed. Mary C. Flannery and Katie L. Walter (Woodbridge, 2013), 60–76.

Von Nolcken, Christina, "Another Kind of Saint: A Lollard Perception of John Wyclif," in *Ockham to Wyclif* (1987), 429–43.

———, "Some Alphabetical Compendia and How Preachers Used Them in Fourteenth-Century England," *Viator* 12 (1981): 271–88.

———, "An Unremarked Group of Wycliffite Sermons in Latin," *Modern Philology* 83 (1986): 233–49.

———, "Notes on Lollard Citation of John Wyclif's Writings," *Journal of Theological Studies* n.s. 39.2 (October, 1998): 411–37.

———, "Richard Wyche, a Certain Knight, and the Beginning of the End," in *Lollardy and Gentry* (1997), 127–54.

Wakelin, Daniel, "Writing the Words," in *The Production of Books in England, 1350–1500*, ed. Alexandra Gillespie and Daniel Wakelin (Cambridge, 2011), 34–58.

Walker, Greg, "Saint or Schemer? The 1527 Heresy Trial of Thomas Bilney Reconsidered," *Journal of Ecclesiastical History* 40 (1989), 219–38.

Watson, Nicholas, "Censorship and Cultural Change in Late-Medieval England: Vernacular Theology, The Oxford Translation Debate, and Arundel's Constitutions of 1409," *Speculum* 70 (1995), 822–864.

———, "Visions of Inclusion: Universal Salvation and Vernacular Theology in Pre-reformation England," *Journal of Medieval and Early Modern Studies* 27 (1997), 145–87.

———, "Lollardy: The Anglo-Norman Heresy?" in *Language and Culture in Medieval Britain*, ed. Jocelyn Wogan-Browne et al. (York, 2009), 334–46.

Waugh, W.T., "Sir John Oldcastle," *English Historical Review* 20 (1905), 434–56, 637–58.

———, "The Lollard Knights," *Scottish Historical Review* 11 (1913–14), 55–92.

Weaver, Rebecca Harden, *Divine Grace and Human Agency: A Study of the Semi-Pelagian Controversy* (Macon, Ga., 1996).

Westphall, Allan, "Reconstructing the Mixed Life in Reginald Pecock's *Reule of Crysten Religioun*," in *After Arundel. Religious Writing in Fifteenth-Century England*, ed. V. Gillespie and K. Ghosh (Turnhout, 2011), 267–84.

Whiting, Michael S., *Luther in English: The Influence of His Theology of Law and Gospel on Early English Evangelicals*, Princeton Theological Monographs Series 142 (Eugene, Ore., 2010).

Wilks, Michael, "The *Apostolicus* and the Bishop of Rome," 2 parts, *Journal of Theological Studies* n.s. 13 (1962), 290–317, and n.s. 14 (1963), 311–54.

———, "Wyclif and the Great Persecution," in *Wyclif* (2000), 179–203.

———, *Wyclif: Political Ideas and Practice*, ed. Anne Hudson (Oxford, 2000).

Williams, Rowan, *Arius: Heresy and Tradition*, 2nd ed. (London, 2001).

Workman, H.B., *John Wyclif: A Study of the English Medieval Church*, 2 vols. (Oxford, 1926a).

———, "Wyclif, Hus, Luther, Wesley," *Proceedings of the Wesley Historical Society* 15 (1926b), 141–46.

Wunderli, Richard M., *London Church Courts and Society on the Eve of the Reformation* (Cambridge, Mass., 1981).

Dissertations, Theses, and Unpublished Papers

Bose, Mishtooni, "The Trouble with Lollardy."

Brady, M. Theresa, "The Pore Caitif, Edited from Harley 2336 with Introduction and Notes" (Ph.D. diss., Fordham University, 1954).

Catto, Jeremy, "William Woodford, O.F.M. (c.1330–c.1397)" (D.Phil. thesis, University of Oxford, 1969).

Crompton, James, "Lollard Doctrine, With Special Reference to the Controversy over Image-Worship and Pilgrimages" (B.Litt. thesis, University of Oxford, 1950).

Cullen, Mairi Anne, "The Lollards of Northamptonshire, 1382–1414" (M.Litt. thesis, University of Oxford, 1989).

D'Alton, Craig, "The Suppression of Heresy in Early Henrician England" (Ph.D. diss., University of Melbourne, 1999).

Hargrave, O.T., "The Doctrine of Predestination in the English Reformation" (Ph.D. diss., Vanderbilt University, 1966).

Illig, Jennifer, "Through a Lens of Likeness: Reading English Wycliffite Sermons in Light of Contemporary Sermon Texts" (Ph.D. diss., Fordham University, 2014).

Jefferson, Judith (ed.), "An Edition of the Ten Commandments Commentary in BL Harley 2398, and the Related Version in Trinity College Dublin 245, York Minster XVI.L.12 and Harvard English 738 Together with Discussion of Related Commentaries," 2 vols. (Ph.D. diss., University of Bristol, 1995).

Kightly, Charles, "The Early Lollards: A Survey of Popular Lollard Activity in England, 1382–1428" (Ph.D. diss., University of York, 1975).

Levy, Ian Christopher, "Were the Lollards Heretics?"

Norris, Kirsti, "Authors of Fate: Episcopal Voices in Lollard Trials."

Reilly, Robert (ed.), "A Middle English Summary of the Bible: An Edition of Trinity College (Oxon) MS 93" (Ph.D. diss., University of Washington, 1966).

Royal, Susan, "John Foxe's Acts and Monuments and the Lollard Legacy in the Long Reformation" (Ph.D. diss., University of Durham, 2013).

Index

Abell, Thomas   177
absolution and penance   39, 67, 125–126, 148
academic heresy   22–23
Adam of Usk   111
Aers, David   120–121
Alnwick, William   54, 63, 116, 119, 129n101, 131, 134, 159, 173, 176, 181–183, 190
Alyngton, Robert   149
Ambrose   151
Amersham   53
Anne of Bohemia   197
Anneys, John   181
anthologies of lollard writings   77n4, 98–101
Antichrist   25, 72, 109, 133, 134, 135, 201
anticlericalism   129–130
Apleward, William   183
apocalypticism   202
Apology for Lollard Doctrines   89, 90
apostles   134
Arnold, John H.   14
    Inquisition and Power   174–175
Arnold, Thomas
    Select English Works of John Wycliffe   77n4
Arundel, Thomas   10, 148–149
    Gascoigne castigates   144–145
    and Kempe   150
    opposition to heresy   48–49
    Provincial Constitutions of 1407/1409   65, 81, 144, 149, 151–153, 210
    and Purvey   39
    and Thorpe   40, 41, 88, 167
    267 Articles against Wyclif   149
Ashwardby, John   88, 148, 154
Aston, John   36, 38, 178
Aston, Margaret   10–11, 21–22, 139, 173, 195
    England's Iconoclasts, Volume I   11
    "Lollardy and the Reformation"   205
Audelay, John
    "Marcolf and Solomon"   155–156
Audley, Edmund   63, 184
Augustine of Hippo   113, 128, 151
    De haeresibus   6
authority, spiritual   109–110, 135, 147, 149, 150, 168
Ave Maria   71

Badby, John   49, 156
Bale, John   24, 199–201
    Fasciculi Zizaniorum   199
    The Image of Bothe Churches   199–200, 201, 202
Ball, John   47
baptism   117–119, 182n71
Barnes, Robert   194
Barton, William   147, 148
Bath diocese   183
Batman, Thomas   195, 204
Baxter, Margery   64, 65, 159–161, 166, 173, 182
beguines/beghards   15, 55
Belgrave, John   180–181
beliefs and theology, lollard
    absolution and penance   39, 67, 125–126, 148
    baptism   117–119, 182n71
    celibacy   39
    church endowments (ownership rights)   4, 44
    coherency of corpus of   105–110, 141–143
    confirmation   119–120
    divine election   109
    and English apocalypticism   202
    eucharist   39, 44, 66, 67, 120–125, 148, 150, 168–169
    extreme unction   131–132
    holy orders sacrament   129–131
    images and iconography   4, 41, 74, 139–141
    limitations of evidence of   110–111
    lordship, dominion, and spiritual authority   109–110, 135, 147, 149, 150, 168
    marriage, sacrament of   126–129
    methodology of study of   105–111
    ordination   55, 129–131
    ordination of women   44, 55
    pilgrimage   4
    predestination and free will   73, 109, 110, 111–117, 142
    priesthood of all believers   39
    sacraments   117–132
    sacraments for states of life   126–131
    sacraments of initiation   117–120

INDEX 243

salvation and grace   111–117
tithing   44
transubstantiation   3, 120–125, 147–148
Benenden, Kent   64
Bernham, William   181
Bethom, Agnes   160
biblical exegesis   73–74
Bikenore, Thomas   116, 134
Bilney, Thomas   195, 204
Binham, William   147
Birch, John   152
Blackfriars Council (1382)   4, 37, 38, 47, 110, 147–148, 151, 178
Blood of Hailes   182
Blythe, Geoffrey   184, 185, 189
Blythe, John   183
Bocher, Joan   204
Bodley, Thomas   9
Bohemia   43, 196–198
Books under Suspicion (Kerby-Fulton)   13
Book to a Mother   93–94, 100, 101, 102
Bowet, Henry   150
Boxley, Kent   64
Boyle, Leonard   172
Braybrooke, Robert   167
Brinton, Thomas   111, 145
Bristol   4
Brown, Andrew   54
Browne, John   184
Brut, Walter   44–45, 48, 88, 115–116, 121
Buckingham, John   43
Buckinghamshire   190
Burell, John   177

Calvin, John   111
Campbell, Kirsty   156
Campi, Luigi   198
Cannon, H.L.   61
Canterbury College   3
Canterbury convocation (1396)   110, 118–119
Canterbury diocese   62, 184, 189, 195
Cardinal College (Oxford)   193
Cathars/Catharism   13–14, 55, 162, 172, 174
"Catholic"   7n9
Catto, Jeremy   11n26, 16–17, 40
celibacy   39, 128
censorship   48–49
Cermanova, Pavlina   198

Certeau, Michel de
  The Practice of Everyday Life   61n4
Chedworth, John   53, 179, 183
Chichele, Henry   63, 149, 181
Christ, imitation of   71–72
Christianson, Paul   201–202
Christ's law   71
the church, lollardy and
  about   132–133
  authority of and within   135–136, 148, 168, 169
  ecclesiastical finance   136–137
  images and iconography   139–141
  the papacy   133–135, 148, 201
  religious orders   137–138
  tithing   136–137
church endowments (ownership rights)   4, 44
civil courts   162
Clanvowe, John   46
  The Two Ways   89, 93
Claydon, John   93, 116
Clebsch, William   194, 205
clergy
  absolution of sins   39, 67, 125–126, 148
  celibacy   39, 128
  clerical marriage   127–129
  ecclesiastical finance and   136–137
  ordination   55, 129–131
"The Clergy May Not Own Property"   92
Clerke, Robert   185
Clifford, Lewis   45
Clifland, Joan   64, 160
Clopper, Lawrence   93
Cloud of Unknowing   103, 104
Cole, Andrew   17
Colet, John   164n18
Collinson, Patrick   190
Colyn, William   129, 182
communities, lollard
  about   51–57, 211
  family and social relationships   54–57
  godparenthood in   56
  itinerant preachers and   61–63
  in sixteenth century   189–196
  social and economic status   53–54
  textual nature of   52
  theological discussion among   63, 65–66
  trade and commerce   56–57

confession. *See* absolution and penance
confirmation   119–120
Contre les lollardes (statute) (1401)   43, 48, 49, 63, 149
contrition   126. *See also* absolution and penance
Copeland, Rita   65
Council of Basel-Ferrara-Florence (1431)   19, 179
Council of Constance (1415)   4, 8, 38, 110, 113, 116, 119, 149–150
Courtenay, William   36, 47, 147–148, 152, 180
Coventry diocese   4, 53, 54, 142, 183, 184, 185, 186, 189
Cranbrook, Kent   184, 190
Crashawe, William   97
Crump, Henry   146, 147, 148

D'Alton, Craig   191
Davies, Richard G.   16, 54
Davis, J.F.   196, 204
Denys, Thomas   185, 186
De Officio Pastorali   136
"De Pontificum Romanorum Schismate"   126
De pusillanimitate   103
Deveros, John   149, 158
devotional practices, lollard criticism of   139–141
Dialogue between a Clerk and a Knight   97
Dialogue between a Friar and a Secular   96, 97, 153
Dialogue between a Wise Man and a Fool   72, 97
Dialogue between Jon and Richard   96, 97, 99
Dialogue between Reson and Gabbyng   87, 96, 97
dialogue genre   154
Dickens, A.G.   195, 204, 205
    The English Reformation   204
    Lollards and Protestants in the Diocese of York   204
Dillon, Janette   156
Divine election   109
Doctrinale (Netter)   39–40
dominion   109–110, 135, 147, 149, 150, 168
Donation of Constantine   135, 136
double predestinarianism   112
Duffy, Eamon
    The Stripping of the Altars   2, 205

Dymoke, Roger   150
    Liber contra XII errores et hereses Lollardorum   148

Eagleton, Terry   152
Earsham   54, 176–177
East Anglia   53, 62–63
Easton, Adam
    Defensorium ecclesiasticae potestatis   147
ecclesiology. *See* church, lollardy and
Edward III   45
Edwards, A.S.G.   76n1
Egerton sermon   68
England's Iconoclasts, Volume I (Aston)   11
English Reformation, lollardy and   202–207
    The English Reformation (Dickens)   204
    English Wycliffite Sermons   69, 79, 82–83, 86, 87, 91, 123, 154, 212
Epiphanius of Salamis   6
eucharist   39, 44, 66, 67, 120–125, 148, 150, 168–169
"evangelical"   7n9
Exeter, John   176–177, 181, 182
extreme unction   131–132

Fairfield, Leslie   199
Farnham   186
Fasciculi Zizaniorum   158
Faulfiš, Mikuláš   197–198
Feeling Like Saints (Somerset)   70, 209
Fifth Lateran Council (1512)   164, 179, 184
First seiþ Bois   99
Firth, Katherine   200
Fishbourn, Thomas   66
Fitzjames, Richard   63, 184
Five Questions on Love   87
Floretum   79, 80–81, 84, 87
Folkhyrde, Quentin   197n33
Forest of Dean   53
Forrest, Ian   12n26
    The Detection of Heresy in Late Medieval England   163
Foucault, Michel   14, 174
Four Errours Whiche Letten þe Verrey Knowying of Holy Writt   103–104
Fourth Lateran Council   125
Four Wycliffite Dialogues   97
Fox, Richard   63, 65, 184, 185, 189

INDEX

Foxe, John   2, 37, 106–107, 117–118, 161, 171, 173–174, 202, 208
   Actes and Monuments   7–8, 200, 201
   Rerum in ecclesia gestarum   201
Freeman, Thomas   173
Free Spirit heretics   162
free will and predestination   73, 109, 110, 111–117, 142
Friar Daw's Reply   95
"Friar's Answer"   96
Frith, John   193–194

Gairdner, James   203
Gascoigne, Thomas
   Loci e Liber Veritatum   144–145, 150
Gasquet, Francis Aidan   85, 203
Gaunt, John of   3, 45
Gayk, Shannon   140
Gertz, Genelle   175
Ghosh, Kantik
   The Wycliffite Heresy   108
Gillingham, Kent   62
Given, James   14
Glossed Gospels   79, 81–82, 84, 85, 86, 103
Gloucester Vale   53
Godesell, John   116, 181
Godesell, Sybil   181
godparenthood   56
God's law   71
grace-oriented predestinarianism   112
Gratium
   Decretum   90
Gregory XI   3, 110, 146
"Gret Sentence of Curs"   120
Grosseteste, Robert   20, 151
groundid/ungroundid   74
Grymle, Joan   160
Gui, Bernard
   Practica inquisitionis hereticae pravitatis   174

Haigh, Christopher   206
Hales, John   185
Haller, William   200
Hampshire   190
Harpsfield, Nicholas   161
Havens, Jill C.   18
Henry IV   48, 49
Henry V   49
Henry VII   183

Henry VIII   4, 164, 179–180, 184, 191, 199
   Assertio septem sacramentorum   191
Hereford, Nicholas   115, 137, 178
   Ascension Day sermon   68, 88
   biographical information   36–37
heresy
   academic vs. popular   22–23
   beliefs and   105
   Christian discourse on   5–6
   Christianity's erroneous presuppostions about   210–211
   and heterodoxy   19–21, 164–165
   pre-Wycliffite charges of   178n63
   trials   161–168
Herrick, Peter   181
heterodoxy   20–21
"Heu quanta desolacio"   96
Hilton, Walter   103
Holi Prophet David   103
holy orders sacrament   129–131
Holy Roman Empire   197
Honorius Augustodunensis
   Elucidarium   97
Hope, Andrew   196, 205
Hornbeck, J. Patrick, II
   What is a Lollard?   107, 141–142, 176
Hudson, Anne   11, 16, 17, 18, 39, 41, 66, 120, 167–168
   "Five Problems in Wycliffite Texts and a Suggestion"   78n5
   The Premature Reformation   1, 11, 16, 59n1
human dignity   74
Hus, Jan   41, 196–198
Hussite movement   13, 43, 196–198
Hutte, John, Junior   181
Hyllyng, Richard   184

images and iconography   4, 41, 74, 139–141
imitation of Christ   71–72
Innocent III   126
Islip, Simon   3

Jack Upland   94, 95, 198
James, Thomas   9
Jerome   151
Jerome of Prague   198
Joachim of Fiore   13, 200, 201, 202
John XXIII   149
Jopson, Margery   74

Jurkowski, Maureen   40, 54, 62
justice   72–73

Kelly, H.A.   161, 164n19
Kempe, Margery   188
   Book   19, 150, 153, 155
Kenny, Anthony   151
Kerby-Fulton, Kathryn   212
   Books under Suspicion   13
Kightly, Charles   106, 107
King, John   200, 205
King, Oliver   183
Kingston-upon-Thames   185–186, 189
Knêhnice, Jiri   197–198
Knighton, Henry   2, 6, 38, 45–46, 64, 106–107, 110, 156, 171, 208
Kravar, Paul   197n33
Kynyngham, John   146

Lahey, Stephen E.   2, 109–110
Lancaster, House of   37
Lancastrian Kings and Lollard Knights (McFarlane)   46
Landesdale, Roger   177
Lanfranc   151
Langham, Simon   3
Langland, William
   Piers Plowman   137
Langton, Thomas   183
Lanterne of Li3t   73, 93, 114–115, 116, 133, 135, 140, 198
Larsen, Andrew E.   107
Latimer, Thomas   45
Lavynham, Richard   103
Lay Folks' Catechism   98
"Layman's Complaint"   96
Lechler, Gotthard   15, 106
Leff, Gordon   109
Leicester   53, 131, 180–181
Leicester Abbey   43
Leicestershire   47
Levy, Ian Christopher   113
Loci e Liber Veritatum (Gascoigne)   144–145
Lichfield diocese   54, 142, 183, 184, 185, 189
Life of Soul   97
Lincoln diocese   53, 180–181, 182
Little, Katherine C.   108
liturgical rituals, lollard   66–67

Lollard Chronicle of the Papacy   92
"Lollard Disendowment Bill"   137
Lollard knights
   about   45–46
   political dissent and   49–50
   Repingdon and   38
Lollards and Protestants in the Diocese of York (Dickens)   204
Lollard Sermons   86, 91–92, 128, 140
"Lollards of Kyle"   53
lollard studies
   Bohemian connection   196–198
   contemporary scholarship   11–14
   developments in   5–14
   historical professional mindset in   9–10
   historiography   202–207
   Hudson's influence   1
   presuppostions in   208
   recent advances in   208–213
   skepticism about importance   2
   terminological quandries   15–23
lollardy
   campaign against   46–51
   coherence as social movement   57–58
   early assumptions about   6–7
   history of writings about   7–11
   later lollard sympathizers   46–51
   and later reformations   10, 14, 188, 196–198, 202–207
   lollard communities   51–57
   lollard communities in 16th century   189–196
   "lollard" epithet   15, 18, 47
   membership gradience and   18–19
   as multifaceted and dynamic subculture   209–210
   opponents of   144–158
   Oxford as a center of   35–36, 40
   political dissent and   49–50
   as sect   21–22
   sect vocabulary   73–74
   spirituality   12
   stigma of   188
   traditional tale of   3–5
   women and   55–56
   writings printed in sixteenth century   198–200
   and Wycliffism   15–18

Wyclif's contemporaries and
  supporters 40–45
"Lollardy and the Reformation"
  (Aston) 205
London diocese 4, 53, 56, 184, 185–186
Longland, John 53, 191n9
lordship, dominion, and spiritual authority
  109–110, 135, 147, 149, 150, 168
Love, Nicholas
  The Mirror of the Blessed Life of Jesus Christ
    149, 157–158
  Treatise on the Sacrament 149, 157
Lucidarie 97
Luther, Martin 8, 178, 191, 196
Lutheranism 191–192
Lutterworth, Leicestershire 3
Lutton, Robert 54, 57

MacCulloch, Diarmaid 7n9
Maid of Kent 204
Maidstone, Kent 56, 64, 184
Maidstone, Richard 88, 148, 154
Manipulus Florum 80
marriage, sacrament of 126–129
Marshall, Peter 9, 188, 203, 206–207
Martham 159
Masse, William 176–177
Matthew, F.D.
  *The English Works of Wyclif Hitherto
    Unprinted* 77n4
Maxfield, Ezra Kempton 16
McFarlane, K.B. 10
  Lancastrian Kings and Lollard Knights
    46
McGrade, A.S. 20
McHardy, Alison 40, 62
McNeill, John Thomas 122
McSheffrey, Shannon 54, 55–56, 172
membership gradience 18–19
mercy 72–73
Merton College (Oxford) 40, 62, 68
Minnis, Alastair 44
Mirk, John 111
Mone, Hawisia 132, 181
Mone, Thomas 181
Montaigu, John 45
Moore, R.I. 163
More, Thomas 8

Morton, John 184
Mum and the Sothsegger 94, 95–96
Mundy, William 129

Netter, Thomas 17, 111, 145, 151, 157
  Doctrinale antiquitatum fidei ecclesiae
    39–40, 144, 150, 154
Nisbet, Mudroch 195
Nolcken, Christina von 78
No Man May Serve Two Lords 103
Norfolk 53, 54, 194
Northampton 56
Norwich diocese 4, 53, 54, 62, 116,
  119, 129, 131, 132, 134, 181–182,
  183, 186, 190, 195
Nykke, Richard 183

O'Day, Rosemary 203
Of Mynystris 83, 86, 134
"Of Poor Preaching Priests" 137
"Of Thes Frer Mynours" 96
Of Weddid Men and Wifis 128–129
Oldcastle, John 4, 39, 41, 43, 49–50,
  116, 124, 149, 162n11, 170–171,
  181, 200
Omnis Plantacio 92
On Holy Prayers 71
Oon of Foure 85
"The Opponents of John Wyclif"
  (Bose) 145–146
opponents of lollardy
  about 144–146
  analysis of 150–158
  chronology of 146–150
  Ricardian *vs.* Lancastrian phases 153–154
Opus Arduum 90–91, 201, 202, 212
ordination 44, 55, 129–131
ordination of women 44, 55, 131
Oxford 80, 151
  as center of lollardy 35–36, 40
  scattering of lollardy from 51
  theological censorship at 48
Oxford committee (1411) 110, 119

Palmer, Thomas 149
the papacy 133–135, 148, 201
Partridge, Peter 43
Pavlicek, Ota 198

Payne, Peter   43, 153, 198
Pecock, Reginald   150, 151, 154, 156–157
pedagogy, lollard   61–69
Pegg, Mark Gregory   14, 59n2
Pelagianism   112
penance. *See* absolution and penance
Perett, Marcela K.   198
Perkins, William   50
Peter   134
Piers Plowman (Langland)   137, 199
Piers the Plowman's Creed   94, 95, 106, 115
pilgrimage   4
Plowman's Tale   94–95
popular heresy   22–23
Pore Caitif   86, 102, 104
power   14
practical theology   59–61
practices, lollard religious
   about   59–61
   beliefs and   60
   continuous prayer   71
   emphasis on biblical exegesis   73–74
   gatherings   65–66
   God's or Christ's law   71
   human dignity and spiritual simplicity   74
   imitation of Christ   71–72
   liturgical rituals   66–67
   positive spiritual ideals of   69–75
   preaching and teaching   61–69
   reading aloud of vernacular texts   63–65
   social reform aspirations   73
   spirituality   69–71, 74–75
   works of individual mercy and social justice   72–73
prayer   71
preaching, lollard   61–63, 68–69, 107
predestinarianism   112, 142
predestination and free will   73, 109, 110, 111–117, 142
   The Premature Reformation (Hudson)   1, 11, 59n1
Pride, Wrath, and Envy   100, 101, 102
priesthood of all believers   39
"Protestant"   7n9
Pseudo-Dionysius   151
pseudo-Hildegard
   Insurgent gentes   99
Purvey, John   38–40, 76n2, 115, 124, 131

Queen's College (Oxford)   40
Qwyrk, John   124, 183

Radcliff, Nicholas   147, 148, 158
Ramsbury, William   66–67
Ramsey Abbey   180
readings, lollard   64–65
reformations, lollardy and   10, 14, 188, 196–198, 202–207
religious orders   137–138
Repingdon, Philip   36, 37–38, 43, 53, 148, 150, 178, 179, 180–181
Reve, John   119
Rex, Richard   41, 66–67, 206
Richard II   45, 46, 49, 197
Rolle's *English Psalter*   79, 83, 84, 86–87
Rosarium   79, 80–81, 84, 87, 134
Royal, Susan   203
Rubin, Miri   120
Rupert of Deutz   201
Rupp, Gordon   117
Rygge, Robert   148
Rymington, William
   Dialogus inter catholicam vertiatem et haereticam pravitatem   148
   Quadraginta quinque Conclusiones   148

sacraments
   sacraments for states of life   126–131
   sacraments of initiation   117–120
   transubstantiation in eucharist   120–125
Salisbury diocese   63, 124, 134, 142, 183, 184
Salter, H.E.   152
salvation and grace   111–117
Sarum Rite liturgy   66, 82
Sawtre, William   48, 49, 115
Scarisbrick, J.J.   206
Scattergood, John   106
Schirmer, Elizabeth   127
Schort Reule of Lif   101
Scotland   53, 190
Scott, James C.   14
Second Vatican Council   20
sect 21–22
Sermon of Dead Men   91
Seven Works of Mercy   100, 101
Severs, J. Burke   76n1
sexuality   127–129
sexual vice   128

INDEX

Seynon, John   124
Sharp, Jack   50
Simon Magus   6
sin, social consent to   72–73
single predestinarianism   112
Sixteen Points   90, 99
"Sixteen Points on Which the Bishops Accuse Lollards"   174
Skirlawe, Walter   41, 169–170
Šmahel, František   43
Smeeton, Donald Dean   192–193
Smith, William   181
Snappe's Formulary   152
social reform   73
Somerset, Fiona   1, 3, 12, 71, 169
    Feeling Like Saints   70, 209
soteriology. *See* predestination
spiritual authority   109–110, 135, 147, 149, 150, 168
Spiritual Franciscans   13
spirituality, lollard
    about   69–71, 74–75
    continuous prayer   71
    emphasis on biblical exegesis   73–74
    God's or Christ's law   71
    human dignity and spiritual simplicity   74
    imitation of Christ   71–72
    social reform aspirations   73
    works of individual mercy and social justice   72–73
spiritual simplicity   74
St. Paul's Cathedral (London)   37
Stanbury, John   183
Standard Orthodox Commentary   87
Statute of Labourers (1351)   47
Sterne, Augustine   183
Stillington, Robert   182
Stilman, John   51, 63, 68
Stock, Brian   52
Stokes, Peter   148
    The Stripping of the Altars (Duffy)   2, 205
Strode, Ralph   146
Strohm, Paul   48, 121, 172
Stury, Richard   45
Swaffer, Elizabeth   186
Swaffer, Laurence   68
Swanson, R.N.   14, 172
Swinderby, William   43–44, 48, 62, 68, 88, 119, 134

Tailour, Thomas   183
Talbert, Ernest W.   76n1
Tanner, Norman   172, 184
Taylor, William   68, 88
teaching, lollard   61–69
ten commandments   71, 87
Tenterden, Kent   57, 62, 184
The Testimony of William Thorpe (Thorpe)   41, 88, 135, 167–169, 171, 193
theology, lollard. *See* beliefs and theology, lollard
Thirty-Seven Conclusions   89, 134
Thomson, John   106, 117–118, 173
Thomson, S. Harrison   76n1
Thorpe, William   38, 39, 121, 124, 136
    biographical information   40–41
    public sermon of   68
    The Testimony of William Thorpe   41, 88, 135, 167–169, 171, 193
tithing   44, 136–137
Tractatus de oblacione iugis sacrificii   92, 123, 137, 201
Tractatus de regibus   87
transubstantiation   3, 120–125, 147–148. *See also* eucharist
Trefnant, John   43, 44, 88
Tretise of Miraclis Pleyinge   93
trials, of lollards
    abjurations   165, 167, 175
    about   186–187
    detection   163–165
    frequency of   178–179
    inquisitorial process   161–167
    of John Oldcastle   170–171
    Letter of Richard Wyche   169–170
    of Margery Baxter   159–161, 166, 182
    punishment   166
    records' accuracy and biases   167–178
    survey of extant records   178–186
    The Testimony of William Thorpe   167–169
Trueman, Carl   194
Tryvet, William   180–181
Tudor, Henry   179
Twelve Conclusions   45, 48, 89–90, 148, 150
Twenty-Five Articles   90
267 Articles against Wyclif   149
Tyball, John   194
Tyconius   201

250

INDEX

Tyndale, William 8, 192–194
Tyssyngton, John
    Confessio 147, 150–151

Ullerston, Richard
    Defensorium dotacionis ecclesie 149
Unremarked Sermons 91
Upland series 94, 95, 135
Upland's Rejoinder 95
Urban VI 36, 148
Usk, Adam 6

Vae Octuplex 83
Valla, Lorenzo 135
Van Dussen, Michael 197
vernacular primers 65

Walker, Edward 64
Walsh, John 184, 192
Walsingham, Thomas 24, 45, 110–111
Warham, William 64, 129n101, 132, 140, 184, 189, 190, 193
Wars of the Roses 179
Wasshingburn, Joan (Warde) 56, 185
Watson, Nicholas 23, 48
Wattes, Thomas 68
Waugh, W.T. 46
Weald of Kent 4, 53, 190, 204
Wells, John 148
Wells diocese 183
West Midlands 190
Westphall, Allan 156
What is a Lollard? (Hornbeck) 107, 141–142, 176
White, William 51, 62–63, 129, 131, 159, 160
Williams, Rowan 175
Winchester diocese 63, 65, 124, 142, 184, 185, 186, 189
Winterton, Thomas
    Absolutio 147, 151
Wittgenstein, Ludwig 18–19
Wolsey, Thomas 193
women
    held in common 129
    lollardy and 25n6, 55–56, 127, 193
    ordination and priestly powers of 44, 55, 131
Woodford, William 95, 118–119, 121, 144, 147, 151, 158

De causis condempnationis articulorum XVIII damnatorum Joannis Wyclif 149
De dominio civili clericorum 147
Quatuor determinationes in materia de religione 148
Responsiones 148
Septuaginta duae quaesitones de sacramento altaris 148
"Wordes of Poule" commentary 100
Workman, H.B. 109, 114, 122, 203
Works of a Lollard Preacher 154
works-oriented predestinarianism 112
writings, lollard
    about 76–79
    anonymous declarative or confessional writings 89–90
    anthologies of 77n4, 98–101
    apocalyptic nature of 201–202
    authorship attribution 76n2
    English Wycliffite Sermons 69, 79, 82–83, 86, 87, 91, 114, 123, 212
    Floretum 79, 80–81, 84, 87
    Glossed Gospels 79, 81–82, 84, 85, 86, 103
    identifying 76–77, 78–79
    literary forms 70
    lollard learning 90–94
    Of Mynystris 83, 86
    by named authors associated with Wycliffism 88–89
    Oxford as locus of early 80
    phases of 78
    prose dialogues 96–98
    recension and diffusion 101–104
    Rolle's *English Psalter* 79, 83, 84, 86–87
    Rosarium 79, 80–81, 84, 87, 134
    spinoffs from phase 1 projects 84–87
    translations or citations of Wyclif 87
    Unremarked Sermons 84
    Vae Octuplex 83
    in verse 94–96
    Wycliffite Bible 79, 81, 85, 198
Wyche, Richard 42, 43, 197n33
    Letter of Richard Wyche 88–89, 169–171
Wycklyffes Wycket 123–124, 125, 142, 198
Wyclif, John
    about 24
    authorial attribution 76n2
    on authority within church 135
    Bale's depiction of 200

INDEX

on baptism 118
biographical information 26–35
condemnations and criticisms 24–25
on confirmation 119–120
De amore 87
De blasphemia 125
De civili dominio 146
De dominio divino 197
De ecclesia 197
De eucharistia confessio 121, 125, 147
De officio regis 87
De veritate sacrae scripturae 197
Dialogus 87, 154
distinct from those who came after 15–16
on the eucharist 121–123
exhumation and burning 150
on images 139
on marriage 128
opponents of 146–149
Opus evangelicum 128

on ordination and true priesthood 130
on the papacy 133, 201
on penance 125
philosophical realism 113
and predestinarianism 113
Responsiones 148
Supplementum Trialogi 148
traditional tale of 3–5
Trialogus 118, 120, 125, 131–132, 148, 154
on unction 131–132
Wycliffite Bible 4, 24, 36–37, 79, 81, 85, 198
Wycliffite Glossed Gospels 11
The Wycliffite Heresy (Ghosh) 108
Wycliffites/Wycliffitism. *See also* lollardy
assumptions about 6–7
terminological considerations vis a vis lollardy 15–18
Wyclif Society 9
"Wyclyf and His Followers" (Talbert & Thomson) 76n1

Printed in the United States
By Bookmasters